Samizdat

Left Oppositionists at an exile colony (Yeniseisk, in Siberia) demonstrate on the anniversary of the Bolshevik revolution. The year is apparently 1928: the banner on the left, with its slogan "Turn the Fire to the Right, Against Kulak, Nepman, and Bureaucrat— Not in Words but in Deeds," refers to a hesitant "leftward" move by the Stalin regime that year. The center banner, with portraits of Lenin and Trotsky, proclaims "Long Live the Dictatorship of the Proletariat."

SAMIZDAT

Voices of the Soviet Opposition

Edited by
George Saunders

MONAD PRESS, NEW YORK

DISTRIBUTED BY
PATHFINDER PRESS, INC., NEW YORK

To all those Soviet Communists and Marxists who have given their lives or sacrificed their well-being in the fight against Stalinism. In particular, to the anonymous author of "Memoirs of a Bolshevik-Leninist," who survived Stalin's camps to tell the truth about the revolution and the party; to Aleksandra Chumakova, who has done likewise; and to former Major General Pyotr Grigorenko, who gave up a position of privilege in order to speak his convictions and has refused to abandon his ideas despite four years in the hell of a Brezhnev "special" psychiatric hospital.

Copyright © 1974 by the Anchor Foundation, Inc.
All rights reserved
Library of Congress Catalog Card Number 75-186692
Manufactured in the United States of America

Published by Monad Press
for the Anchor Foundation, Inc.
First Edition, 1974

Distributed by:

Pathfinder Press, Inc.
410 West Street
New York, N.Y. 10014

CONTENTS

FOREWORD

The political development of the Soviet Union from its birth in 1917 has passed through three phases: the formative period of the first workers' state, under the Bolshevik leadership of Lenin and Trotsky, from 1917 to 1923; the rise and consolidation of the bureaucratic caste under Stalin's personal dictatorship from 1924 to his death in 1953; the post-Stalin decades from 1953 to the present. One of the most remarkable features of the post-Stalin years has been the emergence — and the endurance under extremely adverse conditions — of an articulate, if diverse and disorganized, opposition to the powers that be in the USSR. This antibureaucratic opposition heralds a new chapter of political progress in the second most powerful country in the world.

The difficulties in assessing the present political opposition movement in the USSR are obvious. The official press, controlled by the privileged bureaucracy, with its monopolistic hold on power, hardly gives reliable information. First-hand interviews from those of oppositionist views are hard to come by — even if not in jails, camps, or "special" psychiatric hospitals, they are not likely to speak freely with foreign reporters, because of the ever-present police threat. And of course the capitalist press and intelligence agencies can be expected to distort or suppress what information they do get. The best source to judge from is samizdat.

Samizdat is a Soviet term coined by post-Stalin dissidents for the old Russian revolutionary practice, from the days of the czarist censorship, of circulating uncensored material privately, usually in manuscript form — nonconformist poetry and fiction, memoirs, historical documents, protest statements, trial records, etc. The name "Samizdat" — Self-Publishers — is an ironic parody of such official acronyms as "Gosizdat," meaning State Publishers (short for Gosudarstvennoe Izdatelstvo). More col-

7

loquially, one might translate samizdat as the Do-It-Yourself Press. The message is clear: "If the bureaucrats won't print it, we'll get it around *ourselves*." Today's samizdat has post-October antecedents as well as prerevolutionary ones — in the private printing and circulation of manuscripts done by the Left Opposition in the twenties and thirties after it was denied the use of the party's printing facilities (the "illegal" printing and circulation of its program was one of the charges that led to the expulsion of the Left Opposition).

In the late twenties and early thirties many Left Opposition documents passed from reader to reader by the same methods that today are called samizdat. Here is how Trotsky described the fate of his 1927 "Letter to the Bureau of Party History": "It circulated from hand to hand in the USSR. In hundreds of copies, either retyped or copied by hand. Single copies, often inexact, filtered abroad. Translations of them appeared in several languages." How contemporary this description sounds! It could refer to any of dozens of samizdat documents of recent years.

The fact is that samizdat is nothing more than the revival, whether conscious or not, of the methods used by the opponents of the Stalin bureaucracy in the period before all vestiges of criticism were stamped out by mass terror.

Even in the early thirties, when most Oppositionists were in prison or exile, their political documents were passed around. Moreover, as late as 1932, they were able to smuggle materials out to be published in the Russian-language *Bulletin of the Opposition*, edited by Trotsky. (In one case, a lengthy theoretical tract, written on cigarette paper in microscopic lettering, was mailed out in a matchbox.) And at the Verkhne-Uralsk "isolator" — a prison described here in the "Memoirs of a Bolshevik-Leninist" — the political prisoners circulated their own manuscript publication, "The Militant Bolshevik" (*Voinst-vuyushchiy Bolshevik*). Its issue no. 2 was reprinted in the Russian *Bulletin* no. 27 (March 1932).

In fact, like the *Chronicle of Current Events* today, the *Bulletin of the Opposition* in 1929-32 found its way into the USSR and "passed stealthily . . . from hand to hand, eagerly read and commented upon even in Stalin's entourage. . . . If only readers in the West had, in the early 1930s, paid more attention to the Letters from Exile from various 'isolators' and camps [reprinted in the *Bulletin*], the 'revelations' of Khrushchev, *The Tales of Kolyma* or the story of Ivan Denisovich would have been much less startling." (*Times Literary Supplement* [London], November 23, 1973).

There is a key difference, of course. The unauthorized circulation of Opposition literature in the thirties was part of the last resistance to the Thermidorian undertow in the Soviet Union fostered by the international recession of anticapitalist revolution. This rise of samizdat, its steady spread, and the deepening politicization in post-Stalin Soviet society are part of a worldwide revolutionary upswing.

The struggle for socialist democracy in the Soviet Union in recent years has centered around samizdat to a great extent. Most of the trials have been aimed at intimidating dissidents involved in producing or circulating uncensored literature. The most prominent figures among the oppositionists have relied on the samizdat network in their battle for free speech, freedom of the press, and basic democratic rights.

The stress in this collection is on dissident Marxist writings. The aim is not to give a sampling of all the different viewpoints that have been expressed in samizdat in recent years. The range of viewpoints that has emerged in Soviet society is quite wide. Other samizdat currents such as the literary-cultural, religious, neo-Slavophile, Great Russian chauvinist, Zionist, neo-Stalinist, and even outright fascist are not represented here. Other collections of samizdat in English have already provided a good sampling of most of those points of view.

This anthology centers around documents of the post-Stalin period which hark back to the revolutionary tradition, documents which protest and expose the decades of Stalin's rule, and which indicate some of the directions the struggle for *socialist* democracy is taking in the USSR. Its stress is on the survivals of early Bolshevism and subsequent manifestations which various authors have called neo-Bolshevism or neo-Leninism.

Central to the book are the "Memoirs of a Bolshevik-Leninist," an anonymous account by a survivor from Stalin's camps who had been in the ranks of the Left Opposition in the twenties. It is a fact that although Stalin has been denounced by the highest official bodies in the Soviet Union, and many of his victims have been posthumously "rehabilitated," the chief Old Bolshevik opponents of Stalin (Trotsky, Zinoviev, Kamenev, Bukharin, etc.) have remained under a ban, whether that of the Khrushchev regime or of Brezhnev-Kosygin. After the war there was reason to think that the entire old Left Opposition had perished in Stalin's prisons and camps. The post-Stalin amnesties at first brought news only of the systematic massacre of the Trotskyists in the camps at the time of the great purges of 1936-38, during the Moscow trials.

If any Oppositionists had survived, it was assumed that the continued ban on "Trotskyites, Zinovievites, Bukharinites, and bourgeois nationalists" (as Khrushchev labeled the still unrehabilitated oppositionists in his famous "secret speech" to the twentieth Soviet party congress in 1956), would prevent them from raising their heads or making themselves heard.

Then, against all expectation, this unique manuscript appeared. And not only has a single Left Oppositionist survived and anonymously recorded the tale of his experiences. A second voice is heard, confirming the first—that of Aleksandra Chumakova, a survivor who even dares to sign her name. (Although she herself was not in the Opposition, her husband was, and her fate was linked to his and to that of other Oppositionists close to them.)

The anonymous memoirs—written over a period of years and completed in the late sixties—became known to the world in 1970 (they were published in a French edition by Maspero that year). Chumakova's are here appearing for the first time in a Western language. Recently other samizdat documents, particularly Roy Medvedev's monumental work *Let History Judge*, have made information public that suggests the existence of still more documents by Oppositionist survivors. But these have not yet reached us. The accounts by the anonymous Bolshevik-Leninist and Chumakova remain the only first-hand word from the historic Soviet Opposition movement to be heard since the time of the purges.

For students of the Soviet Left Opposition, in which the world Trotskyist movement had its origins, the publication and distribution of these unprecedented memoirs is especially significant.

These first two documents, the major part of our book, are followed by two others that are not samizdat texts. But they shed important light on the samizdat documents proper. The eyewitness account of "Trotskyists at Vorkuta" by M.B. might have been a samizdat work, if its author (an old Menshevik who survived Stalin's camps) had stayed in the Soviet Union and passed his papers around privately. The special significance of M. B.'s account is its corroboration of similar passages in the anonymous "Memoirs."

The reason for including Brigitte Gerland's memoirs of life in Stalin's prisons is somewhat different. Such records are what a large part of samizdat consists of, and if Gerland, an East German Communist, had remained in the Soviet bloc and dared to risk repeating her term, she might have circulated her account in samizdat. But she published her account in the West, in a Trotskyist newspaper. The value of her memoirs is threefold. It shows what life was like in the postwar period at the same Vorkuta camps described by the anonymous Bolshevik-Leninist. It shows what kind of opposition groups existed after the war, even quoting from their uncensored publications. And it provides information about the elements of continuity and the loss of it between the three waves of opposition: the first, which perished in the purges, the postwar opposition elements whose strike-organizing efforts helped inaugurate "de-Staliniza- tion," and the new opposition movement of the post-Stalin period.

Two shorter documents from the mid-sixties included with these memoirs show how the young rebels who created samizdat regard the early Bolsheviks, Trotsky, and the Left Opposition. The essay by E. M., "Who Killed Trotsky?," is the first samizdat document in the post-Stalin period, so far as we know, to defend Trotsky's record against the regime's current attacks. (Polemics against Trotsky and Trotskyism have been a continuous feature of the Soviet press since the early sixties; in the fifties, one might have thought from the Soviet press that Trotskyism had finally been buried.) The excerpt from a poem by Vadim Delone (who in 1967-68 became prominent in two political trials) shows the favorable regard among rebel lit- erary youth for the anti-Stalin Bolsheviks, including Trotsky.

The statement by the forty-three children of Old Bolsheviks protesting against any rehabilitation of Stalin is reprinted in this same "historical" section to illustrate another element of continuity between the Bolshevik tradition (best represented by the Left Opposition) and the opposition elements of today. Finally, the reprint from the samizdat journal *Kolokol* rep- resents the only document by a neo-Bolshevik youth group, the Union of Communards, to have thus far become available outside the Soviet Union.

The second section of our collection comprises documents

of the group around Pyotr Grigorenko and Aleksei Kosterin. These center on the year 1968 — when a movement surfaced involving thousands of Soviet citizens in open, public protest in defense of democratic rights, in support of the democratization process in Czechoslovakia, and in opposition to the Kremlin's invasion of that country and its suppression of protest at home. Among the leading figures who inspired this movement were the Old Bolshevik Aleksei Kosterin and the former Red Army General Pyotr Grigorenko. Both of them are dissident Communist Party members, whose theme was Leninism, yes! Stalinism, no! Joining them were such figures as Leonid Plyushch, a Ukrainian civil rights fighter, and Pyotr Yakir, son of a Red Army general shot in Stalin's purges. The young Yakir, freed in 1954 after spending seventeen years in prisons and camps simply because he was the child of an alleged "enemy of the people," came forward as one of the most outspoken opponents of the rehabilitation of Stalin under Brezhnev and Kosygin. Yakir's subsequent capitulation and abandonment of the struggle for democratic rights, after a year in prison in the hands of the secret police and a show trial in September 1973, is well known.

The central feature of this section of documents is the collection of speeches made at memorial services for Aleksei Kosterin in November 1968. Compiled by Grigorenko, who was one of the main speakers, the collection includes a speech by Pyotr Yakir that is of considerable interest in the light of his subsequent forced capitulation to the regime. The Kosterin funeral became an opposition rally that the police were unable to control. It marked the high point of the protest movement of 1968. After it, a series of arrests began — including Grigorenko in May 1969. Documents describing the harassment and persecution (including "special" psychiatric hospitalization) meted out to such victims are included. The struggle to free Grigorenko from psychiatric incarceration is still, in 1974, a central task of solidarity with the Soviet oppositionists of today.

The last part of this book is a sampling of the documents of the post-1968 resistance against repression. The Initiative Group for the Defense of Human Rights in the USSR, in which Pyotr Yakir played an important role, was formed in the wake of and largely spurred by the arrest of Grigorenko. Some of the central documents of the Initiative Group are included here. Most of the members of this group, like Yakir and Plyushch, have been imprisoned, sent into internal exile, pressured into leaving the USSR, broken and forced to capitulate, or forcibly confined in mental hospitals.

The years 1968-72 saw a unique phenomenon — the *Chronicle of Current Events*, a samizdat publication that managed to appear bimonthly with a few exceptions for almost five years (twenty-seven issues in all). It attempted with remarkable success and scrupulous objectivity to document as many cases of political persecution and violation of rights as its editors received information about, as well as all manifestations of struggle to exercise or assert democratic freedoms (in such spheres as political expression, national rights, the right to emigrate, etc.). We have included several excerpts from the *Chronicle*.

A moderate opposition tendency within Soviet society is represented by Academician Andrei Sakharov and dissident historian Roy Medvedev. A program of gradualist democratization proposed by them in 1970 is reprinted here, along with the extremely restrained statement of principles of the Human Rights Committee, founded mainly on Sakharov's initiative in Moscow in 1970. While it shares the same sort of aims as the Initiative Group, the difference in tone between the two groups' statements of principles makes a notable contrast.

Several documents of the post-1968 period illustrate the militancy and high level of consciousness, solidarity, and determination with which political prisoners have continued their struggle even from the labor camps.

A publication similar to the *Chronicle* began to appear in the Ukrainian Soviet Republic in 1970 — *Ukrainsky Visnyk (Ukrainian Herald)*. Its statement of principles was more explicitly pro-Marxist than the *Chronicle* and is reprinted here, along with an assessment by the *Visnyk* of the political trends in the Russian-speaking opposition. The dramatic letter by Latvian Communists to Communists of the West is included here as a further illustration of the severity and explosiveness of national oppression (Russification) in the USSR.

The final documents reflect the reaction of democratic oppositionists to the Kremlin campaign of 1972-73 to suppress the *Chronicle* and the *Visnyk* and destroy the two civil rights groupings.

In response to the repressive policies intensified after 1968 and deepening in 1972-73, a debate arose in samizdat over what tactics the "democratic movement" should follow — what organizing methods it should use, what program it should adopt, how it should relate to the regime and to different social layers. This debate was reflected in the summaries of samizdat material regularly published by the *Chronicle*.

In connection with this attempt to grapple with the program, slogans, and orientation of a struggle for democratization, we have added an appendix — a discussion of a transitional program for the antibureaucratic struggle in the Soviet Union elaborated by Leon Trotsky in 1938. Trotsky's method and approach, and many of the ideas he sketched out, still have as much relevance for the struggle against Stalinism and for a return to the standards of promotion of the socialist democracy envisaged by Lenin as they did thirty-five years ago.

G. S.

INTRODUCTION
Currents in the Soviet Opposition Movement

Is there any connection between the Left Opposition destroyed in the purges of the 1930s (as described in the "Memoirs of a Bolshevik-Leninist," Chumakova's memoirs, and the account by "M.B.") and the "democratic movement" in the Soviet Union today? This is a highly important question for Soviet history and politics.

The Left Opposition was led by a group of prominent Bolsheviks who had played major roles in the October Revolution, civil war, and construction of the Soviet state. Its ranks consisted largely of a younger generation that had fought in the revolution and civil war. In the twenties these young people remained the most active, devoted, and internationalist-minded of the young Communists, both workers and students. (Survivors of that generation of anti-Stalinist Communists include two of our authors, Chumakova and the anonymous memoirist.)

By contrast with the Left Opposition of old, the best-known Soviet "dissidents" today are not veteran party leaders or revolutionary-minded Marxist activists. Writers like Aleksandr Solzhenitsyn, Andrei Sinyavsky, Yuli Daniel, Lidia Chukovskaya, and scientists like Andrei Sakharov and Zhores Medvedev, highly publicized by the mass media in America and the West generally, give the impression that most of Soviet dissent today is centered in literary and cultural circles and among some of the "technical intelligentsia" of Moscow and the main Russian cities. However, more radical forms of dissent, and expressions of discontent among the masses, definitely exist, though they have received far less attention.

Throughout the Stalin and post-Stalin eras, there has been a continuing tendency for radical opposition to crop up among students and workers, not least of all among the nationally oppressed. The conditions of bureaucratic rule, as well as the surviving traditions of the Bolshevik revolution and of true Marxism and Leninism, have guided such tendencies toward ideas and activities often closely parallel to those of the Left Opposition. (One expression of such "neo-Bolshevik" trends, the circle consisting of Grigorenko, Kosterin, and their friends — which was closely linked with and influenced the "democratic movement" — has even received considerable publicity. For details see Section Two.)

Likewise, protest actions in the USSR involving large numbers of workers and members of oppressed nationalities have occurred rather often in the past two decades, although Western public opinion is not nearly so aware of those as of similar outbreaks in Eastern Europe.

Without denying the importance of the ferment in the upper intellectual establishment of the Soviet Union, or the courageous role of the most prominent dissidents, this essay attempts to acquaint the reader with the more radical, often "neo-Bolshevik" groupings, especially among the youth, and the instances of mass outbreaks that have occurred in the Soviet Union, even though detailed information is often lacking.

A look at the opposition currents that grew up among Soviet youth in the last period of Stalin's rule (1945-53), especially the testimony provided by Brigitte Gerland's memoirs of life in the Vorkuta camps in the early fifties, shows that militant anti-Stalinist struggle soon revived in spite of the destruction of most of the old Opposition cadres. Several clandestine youth organizations appeared in the early forties which had arrived "independently" at positions very close to Trotskyism. We say "independently" in quotes because it is impossible to know where the ✳ideas came from that finally took shape in underground student groups functioning in several major cities.

But before looking more closely at the opposition groups of the early postwar period, a review of the background to their struggle is necessary.

The years 1938 and after saw the final defeat of the Spanish revolution, the Munich agreement, the Stalin-Hitler pact, and the opening of World War II. Simultaneously, inside the USSR, the bloody purges of 1936-38 subsided into a more "normalized," routine pattern of repression and execution.

The Nazi invasion of the Soviet Union in June 1941 precipitated a new crisis. In the face of the disastrous early setbacks of the Nazi-Soviet war, Stalin was forced to release many of his prisoners — those who were able to serve the defense of the workers' state more effectively than Stalin's old cronies in charge of Soviet defense, incompetents like Budenny and Voroshilov, who were set aside by late 1941. (Not all of Stalin's revolutionary prisoners, however, were allowed to participate in the fight. Many of the surviving Oppositionists volunteered for duty, but some were immediately executed and others assigned to suicide missions.)

The war also produced new droves of prisoners for the camps, the generation of the "Ivan Denisoviches." Anyone who had been captured by the Germans or exposed to the West became suspect and was jailed. In addition, many military personnel who, like Solzhenitsyn, fought to defend the Soviet state, but were caught expressing criticism of Stalin's calamitous misleadership, were sent to the camps, if not shot outright.

Political life went on in the society, beneath the surface. And in the camps, all the most politicized elements were gathered. There, even if in tenuous and distorted ways, and despite the murderous conditions, the revolutionary heritage passed on to new generations.

In the postwar years, antibureaucratic moods and struggles grew stronger. After a slight relaxation in 1945-46, Stalin introduced a new reign of terror — a brutal anti-Semitic campaign in which the cream of Soviet Jewish culture was exterminated; a campaign against "bourgeois nationalism" aimed particularly against the newly assimilated territories of the Western Ukraine, Western Byelorussia, the Baltic republics, and Moldavia. All who resisted the policy of Russification in those areas — or any other non-Russian areas of the Union — were likewise purged for "bourgeois nationalism," even if they were Communists, as the 1972 letter by Latvian CP members has shown.

Stalin's ferocious intensification of terror in the postwar period culminated in the notorious Doctors' Plot. Several Jewish doctors who attended top leaders in the Kremlin were accused of planning to poison their eminent patients. Here anti-Semitism, one of Stalin's long-time devices, was combined with plans for generalized terror, arrests, and executions on an unparalleled scale.

Stalin's timely death in March 1953 interrupted the plans for the massive Doctors' Plot purge. His heirs dropped the whole scheme, cleared the accused physicians, and began a whole series of reforms and concessions to mass discontent that finally peaked in the "de-Stalinization" revelations of the twentieth and twenty-second congresses.

Behind the ferocity of the terror in Stalin's last years stood an insoluble crisis of the system — economic, social, and political strains that reflected the persistent pressures of imperialism and the impossibility of building "socialism in one country." In the face of U.S. imperialism's postwar expansionist drive, and the U.S. nuclear threat, the inefficient Soviet bureaucracy, with its swollen military apparatus, continued to employ only military-diplomatic methods and intensified political repression, once again showing its hostility to a revolutionary internationalist strategy based on socialist democracy.

The Stalin regime incorporated the East European buffer states, according to its military-diplomatic perspective, with no regard for the special conditions or national feelings of the incorporated nations. Its arbitrary, Russian chauvinist, military-bureaucratic methods provoked the Tito split in 1948; and to prevent similar developments in other East European countries, the Stalinist police then engineered show trials against "Titoites and Trotskyites" (i.e., unreliable local CP leaders) throughout Eastern Europe.

The same cold war pressures, and military-bureaucratic responses, led the Kremlin high command to introduce a five-year plan with impossible targets that once again brought Soviet agriculture to a state of crisis, causing famine in the countryside just as forced collectivization had done in the early thirties.

These pressures and crises continually regenerated opposition from below. The police-bureaucratic management of the economy, and the unproductive approach to the domestic and international problems of state drove thinking people, especially the young, to revolutionary conclusions. In the Western Ukraine and in Lithuania, Russian chauvinism and the bureaucratic establishment of Soviet power led to guerrilla resistance involving tens and hundreds of thousands against the Stalin regime.

Against the social and historical background outlined above, the significance of the revolutionary underground groups known to have emerged in the 1945-53 period is better understood. An echo of the Bolshevik-Leninist tradition reappeared in them, and they foreshadowed the "neo-Bolshevik" or "neo-Leninist" groupings of the post-Stalin period.

Revolutionary Underground Groups of 1945-53

The most detailed description of the political ideas of dissident Soviet youth in the early postwar years is given by Brigitte Gerland, in her memoirs of life at Vorkuta in 1948-53, published here as "Vorkuta (1950-53): Oppositional Currents and the Mine Strikes." Most interesting is the fact that a neo-Leninist group, numbering some hundreds of students at major universities in Moscow, Leningrad, Kiev, and Odessa arrived at a program very close to that of the Left Opposition, even though, as Gerland believes, "the young Leninists had no contact of any kind with the old Opposition."

Many of these young Leninists had been children of "enemies of the people," i.e., their parents had been prominent in the party, government, and military but had been purged in 1936-38. (Stalin had feared the potential challenge to his apparatus from the entire older generation of revolutionists from October and the civil war years.)

"The whole movement is said to have started in 1948 from a discussion between five Moscow University students on the long-banned poetry of Boris Pasternak, in which the idea is developed that spiritual freedom is incompatible with social justice," Gerland relates in her book on Vorkuta published in Germany in 1955. In response to the pessimism prevalent all around them and expressed in Pasternak's poetry, the students resolved to find "a way of making room for spiritual freedom in a collectivist society by decentralization of state power."

This episode is a remarkable forerunner of events to come. The struggle for greater freedom of literary and cultural expression became a major feature not only of the anti-Stalinist movement under Khrushchev (and around Pasternak's poetry then, as well as other "unapproved" literature) but also in the struggles in Eastern Europe for socialist democracy.

Program of the "Lenin's True Work" Group

The program these orphans of the "generation of 1937" developed, called Istinny Trud Lenina (Lenin's True Work), paralleled that of Trotskyism in many ways. Gerland quotes from it and describes it in full in her memoirs of Vorkuta included here. Briefly, it advocated political revolution to replace the bureaucracy with full Soviet democracy, based on soviets (councils) in every plant and collective farm. These councils were to be elected by the workers and peasants by secret ballot, with all council members subject to immediate recall by the voters. Instead of salaried professionals there would be committees of workers and peasants to carry out administrative tasks. The standing army — whose officer caste had generally proved to be a mainstay of the privileged bureaucracy — was to be replaced by a workers' and peasants' militia (an idea paralleling a proposal by Trotsky in the early twenties).

"Bourgeois democracy, . . . parliamentary forms, and the capitalist economy of the West held little attraction for these young people thirsting for social justice," Gerland stressed in her book.   ,

On the international level, they decisively rejected the dogma of "socialism in one country." They asserted that the transition to communism "can be achieved only by the working classes of all countries, acting in common, in a revolution embracing the whole world." The Istinny Trud Lenina (ITL) supporters were also convinced that "the world revolution was impossible without a world Communist party, leading the proletariat in the struggle."

The consistency of Bolshevik-Leninist line they had reached is strikingly apparent not only on the question of international revolution but also on the question of *nationalities policy* within the sphere of postcapitalist society. Here they opposed the military-bureaucratic methods, the bureaucratic supercentralism, and the Russian chauvinist policies of the Kremlin, not only in relation to non-Russian nations within Soviet borders but also toward the nations of Eastern Europe where capitalism had been abolished. Insofar as the Kremlin's postwar annexations (Western Ukraine, Western Byelorussia, the Baltic states) violated national self-determination, the young Leninists condemned them.

Other Neo-Leninist Groups

The ITL was not the only neo-Leninist grouping to have its origins among young Communists affected by the purges. The "Lenin Group," an underground youth organization that was discovered and smashed by the secret police in 1947, is another group that had its origins in a reaction against the purges, if only a delayed one.

Less is known about the "Lenin Group" than about the ITL but its origins are indicated in its program, which was described in an anonymous "Letter to Stalin" that apparently circulated in the USSR before 1947. The author of the letter was a young Communist who had gone along with the purges of 1936-38, because the Soviet Union had seemed the "only rampart of the forces of progress in the world" at that time, encircled by world capitalism and threatened by fascist invasion. In that atmosphere the purging of the Old Bolsheviks and all oppositionists had been tolerated because the external threat appeared to make monolithic unity imperative.

Once the war had been victoriously concluded, however, and the Soviet state was no longer isolated and encircled, the anonymous author of the letter, this once-loyal Stalinist, revived many of the very criticisms made by the purged opposition: The bureaucracy has become a privileged caste, ever more estranged from the working masses, an aristocracy that ruins agriculture and disorganizes industry. The letter writer even predicted that Stalin's successors would disavow him in order to maintain their bureaucratic power!

The groups we have named are not the only ones known to exist in the early postwar period. One of the most interesting was a clandestine organization in the camps in 1947-48, made up of veterans of the war against the Nazis, that took the name "Democratic Movement of the North of Russia." Its composition reflected the fact that Stalin's camps had been swelled by Soviet soldiers arrested during and after the war. Whole units cut off and surrounded by Germans in the first period of the war, after fighting their way back to their own lines, would find themselves arrested on charges of desertion or treason — all in order to cover up for the bureaucracy's own disorganization of the army by wiping out the top military leadership in the purges and failing to prepare for the invasion.

Veterans like the ones organized in the secret Democratic Movement of the North of Russia staged a desperate revolt in 1948. Seizing their guards' weapons, they tried to take a town in the vast Norilsk labor-camp region, east of the Urals. The effort failed, and they fled toward the mountains — reportedly over 2,000 strong — but were annihilated by the Kremlin's airpower. A similar revolt apparently occurred in the eastern Siberian region of Kolyma, according to the Soviet writer Varlam Shalamov, whose *Notes from Kolyma* have circulated in samizdat and been published outside the USSR.

All-out mobilization of the forces of the bureaucratic machine managed to break up such opposition groups and crush the isolated revolts of 1948-53. But as the strains and tensions persisted, the bureaucracy finally had to take a new tack. With Stalin's death, they began a relaxation. But this encouraged the rebels in the camps to organize strikes that were partly successful — and incidentally were strengthened by the example of the East Berlin workers' revolt of June 1953. Although the regime smashed the strikes, it also was forced to grant some concessions. New strikes kept breaking out through 1954 and 1955, until finally a general amnesty of political prisoners was granted and the camp system partly dismantled. Thus the stage was set for the twentieth congress and the official repudiation of Stalin by his heirs and former henchmen.

Bolshevik Traditions and the National Question

Nationalities policy has always been a central index of the struggle between revolutionary internationalist tendencies and bureaucratic-reactionary ones in the Soviet Union. It was one of the key issues that caused Lenin to break with Stalin in late 1922 and early 1923, and to prepare an all-out fight against bureaucracy in the party and government. Lenin's illness and death meant that the first step in that fight — removal of Stalin from the post of "general secretary" because of his great-power chauvinism and abuse of authority — was not carried through.

Stalin retained and augmented his power and the bureaucratic, Russian-centralizing tendency he represented grew stronger as the general trend of reaction deepened. Stalin imposed his great-power chauvinist concept upon the USSR in spite of the struggle by the Left Opposition and revolutionary elements in the national republics to fight for implementation of Lenin's policy, as adopted by the 1923 twelfth party congress.

The Left Opposition carried on Lenin's struggle for a correct nationalities policy, and the 1927 *Platform of the Left Opposition* raised eleven demands on this question. It is a significant fact that "a larger proportion" of Trotskyists "than in other parties were members of national minorities," as Joseph Berger observes.[1] *

---

*Notes to the Introduction begin on page 44.

The defeat of the Left Opposition and the strengthening of the narrow, Russian-chauvinist bureaucracy's stranglehold on the party, government, and economy in the early thirties meant an end to whatever progress in Ukrainization, Turkification, and so on, had actually been achieved in the twenties under the impact of Lenin's fight and the best Bolshevik traditions. Ivan Dzyuba in his *Internationalism or Russification?* describes the crude brutality with which Stalin in 1932-33 cut short the highly positive Ukrainization program — a term that Dzyuba says is still mentioned only in whispers to this very day. Thousands of prominent figures in the cultural life of the Ukraine were slaughtered in a blood purge of the Ukrainian Republic promoted by Stalin, several years before the infamous unionwide blood purges of 1936-38.

But the complexities and difficulties for the Soviet state and for the course of world revolutionary developments in general caused by the national question did not disappear even with Stalin's attempts to wipe it out physically. The coming of World War II brought Soviet expansion into the Western Ukraine, Western Byelorussia, and the Baltic republics. In the postwar period, Soviet influence dominated most of Eastern Europe, and under Stalin's direction played a major role in Iranian Azerbaidzhan, Mongolia, Manchuria, Korea, and in relation to the Chinese and Vietnamese revolutions. These and similar events continually placed the Russian-centered, narrowly chauvinist Kremlin bureaucracy in conflict with the national aspirations and needs of masses of people, often moving in revolutionary directions.

The bureaucratic-military approach of the Stalinist bureaucracy in overturning capitalism in the Western Ukraine and the Baltic republics drove peasants in those areas to organize guerrilla warfare against the Stalin regime. It is of great significance that the neo-Leninist youth group that evolved at Vorkuta in the late forties and early fifties, arriving at positions close to those of the old Left Opposition, should have found the national differences with the Ukrainian and Baltic guerrilla veterans to be the most difficult problem in coordinating a fight against the regime. The fact that they were able to ultimately forge an alliance with those "national" elements was also of enormous significance, and was clearly the key to the substantial gains won in that fight.

The revolutionary socialist tendency among the postwar Ukrainian guerrillas is not so evident in Gerland's account, but it was significant. A major tendency in the Ukrainian

Partisan Army (UPA), which survived into the early fifties, based its struggle on an anticapitalist and anti-Stalinist program in favor of socialist democracy.[2]

The post-Stalin period, and the half-hearted "de-Stalinization" concessions, created an opening in which the struggle for national rights could reassert itself. On the one hand this was spurred by the continuing policies of Russification pursued by the bureaucratic regime — Stalin's heirs remained true to his program in that respect. On the other hand, the total non-Russian population, by the 1970 census, was threatening to turn the dominant Russian nation's majority into a plurality.

The revival of struggle against Stalinism around the national question was most dramatic in two areas: the new "cultural" opposition in the Ukraine; and the linkup between neo-Leninist oppositionists in Moscow and the struggle for "rehabilitation" of nationalities deported wholesale by Stalin during World War II. (Entire populations had been accused of collaboration with the Nazis.)

The present collection cannot do justice to the complexity and variety of the national question in the Soviet Union today. But some of the uncensored materials reprinted here from the USSR show that it is an explosive issue. The struggle for a correct revolutionary policy on this issue, uncompromisingly opposed to Russian chauvinism, as Lenin's example showed, is of vital importance in the struggle against the bureaucracy. All "neo-Leninist" tendencies must grapple with this problem and solve it correctly. In fact, on the central problem of mobilizing masses of people into a struggle against the bureaucracy and for a political revolution to institute socialist democracy, the national grievances have thus far produced the nearest thing to mass movements in which the more conscious elements, coming first from the ranks of the intelligentsia and party, have been able to find a common voice with the workers and peasants.

"De-Stalinization" and the Upsurge of 1956

We come now to the watershed between two periods of Soviet history — Stalin's death. "De-Stalinization," made official at the twentieth congress (1956) with Khrushchev's denunciation of Stalin, created a new situation for opposition elements in the struggle against bureaucratism and for socialist democracy, a framework in which certain legal opportunities became available. This is by no means to imply that the bureaucracy could, or wished to, reform itself out of existence, as some thought or hoped. The bureaucracy's "de-Stalinization" was not self-motivated, but a *concession* to mass pressure—and it grudgingly conceded as little as possible. Khrushchev and his apparatchiks tried to retain maximum control over the process by which the worst excesses of the Stalin era were halted while the basic structures of the Stalin system were retained. (Soon Khrushchev's accomplices would restore the Stalin figurehead—though on a much smaller scale.)

How much leeway was there for antibureaucratic oppositionists in this new situation? Despite Khrushchev's claim that there were no more political prisoners, the repression continued. And it took the form of savage violence by the terrified police regime whenever mass movements began to get "out of hand." But day-to-day repression was modified and pulled back; the bureaucracy tried to adopt a more legalistic form, to be less obviously high-handed. A certain level of grumbling, or mild dissent, was allowed—within limits—as long as it did not become coherent, vocal, organized, or massive.

Thus, in the post-Stalin era, some critical ideas could be expressed, without running the risk of harsh reprisals. The possibility of fighting one's case in court and appealing for public support even opened up. Some oppositional ideas found an avenue of expression—especially when couched in the regime's own terminology: "the cult of personality," "overcoming harmful vestiges of the past," restoring "Leninist norms in the party and state," observing "socialist legality." In the worst periods under Stalin, extreme clandestinity had been required. In the post-Stalin situation, by contrast, rebels against the system could more easily hear about one another, establish contact, hold discussions, make their ideas known, if only in disguised and allegorical fashion.

Another important new feature of the post-Stalin situation was its world context. There was some relaxation of border controls. Information from abroad entered more easily. At the same time, divergent currents arose within "official" world Communism, even in "fraternal" countries—lands that were no longer jumping-off points for imperialist invasion, where "bourgeois ideology" could no longer be said to prevail. If certain ideas—or a certain status as "independent" socialist republics—were permissible in the case of Yugoslavia or Poland, then why not for individuals or nations within the USSR? This heterogeneity and multipolarity in the world Communist movement continues to play a significant role to the present day.

The initial response to de-Stalinization was explosive — reflecting the high pressures that had built up among the masses. The East Berlin uprising and the Vorkuta and other labor camp strikes in summer 1953, and then on a greater scale, the uprisings in Poland and Hungary in October-November 1956, were like the first rush of steam through a half-opened valve.

The Polish and Hungarian workers' revolts raised the specter of political revolution, which could have replaced the bureaucratic caste with workers' democracy and institutions of self-management. The uprisings came very close to succeeding; they were prevented only by the repressive forces thrown in by the Kremlin and the lack of revolutionary leadership at the head of the insurgent masses.

This high point of antibureaucratic revolt had reverberations inside the Soviet Union itself. Mass protests were reported in some areas, such as the ancient Lithuanian city of Kaunas. During the Hungarian events entire Soviet military units, sympathetic to the rebels, had to be pulled out of Hungary; there were also reports that Soviet railway workers refused to run military supply trains in for the repressive forces.

These turbulent developments were reflected in the reappearance among Soviet youth of a strong "neo-Bolshevik" current, with ideas close to those of the Left Opposition. Clandestine neo-Leninist groups, strikingly similar to the ITL of the late forties, were once again reported from Moscow student circles.

It is worth taking a closer look at the neo-Bolshevik currents of 1956-57, for similar groupings have been consistently reported throughout the sixties and into the seventies.

Neo-Bolsheviks of 1956-57

At Moscow University in November 1956, students at a compulsory session on Marxism-Leninism began to bombard the professor with questions about the suppression of the Hungarian revolt, refuting his apologies with — quotations from Lenin! The lecturer was forced to leave, and the class was dismissed. The next day a Communist Youth (Komsomol) meeting was called to discuss the "shameful" incident. The student audience again took over the meeting from their official leaders, converting it into a solidarity demonstration with the Hungarian workers and drawing analogies between the regimes in Hungary and the USSR. Despite expulsions and other reprisals against hundreds of student activists, open protests continued for a while. Similar student meetings were reported in Leningrad (where there was also a demonstration supporting the Hungarian workers, held in front of the Winter Palace) and in other major Soviet cities, including in Central Asia, as well as in the Komsomol of the Moscow army garrison.

A dramatic first-hand description of the student turbulence in Moscow at that time has been given by David Burg, pseudonym of a Soviet exile now living in Britain who was a student at Moscow University in the period 1951-56.

"In 1956-57, after the XXth Party Congress," Burg writes, "opposition elements within the institutes and universities began to wage an open battle against [the] Komsomol leadership. They sought, first of all, to gain freedom of criticism and expression, and second to introduce a degree of intra-Komsomol democracy that would make the Komsomol a truly representative organization with an honestly elected leadership. Freedom of expression was in fact gradually achieved at that period by a kind of procedure of protestation, and extraordinarily sharp critical comments were heard more and more commonly at meetings. At the same time, illegal and semilegal student journals with such characteristic titles as *Heresy* and *Fresh Voices* began to appear; they discussed art and ideology, ridiculed socialist realism, and attacked the local Komsomol leaders. . . ."[3]

Burg estimates that between one-third and one-fourth of the student body evinced open political discontent during "the thaw of 1956." The attitude of the rest of the students toward the political avant-garde was "sometimes sympathetic, sometimes uncomprehending, but rarely hostile."

It is worth noting that demands for the rehabilitation of the major defendants of the purge trials were widely raised by the student protesters. Burg also comments that previously unmentionable names like Trotsky and Bukharin began to be mentioned, and that the open and semi-"legal" tactics of 1956 were supplemented in some cases "by the creation of illegal political groups that had far-reaching political aspirations. In the history faculty at the University of Moscow, for example, a group of some ten to fifteen graduate students and young research workers printed and distributed leaflets directed against Khrushchev personally and the party dictatorship generally, and calling for the establishment of Soviet democracy and a return to the 'Leninist line.'" This apparently refers to the group around the history students Krasnopevtsev and Rendel; the group was eventually discovered and broken up by the secret police in summer 1957; most of its members were arrested and sentenced to rather harsh prison terms. This group reflected the predominant view among student oppositionists. "The leaflets issued by clandestine groups," Burg reports, "generally expound the neo-Bolshevik line, as did the history students at the University of Moscow."

The neo-Bolshevik line was reported the strongest of the three main political currents among Soviet students at that time. Burg describes these three viewpoints in some detail. They were, to use his terminology, the "neo-Bolsheviks" (or "neo-Leninists"), the "liberal socialists," and the pro-Western "antisocialists."

Burg's account is confirmed by a description in the German socialist youth paper, *Junge Gemeinschaft*, of November 1957: "The oppositional youth consider themselves Marxists, but they feel that the present Soviet social order does not correspond to Marxist ideals. They seek a genuine Marxism and have therefore turned to the pre-Soviet period and to the twenties. . . . They consider the purges of 1937 as an annihilation of the true leaders of the Revolution by Stalin's bureaucratic clique—as a kind of Thermidor."

The program of the "neo-Bolsheviks" of 1956-57 was remarkably similar to that of the Istinny Trud Lenina group of 1948-53, and to that of the original Bolshevik-Leninists destroyed in the purges. They advocated: retention of the planned economy with workers' control of industry and the transformation of the collective farms into real cooperatives managed by their members; political power in the hands of democratically elected and genuinely representative soviets; an end to persecution of dissenters; and free discussion of all interpretations of Marxist thought, as well as freedom of discussion in science and art. The neo-Bolsheviks, according to Burg, did not favor a multiparty system, but rather, full internal democracy within the Communist Party. They also opposed introduction of market mechanisms into the economy, believing these would lead to inequality.

Their attitude toward the major centers of world capitalism in particular is worth noting. "The neo-Bolsheviks," reports Burg, "usually argue that while the West is politically freer than the USSR, the Soviet economic structure is more progressive because it is no longer under capitalist control. All that remains to be accomplished, therefore, is the modification of the political structure to prevent the consolidation of power in the hands of a new exploiting class. In contrast, the West is still faced with the problem of wresting economic power from a strongly entrenched bourgeoisie." This is exactly the kind of distinction, it should be noted, that Trotsky drew with the characterization of *political* rather than *social* revolution for the bureaucratized workers' state.

The second political tendency that Burg describes is that of the "liberal socialists" whom he likened to Mensheviks under changed historical circumstances. They do not think a return to October is possible or desirable; instead they favor introducing market-type modifications in the economy and a Western-style parliamentary democracy. Their ultimate goal is individual political freedom, defined rather narrowly. In general, the "liberals" fear revolution and advocate gradual reform as a near-universal solution. They tend to have illusions about life in advanced capitalist societies and a concomitant inability to see the Soviet working class as the potentially mighty force that could topple the bureaucracy.

The openly procapitalist "antisocialists" are the third tendency Burg describes. They tend to think in more simplistic terms: Whatever they dislike in their environment they attribute to evils inherent in the system of planned economy; whatever they wish for but do not have, they believe that capitalism, private property, a "free economy," could provide. According to Burg, this attitude was found more frequently among the *technical intelligentsia* — students at engineering, technical, and similar schools.

Such divergences of viewpoint among oppositionist elements developed further in the Khrushchev and Brezhnev eras. Roy Medvedev in his 1970 book *On Socialist Democracy* described similar currents in the late sixties.

The upsurge of 1956-57 was beaten down, and thousands of student oppositionists swelled the population of the camps and prisons for politicals.

Clandestine Neo-Leninist Groups Since 1956

Andrei Amalrik, a dissident historian now serving a prison term under very harsh conditions, wrote a brief account of the rise of what he calls "the democratic movement" in his well-known essay, *Will the Soviet Union Survive Until 1984?* In it he refers to a number of underground organizations which, "despite the secrecy surrounding their trials," have become known since 1956. Besides the Krasnopevtsev-Rendel group, he mentions the Leningrad group that published *Kolokol* (The Bell) in 1964-65. *Kolokol* had been the name of one of the clandestine journals that appeared in the 1956-57 period in Leningrad, apparently of neo-Bolshevik viewpoint. Its title was taken from Herzen's famous anti-czarist emigre publication of the mid-nineteenth century. The later *Kolokol,* of 1964-65, was put out by a group called the Union of Communards, which based its Marxist program on Lenin's *State and Revolution*. It was presumably a revival of the 1956-57 publication. We have included in this collection material from the only issue of the 1964-65 *Kolokol* to come out of the USSR.

Clandestine, usually "neo-Leninist" groups have continued to exist or come into being as a regular feature of Soviet political life. Little first-hand information about them has become available. The exceptions are the group around Kosterin and Grigorenko in 1968 and the Ukrainian group of 1960-61, called the Union of Workers and Peasants of the Ukraine.

The bureaucracy surrounds such groups with the strictest secrecy because it fears them the most. Sometimes the only information about them appears as a few lines or a few paragraphs in *The Chronicle of Current Events.*[4]

In the late fifties and early sixties several clandestine organizations appeared in the Ukraine. These groups were especially significant because workers were involved.

We have reprinted here excerpts from the *Chronicle* with more detailed information on three opposition organizations that appeared in Central Russian cities in the 1968-69 period.

There have been reports that a clandestine organization of young neo-Bolsheviks played an important role in mass strikes and protests by workers in the Donbas region in 1962. One report, although unverified, described students in a role strikingly reminiscent of the one played by the young Leninists in the Vorkuta strikes, even including collaboration with "Ukrainian nationalists."

"In June of 1962, an uprising occurred in Novocherkassk. There a large part of the population joined in a massive demonstration [against price increases on meat and dairy products] that was brutally suppressed. Almost helpless in cases like this, the military was forced to call up reinforcements. But even these additional troops allegedly refused to fire into the crowd after the commanding officer shot himself in front of their eyes. Accompanied by tank units, the MVD [internal security] troops . . . finally put an end to the mass demonstrations. According to unofficial reports, several hundred people were killed.

"The insurgents in the Donbas region [where a wave of protest strikes had occurred] reportedly considered . . . the demonstration in Novocherkassk unsuccessful mainly because they rebelled there without the consent of the strike organization offices in [nearby] Rostov (on the Don), Lugansk, Taganrog, and other cities. This would confirm rumors and reports concerning a headquarters for organized opposition in [the] Donbas and also explain that a planned co-ordinated demonstration didn't develop because of tumult breaking out over the price increases before final preparations could be made. (*The agitation was supposedly instigated for the most part by students and intellectuals, abetted by a few Ukrainian nationalists.*)" [Emphasis added — G. S.]5

Mass Discontent — the Power Behind the Opposition

The oppositional activities of the intellectuals and students have usually been the first to reach our ears. This is not only because they are harbingers of the movements in the depths of the working class, but because they are more articulate and have easier access to means of publicity. In fact, however, they draw inspiration and courage from the mood of the workers and the knowledge that they have the support of the workers. Behind the continual reappearance of clandestine revolutionary grouping in the USSR stand the much broader, general discontents of the masses, especially the hostility of the workers toward the privileged bureaucracy. Such feelings are widespread and just below the surface.

As the economy becomes more complex, as the consumer demands of the ever larger, more educated and confident working class (50 million strong) become greater, the privilege-seeking bureaucrats are under more and more pressure to produce efficiently. But the total monopoly on decision-making, which the bureaucracy needs to protect its privileged position, necessarily means inefficiency. For in the planned economy, full, democratic self-management by the workers is ultimately the only way the economy can function to the optimum.

It is against this background of the economic and social crisis of the bureaucracy that the student and intellectual protests of today must be seen.

There have been literally hundreds of occasions in the last

decade when the Soviet working class has broken out into open protest, often in the form of violent spontaneous outbursts. "It is interesting to note," one observer writes, "the speed with which these outbursts develop and how quickly they spread if the bureaucracy fails to contain them by cordoning off the city in which they occur." He goes on to describe working class protests in several cities. In Kiev the striking workers of the hydro-electric plant "actually organized mass meetings which were addressed by their own elected representatives, and where the bureaucrats who tried to address the workers were physically evicted from the platform. The strike was about housing shortages. But during demonstrations which the workers organized, banners were raised calling for 'All Power to the Soviets'." [6]

In this action and others, it is the women, who receive on the average 50 percent of men's wages and still bear the burden of housekeeping, cooking, and shopping, who have felt the shortages more acutely than the men and have taken the initiative to protest.

Another example of such outbreaks was the one that occurred in Temir-Tau, Kazakhstan, were a strike began in October 1959 involving several thousand young women and men at a metallurgical center under construction. This was the region where the Karaganda network of Stalin-era labor camps had functioned. The Khrushchev regime, instead of shipping people off to labor camps, applied various kinds of pressure, including appeals to youthful idealism, to get workers out to such remote industrial areas. At Temir-Tau they were stuck living in a tent colony without sanitation facilities or adequate supplies. On October 3, some fifty young workers began a demonstration, including expropriation of goods from stores. When the police interfered, the number of rebels grew to over fifteen hundred, barricades were set up, and the police chief and director of the tent colony were seized. On October 4, troops from Karaganda arrived but were disarmed by the rebels (apparently by fraternization tactics). The rebels took over the whole town. Only on the evening of October 5 did reinforcements — special detachments of security police — suppress the rebellion, after cordoning off the city.

At the March 1960 congress of the Communist Party of Kazakhstan, a few months later, the new party secretary Kunaev, who had replaced his predecessor Belyaev in January, laid the blame for these explosive events on "the scornful attitude of the director of the tent colony toward the living conditions of the workers."

Many other specific instances of such explosions have become known, despite the secrecy with which the bureaucracy tries to hide them. [7]

Dissident author Andrei Amalrik has given a valuable firsthand impression of the mass moods behind these outbreaks, though he qualifies his assessment with the observation that "no one, not even the bureaucratic elite, knows exactly what attitudes prevail among the wider sections of the population." (*Will the Soviet Union Survive. . . ?*)

Writing during the period 1966-69, Amalrik used the rather apt term "passive discontent" to summarize his impression of popular attitudes. Mass discontent was not at that time directed against the regime itself, in Amalrik's opinion, but against certain *aspects* of conditions in society.

"The workers, for example, are bitter over having no rights vis-a-vis the factory management. The collective farmers are resentful about their total dependence on the kolkhoz [farm] chairman. . . . Everybody is angered by the great inequalities in wealth, the low wages, the austere housing conditions, the lack of essential consumer goods, compulsory registration at their places of residence and work, and so forth."

The slow rise in the standard of living, Amalrik felt, had neutralized popular anger but not removed it. If such improvement stopped or was reversed, explosions of mass discontent would follow. He speculated that fear of such an explosion had induced the regime not to introduce a big price increase in early 1969, but to let creeping inflation go on instead. The regime learned a lesson in 1962, he argued, when Khrushchev's raising of meat and dairy prices had sparked the series of strikes and mass protests we have referred to earlier.

In a 1970 television interview Amalrik spoke further on the discontent among the masses. "[There is] a great deal of dissatisfaction on account of the wide discrepancies in wage levels, extreme annoyance at the existence of special closed shops and stores, in which the ruling elite are able to buy goods which cannot be bought in the ordinary shops, and with other ways in which the nation's wealth is unfairly distributed."

"The workers are discontented because of their low wages, high work quotas, and the efforts to force them to stay at their workplaces. The farm workers are discontented also because they are forced to remain at one place of work and [because of] their very hard working conditions. Some people are discontented at having so little money; others because there is nothing to spend it on."

The possibility of "passive discontent" erupting into strikes and revolts in reaction to unpopular economic measures was clearly demonstrated in the USSR's neighbor Poland in December 1970. In response to sharp price hikes on food, fuel, and other essentials, dockworkers in Gdansk, Gdynia, and Szczecin went on strike. Police attempts to repress the strikers led to large-scale street fighting and the spread of strikes to other areas. Only the resignation of Gomulka and the concessions introduced by his successor Gierek, above all a rescinding of the price increases, brought the situation under the regime's control again in early 1971. And since then the Polish workers have remained combative, asserting increasing independence.

If the lesson of Novocherkassk in 1962 was not enough, that of Poland in December 1970 clearly influenced the Brezhnev regime in the USSR. In March 1971, at the twenty-fourth Soviet party congress, a plan for increased consumer goods supplies and other guarantees of improved living standards for the Soviet population received a great deal of emphasis, largely due to the Polish events and the concomitant wildcat demonstrations in the Soviet Union for better living conditions and better consumer goods. [8]

From "Cultural" Opposition to Political Opposition

After the 1956-57 upsurge among students and intellectuals, the late fifties and early sixties saw a relative decline of overt protest as many of the more militant dissidents were expelled from universities or other institutions and sent off to labor camps, and as articulate opposition elements that remained turned to less explicitly political activities. A broader, more diffuse, more "culturally" oriented ferment among young rebels then arose. It was permitted a semilegal existence: though constantly harassed by "selective" arrests and trials, it was not crushed completely. That was how Khrushchev's "thaw" developed, with a relative relaxation of censorship and a partial alliance between the regime and liberal elements in the "cultural" establishment. And alongside them emerged the unofficial, privately circulated literature of the "cultural opposition," evolving gradually, growing more and more daring.

At first, unauthorized student publishing ventures were concerned mainly with literature and the arts. They criticized or parodied official "socialist realism" and reproduced literary works that departed from the official school in order to express real attitudes and feelings, not those dictated from on high.

The loose, unstructured phenomenon of the "cultural opposition" — spontaneous public readings; the passing around of a piece of poetry or other writing among friends, etc. — with time became more widespread and systematic, developing into the social phenomenon of samizdat, a regular network by which uncensored material was duplicated and passed around to the interested audience. [9]

The vague ferment in the rebel circles that produced and read underground literature gradually became more organized, focused, and political, especially around the time of Khrushchev's ouster, in 1964-65. This was a time of growing discontent, not only among the more politicized intellectual layers, but among the masses of workers. There were reports of strikes and slowdowns, for example, at an automobile plant in Moscow, that apparently contributed to the decision to replace Khrushchev with the bureaucratic team of Brezhnev-Kosygin.

An example of the trend toward greater organization and coherence among literary dissidents in 1964-65 was the formation of a loose organization called SMOG. (The acronym has been variously explained.)

Like their hero, Mayakovsky, the SMOGists wanted to break from conventionalism and had revolutionary impulses: "Today we have to fight against everything from the Chekists [secret police] to the bourgeoisie, from ineptitude to ignorance," said one of their manifestos. The idea of forming SMOG groups apparently caught on among young rebels in many parts of the Soviet Union. While the movement was centered in Moscow and Leningrad, there were also reports in 1965 of SMOG groups that put out uncensored newsletters in the Urals, Odessa, and "southern Russia."

In April 1965, on the anniversary of Mayakovsky's death, SMOGists organized a "literary-political" meeting, as they described it. About a thousand young people turned out to hear SMOG speakers demand recognition from the official Writers Union, and the right to discuss ideas freely and to set up their own press. Among the SMOG demands was freedom for figures like Vladimir Bukovsky and Joseph Brodsky. [10]

The new wave of rebel youth in the post-Stalin period look back with strong affinity to the native revolutionary tradition, starting with the Decembrists and ending with Lenin and the October Revolution. They are also quite curious about and sympathetic to the post-October leaders who opposed Stalin.

Both the trend toward greater organization and the increased political interest in revolutionary traditions were reflected in the formation of the Ryleev Club in June 1964 by young rebels of the SMOG circles, in particular, Evgeny Kushev and Vladimir Voskresensky. This organization was interested in social criticism as well as literature, and claimed to stand in the tradition of the Decembrist secret society, the Society of the Russian Word, which had been led in the 1820s by the poet and Decembrist leader, Kondraty Ryleev. They accordingly published a samizdat journal called *Russkoe Slovo* (Russian Word) in July 1966.[11] Many of its articles were devoted to investigating and describing the lives and experiences of nineteenth-century revolutionaries, and relating these to the struggle of young rebels in post-Stalin Soviet society.

A similar underground journal of 1964-65 was *Tetradi Sotsial-Demokratii* (Notebooks of Social Democracy). Kushev was also one of its editors, and the same circles of rebel youth and literary-cultural dissenters contributed to it. Like *Russkoe Slovo*, the *Notebooks* editors were interested in bringing relevant interpretations of revolutionary traditions to the rebel youth of the sixties. But unlike *Russkoe Slovo*, the *Notebooks* dealt mainly, not with the Narodniks and Decembrists — if we judge by its title — but with the Marxist wing of the nineteenth-century revolutionary movement.[12]

As part of its exploration of the early Marxist traditions in Russia, the magazine found itself defending that anathema of anathemas, Trotsky, against an official attack in the Soviet press of 1965, which it did fairly ably in its eighth, and apparently final, issue. We have reprinted this essay, "Who Killed Trotsky?" by E.M., in the present collection.

It was undoubtedly to circles of rebel youth like the producers of these publications that the anonymous author of the "Memoirs of a Bolshevik-Leninist" addressed himself when he produced his samizdat account in the mid-sixties.

The appearance of journals like *Russkoe Slovo* and *Notebooks of Social-Democracy* (and the more clandestine journal of the Union of Communards in Leningrad in 1964-65) marked a trend from broader "cultural" concerns toward specifically political ones. At the same time, the young rebels were getting to know older, more "hardened" elements, who had spent years in the camps and were making their influence felt in a society that was increasingly interested in politics.

Just to mention some of the names of these returnees from

the camps is to indicate their political impact on the youth: Solzhenitsyn, whose stature has become comparable to that of Tolstoy; Lev Kopelev, a writer whose analysis of Stalinism, written for the Austrian CP magazine *Tagebuch*, led to his expulsion from the CPSU in 1968; Evgenia Ginzburg, an old Communist, whose *Journey into the Whirlwind* is a samizdat memoir of Stalin's purges; A.V. Snegov, an unreconstructed anti-Stalinist who in open discussions at the Institute of Marxism-Leninism in 1966 denounced Stalin's counterrevolutionary policies in the Spanish Civil War and in Germany on the eve of Hitler's takeover; Aleksei Kosterin and Pyotr Yakir, whose experiences in Stalin's camps and role in the post-Khrushchev protest movement are well known and documented in the present collection.

The early and middle sixties were a time when many memoirs by Old Bolsheviks and oppositionists telling the truth about the revolution, the twenties, and Stalinism began to circulate. It was people of that pre-Stalin generation who joined with young rebels in early 1966, on the eve of the twenty-third congress, to demonstrate in Moscow against the rumored plans to "rehabilitate" Stalin at that congress.

The ferment of the early sixties, stirred by veterans returning from the camps, affected not only advanced sections of the youth. Inside the CP, in the ranks of the bureaucracy itself, older members were having their thinking shaken up, or were feeling that their previously restrained critical views could get a hearing with the relaxation of police controls (Grigorenko was one of these). New, "reformist" elements also were brought into the CPSU after 1956, in an effort at cooptation. Roy Medvedev and Ivan Yakhimovich are examples of the youth, filled with hopes of antibureaucratic reform, who joined at that time. Others, such as Lev Kopelev, Evgenia Ginzburg, and Aleksei Kosterin were readmitted.

Later, after the 1968 protest movement, most of these individuals found themselves outside the party again.

The Rise of the Public Protest Movement (1965 to the Present)

A brief resume is needed here to clarify the forces giving rise to the new stage—the so-called "democratic movement."

After the defeat of the Hungarian revolution, the intensity of student protest, which had given rise to groups like that of Krasnopevtsev-Rendel at Moscow University and the first publication of *Kolokol* in Leningrad, subsided.

The bureaucracy accompanied arrests and trials with the expulsion of several thousands from universities and from the party (loss of career possibilities) and by a strident campaign to "straighten out the ideological front."

For the moment it seemed that the possibility of action from below was closed off. Although a radical current continued to engage in underground organizing and publishing, and thus prefigured samizdat, these young underground editors and poets of the late 1950s (Galanskov, Ginzburg, Bukovsky, Delone) were not the dominant trend. The main disposition in the 1958-62 period was to wait for the promised reforms from above, in the belief that the bureaucratic dictatorship would liberalize itself. The criticism of Stalinism that the twentieth congress had made legitimate seemed to offer a "normal" way to restore the Soviet democracy of Lenin's day. It also seemed that improvements in living standards would be made available to the masses. The legal "cultural opposition" appeared, centered around Tvardovsky's *Novy Mir*, as did the "legal" rebel poets Yevtushenko and Voznesensky.

By 1962 and 1963 those illusions were becoming tarnished. The failure of Khrushchev's economic policies brought a sudden halt in the improvement of living standards; the price rises on basic foods, provoking strikes and protests in the summer of 1962, came only a few months after Khrushchev promised that "communism was being built" within the borders of the USSR after the consummation of socialism.

Even before Khrushchev fell in October 1964, a hardening on the "ideological front" began, accompanied by a rehabilitation of Stalin and a continuous counterreform aimed against the most advanced sectors of the intelligentsia and the anti-Stalinist Communist militants (among the youth as well as the Old Bolsheviks).

This counterreform, which is still in progress, cut short the illusory belief in the re-establishment of Soviet democracy from above. As early as 1963 one of the leading figures in the new Communist opposition in the USSR, former Major General Pyotr Grigorenko, thought of constituting an underground Bolshevik organization, reflecting the loss of confidence in Khrushchev-type "liberalization."

In 1965 the Brezhnev-Kosygin regime decisively stepped up the counteroffensive with the arrest of Sinyavsky and Daniel, samizdat authors who were typical of the semilegal circles of "cultural ferment" in Moscow; the arrest of dozens of anti-Stalinist Ukrainian intellectuals for reaffirming the national cultural traditions and opposing Russification; and in Leningrad, the arrest of the leaders of the Union of Communards, editors of *Kolokol.*

But in response to this official hardening, 1966 and 1967 saw a new flowering of opposition in protest against the Sinyavsky-Daniel trial and, in the Ukraine, against the imprisonment of dissident intellectuals. That is, the move toward tighter controls sparked a more intensified resistance. Out of this developed a more politicized samizdat, reflecting a network of thousands, the most active elements of which became central figures in the "democratic movement." A movement of open, public protest in behalf of democratic rights began which has been the center of attention into the early 1970s.

For all the severity of the Brezhnev "counterreform," the worst forms of the Stalinist dictatorship have not been restored, and it is unlikely that they will be, because of the changed relationship of forces between the masses and the bureaucracy. But the gradual retracting of concessions that the masses had won through struggle in the 1953-62 period stimulated the developing vanguard, the more conscious elements among the youth, the workers, the intelligentsia, and the party rank-and-file, to resist. These elements became convinced that they had to take a stand; the reimposition of the repressive police regime had to be prevented at all costs. Thus rose the opposition which chose to act *in the open,* not just underground, but to appeal to the population at large.

The tactic adopted by this opposition was to take the text of the 1936 constitution and demand all the freedoms that it guaranteed; to declare that it, the opposition, was adhering to law and that the bureaucratic authorities were the violators. This initial tactic was politically well founded, because the aspiration for Soviet democracy is undoubtedly the chief common denominator of the various social layers in opposition, and of the different ideological currents within what is now given the name "democratic movement."

This tactic is also consistent with the basic political logic of the most consistent elements among the new opposition who approach fundamentally the same point of view as that held by the Left Opposition. That is, it regards Soviet society as a social structure resulting from the October Revolution and denies that Stalinist terror is the product of October or of Leninism.[13] The proof is that Stalin had to destroy the Bolshevik Party and exterminate the entire generation that led the revolution in order to consolidate his power. The opposition focuses its attacks on the phenomena of bureaucratic degeneration and considers the establishment of full democratic freedoms for all the workers and citizens under the socialist constitution as the central aim of its struggle. Stalinism appears to the new oppositionists primarily as the violation of legality; they do not always detect or point out the institutionalized material privileges of the bureaucracy.

The struggle against the arbitrariness of today, by the same logic, is related to the struggle against past injustices. Hence the great importance attached by the new opposition to resisting the rehabilitation of Stalin, to calling for posthumous condemnation of Stalin as a criminal and full rehabilitation for all his victims.

Inevitably the rise of the antibureaucratic political revolution in the Czechoslovak Socialist Republic in 1968 met with a sympathetic response among the rebellious Soviet intelligentsia. The trend toward establishing the norms of socialist democracy in the state and party was the main aspect of the Prague Spring and directly corresponded to the central concern of the Soviet oppositionists. These oppositionists, isolated, poorly informed, if at all, about the changes that had been occurring in the relationship of forces on the world scale in recent years, participated indirectly, through Czechoslovakia, in the worldwide phenomenon of youth radicalization and a new rise in international revolutionary struggles.

Besides these events, with Czechoslovakia being the strongest impulse, there were some more basic causes that stirred the new opposition to public political action in the Soviet Union.

During the postwar period, when the Soviet economy, ravaged by the war, was being rebuilt, the borrowing of Western industrial technology still characterized much of Soviet industry. There was unquestionable progress in the top-priority fields of armaments, aeronautics, and space. But behind that, a structural crisis appeared. The decline in economic growth rates was one symptom. In early 1970, Brezhnev himself revealed a serious decline in agricultural production and delays in the rise of labor productivity. The regime even flirted with the idea of calling for a full discussion of economic problems. (It was at that time that Roy Medvedev, Sakharov, and Turchin submitted their document, included in this collection, on the relation of democratization to the economic difficulties.)

The essence of the crisis is that Soviet society — with a bureaucratically degenerated regime fastened onto a society in transition between capitalism and socialism — is threatened in

most fields by the consequences of the absence of both workers'
democracy and democratically centralized self-management by
the producers.

In *The Revolution Betrayed*, Trotsky wrote that "under a
nationalized economy, *quality* [or higher productivity] demands
a democracy of producers and consumers, freedom of criticism
and initiative—conditions incompatible with a totalitarian regime of fear, lies, and flattery. . . . Behind the question of
quality stands a more complicated and [elaborate] problem
which may be comprised in the concept of *independent, technical* and *cultural creation*. The ancient philosopher said that
strife is the father of all things. No new values can be created
where a free conflict of ideas is impossible. . . . The dictatorship of the proletariat opens a wider scope to human genius
the more it ceases to be a dictatorship. Socialist culture will
flourish only in proportion to the dying away of the state.
In that simple and unshakable historical law is contained
the death sentence of the present political regime in the Soviet
Union. Soviet democracy is not the demand of an abstract
policy, still less an abstract moral. It has become a life-and-
death need of the country."

This impasse of the system is manifested in many ways—
among them, the lag in research and technical innovation in
some key fields, such as computers; the striking disparity between the high level of technological development in some
areas and the mediocre living standards of the masses; the
multiplication of waste and loss in production and distribution;
the tension around access to university education; and the increasing disproportions in employment.

The courage shown by the new oppositionists in openly
espousing their aims is a reflection of this social crisis. They
sense that they can win sympathy and support. Individual
promotion through education no longer seems available to
millions of sons and daughters of workers and collective farm
peasants. Not only individuals but entire social layers feel
there is no way out. Although the increasing levels of repression are aimed at cauterizing such feelings, they are nevertheless bound to become increasingly articulate.

There is still a very wide gap, however, between the minority
of courageous oppositionists and the large masses. This is
not only the result of the break in continuity between the older
Bolshevik generation and the present-day mass of workers—
the result of the bureaucracy's conscious massacre of the cadres
of the entire revolutionary generation. It is also true that Marx-

ism has been seriously discredited in the eyes of the masses by the bureaucracy, which has debased it to the status of a state religion. The prolonged isolation of the politically inactive masses from the international labor and revolutionary movements has served further to aggravate the situation.

This explains the pronounced confusion of wide layers among the intellectuals and in the populace at large—and the wide range of viewpoints that have emerged, from Slavophile and semifeudal nostalgia to Communist trends quite close to revolutionary Marxism.

Within the prosocialist democratic movement the political spectrum is still quite varied. A right wing may be seen in Academician Andrei Sakharov, advocate of convergence between Western "democracy" and Soviet "socialism," who does not seem to understand many central issues of the world revolutionary movement and who shies away from any involvement of the masses in democratization, unless strictly limited and controlled.

The left wing in the democratic movement is represented by those like the former collective farm chairman Ivan Yakhimovich, whose call is "Stalinism no, Leninism yes." The most outstanding representatives of this current so far have been Pyotr Grigorenko and the late Bolshevik writer Aleksei Kosterin.

In a certain sense the funeral of Kosterin constituted the first public opposition rally in the USSR since the Left Opposition demonstrations of 1927. (The full text of the speeches at Kosterin's funeral are printed here in English for the first time.)

The oppositionists are still a small minority, fighting from a weak position. The regime has opened an offensive against them, especially since January 1972, determined to destroy the civil rights groups that tried to establish an open existence. In the same way the police did destroy the organization in the city of Vladimir that claimed the right to "legal" existence— the Independent Youth for Socialist Democracy —and has broken up and tried several large neo-Marxist youth groups, in Gorky, Samara, Saratov, and, again in 1971, Leningrad. Even more, the regime made it a central objective to stamp out the regular underground publications, particularly the *Chronicle of Current Events* in Russia and *Ukrainsky Visnyk* in Ukraine. For the moment, it has apparently succeeded in that aim.

Although the antibureaucratic opposition assumes a much

larger scale among some of the non-Russian nationalities — and has been able to win some concessions from the bureaucracy as a result — and although there is a certain level of popular sympathy with the oppositionists, still the regime is able to physically break up the initial formations of these groups.

How large is the democratic movement? And how much support does it have? Its activists have been variously estimated at from several hundred to a couple of thousand.

Besides those who protest openly there are certainly many more who sympathize silently. The ups and downs of repression and relaxation also, obviously, affect the number who will openly associate themselves with the protest movement.

What is the social composition of the movement? What social layers, if any, does it base itself on? What chance does it have to win mass support, to become a force that can influence or change policy in the Soviet Union?

It is rather obvious that most of the protesters come from the ranks of the intelligentsia — that is, people with professional training and a higher education. A good number were party members, usually a prerequisite for a "good job." Many worked at institutes or were teachers or technicians, or worked at publishing houses.

There is nothing unusual in this. Most revolutionary movements have started in layers of society which have had the leisure time and interest or sensitivity to ideas and social problems to become aware of the need for change before the mass of the population began to stir. An odd feature of the Soviet movement is that students have made up a relatively small proportion so far. Although some of the best-known figures began their oppositional activities in the student milieu in the late fifties, during the sixties the students as a whole remained quiescent. One reason is that it is extremely difficult to get into a university or institute of higher education. Only a small percentage of those who apply are admitted — after a series of extremely rigorous exams. Thus, there is a strong tendency not to rock the boat and lose the rare career opportunity of university admission. One of the first steps the regime takes against dissenters is to have them fired from their jobs or, if they are students, expelled from their university. The extremely limited access to higher education, especially in comparison with the high number of secondary school graduates, has up to now apparently had a dampening effect on student participation in the civil rights movement. But this is a factor that in the future could turn from a deterrent into an explosive protest issue.

Amalrik draws some conclusions from the high proportion of intellectuals, "academics," and "specialists" from the layer of "new scientific and technical personnel" in the protest movement. These social types, in Amalrik's view, are the "least capable of purposeful action." While the "middle class" of technicians and specialists is "capable of comprehending the principles of personal freedom, rule of law, and democratic government . . . needs those principles, and provides the emerging Democratic Movement with its basic contingent of supporters, the vast majority of this class is so mediocre . . . and [even] its intellectually most independent members are so passive that the success of a Democratic Movement based on it seems to me to be gravely in doubt."

Amalrik holds that the movement's base in a part of the "middle class" leaves it too weak and too ridden by contradictions to be able to engage in a real struggle with the regime. Can it, he asks, find a broader base of support among the masses?

That is a central question. And the answer depends in part on what policies the democratic movement adopts, and which of the tendencies within it can learn to mobilize the masses. In the present stage, since 1972, as the Brezhnev regime resorts to the harshest repressive measures used since Stalin's purges, it is too early to say what the final outcome of the effort to create a public movement for democratic rights will be. The full impact of the 1965-73 phase of struggle, which may have ended with the trial of Yakir and the apparently successful suppression of *Ukrainsky Visnyk* and the *Chronicle of Current Events,* cannot yet be assessed. The protest movement may prove to have had more deep-going effects than are immediately evident. Certainly a new turn and change of tactics is dictated for oppositional elements, as the Nixon-Brezhnev detente, and the harshest repression for a generation, create a new and contradictory situation.

Regardless of the momentary ups and downs, however, the general perspective remains unpromising for bureaucratic rule. As the young Communist Ivan Yakhimovich said in 1968, "The genie is at large and cannot be confined again."

George Saunders
January 1974

NOTES TO THE INTRODUCTION

1. Berger was a founder of the Communist Party of Palestine who lived in the USSR, doing Comintern work, and knew the Trotskyists well in the twenties and thirties, including in the camps and prisons.

2. For details on that program, especially as reflected in the anti-capitalist and anti-Stalinist Ukrainian paper *Vpered*, see "The Future of the Soviet Union" (an interview with W. Wilny, a young Ukrainian emigre and supporter of *Vpered*), and "Inside the Soviet Union— Interview with Two Ukrainian Refugees" (Wilny and A. Babenko, an emigre Ukrainian Old Bolshevik, also a supporter of *Vpered*), in *Fourth International* (New York), May-June 1951, pp. 77-84, and September-October 1951, pp. 156-60 respectively.

3. *Daedalus*, Summer 1960.

4. For documentary materials on the Ukrainian group, see *Ferment in the Ukraine* (New York: Crisis Press, 1973). Other groups that have become known are: The "Young Workers' Party of Alma Ata," in Kazakhstan; the "Russian Socialist Party," which distributed leaflets in Leningrad calling on workers to launch a general strike; the "Party of Non-Party Workers Struggling for the Restoration of Socialism"; the "Struggle Committee for Socialist Democracy," which put out a leaflet in Moscow in August 1970 protesting the appearance of a bust of Stalin at the Lenin Mausoleum and calling for an all-out struggle for socialist democracy on a Leninist basis; the "Democratic Union of Socialists"; a group of seven "neo-Leninists" around the Leningrad engineer Dzibalov, arrested in March 1971 and tried in January 1972; the 1968-69 "Union of Independent Youth" of the town of Vladimir—an attempt at a legal organization fighting for socialist democracy based on the constitutional guarantee of "freedom of organization" (its leader, the young worker Vladimir Borisov, was arrested, forcibly confined in a mental hospital, and driven to suicide). In the late fifties and early sixties several clandestine organizations appeared in the Ukraine. The "United Party for the Liberation of the Ukraine" and the "Ukrainian National Committee" were two organizations in the Lviv region composed mostly of industrial workers. Two members of the UNC were shot, after being arrested, allegedly for planning terrorist attacks; the remainder had their death sentences commuted to long prison terms.
Another group, the Ukrainian National Front, functioned in

1965-67. Sixteen issues of its uncensored publication, *The Homeland and Freedom*, appeared before the group was uncovered by the police and broken up.

5. Cornelia Gerstenmaier, *Voices of the Silent* (New York, 1972), pp. 97-98.

6. Ted Harding, "Opposition Currents in the Soviet Union," *Intercontinental Press*, September 17, 1973.

7. Other examples of recent mass actions inside the Soviet Union include a building trades strike in Moscow in 1960; a dock workers' strike in Odessa in late 1961; a strike at the Eletrosila power plant in Leningrad, apparently in 1963; a strike for lower prices that reportedly involved over 100,000 workers in Kharkiv, in the Ukraine, in autumn 1967, which won its demands; a mass demonstration by Crimean Tatars in Chirchik, Uzbekistan, on Lenin's birthday in April 1968 (one of many mass demonstrations by this nationality, demanding the right to return to its native region and have its own autonomous region, abolished by Stalin, restored to it); and the demonstrations involving thousands in Kaunas, Lithuania, in May 1972 to protest Russification and demand independence for Soviet Lithuania. Other cities where protest demonstrations over food and other shortages occurred in the sixties include Archangel and Murmansk (reported dock strikes), Gorky, Ryazan, Volgograd, Kriviy Rih, Donetsk, Zhdanov, Tashkent, Omsk, and Vladimir.

8. Samizdat historian and gradualist dissenter Roy Medvedev explained this development in a very interesting way, reporting incidentally on a number of additional mass protests of recent occurrence. "The fact that pressure 'from above' can to some extent modify the policies of the 'high ups' is shown by the Twenty-fourth Congress of the CPSU. Many of the important social programs and plans for a more rapid rise in living standards for the workers, which were announced in two reports at the congress, were adopted even before the congress itself. These promises and programs looked quite different before December 1970 in the first variants and drafts of the Directives and the Official Report. Here, undoubtedly, effects were felt from both the Polish events of December 1970 and from certain wildcat demonstrations by workers in our own country who were dissatisfied with the difficult living conditions and the frequent interruptions in supplies of meat and dairy products (such demonstrations, as far as we know, took place in Ivanovo [Central Russia], Sverdlovsk [Urals], Gorky [on the Upper Volga], and several other cities" (*On Socialist Democracy* [Amsterdam, 1972], p. 376).

9. On December 23, 1955, the Soviet youth paper *Komsomolskaya Pravda* complained about an uncensored publication bearing the

title *Fig Leaf* (*Figovy List*) that was being circulated at the University of Vilnius (in Lithuania). The same newspaper referred three times in 1956 to uncensored journals appearing at educational institutions in the Leningrad area with names like *The Blue Bud* (*Goluboy Buton*), *Fresh Voices* (*Svezhie Golosa*), and *Heresy* (*Yeres*). In Moscow, an uncensored publication called *Culture* (*Kultura*) was reported.

These initial unauthorized student ventures were apparently concerned above all with literature and the arts — that is, they criticized or parodied official "socialist realism" (which might better be termed "bureaucratic romanticization"). They reproduced literary works that departed from the official school in order to express real attitudes and feelings, instead of those dictated from or approved on high, including satire and criticism with political implications.

In the early sixties, uncensored literary-cultural publications like Ginzburg's *Syntax* and Galanskov's *Phoenix* proliferated. Usually these were collections of literary pieces that had circulated separately. In the Moscow samizdat milieu of those years, there was a monthly called *Cocktail*, three issues of a journal entitled *Siren*, and another publication, *The Seasons*. In February 1963 *The Lantern* was issued, *Bomb* in March 1964, *Workshop* in October of the same year, and in August 1965, *Neck*, as well as several issues of *Sphinxes* in 1965. Meanwhile, dissident literary circles in Leningrad circulated a publication called *Anthology of Soviet Pathology* in 1963 and another anthology of the same name in 1964.

10. For Bukovsky, see note 77 of text. Brodsky was a nonconformist Leningrad poet whose 1964 trial for "parasitism" gained international notoriety.

11. The *Russkoe Slovo* founded a hundred years earlier had been a legal journal of the revolutionary-democratic Narodnik movement of the 1860s.

12. The Marxist opponents of populism, of course, used the name Russian Social Democratic Labor Party until World War I.

13. Even observers hostile to Leninism have noted this feature of most currents in the Soviet dissident movement. Abraham Rothberg, for example, in his *Heirs of Stalin* (New York, 1972), commented on Pavel Litvinov's declaration at the 1968 trial in which Litvinov was sentenced to penal exile for demonstrating against the Kremlin's invasion of Czechoslovakia. "The prosecutor says also that we [demonstrators] were against the policies of the party and government but not against the social state system. Perhaps there are people who consider all our policies and even our government's mistakes to be the result of our state and social system. I do not see it this way.

And I do not think the prosecutor himself would say this. For then he would have to say that all the crimes of the Stalin era resulted from our . . . system."

Rothberg comments: "[Such a] fundamental criticism of Soviet life and institutions [i.e., equating Stalinism with the postcapitalist social system itself] was almost everywhere avoided like the plague, by regime spokesmen and dissidents alike. Ironically [this line] was almost 'Trotskyist'; it called Stalinism a 'distortion' instead of seeing it as a direct outgrowth of the Revolution, the institutions imposed on the Soviet Union by the Bolsheviks, and the character of the Bolshevik leadership and of the Russian people" (p. 248).

Gerstenmaier too observes that the "majority of dissident intellectuals and artists of the 1950's (and *even thereafter*) did not fight the Communist system, but rather, a privileged caste, which had taken advantage of this system to pursue its own personal power. The political views of the [majority of] rebels can be described as 'neo-Leninist' inasmuch as they acknowledge the basic precepts of Leninism and the goals of the October Revolution" (*Voices of the Silent*, p. 93).

Part I:

From the
Old Opposition
to the New

A "corrective" labor camp in the Soviet Far North. In the years of reaction under Stalin, those who fought to continue the best traditions of the Soviet revolution and Marxist movement were isolated, silenced, and eventually killed in places like this. Complexes of such camps and prisons dotted the USSR, under the jurisdiction of GULAG (Chief Administration for Corrective Labor Camps)—whence Solzhenitsyn's ironic term "Gulag Archipelago." A survivor of such camps in the Pechora-Vorkuta region, where most Left Oppositionists perished in 1936-38, is the anonymous author of "Memoirs of a Bolshevik-Leninist."

PREFACE

This section of samizdat documents consists mainly of writings on historical questions, centering on Trotsky, the Left Opposition, the struggle against Stalinism in the twenties, and Soviet anti-Stalinist ideas and traditions in general. Part of the battle for freedom of discussion. within the context of support to the Soviet system (not "anti-Soviet" slander or propaganda, as the regime charges), has been around historical questions, especially the right to critically examine the Stalin era.

In the immediate post-Stalin period, the bureaucracy itself, under Khrushchev, began to reveal some of the truth about past events or to republish historical documents that had been buried for years (not least, Lenin's writings of 1922-23 against Stalin and John Reed's *Ten Days That Shook the World*). The Stalin machine had of course piled up an unprecedented mountain of lies in its years of rewriting history. Stalin's heirs were tempted to overturn their former master — to transfer him from universal idol to all-purpose scapegoat — in order to win popular support for themselves. But such a move would also tend to endanger their own pedigrees. They had all made their careers on Stalin's coattails. Condemning Stalin might even suggest that some of Stalin's opponents in the party had been correct against him — and that the ideas of the 1920s oppositions might still be correct against his successors.

The pressure the new masters of power felt to dissociate themselves from Stalin proved irresistible. But they tried to wrap themselves in the mantle of Lenin, to establish a "new" legitimacy, and to impose limits on "de-Stalinization." The rehabilitation of Stalin's victims stopped short of the main defendants of the Moscow frame-up trials — Trotsky, Zinoviev, Kamenev, Bukharin, Rakovsky, etc.

Khrushchev in his "secret speech" to the twentieth congress made clear the limits of this new Stalinism without Stalin: "It is known that Stalin, after Lenin's death, especially during the first years, actively fought for Leninism against the enemies of Leninist theory and against those who deviate. . . . The

51

party had to fight those who attempted to lead the country away from the correct Leninist path; it had to fight the Trotskyists, Zinovievists, and rightists, and the bourgeois nationalists. This fight was indispensable."

Within these limits, then, a certain amount of critical discussion of the Stalin era was permitted in the controlled press. But there were currents in Soviet society pressing for much more. "De-Stalinization" itself was a partial concession in the direction of strong moods of discontent in the population. One expression of the desire to go much further than Khrushchev's twentieth congress formula was an incident not long after Khrushchev's speech.

"A group manifesto against distortion of Soviet history, including the role of Trotsky" appeared on a wall-newspaper board at Moscow University, reported Cedric Belfrage in September 1957 in the American radical weekly the *National Guardian.* "This [manifesto] was removed and put back again, and finally the expulsion of five students connected with it was announced. A protest against this, which even the university Komsomol [Young Communist League] leader signed was successful."

After the twenty-second congress, in late 1961, with its highly publicized revelations of Stalin's crimes, a group of Moscow students again went further than officialdom desired. They passed a resolution that Stalin's body be removed from the Red Square mausoleum. It was removed a short time later. In 1968, students at Gorky University passed out leaflets calling for rehabilitation of all the defendants in the Moscow show trials, once again giving expression to a desire to go much further than the authorities wish in this "historical" matter.

But the most dramatic illustration of the pressure from below for the truth to be told about the Stalin era came in 1962-63. In a fit of liberalism in late 1962 (an attempt to shore up his tottering position by winning some popular support) Khrushchev authorized the official publication of a manuscript describing conditions in a Stalin-era labor camp. Its title was *One Day in the Life of Ivan Denisovich,* and its author was Aleksandr Solzhenitsyn, a former camp inmate whom no one had ever heard of. This created a sensation. The magazine in which the "fictional" account appeared sold out overnight.

It soon developed that Solzhenitsyn's manuscript was not the only one of its kind. Thousands of such manuscripts, personal accounts of what really happened under Stalin, came flooding into publishing houses and magazine offices, as though a sluice had been opened. To send such a manuscript to an editorial office, where dozens of people might see it, and start it circulating privately, was in itself a political act. By March 1963, Khrushchev had to make a public speech to the entire Soviet Union, announcing that no more literature on the "camp theme" would be published. (It was not a suitably uplifting subject for Soviet literature, he explained.)

This flood of manuscripts was a major manifestation of the social pressure to which "de-Stalinization" had catered. Those concessions had only encouraged discontent and made it bolder. So the regime tried a new tack: to reimpose censorship. The result was unofficial circulation in the form of samizdat.

The private circulation of personal accounts of the Stalin years and before, both fictionalized and in memoir form, had become very widespread even before the publication of *Ivan Denisovich.* But after that, we can assume, many of those thousands of manuscripts exposing the crimes of the Stalin era continued to circulate. Some of the more outstanding samizdat works of this genre have been published outside the Soviet Union — among them Evgenia Ginzburg's *Journey into the Whirlwind,* Lidia Chukovskaya's *Deserted House,* Solzhenitsyn's *First Circle,* and Varlam Shalamov's *Notes from Kolyma.*

It was in the post-Khrushchev period, as part of the genre we have described, that the "Memoirs of a Bolshevik-Leninist" was completed. Although these "Memoirs," and those of Aleksandra Chumakova, are unique in that they concentrate on the history of the Left Opposition and share the views of the Opposition, they are part of a whole body of historically oriented samizdat memoirs and writings.

A good picture of the number and variety of manuscripts in this genre can be gathered from Roy A. Medvedev's *Let History Judge.* Medvedev's is the fullest and most systematic effort so far by a post-Stalin Soviet dissenter to investigate the origin and meaning of Stalinism. Written from 1962 to 1968, *Let History Judge* is itself a product of samizdat; Medvedev wrote it in hope of official publication, but it was rejected and he himself was expelled from the CPSU in 1969.

Medvedev quotes and describes dozens of uncensored personal memoirs about the Stalin and pre-Stalin eras. Thus his book constitutes, among other things, an extensive review of

the samizdat material on this subject. Medvedev indicates, for
example, that there are a few rank-and-file survivors of the
"opposition movement of the twenties" who are "now trying
to vindicate certain opposition leaders, on the grounds that
they were correct and bold, though unsuccessful, in their criticism of Stalin."

As an example of such a person, Medvedev cites Professor
A. I. Dashkovsky of Kharkov, who is described as a survivor
of the Democratic Centralist group of 1920-21. Dashkovsky
exemplifies the "tendency to exaggerate Trotsky's importance
in organizing the October 1917 insurrection in Petrograd,"
reports Medvedev. Among the historically oriented works that
circulate privately is an unpublished 1967 letter by Dashkovsky
to *Pravda* objecting to a radio talk that described Lenin and
Trotsky as enemies in 1917. Accompanying Dashkovsky's
letter is a reply by the radio commentator and Dashkovsky's
rebuttal.

The memoirs of the surviving Left Oppositionist and those
of Chumakova, then, are not only part of a whole body of
samizdat historical memoirs; they are also part of a definite
current in samizdat that views Trotsky and the Trotskyist
Opposition favorably. And there may be other survivors of
the Left Opposition who have not dared to raise their
voices yet.

It would be wrong to exaggerate the strength or significance
of the pro-Trotskyist moods among Soviet dissidents. Human
rights and the struggle against repression today are the main
themes of samizdat, along with a historical critique of Stalinism that expresses several different viewpoints. But the impression one might receive from Western media coverage of the
dissident movement is that its members are totally unaware
of or indifferent to Trotsky. That, too, is incorrect. Several
sympathetic references to Trotsky have been noted in samizdat
publications.

For example, three Soviet dissidents who were central figures
in the human rights movement of recent years — Ilya Gabai,
Yuli Kim, and Pyotr Yakir (before the latter was broken by
the regime and forced to recant) — included the following passage in an open letter to the Soviet public against the rehabilitation of Stalin: ". . . [for] some reason, there is not enough objectivity to permit telling the truth about the major political
leaders of the first decade of Soviet power. It would, after all,
be possible, without violating the proper bounds of party dis-

cussion, to say honestly of various persons that they did not organize terrorist actions, did not engage in espionage, and did not sprinkle broken glass into foodstuffs. It would, after all, be possible to relate also what they accomplished while in their high positions. But the great civil war services of the People's Commissar for National Minorities J.V. Stalin remain with us to this day alongside the unrelieved wrecking activities of the then People's Commissar of War and Chairman of the Revolutionary Military Council, L.D. Trotsky."

The reason for the definite reservoir of sympathy for Trotsky is not hard to find. Even Medvedev, who makes clear his many strong disagreements with Trotskyism, states it quite plainly: of all the leaders of the united opposition, "Trotsky alone tried to continue the struggle." "Neither Kamenev, Zinoviev, Radek, nor Piatakov spoke out against" Stalin after capitulating to him, Medvedev observes.

But of course Trotsky did not stand alone. Although the top leaders of the Opposition—placed under the greatest pressure by the bureaucracy—either broke, committed suicide, or were driven to their deaths, a whole layer of younger leaders remained firm (as in the cases of Socrates Gevorkian and Virap Virapov cited in the anonymous "Memoirs" and in those by "M. B."). Moreover, thousands of Oppositionists, young and old, continued an organized struggle within the prisons and camps down to the bitter end in Stalin's massacres.

Another samizdat writer has memorialized—with a touch of humor and irony—those anonymous Oppositionists who remained true to the revolution in the depths of the Stalinist reaction. Solzhenitsyn does this in his portrait of a Left Oppositionist who survived (chapter 51 of *First Circle*). In describing this figure, whom he names Adamson, Solzhenitsyn hints at the struggle and fate of the Bolshevik-Leninists as a whole. Whether Solzhenitsyn takes up the question of the thousands of Trotskyists who never capitulated to Stalin in his recent monumental *Gulag Archipelago* is unclear. The complete text was not available at the time of publication of this collection.

The appearance of memoirs by a survivor of the Left Opposition is a historic occasion. The last direct word from the organized anti-Stalinist Bolsheviks reached the outside world in 1935-36, when a Bolshevik-Leninist named A. Tarov, a mechanic by trade, managed to get out of the Soviet Union. He contacted the Russian *Bulletin of the Opposition*, edited by Trotsky, and wrote a number of statements describing the conditions in which Soviet Oppositionists had to live.* Tarov's evidence independently corroborates many factual details in the "Memoirs of a Bolshevik-Leninist." For example, Tarov mentions two Tsintsadze brothers and Roza Rozova among the prisoners at the Verkhne-Uralsk isolator.

In January 1936 the Russian *Bulletin* carried the first of several articles by Anton Ciliga,** a Yugoslav Communist who had joined the Left Opposition in the USSR in the late twenties. Arrested, he had shared prison life with the Soviet Left Oppositionists. Ciliga's information, too, corresponds in many respects to that of the anonymous Bolshevik-Leninist.

In July-August 1936 the *Bulletin* carried one more batch of direct communications from Oppositionists — letters from anonymous cothinkers in exile and from Victor Serge, a Belgian writer of Russian origin who had been active in the Comintern and joined the Left Opposition in the twenties in the USSR. He had been in prison and exile since 1933, but was finally released as a result of protests by French literary and radical circles. Arriving in Belgium in April 1936, he apparently brought messages to the *Bulletin of the Opposition* from Trotskyist exiles in Orenburg.

The information that came out through Tarov, Ciliga, and Serge was the last direct word before the notorious Moscow trials, between 1936 and 1938, ushered in the final bloody phase.

Why is it that nearly two decades went by, even after the death of Stalin, before any direct word from surviving Left Oppositionists was heard? First of all, the expression of Trotskyist ideas still involves serious dangers wherever a Stalinist regime dominates. Even in "liberal" Yugoslavia today, as in Husak's Czechoslovakia under Kremlin occupation, in Mao's China, and until recently, in "liberal" Poland, people holding Trotskyist or semi-Trotskyist views have been imprisoned. The

---

*A translation of Tarov's first letter to the *Bulletin* may be found in the *New Militant*, October 19, 1935. His testimony to the Dewey Commission investigating the charges in the Moscow trials of 1936-37 may be found in *Socialist Appeal*, September 11 and 18, 1937. Trotsky's comment on Tarov's first letter, translated from the *Bulletin*, may be found in *Writings of Leon Trotsky (1935-36)*, first edition, 1970, p. 97.

** The *Bulletin* published three reports by Ciliga, in its January, February, and April issues for 1936. These may be found in the four-volume reprint of the Russian *Bulletin* (Monad Press, 1973).

mere mention of Trotsky's name can still produce a reflex action of alarm and tension, even among young people, in the Soviet Union. That was the name, after all, of the cardinal sin for which millions were arrested and shot in the purges.

It took a decade or more after Stalin's death for the samizdat network to develop, and for the circulation of critical writing of all kinds to achieve a fairly massive scale. It was only then that works like the present "Memoirs" must have seemed safe, or at least not suicidal, to circulate.

Still, the anonymous memoirist and Chumakova have taken a definite risk. Solzhenitsyn revealed in September 1973 that he had compiled the "multivolume research work about Soviet prison camps," based on interviews with "about 200 persons still alive," called *The Gulag Archipelago*. People had given their information to him ten years ago, he said, but "in the last few days" the secret police had tracked down a copy of the manuscript.

Solzhenitsyn expressed his "fears that the persecution of these [227] persons will now begin. . . . Information on the whereabouts of the [manuscript] was provided by Yelizaveta Voronyanskaya, who was interrogated by the KGB [secret police] for five days without interruption. On returning home, she hanged herself."

Keeping in mind this general background, the historical milieu out of which the "Memoirs of a Bolshevik-Leninist" appeared, let us take a closer look at some features of the document itself.

The "Memoirs of a Bolshevik-Leninist," the main text in the present collection, reached Trotskyist circles in the West—as have many samizdat documents—by means that for obvious reasons cannot be discussed. But it is authentic beyond any doubt. Confirming its authenticity are all the details of the author's personal biography—which Soviet authorities could easily check and refute. There has been no challenge.

Beyond that, the authenticity of the "Memoirs," as Pierre Frank says so well, in the preface to the French edition (*Renaissance du bolchevisme en URSS: Memoires d'un bolchevik-leniniste* [Maspero: Paris, 1970], "can be sensed, above all, in the text itself, its tone, its composition. The author does not use a labored style. He expresses himself as someone who . . . bit by bit, has gathered together memories spreading over several decades. In the middle of a story, suddenly he will remember something else and write that down too. From this spontaneous production has come a text that is neither a literary nor a specifically political document."

We have omitted a section of this document, which may be found in the first part of the French edition (pp. 29-59). This deals with the anonymous author's experiences in the civil war, and is of far less political interest than his account of the internal party struggle in the twenties or than his opening of the hidden book on what happened in Stalin's prisons and camps. His civil war reminiscences, while interesting, raise a number of problematic questions.

He concentrates on restoring the good names of three Red Cavalry commanders condemned by Soviet authorities in 1920-21. Two were executed — Boris Mokeevich Dumenko in 1920, and Filipp Kuzmych Mironov in 1921. (Both were rehabilitated in the post-Stalin era.) The third, Dmitry Petrovich Zhloba, was removed from his command under a cloud of suspicion in 1920, but later was able to continue his military career.

The memoirist argues that all three were victims of early intrigues by Stalin and his associates.

The difficulty is that their cases may have been more complicated than the memoirist indicates. Trotsky himself wrote, incidentally, about both Dumenko and Mironov from a point of view that makes it surprising to find a Trotskyist defending them rather uncritically. All the information about their cases is not available, and the reason for their post-Stalin rehabilitation may be not that their records were free from error, but that capital punishment in their cases was not justified.

At any rate, their cases do not raise the pressing and important political issues that are raised in the sections of the "Memoirs" we are printing. The author's connections with the Left Opposition are enormously significant, especially as one of the few survivors. In contrast, many authors have written about the Cossack-based Red Cavalry (Sholokhov and Isaac Bebel being the best known).

The many biographical details the Bolshevik-Leninist gives about himself mean that he is probably as well known to the secret police, despite his anonymity, as are the authors of similar memoirs who sign their names. A common attitude among samizdat authors in the middle and late sixties, when these memoirs were completed, was to exercise their "constitutionally guaranteed" right of free expression — often in the form of privately circulated papers — while avoiding any effort to build an opposition organization.

The scattered references throughout the "Memoirs" add up to the following picture. The author grew up in a family of poor peasants in a region some 100 miles southwest of Moscow.

In 1914, after his father's death, relatives sent him to Petrograd to become an apprentice in the hatmaking business. It was there, as a youth, after the February revolution, that he first heard of Trotsky. The impact of Trotsky's powerful speeches to the crowds at the Cirque Moderne—as the masses awakened to political life and revolutionary perspectives in the stormy year 1917—are reflected in the memoirist's description of a typical streetcar discussion in the Petrograd of those days.

With the coming of the civil war, the memoirist, despite his youth, served in the Red Army as a code specialist. He names the various military formations he served in during the civil war, and describes his work at the central staff headquarters in Moscow in the early twenties. Later, as a student, he joined the Left Opposition and acted as a representative of Moscow student Oppositionists on a few occasions. He does not describe his first arrest or trial, but names the prisons and camps he was in during the thirties. With the Nazi invasion in June 1941, his military experience presumably was recognized, for he was able to leave the camps and serve in defense of the Soviet Union against the imperialist invader, as all consistent revolutionaries would have wanted to do.

Free for a time after the war, perhaps by an administrative oversight, as in the case of *The First Circle*'s Adamson, the memoirist was, as he puts it, "unjustly subjected to repression [in 1949] and confined in the Karaganda concentration camp," where he apparently remained until the strikes in the labor camps after Stalin's death in 1953 won a general dismantling of the camp system.

A few words are in order on the physical appearance of the "Memoirs" manuscript itself. Two hundred pages of onionskin, double-spaced, crowded with type, and having only narrow margins at top and bottom, it is eloquent testimony to that selfless labor of samizdat typists of which Solzhenitsyn has spoken. Here and there on the manuscript there are typographical errors, or corrections made by striking over or retyping above the line, but for the most part it is remarkably clean— testimony to the great care taken. Now and then a typed footnote or interpolated passage appears. One does not know whether this is the original author's work, or an addition from someone else along the "chain" of samizdat readers and copiers. At other times, notes are added in handwriting, in the margin or on the reverse side of the page. Again, their authorship is unclear. Thus, in a very literal sense this work represents a collective effort toward the restoration of historical truth.

Obviously the "Memoirs" are not the product of professional writing. Some of the random reminiscences seem to have been transcribed from tape, and in general there is no overall system, not even a chronological one.

While truthful on the whole, this document includes a number of factual errors, indicated in the notes, which are quite understandable. In the first place, the multiple transcription and circulation from hand to hand result in all kinds of mistakes. Furthermore, this is not the work of a historian, with the time to do research and carefully compare sources. What archives would an old Oppositionist, with a "record," be admitted to, especially to look into subjects that for decades have been restricted to the initiated only. The author is forced to rely mainly on memory; he transmits conversations, recalls incidents, etc. What he has recorded is information that survived only with the greatest difficulty through the oral tradition of a few people.

The historical significance of the document and its overall subject matter more than make up for the roughness of style and occasional errors of detail. Quite a few issues and episodes are taken up and presented more or less accurately. Many of these are subjects that have been hidden away or blown up out of all proportion by Stalinist falsification. The same issues have claimed the attention of many recent anti-Stalin writers in the Soviet Union (for example, the role of Stalin and Kamenev in March 1917).

A final word is called for concerning the "episode from Yesenin's life," which the memoirist tacks on at the end of his recollections. This passage reflects the strong interest in literary and cultural questions that grew up in the post-Stalin era, especially the revolt against "socialist realism."

Even in cultural questions, the Soviet rebels of the sixties and seventies look back to the anti-Stalin Bolsheviks of the twenties. Significantly, the Trotskyist literary critic, Voronsky, has been rehabilitated and some of his works republished. And one samizdat publication has circulated Trotsky's 1926 article in memory of Yesenin and a 1927 piece by Bukharin on the same subject. Bukharin differed with Trotsky in his assessment of Yesenin and generally supported the campaign against Yesenin's "hooligan" influence, though Bukharin did criticize the dreary official "proletarian" poets, who drove young people to prefer Yesenin's "hooligan" verse out of boredom. It is obviously in response to this kind of interest that the memoirist chose to discuss Trotsky and Yesenin's attitudes toward one another, however inaccurately he may have presented these, going by memory alone.

A passage from the omitted civil war section of the "Memoirs" should be cited here. It comes at the end of that section and makes the transition to his account of work in Moscow and the struggle of the Left Opposition. It also serves as a general statement of his aims in writing.

"The present memoirs do not pretend to be exhaustive, complete, or stenographically accurate. They are the memoirs of a participant and witness of the heroic struggle of the Red Army against its enemies. . . .

"Since in my subsequent military service at the central headquarters of the Red Army high command, I also met and had dealings with both Tukhachevsky and Trotsky, who aroused my admiration by their unbounded self-sacrificing work for the good of the world revolution, I cannot help having something to say about them *to preserve a favorable memory of them for the new generations, who will be seeking and discovering the historical truth* about these heroes of the Soviet Republic, who perished amid slanders" (Emphasis added).

The "Memoirs of a Bolshevik-Leninist" was translated for this volume by the editor. All notes on the Russian manuscript are here kept as footnotes. Editor's notes are in brackets.

MEMOIRS OF A BOLSHEVIK-LENINIST
The Twenties: Years of Inner-Party Struggle (and Actual Split)

The October Revolution at the time of its birth left no doubt about its historical justification inasmuch as it declared its *international* essence to the whole world.

But when a certain "someone" in the leadership, after Lenin's death, began to take advantage of his "enormous power" in the party's Central Committee and to replace the international banner of the October Revolution with a national banner (national socialism in one country)—that was all it took to make doubts flare up immediately among Communists around the world and for a struggle to begin.

The internal struggle led in fact to a split in the world Communist movement, and especially in the ranks of the Russian Communist Party, which split into three parts: left, right, and center.

The *left wing* of the Russian Communist Party, led by L. D. Trotsky, was the representative of the interests of the city proletariat, the rural poor, and the agricultural workers. The Left Opposition proposed a plan for the industrialization of the country, which flowed from the vital need to transform Russia technologically and improve the standard of living of the workers and peasants. The Left Opposition called on the party to render direct assistance to the world proletariat in the effort to establish throughout the world the power of the proletariat and peasantry — Soviet power. In this respect it based itself on a situation that favored the seizure of power in the weakest link in the chain of the capitalist world — bourgeois Germany in the first years of the 1920s.

"All the capitalist powers of what is called the West are pecking at her and preventing her from rising," Lenin wrote in March 1923 in his article "Better Fewer, But Better" (*Collected Works* [Progress Publishers, 1966], Vol. 33, pp. 487-502). "The whole world is now passing to a movement that must give rise to a world socialist revolution" (p. 499).

However, Stalin's intrigues against Trotsky, begun even during the civil war and expanded to their full after Lenin's death, had a pernicious effect on the international Communist movement and first of all on the German Communist Party, from whose leadership the old, experienced Bolshevik cadres — those loyal to Lenin's legacy — were removed. The split in the German party threw the working class of Germany into confusion. Through the hole thus opened, the fascists poked in, taking advantage of the disarray and vacillations in the ranks of the German proletariat sown by Stalin's intrigues. At that time the German Communist Party was the largest, the most active, and the most crucial to the fate of the world socialist revolution. While proponents of the Stalinist theory of socialism in one country gradually came to predominate in the Russian Communist Party, a domination brought about by chopping off supporters of Lenin's heritage from the Communist Party, in Germany a process was under way in which the proponents of national socialism were building up, resulting in Hitlerite fascism coming to power in 1933.

Not by accident did Lenin write in his testament: "I think

that from the point of view of preventing a split and from the point of the view of the relations between Stalin and Trotsky which I discussed above, it is not a trifle, or it is such a trifle as may acquire decisive significance."

Lenin's prediction proved farsighted and accurate. One can only regret that the party did not heed these words of Lenin's. The basic reason for this was the concealment of Lenin's testament from the party in the 1920s by the Septemvirate, formed within the Central Committee immediately after Lenin's illness. This factional Septemvirate, about which Zinoviev told us when he, along with Kamenev, came over to Trotsky, was made up at first of rightists and centrists, supported to a considerable extent by the authority of Zinoviev, Kamenev, and Yaroslavsky.[1] Among them, Bukharin, Rykov, and Tomsky were of the right.

The right wing of the Russian Communists, led by N. I. Bukharin, represented the interests of the private property-holding classes — the kulaks (better-off peasants), the NEPmen,[2] and the old intelligentsia. The Right Opposition was against industrializing the country by using the resources of the state and insisted on a free hand for the private entrepreneur and on the abolition of the state monopoly on foreign trade. The Right Opposition considered it possible (in the light of the delay in the world revolution) to preserve private capitalist

---

1. [The Septemvirate consisted of the six members, other than Trotsky, on the Politbureau after Lenin's death — that is, Zinoviev, Kamenev, Stalin, Bukharin, Rykov, and Tomsky. The seventh member was Stalin's henchman Kuibyshev, who was chairman of the Central Control Commission. The memoirist here mistakenly names Yemelyan Yaroslavsky instead of Kuibyshev. The error is logical. Yaroslavsky was in Stalin's inner circle, and from 1924 to 1931 was the chief official in charge of the rewriting of history.]

2. [The New Economic Policy (NEP) was initiated in 1921 to replace the policy of "Military Communism," which prevailed during the civil war and led to drastic declines in agricultural and industrial production. To revive the economy after the civil war, NEP was adopted as a temporary measure allowing a limited revival of free trade inside the Soviet Union and foreign concessions alongside the nationalized and state-controlled sections of the economy. The NEP stimulated the growth of a class of wealthy peasants and of a commercial bourgeoisie (NEPmen) and produced a long series of political and economic concessions to private farming and trade. It was succeeded in 1929 by forced collectivization of the land and the first five-year plan.]

property in peasant Russia—for the time being. In this connection they put forward the new slogan of *kulak and NEP-
man growing over peacefully into socialism.*

Subjectively Bukharin, Rykov, and Tomsky were not bad
people, nor bad Communists. Having lost faith in the world
revolution, however, they objectively headed down the false
road of accommodating the Soviet system to the interests of
the capitalist elements, who, in Lenin's view, could be utilized
through the New Economic Policy only for a certain length
of time.

The basic danger from the Right Opposition was that it
defended slow tempos for the industrialization of the country,
when what was necessary were accelerated, rapid tempos to
ensure, first of all, a defense industry and an air force in the
event of an attack on Soviet soil by enemies from the surrounding capitalist world.

Through the technological transformation of the country
and by arming agriculture with technology, and organizing
it on the basis of Lenin's plan for cooperatives, it would have
been possible to assure the consolidation of the October victory
and be ready not only to repel a blow from the capitalist
encirclement but also to give really effective support to the
world proletariat—which was of a mind to seize power from
the bourgeoisie, shattered and falling apart as a result of the
imperialist war.

Today it is completely clear to everyone that the failure,
resulting from the influence of the rightists and centrists, to
industrialize the country at the necessary rate, as advocated
by the left wing of the party headed by L. D. Trotsky—this
failure had a telling effect even during the Civil War in Spain
and at the beginning of the assault on us by Hitler Germany.

The center wing of the party, under Stalin's leadership, represented the interests of the significant layer of state and party
functionaries, in whose hands rested both party and government power in the capital and in the outlying areas. This
influential bureaucratic hierarchy was a force to be reckoned
with in the country and could muster all sorts of resistance
to measures proposed either from the left or from the right.

The centrists had no economic program of their own and
were forced to borrow particular ideas from the right or the
left, and put them into effect in distorted form, with a certain
"original twist" added. All the while, they hypocritically presented these ideas as their own "general line," . . . calling it
"Leninist." . . .

But in essence the entire conduct of the centrists was anti-

Leninist, not only their inner-party crimes, consisting first of all of using their enormous power to hide from the party Lenin's testament and the other fundamental documents he wrote before his death; but also in their splitting of the world Communist movement in all sorts of ways, preventing the realization of the world revolution, and then basing themselves on the supposed "delay in the world revolution" to put into circulation the theory of "the victory of socialism in one country," in order to take further criminal steps in matters of economic reconstruction and industrialization of the country, and along the lines of discrediting the idea of communism by the bloody deeds of the period of the personality cult.

In the course of bitter factional struggle between opposing groups in the party a situation arose of organizational differentiation between the three wings of the party, each with its own leaders and organizational centers.

This internal dissension was the fruit of differences in the Bolshevik Party that began as far back as April 1917, when the discussion was going on over Lenin's *April Theses* and the basic question of armed insurrection.[3] As has now become generally known, Stalin even in those days supported the "strikebreakers of October" who came out against Lenin and Trotsky, adhering instead to the line of "putting pressure on the Provisional Government."

Later, in admitting his "error," Stalin did not fail to add that he had "erred together with the majority of the Bolshevik Party Central Committee," thus in essence confirming what was said by Trotsky in *Lessons of October*.[4]

---

3. [Lenin's Theses of April 4 (1917) precipitated a crisis in the Bolshevik Party. Newly arrived from Switzerland, Lenin condemned the Provisional Government that had been established by the February revolution, called for an end to the war, and defined the task of the Bolsheviks as preparing for the soviets to take full power and establish a workers' state. In his call for the establishment of a dictatorship of the proletariat, Lenin was initially opposed by virtually the entire Bolshevik leadership.]

4. [Trotsky's 1924 essay *Lessons of October* was printed in response to the Stalinist falsification of party history. In it, he related the two major crises the party had gone through in 1917: in April, when Lenin had had to overcome the resistance of the party's right wing before he could persuade the party to set its course for socialist revolution; and on the eve of October, when the same right wing balked at insurrection. Trotsky exposed the role that Stalin, Zinoviev,

After Lenin fell ill during the celebrated "Georgian affair," and later died, during the reading of the resolution of the thirteenth party conference, his opponents of October 1917 — the very same ones who were to oppose his testament — blocked together against Trotsky and "the forty-six" — the Central Committee members and Old Bolsheviks who advocated the fulfillment of Lenin's testament and a program of rapid rates of industrialization — and they established their own factional center within the Central Committee in the form of the Septemvirate, which laid the basis for the actual split in the leadership of the party and in the party itself.

Thus the Stalinist leadership of the CC created a situation in the party that led to a complete break with the organizational principles of Bolshevism: each oppositional group, both in the capital and in local areas, had its own conspiratorial apartments where political questions were discussed. In the same way, the factional Septemvirate within the CC, before bringing a question to the Politbureau of the CC, made its own decisions, in preliminary fashion, behind its back, and laid the basis for cutting the adherents of Lenin's testament out of the leadership, those of the "forty-six."

I belonged to the group that advocated the fulfillment of Lenin's testament, which was led by Trotsky. I recall how after the fourteenth party congress the Leningraders led by Zinoviev and Kamenev split from the bloc with Stalin, admitting their factional activity within the CC against the party, against Lenin. They came over to the Left Opposition.

At that time in Moscow, Communists from the factories and plants of the city and from its institutes of higher education gathered at numerous apartments of the Left Opposition in conspiratorial fashion. The leaders of the Left Opposition came to these — Trotsky, Zinoviev, Kamenev, Radek, Lashevich, Piatakov, Muralov, Sapronov, and others.

At such an apartment on the Petrovka I often saw that leading figure of the Russian Communist Party, Kamenev. Those meetings took place in the autumn of 1926. Particularly unforgettable were his discussions with us on the party and its leading cadres.

All that I heard then I shall try to relate in my own words in ten letters.

---

and Kamenev had played in 1917; and thus he challenged the right of the Stalinist faction, which had been the party's right wing in 1917, to speak as the only authentic interpreters of Bolshevik doctrine.]

WHAT I HEARD FROM THE LIPS OF
L.B. KAMENEV AND G. YE. ZINOVIEV
AND KNOW FROM THE DOCUMENTS OF LENIN

Letter One

The leading center of the Bolshevik Party — the Central Committee Bureau — was located in Petrograd in 1917. It was made up of leading figures from the Old Guard. Among them was Molotov, a lethargic and mediocre person. The political situation in those days was red-hot and revolutionary. The Provisional Government had just come to power.

History imposed a task of enormous importance on the Bolshevik Party — to keep pace with the events, influence them, and establish jumping-off points for the proletariat's future battles with the bourgeoisie for power.

But the Central Committee Bureau did not measure up to this task. It did not propose a single slogan to the aroused people but through inertia repeated the party's slogans of yesterday.

It was not surprising that Stalin and Kamenev, just returned from penal exile, did not long put up with such inaction by the Bureau. Using force, they took over from Molotov the apparatus of the Central Committee Bureau and the editorial office of *Pravda*. Losing no time, they developed a "stormy activity" in the plants and factories of Petrograd . . . in defense of the bourgeois Provisional Government and its policy of war until final victory. . . .

This amounted to adoption by the Bolsheviks of defensist positions. [5]

Following the Petrograders, the Old Bolsheviks of Moscow also supported Stalin and Kamenev. Bubnov, Rykov, Piatakov, Nogin, and others made declarations of support to the Provisional Government which was trying to continue the war "to a victorious conclusion."

This was not only a major political error by the Bolshevik

---

5. [On the internal struggles within the ranks of the Bolshevik Party during 1917, see Trotsky's *History of the Russian Revolution*. The term "defensist" was applied to those who after February 1917 supported the Provisional Government's policy of national defense, i. e., pursuit of the war, which remained, as far as Lenin was concerned, an imperialist war on Russia's part since the Provisional Government remained in the service of the Russian bourgeoisie.]

Old Guard; it was an outright betrayal of internationalism, for it signified a refusal to comply with the decisions of the international conference of socialist-internationalists.

The Bolshevik Old Guard knew that in 1915-16 at Zimmerwald a conference had been held, attended — along with thirty-eight delegates from eleven countries — by representatives of the Russian Social Democratic Labor Party, including Lenin and Trotsky, who stood on internationalist antiwar positions. The decisions of that conference were binding on the Central Committee Bureau.

The defensism of the Bolshevik Old Guard in the first months of the February Revolution placed Lenin, who was still in exile abroad, in a difficult position. He tried to correct the political positions of the Old Guard in Russia and wrote letters from Switzerland to Petrograd, addressed to the CC Bureau and to *Pravda*. He condemned the support given by the Bolsheviks to the bourgeois Provisional Government, and he called on the workers and peasants to turn the imperialist war into a civil war. However, Lenin's appeals did not meet with any understanding from the CC Bureau leadership of that time. Lenin's letters and articles were published in *Pravda* in altered form. From them it was difficult to understand Lenin's actual position in those historic days of the February Revolution.

Such is the truth, and there is no getting around it. Bolsheviks have never feared the truth, and this can be spoken openly.

The causes of the Old Guard's mistakes were not accidental. They flowed from the resolutions of the party on the attitude Bolsheviks should take toward the bourgeois-democratic revolution.

The Old Guard regarded these party resolutions much as a Christian does the Gospel. Not knowing the laws of social development, and not taking them into account, the Old Guard failed to observe certain very important historical developments. They did not see that the bourgeois-democratic revolution in Russia came to an end the very day after its victory, having accomplished its historic mission in full.

Not having understood that, a part of the Old Guard which found itself in the leadership of the party at the most crucial moment, also failed to understand that the party resolutions on this question had also served their purpose and were outdated on the very first day after the February Revolution. What lay behind the mistakes of the Old Guard was its political immaturity and inability to understand the dialectic of revolution.

Letter Two

For many years Lenin found himself in emigration in Switzerland. The fact that he was far away from his native land and from the party did not have a decisive meaning for the fate of the revolution. Lenin kept himself informed on the situation in Russia by the reports of party members arriving from Russia, by letters from workers in Petrograd and Moscow, and by constantly following the press of Switzerland and other countries.

From the very first day of the February Revolution he unerringly made out the *disposition* of political forces in the new Russia and the results of the bourgeois revolution, which had not given the working people anything worthwhile.

The land as before remained in the hands of the landlords, the plants and factories in those of the bourgeoisie. In place of the czar and his court a bourgeois Provisional Government had come to power.

Life itself impelled the Russian workers and peasants toward a new revolution which would mark the opening of the era of proletarian revolutions throughout the world. Such was Lenin's thinking on April 3, 1917, when he climbed to the roof of the armored car at the Finland Station.

From the roof of the armored car, Lenin hurled six words of wisdom to the Russian and world proletariat, which have become the banner of our time: "Long Live the World Socialist Revolution." A new period of world history had begun.

Lenin made a sharp turn to the left. The Bolshevik Old Guard was not prepared for such a sharp turn on the part of its leader. In its ranks, panic, vacillation, and confusion arose. They accused Lenin of "adventurism," and of passing over to the positions of Trotsky and his theory of "permanent revolution."[6]

---

6. [The Marxist theory of permanent revolution elaborated by Trotsky states, among other things, that in order to accomplish and consolidate even bourgeois democratic tasks such as land reform in an underdeveloped country, the revolution must go beyond the limits of a democratic revolution into a socialist one, which sets up a workers' and peasants' government. Such a revolution will therefore not take place in "stages" (first a stage of capitalist development to be followed at some time in the future by a socialist revolution), but will be continuous or "permanent," passing immediately to a

Since then many years have passed. But this crucial period in the history of our Communist Party has not been given a just and truthful presentation in the pages of the party press.

Is it permissible to hide from the party such an important, dramatic event in its heroic history? No, it is impermissible!

The party should know the full truth about Lenin and the Old Guard, more precisely, the upper layer of the Old Guard, which did not reflect the hopes and *aspirations* of the Bolshevik Party at the moment when the October overturn was being accomplished by Lenin and his true collaborators.

The party should know that for its chief, for Lenin, theoretical dogmas had no meaning if they did not correspond to vital necessity and if they were out of touch with life.

Lenin approached the October Revolution not by following the prearranged schema of Marxist literalists, but by guiding himself with the compass of historical reality, which was arranging the contending forces in a new way. He acted with an eye to this new disposition and interrelation of the forces that had been drawn into the revolution.

Lenin never forgot for a moment that Russia was the weakest link in the chain of world imperialism, which could and must be broken with all possible Bolshevik decisiveness, something very much lacking in the leading nucleus of the older cadres.

Relying only on the Russian proletariat, and on the revolutionary working people of all the nations of the empire, Lenin, along with his true cothinkers and collaborators in the October armed insurrection, was able to organize the seizure of power by a revolutionary party of the workers and peasants — as the Communist Party was in those days.

Letter Three

Lenin was gifted with a very accurate political compass. The Old Guard refused to follow the direction its arrow pointed, failing to understand Lenin and coming out against him in the most critical days.

Lenin wrote his *April Theses* in Switzerland on the eve of his departure for Russia. On the day of his arrival in Petrograd, April 3, 1917, he made his theses public at a

---

postcapitalist stage. For a full exposition of the theory, see Trotsky's *Permanent Revolution and Results and Prospects* (Pathfinder Press, 1972).]

meeting of delegates to an All-Russian Conference of Soviets, at which representatives were present from all three factions of the RSDLP — Bolsheviks, Mensheviks, and internationalist-Mezhrayontsy. [7]

Lenin's theses called for Russia's immediate withdrawal from the war, for the immediate confiscation of the landlords' estates, and for peaceful transfer of state power from the bourgeoisie to the proletariat. There was not one word in Lenin's theses about forceful overthrow of the Provisional Government.

In spite of that the Menshevik leaders — Martov, Chkheidze, and others — called Lenin's *April Theses* "adventurist" and left the conference in protest against them.

After the departure of the Mensheviks, several Bolsheviks came out with criticism of the theses — Zinoviev, Kamenev, Stalin, Rykov, Nogin, and others. They charged that Lenin and his theses were out of touch with reality and were sliding over into left adventurism. They said that Lenin's theses did not represent the view of the party but merely his personal view.

Against Lenin stood all his closest disciples and the not untalented leaders of the party organizations in Russia.

This caused Lenin great distress, and for a time he felt that he had been abandoned by all his comrades. It was painful for him to see that the Old Guard was not measuring up to the historic tasks of the Bolshevik Party and was tail-ending the Menshevik defensist position, opposing the seizure of power by the proletariat.

At that moment, at the rostrum of the conference, L. D. Trotsky appeared. In the name of the internationalist-Mezhrayontsy group he declared full support to Lenin's *April Theses.* [8]

---

7. [The Mezhrayontsy (Inter-District Organization), Trotsky's group, merged with the Bolsheviks in August 1917. It had maintained an internationalist opposition to the imperialist war throughout the war, and opposed the Provisional Government. In 1917 the name of its journel was *Vperyod* (Forward).]

8. [Trotsky was not in Russia in April 1917 but in a Canadian prison camp for German prisoners of war. It was after his return to Russia in May that he expressed his total agreement with Lenin's *April Theses.*]

This was a portentous event.

It was the most dramatic day in the history of the Bolshevik Party. On this day the Old Guard moved away from Lenin, while Trotsky at the head of the internationalist-Mezhrayontsy came closer to him, on the way to becoming his most faithful and devoted collaborator.

In our party literature nothing is written about this. They want to bury this event in the archives. Every year our party publishing organs put out every kind of thing imaginable — where lies are presented as truth and vice versa. On the dispute between Lenin and Trotsky, mountains of books have been written, but on their amicable joint work in October and during the civil war not one true word is written. We do not have a truthful presentation of the historical events connected with the name of Trotsky. Political figures in the party are railed against and slandered. In all this there is a monstrous conspiracy by the enemies of historical truth.

A typical example of this may be found in the commentary and notes to the book by John Reed, *Ten Days That Shook the World.*

In his introduction to this book, Lenin writes: "Here is a book which I should like to see published in millions of copies and translated into all languages. It gives a truthful and most vivid exposition of the events . . ." (International Publishers, 1926, p. v).

But on page 52 [of the Russian edition] the Stalinist-minded annotators hasten to make a liar of Lenin, slanderously claiming, in spite of what was said in the introduction, that "the course of the discussion about the armed uprising of October 1917 is portrayed *incorrectly.*"

Or here, for example, is how John Reed describes the course of the discussion on the question of the seizure of power. The description, as Lenin asserted, is a "truthful" one.

"All the livelong afternoon Lenin and Trotsky had fought against compromise. A considerable part of the Bolsheviki were in favor of giving way so far as to create a joint all-Socialist government. 'We can't hold on!' they cried. . . .

"But Lenin, with Trotsky beside him, stood firm as a rock. 'Let the compromisers accept our program and they can come in! We won't give way an inch. If there are comrades here who haven't the courage and the will to dare what we dare, let them leave with the rest of the cowards and conciliators!'" (pp. 124-25).

That was how Lenin spoke.[9]

And yet, I have in front of me a book, published nowadays, which repeats Stalin's slanders against Trotsky: "In those days of preparation for the insurrection, Trotsky came out against Lenin. . . ."

Such brazen rubbish aimed against both Lenin and Trotsky continues despite the fact that everyone knows about the letters and articles in which Lenin frequently spoke of Trotsky, addressed himself to Trotsky, held counsel with Trotsky, and expressed alarm that a satrap, a rude Great Russian bully, was sitting at the head of the party's Central Committee, and was capable of misusing his "enormous power."

The bulk of Lenin's letters were deliberately kept hidden from the party by Stalin and his accomplices in order to hide the historical truth, the Leninist truth, from the party.[10]

These letters provide the thoughtful Communist who reads them with the key to understanding that Stalin led the party into a political crisis whose terrible consequences have intruded into the reality of our life.

Lev Davidovich Trotsky is a great revolutionary of our time. In the Russian Social Democratic Party he occupied a special place. He approached the October Revolution under the banner of the world proletarian revolution. He did not

---

9. [It was on this occasion, on November 20, 1917, that Lenin said of Trotsky "there has been no better Bolshevik." See the minutes of that meeting, marked to be thrown out by Stalinist editors in the 1920s but preserved by Left Oppositionists and published by Trotsky in *The Stalin School of Falsification* (Pathfinder Press, 1972), pp. 101-22.]

10. [After the twentieth congress (1956) some of Lenin's last articles and letters attacking Stalin in late 1922 and early 1923 were published separately and were included in the fifth Russian edition of Lenin's so-called *Complete Works* and in the English edition *(Collected Works)*, which came out in the 1960s. However, the full significance of Lenin's struggle against Stalin and the bureaucratizing tendency he represented was played down by the official press, and Stalin's heirs continued to spread lies and half-truths about the history of the party and of the Soviet state. Most of the lies and falsifications of the mid-twenties, in fact, were revived in a campaign against "Trotskyism" in the 1960s. Dozens of books, pamphlets, and articles were churned out in this continuing campaign.]

adhere either to the Bolsheviks or the Mensheviks. His popularity in the working class was the result of his revolutionary consistency and honesty in ideological struggle. His oratorical talent won the hearts of the workers of Petrograd.

In 1905 the workers of St. Petersburg elected him chairman of the Petersburg Soviet of Workers' Deputies. For his leadership in the St. Petersburg revolutionary movement in 1905, Czar Nicholas deported Trotsky "to eternal habitation" in Siberia. He escaped from Obdorsk by reindeer sleigh, an event he relates in his book *Flight from Siberia.*

Trotsky came into agreement with Lenin at the most decisive phases of the revolutionary movement in Russia. By the time of the second party congress they were calling Trotsky "Lenin's bludgeon," and in March 1903 Lenin in a letter to G. V. Plekhanov insisted on having Trotsky coopted onto the editorial staff of *Iskra* because he was "unquestionably a man of exceptional ability, full of conviction, energetic, who will develop further. All in all he has been working for *Iskra* in the most energetic way."[11]

It was Trotsky's closeness to Lenin's positions in these prerevolutionary years and his work on *Iskra* that contributed more than a little to his popularity among the St. Petersburg workers and to his election as chairman of the soviet.

After the defeat of the 1905 revolution, in the period of wavering and disarray in the ranks of the Social Democracy and in its Bolshevik wing, when a layer of Bolsheviks moved away from Lenin and grouped around Trotsky, the latter had a number of conflicts and disputes with Lenin and took a position as a conciliator, without adhering to either the Mensheviks or the Bolsheviks. So matters continued until the international conference at Zimmerwald in 1915.

---

11. [The official English edition of Lenin's *Collected Works* (Progress Publishers, 1966) gives the following translation of the relevant part of the letter to Plekhanov: "'Pero' [Trotsky's pseudonym — "The Pen"] has been writing in every issue for several months now. In general he is working for *Iskra* most energetically. . . . He is unquestionably a man of more than average ability, convinced, energetic, and promising" (Vol. 43, pp. 10-11). By translating *nediuzhenny* — meaning "exceptional" or "outstanding" — as merely "more than average," the official translator is trying to underplay Lenin's high regard for the man who later became the Kremlin bureaucracy's principal adversary.]

This was during the first imperialist war, which injected the poison of chauvinism into many socialist parties, causing them to betray their international duty.

Individual socialists who remained true to internationalism opposed the war and "defensist" support for it. At Zimmerwald, thirty-eight such socialist-internationalists gathered from eleven countries of the world.

The Russian delegation consisted of three people — Lenin, Trotsky, and Zinoviev. From the train to the village of Zimmerwald the delegates were transported in four coaches. Trotsky commented: "Half a century after the founding of the international, all the internationalists of the world can fit into four coaches."

Letter Four

The group of internationalist-Mezhrayontsy consisted of very talented and energetic socialists, highly educated and erudite Marxists. Brilliant and outstanding orators and organizers of the workers' movement in Russian adhered to this group. Prerevolutionary Russia knew Trotsky well from his role in the 1905 revolution as chairman of the St. Petersburg Soviet of Workers' Deputies. The revolutionary underground of the Social Democracy and the Bolsheviks knew well the figures of Lunacharsky, Rakovsky, Karl Radek, Preobrazhensky, Joffe, Volodarsky, Uritsky, Krestinsky, Sharov, Serebriakov, Lozovsky, Valentinov, Antonov-Ovseenko, and many, many other active participants in the October overturn, who were among the Mezhrayontsy and whom the majority of workers in the Petrograd Soviet followed in the days of the February Revolution.

As at the time of the 1905 revolution, L. D. Trotsky was elected chairman of the Petrograd Soviet once again in 1917. This spoke convincingly enough of the great influence the Mezhrayontsy group had with the working class of Petrograd. This group of internationalists played a significant role in the political life of Russia in 1917 beginning with the February Revolution, and found itself on the left wing of the revolutionary struggle of the working class.

It was precisely because of this that Lenin came into agreement with Trotsky. And Trotsky, acknowledging the disputes with Lenin that had taken place in the period of confusion and vacillation before Zimmerwald, later declared: "Yes, I came to Lenin through many battles. . . ."

As early as the eve of October it became clear to Lenin that he ought to rely on Trotsky and the Mezhrayontsy — advocates of armed insurrection and opponents of any compromise whatever with the bourgeois Provisional Government and the conciliators.

Long before Trotsky even arrived in Russia, having been detained abroad and prevented by the czarist government's allies from getting back to Russia, long before the sixth party congress, Lenin sought to help speed the arrival of "our comrade Trotsky, the former chairman of the Petersburg Soviet of Workers' Deputies." He wrote letters and articles on this question, aimed especially, it seems, at the British government (see Lenin's *Collected Works*).

Long before the sixth party congress, Ya. M. Sverdlov wrote in a letter (May 4, 1917) to Antonov-Ovseenko: "The question of Trotsky and Lunacharsky's participation on our paper is nearly settled."

And in the report of the Organizational Bureau concerning the call for the sixth party congress, presented by Sverdlov on June 26, 1917, it says: "In Petrograd there exist two internationalist organizations: the Central Committee and the Mezhrayonny Komitet [Inter-District Committee]. The resolutions on fundamental questions adopted by the two organizations do not differ in any essential way. The question of unification had been held over to the party congress, so that now, at the present congress, both Bolsheviks and Mezhrayontsy are in attendance. With the arrival of Trotsky, Lunacharsky, and Chudnovsky, an Organizational Bureau for calling the congress was formed, consisting of five members (three from the Bolsheviks and two from the Mezhrayontsy). The call was put out by both groups. Comrade Trotsky, even before the Congress, joined the editorial board of our party organ, but his imprisonment prevented him from actually participating in the editorial work" (Ya. M. Sverdlov, *Collected Works*, Vol. 2, pp. 10, 32).

At the sixth congress of the party, during the ominous July days,[12] the entire group of internationalists was taken into the ranks of the Bolshevik Party, and a great many former

---

12. [The July days of 1917 in Petrograd broke out without any direction and led to bloody encounters. The Bolsheviks were declared responsible, their leaders arrested, and their papers shut down.]

Mezhrayontsy were elected to the Central Committee. Now Lenin could feel secure about the party. Its ranks had been joined by an energetic group of experienced political figures closely linked with the working class and the revolutionary intelligentsia.

The former Mezhrayontsy became the ideological and organizational backbone of the Bolshevik Party, Lenin's main support in the preparatory work for storming Russian capitalism.

No matter what is now said about Trotsky and the Mezhrayontsy by their opponents among those who orient toward the Old Guard of Bolsheviks, they will never erase from the memory of the Russian people the heroism which Trotsky's internationalist group displayed in the October insurrection and during the civil war for the victory of the socialist revolution in Russia.

They were true Bolshevik-Leninists, as they called themselves after Lenin's death in response to slanderous insinuations by Stalinist sycophants about an alleged attempt to "substitute Trotskyism for Leninism." They did not sit out the revolution and civil war in some quiet corner, taking cover from the storm, the way many did who now lay claim to a monopoly of the leadership for having belonged organizationally to the Old Guard. They threw themselves into the crashing waves of the revolution and perished as fearless fighters for the victory of the socialist cause, for Soviet power.

Comrades Volodarsky, Uritsky, Chudnovsky and a number of others who were later to give their lives for that victory, as well as those who remained alive after the victory of Soviet power, were appointed to the highest posts in the first Soviet government and in the leadership of the Bolshevik Party.

To take Trotsky alone, about whom, even now, every kind of slander and invective is invented—"enemy of Bolshevism," "enemy of Leninism," "Menshevik," "counterrevolutionary"— L. D. Trotsky was appointed people's commissar for foreign affairs in the first Soviet government and elected a member of the Politbureau of the Central Committee, and when the threat of intervention by fourteen imperialist powers arose and domestic counterrevolutionary rebellions began, Trotsky was appointed people's commissar of all the armed forces of the Soviet land. This was the highest and most crucial responsibility and position in the besieged Soviet state. For eight years [actually seven — Ed.] Trotsky stood at the head of the Red Army.

[The author lists the leading Mezhrayontsy and their posts; some, however, like Radek, were not Mezhrayontsy:]

Lunacharsky — was appointed people's commissar of enlightenment of the Russian Socialist Federated Soviet Republic (RSFSR)

Volodarsky — people's commissar of agitation, propaganda, and the press

Uritsky — chairman of the extraordinary commission (Cheka)

Krestinsky — people's commissar of finance

Rakovsky — chairman of the Ukrainian government

Joffe — deputy people's commissar of foreign affairs

Slyansky — deputy people's commissar of the armed forces

Lozovsky — chairman of the Profintern [Trade Union International]

Karl Radek — editor of *Pravda*, chief of the ROSTA press agency

Valentinov — editor of *Trud* [the Soviet trade union newspaper]

Preobrazhensky — secretary of the Central Committee

Serebriakov — secretary of the Central Committee

Sharov — secretary of the Central Committee

Chudnovsky — commandant of the Winter Palace (Together with Antonov-Ovseenko he broke into the room of the Winter Palace where the group of persons who constituted the Provisional Government were to be found. Chudnovsky made a list of arrested ministers. There were sixteen. All present except Kerensky.)

Representatives of the Old Guard were appointed to secondary and tertiary roles in the state, as follows:

Stalin — people's commissar of nationalities and candidate member of the Politbureau

Molotov — no post in the government; deputy of the department of the secretariat of the Central Committee

Kuibyshev — sent to Samara, as secretary of the provincial party committee

Zinoviev — no post in the government; member of the Politbureau; later, chairman of the Comintern

Kamenev — appointed to the All-Union Central Executive Committee and placed on the Politbureau

Rykov, Nogin, and others were appointed to the ministries of internal affairs, trade, and industry.

This distribution of roles in the government and party was carried out by the revolution itself, headed by Lenin.

For their treacherous apostasy from Lenin, their lack of firmness, their vacillations at the most decisive phase of the October Revolution, these people, who considered themselves the Old Guard of Bolshevism, were moved back to secondary roles, and until Lenin's death found themselves in fact at the tail-end of the revolution. . . .

Sufficiently convincing illustration of the aforesaid concerning these people is provided by still unpublished documents of Lenin in the archives, still little known to the party.

Thus for example, Lenin quite often addressed his instructions, proposals, notes for discussion on crucial questions of party work to the Politbureau or Central Committee — beginning in 1922 when Stalin became general secretary: "To Stalin — for the members of the Politbureau," thus assigning Stalin the role of a simple communicating link or technical executor of Lenin's orders or the decisions of the Politbureau.

After Lenin's death Stalin built himself up as "head of the party," belittling Lenin's role as a theoretician and leader of the party in every way.

Also, during the time that Stalin headed the Rabkrin [Workers' and Peasants' Inspection], Lenin constantly kept watch over him, fearing that he would commit mistakes on a massive scale. For this reason he recommended that the selection of cadres for this work be entrusted not to Stalin but to Tsyurupa, Nogin, and others.

It is interesting to compare Lenin's relationships with Trotsky and with Stalin in the entire post-October period, especially in the last years before his death, in order to understand how Lenin related to these two antipodes, exponents of diametrically opposed tendencies within the world Communist movement.

All the more obvious in this light stands out the slander that has been spread about this great collaborator of Lenin's during the October Revolution, the civil war, and the period of transition toward reviving the economy and industrializing the country.

Letter Five

At the doors to the room at Little Hills, the estate where the ailing Lenin was kept, guards were suddenly posted. This was in 1923. The guards were ordered to admit no one to see Lenin without a special pass signed by Stalin.

The hidden purpose of this step is indicated by the fact that from then on, Lenin was under quarantine and his friends and relatives ceased to be admitted to visit him.

At that time Krupskaya was rudely warned that if she came out in support of Trotsky against Stalin the whole country would be informed that, supposedly, Lenin had had two wives: Inessa Armandt and Nadezhda Krupskaya. Only an outright enemy of Lenin could make up such filthy slander. This enemy of Lenin was Stalin. He took revenge on Lenin because of the testament, which he had heard about through devious ways — the testament, in which he had been characterized as a rude person who would misuse his "enormous power" as general secretary to the detriment of the party. And even more than for the testament, Stalin took revenge on Lenin because of the letter entitled "On the Question of Nationalities or 'Autonomization,'" in which Lenin had written:

"The Georgian who is neglectful of this aspect of the question, or who carelessly flings about accusations of 'nationalist-socialism' (whereas he himself is a real and true 'nationalist-socialist,' and even a vulgar Great Russian bully), violates in substance, the interests of proletarian class solidarity . . ." (*Collected Works*, Vol. 35, p. 608).

Krupskaya did not know what she could do to protect Lenin from this vile abuse. Her friends advised her to break through to see him and tell him everything. With Lidia Fotieva, Krupskaya did break through and told Vladimir Ilyich about the foul deeds of this enemy of his. For the first time in her long life with Lenin, she saw tears in his eyes.

The news of Stalin's ugly behavior, tending to intimidate not only Krupskaya but the entire party, wounded Lenin to the quick. By then he could no longer correct the situation. His days were numbered: his last stroke would paralyze him and deprive him of the ability to get around. This was the most difficult thing of all for his active nature to undergo. Still his mind did not betray him. Words came to him with great effort. He dictated a letter to Lidia Fotieva. I will transmit it by memory as it was reported to me then:

"Stalin. After all that Nadya has told me I consider you a person devoid of honor. From this moment, I am breaking off all personal and political relations with you. Lenin." [See *Collected Works*, Vol. 45, pp. 607-08 for the actual text — Ed.]

When, after Lenin's death, an enlarged plenum of the Central Committee and the Central Control Commission was held, Trotsky, a member of the Politbureau and people's commissar for the armed forces, took the floor and hurled in Stalin's face the charge of having committed an outrage against the ailing Lenin in the last days of his life.

Trotsky told the plenum of Lenin's last letter to Stalin (Trotsky's friends had sent him a photocopy of the letter.)

The plenum was shaken by this news and demanded an explanation from Stalin. But he would not admit having received the letter from Lenin and rejected all charges against himself.

Then they sent for Krupskaya and Fotieva. They confirmed the fact that there had been such a letter. Only then did Stalin suddenly remember that he "had received a letter but threw it away without having read it."

Those at the meeting were thrown into confusion; cries of "Shame!" rang out. Some laughed sadistically at what was happening. Trotsky said that perhaps a photocopy should be sent to Stalin so that he could acquaint himself with Lenin's letter. Stalin remained silent. . . .

Letter Six

By a secret agreement among Zinoviev, Stalin, Kamenev, and Bukharin — a session of the Politbureau was convened at the Kremlin.

The fifth member of the Politbureau — Trotsky — was not in Moscow. He was convalescing in the Caucasus.

The sixth member of the Politbureau and its permanent chairman [Lenin] lay on his deathbed at the "Little Hills" estate. [13]

In Lenin's absence the responsibilities of chairman were carried out by his deputy, L. B. Kamenev.

On the agenda there was only one question: the removal of Trotsky from his post as people's commissar of war.

The situation in the party at that time was very tense: in the leading center of the party two rival groups were taking shape — that of Zinoviev and that of Stalin.

Not long before, these groups had stood shoulder to shoulder against Trotsky and, behind the backs of the Politbureau and the Central Committee, had formed the factional Septemvirate composed of Stalin, Zinoviev, Kamenev, Bukharin, Rykov, Tomsky, and Yaroslavsky [a mistake for Kuibyshev — Ed.]. Zinoviev told us about this in a special letter at a later date, when he came over to Trotsky with head hanging in shame.

At the earlier time the Septemvirate was undergoing a differentiation, was beginning to split. But its fear of Trotsky,

---

13. [Before Lenin's death, the Politbureau consisted of seven, not six, full members: Lenin, Trotsky, Stalin, Zinoviev, Kamenev, Bukharin, and Tomsky.]

more precisely, of Trotsky's influence on the party, the working class, and the Red Army united them at this plenum as it always had before that. They knew that a good half of the party placed unlimited confidence in Trotsky, despite the deception practiced on it by the concealment of Lenin's testament, as well as his last, immortal letters, in which he spoke of Trotsky as a voice that should be heeded, and of Stalin as someone who should be removed from the leadership of the Central Committee apparatus.

The Red Army loved Trotsky as its military leader in the victorious civil war. This love of the army for its commander was boundless and sincere.

Zinoviev and Stalin hastened to get rid of Trotsky.

Besides the four members, four [the author apparently meant "three"] candidate members were invited to the Politbureau session with consultative vote — Molotov, Rykov, and Tomsky. . . .[14]

The vote was taken by roll call. All four members of the Politbureau voted for the removal of Trotsky from the leadership of the Red Army.

After the vote had been drawn up in the form of a protocol, they all felt like "victors" . . . and sighed with relief: now, they thought, Trotsky was no danger to them . . . he was disarmed. . . .

Then those present moved on to the nomination of candidates for the post of people's commissar of war.

On this question the Quartumvirate unexpectedly split. This split began in the Septemvirate even before the session of the Quartumvirate. Here it suddenly flared up as a big scandal. Zinoviev proposed Stalin's candidacy for the post of people's commissar of war. Thus he wished at one blow to get rid of both Trotsky and Stalin.

In place of Stalin as general secretary of the party, Zinoviev proposed the honest and devoted party worker and military leader, M. V. Frunze. Zinoviev also stated that this transfer of Stalin would correspond to Lenin's wish expressed in his testament (with which the Politbureau was familiar). Stalin was taken by surprise and severely shaken. He had not expected this stab in the back from Zinoviev. His leaving the post of general secretary would mean the collapse of all his plans

---

14. [Tomsky was a full member of the Politbureau. Molotov was Stalin's chief aide on his secretariat.]

and secret intrigues which he could realize only by using the "enormous power" of the general secretary's position. . . . He felt the end was near for his ambitious schemes and political career, for he was not so naive as to delude himself regarding the situation he would be in as head of the Red Army: the army did not love him and might create obstructions for him that might disgrace him. A critical moment had arrived in the life of J. V. Stalin.

He protested and declared that such an arrangement would only serve the enemies of the party. In these words those present heard an open threat. Stalin's stubbornness had its effect on some of them.

Bukharin, Molotov, and Ordjonikidze (who was also there) supported Stalin, declaring that such a "transfer" in the leadership and army would lead to a split in the party. . . .

Stalin got his way. He had to win time, he needed a respite in which to prepare to repel this assault. Zinoviev backed off. . . . The question was left open.

This retreat of Zinoviev's was his fatal mistake, which subsequently led to his downfall and led the party and country into great upheavals. . . .

The Politbureau session at the Kremlin arrived at no decision. The unanimous vote to remove Trotsky as people's commissar of war was left hanging in the air.

Only a year later in January 1925 did the Politbureau return to this question once more. By that time much water had flowed under the bridge. By his criminal activities Stalin hastened Lenin's death in January 1924.[15]

---

15. [The Russian manuscript of the "Memoirs" contained the following lengthy note, part of which consists of a quote from the fifth Russian edition of Lenin's works:]

In January 1924 the thirteenth all-Russian party conference opened in Moscow. The delegates were painstakingly selected by the factional anti-Leninist Septemvirate headed by Stalin. On its motion the conference approved all the resolutions that had been prepared ahead of time by the Septemvirate — aimed not only against Trotsky but in disguised fashion against Lenin as well. All the decisions of the conference were unanimously accepted. (Trotsky was not at the conference; he was convalescing in the Caucasus.)

Our dramatists (and especially N. Pogodin) have written lies for the people in Stalin's interests for more than forty years regarding

Under these conditions Zinoviev failed in 1925 to muster the necessary resolve to raise again the question of transferring Stalin from the post of general secretary. After forcing Trotsky to submit his resignation from the post of commissar of war, they appointed Mikhail Frunze to that post.

By this appointment Stalin and Zinoviev made mutual concessions to one another. But that vengeful Great Russian bully

---

Lenin's last days and his premature death. From the brief chronology of Lenin's life and work appended to Volume 45 of Lenin's *Collected Works,* fifth edition, pages 716-17, we have taken the following:

*   *   *

1924

"*January 7.* Lenin attends a New Year's party for the children of the workers and employees of the Little Hills state farm and sanatorium.

"*January 17-18.* N.K. Krupskaya reads Lenin the report in *Pravda* on the proceedings at the thirteenth party conference.

"*January 19.* Lenin has a sleigh ride through the woods, observes a hunt.

"*January 19-20.* N.K. Krupskaya reads Lenin the thirteenth party conference resolutions, printed in *Pravda* [among them was a condemnation of "Trotskyism."] 'When, on Saturday, Vladimir Ilyich apparently began to grow disturbed,' Krupskaya later wrote, 'I told him that the resolutions had been adopted unanimously. We spent Saturday and Sunday reading the resolutions. Vladimir Ilyich listened very attentively, raising questions now and then.'

"*January 21.* Sudden acute deterioration in Lenin's condition. 6:50 p.m. — Lenin dies."

[The preceding passage does not appear in the chronology of "Lenin's Life and Work" in his *Collected Works,* English edition, Vol. 33 (1966), which covers the period August 1921 to January 1924. It does appear in the Russian edition, Vol. 45 (1964), as cited by the memoirist and translated here. The corresponding English-language Vol. 45 (1970), containing Lenin's letters, November 1920 to March 1923, does not have a chronology of "Lenin's Life and Work."]

The "heroes" of the factional Septemvirate gave "full personal responsibility for overseeing the regime established by the doctors for Lenin" to the person basically to blame for the serious nervous attacks that Lenin had suffered, that is, Stalin.

"It is not the doctors who give orders to the Central Committee but the Central Committee who instructs the doctors," protested Lenin. What sort of "instructions" these were is not hard to guess from saw in this appointment as well a danger for his own future well-being.

Mikhail Vasilievich Frunze was known among the people as a man of clean conscience. Stalin feared him as a possible rival in the event of a change in the political situation in the party and country. He decided to remove Frunze from his path secretly.

Frunze died unexpectedly at the height of his powers and in full health. I remember how rumors spread around Moscow about Stalin's complicity in Frunze's death. An echo of these rumors, which were not without foundation, was the story by the writer Boris Pilnyak in the journal *Novy Mir* entitled "The Tale of the Unextinguished Moon."[16]

The story tells about a hospital where a certain military commander has been admitted with appendicitis. At night an "unbending man with a Caucasian appearance and accent" secretly arrives and orders the surgeon "in the interests of the revolution" to dispatch the military person during the operation. This was of course a reference to Frunze.

---

reading the diary of Lenin's secretaries [published in the Russian edition of Lenin's works, Vol. 45, 1964].

It is now completely clear who it was that gave "instructions" to the doctors. It was not of course the Central Committee but "the personality," the one who was "personally responsible" for the untimely death of Vladimir Ilyich.

Lenin grew exasperated and upset, but Stalin—making use of Lenin's illness and of his own "enormous powers" as general secretary, both during the period before Lenin's death and for a year afterward — picked uninformed people for the Central Committee apparatus and the provincial organizations to be his temporary fellow-travelers and accomplices, drawing them into criminal intrigues against Lenin and Lenin's closest collaborators and supporters, preparing Stalin's own "glorious ascension" over the corpses of his political opponents, including his own former errand boys and armor-bearers of the Septemvirate and the delegates of the party conferences and congresses, beginning with the thirteenth all the way through the seventeenth.

---

16. [Pilnyak's story is available in English translation in *Mother Earth and Other Stories* (Anchor paperback, 1967). This incident is also described by Trotsky in his *Stalin* (Stein and Day, 1967), and by Roy Medvedev in *Let History Judge* (Knopf, 1972), pp. 47-50.]

Later on, Boris Pilnyak was shot and consigned to oblivion.
In place of Frunze, Voroshilov was appointed head of the Red Army.

No one dared any longer raise the question of transferring Stalin. It seemed that Lenin's testament and his advice about assigning Stalin to other work, removing him from the apparatus of the Central Committee, had been forgotten.

And suddenly . . . Stalin himself proposed that he be re-assigned from the position of general secretary.

"We were thrown into confusion," Kamenev told us later. "We were not ready for this. The voluntary offer to step down from the position of general secretary disarmed us. There was no alternative candidate at hand. We told Stalin, 'there's no need to rush; this is no joking matter; we have to find a candidate for this post, and then we can straighten this all out. . . .' But it turned out that Stalin was toying with us rudely and provocatively. . . . When we realized this, it was already too late."

After that session of the Politbureau, at which Stalin's "voluntary abdication" of the post of general secretary was officially rejected, a colossal purge of the party and state apparatus began. All who advocated the fulfilling of Lenin's testament, united around Trotsky, Zinoviev, Rakovsky, and Radek — predominantly Old Bolsheviks and Communists of the first decade, participants in October and the civil war — these people were all driven out of all positions of responsibility.

Even then it was patently obvious that the greater part of the persecuted Communists still supported Lenin's words — spoken in his letters on the national question and "autonomization" — that this Georgian was himself not only the real, true "nationalist-socialist" but also a vulgar Great Russian bully.

The vacated posts were filled with people who were the vehicles of hierarchical-bureaucratic tendencies and of prejudices of a chauvinist kind, or simply ignorant people, people who did not know the history of the revolutionary movement, of the party, of the civil war, and did not know of Lenin's last appeals, letters, articles, or testament.

All this was served up to these uninformed people third-hand, in distorted form, and as subsequent events showed, as soon as these people began to think more or less for themselves and began to get the truth, Stalin would become aware of the immediate threat they embodied and with every passing year he dispatched and annihilated his former cohorts by the hundreds and thousands, following lists drawn up in advance.

The future demonstrated with full clarity what the real, criminal purpose had been behind that provocative "offer to resign."

Letter Seven

Stalin set up secret surveillance over members of the party Central Committee and the relatives of Lenin. He entrusted this work to the OGPU [Soviet secret police], which subordinated itself to him personally as the general secretary.

This surveillance was carried out in various ways, not least of all by the recruitment of the personal secretaries of the Central Committee members, or those of Lenin's relatives, as OGPU agents. This supplementary "work" of the personal secretaries paid well, quite well in fact.

L. B. Kamenev's personal secretary was also a secret OGPU agent and informed on him to the Lubyanka regularly, telling everything he heard and saw at Kamenev's house, everything he did. . . . Kamenev discovered this treachery on the part of his personal secretary by chance.

Sensing the storm that was building up against him from the direction of the odious personality, Kamenev decided to record for posterity his recollections of Stalin's and Molotov's conduct in the first months of the February Revolution. He wrote down many monstrous and appalling details concerning that period. I remember only a few of those that Kamenev told me:

1. The physical force that Stalin used against Molotov in seizing the apparatus of the Central Committee Bureau and the editorial offices of *Pravda*. In this affair Molotov demonstrated cowardice and a criminal indifference to his own party responsibility. . . .

2. Kamenev described the dramatic episode, not generally known to the party, of Stalin's rapprochement without setting any prior conditions with the Mensheviks in 1917 at a time when he was maneuvering back and forth between Lenin and his enemies.

3. How a number of Old Bolsheviks of Petrograd and Moscow, including Kamenev himself, went over to Menshevik, defensist positions.

Kamenev hid the manuscript of these memoirs in the leg of a bamboo chair he had in his apartment. He thought that no one would think of looking there for these memoirs exposing Stalin. He hid the manuscript in the presence of his personal secretary, who even helped him. An hour later, the OGPU appeared at Kamenev's apartment . . . and confiscated the manuscript. . . .

Letter Eight

Kuibyshev, who was in the Stalin circle, hated Lenin and Trotsky most of all. His hatred for these great revolutionaries began with the first days of Soviet power; the Old Bolshevik Kuibyshev had hoped to receive an important post in the first Soviet government. But he was not given one. In the situation at that time, the "rookie" Bolsheviks from the former Mezhrayontsy group pushed aside the Old Bolsheviks who had proven unequal to the demands of the revolution or the revolutionary tasks, and who were unjustifiably seeking important careers after the victory of the October Revolution.

The basic mass of Old Bolshevik cadres in the outlying districts and in all parts of Russia were alien to any kind of careerist aspirations, or to any intrigues against the Mezhrayonsty and Trotsky simply on the grounds that they had formally entered the Bolshevik ranks only at the time of the sixth party congress. The basic mass welcomed and supported Lenin and Trotsky, joined in the building of the Soviet state, sacrificing their lives on the fronts of the civil war without showing either cowardice or conceit.

Kuibyshev was not like that. He had been appointed to a minor party post as secretary of the Samara province committee of the party, and that did not satisfy him. Soon the civil war began and Kuibyshev began to wear two hats, being appointed a member of the army military council in charge of defending Samara. In the fierce fighting for Samara and the Volga, military council member Kuibyshev displayed cowardice and lack of character: he surrendered the city of Samara to the White Army. For this crime Trotsky branded him a traitor and vowed to have him shot as a coward and betrayer.

Lenin supported Trotsky in this position and Kuibyshev's life hung by a thread. Only blind fate saved him. But his proved to be a vindictive and spiteful character. From that time on he became the personal enemy of Trotsky and Lenin. . . .

During the party discussion in 1923 Kuibyshev came out on Stalin and Zinoviev's side, against Trotsky, in return for which he was brought in closer with the top leadership of the country. Kuibyshev's reasons for opposing Trotsky were purely personal. His old hatred for Trotsky because of the Samara disgrace gave him no rest. Kuibyshev took revenge both openly and indirectly.

He took revenge on Lenin in a vile way. Lenin, at the time he was sick, sent a letter to the Central Committee in which he asked that his article on the Rabkrin be published in *Pravda*. Lenin attached great importance to this article. The article on the Rabkrin signaled the danger of degeneration of the state and party apparatuses.

During the discussion of Lenin's request in the Central Committee, Kuibyshev took the floor. He declared that he was opposed in principle to Lenin's article on the Rabkrin because in his opinion it could provoke discontent among the apparatus workers. In conclusion Kuibyshev proposed that a single copy of *Pravda* be printed with Lenin's article and that copy be sent to Lenin.

It is hard to believe, but the fact that this obscene and brazen proposal aimed at deceiving Lenin was even considered serves as a sufficient example to characterize the attitude on the part of Stalin's Central Committee toward the ailing leader. In this insidious way did Kuibyshev take his revenge on Lenin because of 1918.[17]

In 1935 in the Verkhne-Uralsk prison, Zinoviev told me about Kuibyshev's final revenge on Trotsky. When Stalin decided to expel Trotsky from the Soviet Union in 1929, he made inquiries with almost every government of the world, both East and West, as to whether they would offer Trotsky political asylum. With the exception of Turkey every state in the world refused to admit Trotsky to its territory. Turkey agreed, because Trotsky had played a salutary role in Turkey's national destiny. As commissar of war, Trotsky had rendered military and economic aid to the leader of the Turkish rebels, Ataturk, against the sultanate. As a token of gratitude, renascent Turkey had elected Trotsky and Lenin honorary members of the Turkish Mejlis (parliament). During the discussion in the Politbureau on Turkey's willingness to accept Trotsky on its territory, Politbureau member Kuibyshev introduced a motion "not to deport Trotsky to Turkey but to shoot him in Russia." Even Stalin did not vote for shooting

---

17. [Trotsky mentioned this episode in several places. But he placed it in the Politbureau and not the Central Committee, adding that he had had Kamenev's support against that proposal.]

Trotsky at that time, while Bukharin trembled at Kuibyshev's words.

In relating this, Zinoviev added: "Kuibyshev had an evil and vengeful character like a Chuvash kulak, expropriated during collectivization, and then getting back into power." And today we might add, avenging himself for the past.

Such for the most part were the "kulaks" and "incipient kulaks" whom Stalin in considerable numbers placed in the party and state apparatus. For many years they took revenge and had many people from the Bolshevik Old Guard shot — as well as many old Communists from the first decade after October.

The key to the riddle of Kuibyshev's mysterious death must be sought in the same place as that to the untimely death of Lenin, Frunze's departure, the provocative murder of Kirov, and many others. Historical truth, when its day comes, will have something to say to future generations about this. In the case of Kuibyshev we confidently suppose that, greedy as he was for the summits of power, he became a dangerous rival for Stalin, who saw in Kuibyshev his very own self. There was not room enough in one jar for these two ugly spiders and one devoured the other.

Letter Nine

In the hut in Finland, together with Lenin, Zinoviev hid. He came there not at the order of the Central Committee, but at the call of his own conscience, a desire to share the uneasy fate of his mentor. Lenin and Zinoviev had a friendship of long standing. All through the long years of exile they worked together. Their friendship was based on ideas and goals held in common. Lenin used to discuss all his thoughts and plans first of all with Zinoviev in whom he saw a devoted friend and a highly educated Marxist.

Zinoviev's zigzags of April and October were products of stormy events in which the pupil was not able to keep up with the master. Lenin's sharp turns frightened Zinoviev, although he himself had always been in the extreme left wing of the party. But apparently not everyone is born to live free of mistakes. And Zinoviev made mistakes aplenty.

. . . Kamenev used to make his way to the hut by a secret path. The police were making their sweeps all around, arresting suspects and searching places. They were hunting for Lenin everywhere. A big reward had been posted for his capture.

The Russian bourgeoisie had an elemental fear of Lenin. It whipped up a spirit of mob violence against Lenin by slandering him. It put into circulation false stories about the so-called "sealed train."[18]

Within the hut Kamenev beheld an everyday scene: Lenin and Zinoviev occupied with their usual intellectual labors, the teacher and disciple working in complete accord. They were working out the strategy and tactics of the party in the coming struggle with the bourgeoisie for power. Lenin was sitting on a stump instead of a chair and was working on the book *State and Revolution,* resting his notebook on his knees; he knew the police were hunting for him and fully understood the seriousness of his situation. But he did not fear death. What concerned him was the fate of the revolution and the party. He knew that the proletariat could be victorious only through an armed uprising of the workers and peasants, peasants dressed in soldiers' greatcoats.

According to his old custom, Lenin took Kamenev and Zinoviev by the arms and began to talk with them about the repressive measures the Provisional Government was preparing against the Bolsheviks. He tried to remain calm and hide his inner concern from them. He even tried to joke with them at the expense of the bourgeois police. But his troubled spirit did not subside within him. At one point he suddenly let go of their arms and fell silent. He was thinking about something to himself. [In Kamenev's words] Lenin then "pointed to the pages he had been writing and quietly said to us:

"'I beg you to make known to the party and the working class my . . .' His voice broke off. He had intended to say 'my thoughts in these pages.' We understood that. He said nothing more. He showed such nervous tension only in moments of greatest danger. Zinoviev and I looked at each other in silence. He asked us to excuse him and again sat down on the stump. Within a minute he was again writing animatedly, concentrating his mind and will."

---

18. [When the February revolution broke out Lenin was in Zurich. In order to get back to Russia he had to travel through Germany, with which Russia was still at war. For this purpose he was given a train with a sealed car. The German government was represented in these negotiations by Erich F. Ludendorff, one of the top German generals in World War I. Ludendorff undoubtedly consented to convey Lenin back to Russia in the hope that he would add to the instability of Russia's already-disintegrating military position.]

Kamenev and Zinoviev later used to think about that day in the hut. They tried to guess at the reason for, and the hidden meaning behind, the words Lenin spoke at that time. These words were like a testament before imminent death. Lenin never spoke with anyone about the possibility of his perishing at the hands of the Provisional Government's police. However, the expression on his face and the alarm in his voice expressed the fact that Lenin awaited catastrophe from hour to hour and more than ever hastened to finish his book.

Letter Ten

Soon after the liberation of Georgia by the troops of the Red Army a special commission of the Central Committee, made up of Stalin, Dzerzhinsky, Kuibyshev, and others, went from Moscow to Tiflis. To serve the commission's needs a sizable apparatus of functionaries and an armed detachment of Cheka troops were placed at its disposal. . . . The commission's task was to improve the political atmosphere in Georgia in the wake of the overturn of the Menshevik government.

Complaints addressed to Lenin soon began to arrive from inhabitants of Georgia to the effect that the members of the commission were exceeding their authority. In these complaints, savage arbitrariness and mass shootings of the Georgian population were mentioned.

Lenin in a telegram called Stalin's attention to the impermissibility of arbitrariness, threatening to recall the commission and especially to recall Stalin from the commission. In his answer Stalin justified himself, asserting that his personal enemies in Georgia were slandering him.

However, the complaints continued to pour in, and Lenin recalled the entire commission from Georgia. Later, on Lenin's initiative, a new commission was formed, whose members Lenin himself chose. This commission on the "Georgian affair" was made up of Kamenev, Piatakov, Sokolnikov, and others. The commission went to Georgia in the summer of 1923. After investigating very thoroughly and interviewing numerous inhabitants, Kamenev's commission determined that the previous commission had committed frightful crimes: mass shootings of the population had been organized, entire villages had been burned down, and there had been looting, robbery, rape, and murder on the basis of personal vengeance and blood feuds. Tiny Georgia had found itself for several months in the claws of a ferocious beast, that so-called "personality." . . . Everywhere could be heard the groaning of mothers and the weeping of children over the corpses of those who had been shot and mutilated.

Kamenev's commission informed Lenin and the other members of the Politbureau of its investigatory work. Only then did Lenin learn of his "Georgian wonder's" sanguinary bent of character. As can be seen from the unpublished logbook of Lenin's secretaries, [19] the "Georgian affair," with the evidence that Ordjonikidze had had a hand in it, robbed Lenin of his sleep and left him no peace. He was greatly disturbed and he urged Kamenev to hurry up with his final conclusions. As Kamenev related, this Georgian affair was a heavy blow to Lenin. He fell ill after learning of Ordjonikidze's role in the matter and of Stalin's arbitrariness. Fotieva says that Lenin told her the following: "On the eve of my illness Dzerzhinsky told me about the commission's work and about the 'incident,' and this had a very bad effect on me."

Kamenev said further: Lenin was very ill and wanted to correct his mistake, while he was still alive, regarding the question of Stalin's assignment to the post of general secretary. But he was unable to do so in time. When the report of Lenin's death reached Tiflis from Moscow the commission on the "Georgian affair" put an end to its labors. It returned to Moscow and delivered its materials to the Central Committee.

Where did these materials, so compromising to Stalin, disappear to?

To this day that remains unknown.

---

19. [The notebooks of Lenin's secretaries were published in the Soviet press in 1963 and are included in Volume 45 of the Russian edition of Lenin's works (1964). See the discussion of this historical record, especially in relation to the "Georgian affair," in *Let History Judge*, pp. 21-26. The notebooks are also described in detail in Moshe Lewin's book *Lenin's Last Struggle* (Random House, 1968).]

The Funeral of A. A. Joffe (1927) [20]

. . . The funeral procession traveled from the Commissariat of Internal Affairs across Lubyanka Square, past the Bolshoi Theatre and Moscow University, along the Prechistenka, to the cemetery of the Novo-Devichy monastery. The capital of Russia, Moscow, was saying its last farewell to the outstanding Soviet diplomat and revolutionary — Adolph Abramovich Joffe.

The coffin rested upon a funeral caisson drawn by three bay horses. On the coffin lid lay many wreaths, among which were wreaths from the Soviet government and the Commissariat of Foreign Affairs, from relatives, and from the members of the party's Central Committee. Everyone's attention was drawn to a small wreath with a scarlet ribbon on which was written "From Trotsky and Zinoviev."

The streets of Moscow were filled with people. The funeral procession moved quite slowly. There were no carriages or cars coming along behind. Everyone was on foot. Behind the coffin came the widow, Maria Mikhailovna Joffe. Trotsky walked next to her, holding her arm. Behind them came Zinoviev, Kamenev, Radek, Piatakov, Preobrazhensky, Sapronov, Lashevich. Then came the official delegation representing the government at the funeral, including the minister for foreign affairs, Chicherin, Politbureau member Ryutin, and others. Behind them stretched a long line of many thousands of militant friends of the departed, active participants in the revolution and civil war. They had come to pay their last respects to their comrade in the common struggle for the revolutionary cause.

A. A. Joffe came to the revolutionary movement in the last days of czarist reaction when the bodies of revolutionaries hung from lamp posts, and the flames of the 1905 barricades were flickering out in the Presnya district. Without regret he left the home of his wealthy father, abandoning his peaceful life as a bourgeois for the dangerous life of a revolutionary

---

20. [The speeches at Joffe's funeral proved to be the Left Opposition's last articulate public demonstration. See also the accounts by Isaac Deutscher in *The Prophet Unarmed* and Medvedev in *Let History Judge,* which quotes eyewitness descriptions by other samizdat authors as well. Joffe's suicide letter to Trotsky is in *Leon Trotsky: The Man and His Work* (Merit Publishers, 1969).]

fighter for the proletariat. Fearlessly he walked down this path in life, although he constantly risked exile or death from the bullets of the police.

In the early days of Soviet power, Joffe was asked to work in the most difficult area facing the Soviet state, the sphere of diplomatic work, of foreign policy. Here there was one obstruction or impediment after another. The bourgeois world did not wish to recognize Soviet power. Only Joffe's great capabilities, knowledge, and talent could overcome these obstacles. He was like a sapper on a battlefield, clearing away a road that has been mined, in his efforts to win diplomatic recognition for Soviet Russia. He was the first ambassador plenipotentiary from the land of the Soviets to bourgeois Germany and to other countries. He was assigned by Trotsky, then commissar of foreign affairs, to untangle the knots between Germany and Russia. He played a major role in the peace negotiations at Brest in 1918. For this outstanding work he received Lenin's personal thanks. Not long before his death, Joffe was our ambassador to Japan.

Joffe was greatly troubled by the events in the party in those years. The inner-party struggle threatened to end in a split. The expulsion of Zinoviev and Trotsky signaled the beginning of that split. Joffe proposed to try to stop this dangerous course of events, to bar its way. He began to seek in past history for an example to follow and found it in the courageous death of the Lafargues. [21] . . . In the name of saving the unity of the party . . . Joffe ended his own life, sacrificing himself for it like a sentry at his post at the moment of greatest danger, when the party's future was threatened.

The column at the head of the procession arrived at Novo-Devichy monastery. At the monastery gates were mounted police, armed with rifles. The secretary of the All-Union Central Executive Committee of the Soviets, Yenukidze, stood near the militia. He had given orders to allow only relatives and close friends of the deceased to enter the gate. We were ordered

---

21. [In 1911, Paul Lafargue, an organizer of the early Marxist movement in France, and his wife Laura, Marx's daughter, committed suicide at the age of seventy. Lenin, who spoke at their funeral in Paris, told Krupskaya: "If one cannot work for the party any longer, one must be able to look truth in the face and die like the Lafargues."]

to "immediately disperse and go home." But there were 10,000 of us. We rushed the gates and took them by storm. The police retreated. Within the cemetery we saw an open grave right next to a wall; and on top of the wall stood armed troops of the Cheka. They had laid an ambush for us ("just in case"). As we learned many years later, this was Stalin's vicious plan to provoke bloodletting and murder. . . .

A meeting began near the open grave. First Chicherin spoke. After him Ryutin, a member of the official government delegation to the funeral, got up to speak. He was a "newly risen star" of the first magnitude and he began to speak along familiar lines. His way of speaking was crude and contained many outbursts against the Opposition. It was a funeral oration profuse with insulting allusions and seemed to be a provocation to challenge all of us there. But we kept our indignation to ourselves and remained silent.

Ryutin declared that the entire Opposition was to blame for Joffe's death. Little did we suspect at that time that a few years later we would meet that "star" Ryutin in the same boat as ourselves at the Verkhne-Uralsk prison.

Ryutin's speech dragged on. From rude attacks on the Opposition he proceeded to attacks on Trotsky. When he cried out that L. D. Trotsky "was prophesying the twilight of the revolution," the cemetery echoed with a mighty cry of protest "How dare you! Shut up!" Losing his temper, as though he were the one spat upon, Ryutin got down from the platform without finishing his slanderous speech.

Trotsky, standing next to Sapronov, seemed to awake from some reverie and asked Sapronov, "Why are they yelling at him?" I didn't hear what Sapronov answered, but from Trotsky's appearance one could deduce that he had not been listening to the speakers at Joffe's graveside and saw nothing around him. Deeply immersed in his own thoughts, he had been gazing intently at the open grave. His left cheek twitched nervously. . . . When Chicherin announced that the next speaker was Lev Davidovich Trotsky, everyone fell silent. Even the soldiers on the wall of the cemetery relaxed their stance. . . .

Having climbed to the platform, Trotsky bared his head. His speech flowed like a sad melody and struck us to the very quick. I had heard many of Trotsky's speeches but there had never been one like that. He spoke of his friend, of a revolutionary who had devoted his ardent spirit to the cause of the revolution to the last drop of his blood.

Joffe's death deeply affected Trotsky. This kind of death

could lead to impermissible imitations by others. The noble example of the Lafargues was not a struggle for revolutionary ideals but a protest, a dearly bought protest which could be detrimental, for it removes fighters from the ranks of revolutionaries. This could not be permitted.

And then the sad melody in Trotsky's speech began to give way to a spirited appeal to life, to the struggle for life: Trotsky's scorching words seared into the crowd of 10,000 listeners, ringing out like metal, "No one has the right to follow the example of this death. You must follow the example of this life." [22]

This was the order of the army commander. . . . We never forgot this order, this command, even in the darkest days of the Stalinist repression.

"The Leninist banner of world proletarian revolution has been thrown in the mud and trampled upon," said Trotsky, accusing Stalin of betraying Lenin's cause. The orator's voice rang like a warning bell, raising alarm and trepidation. "How shall we lift it up again? How shall we cleanse it of the mud that soils it?" we thought to ourselves, picturing Lenin's banner in our mind's eye.

Trotsky said further that the leadership of the Central Committee had let slip revolutionary situations in Europe, China, and India, and had thrown back the world revolution many decades. This was a betrayal of internationalism. . . .

Listening to Trotsky I remembered Lenin's wise words on *world revolution.* In April 1917 Lenin had appealed to the Russian proletariat from the armored car at the Finland Station with those words. With those same words in 1919 he had addressed the First Congress of the Communist International. Those words were written into the party program. And as though in tune to my thoughts I heard Trotsky's words: "In Russia the reactionary idea of national socialism in one country is winning out. In the last analysis this could lead to the restoration of capitalist relations in the country." Trotsky's last words at Joffe's grave rang out like a sacred

---

22. [Up to this point, the memoirist's memory is fairly true to the text of Trotsky's speech as preserved in the Trotsky Archives at Harvard University. However, the Archives text contains nothing like the following passages about "world revolution." The memoirist might be confusing Trotsky's speech with Zinoviev's, which was reportedly very fiery and full of hyperbole.]

oath: "We will raise high the Leninist banner of the world proletarian revolution and carry it forward to world communism. Long live the revolutionary communist party!"

The cemetery erupted in a burst of stormy applause. For a long time the shouts of solidarity with Trotsky resounded, of solidarity with his words, which coincided so well with the thoughts and aspirations of those who had gathered. Trotsky was being filmed during that time.

When silence fell at last Zinoviev and Kamenev rose to the platform. After their speeches, we lowered the coffin into the grave and threw a handful of cold earth upon it.

"Your path has ended, but for us the struggle still lies ahead." Such were our thoughts. We had no illusions about our struggle on the morrow and we foresaw that we would drain the cup of suffering to its dregs.

The cemetery did not fall silent but grew more tempestuous. Trotsky's presence among us raised our spirits and our faith in the victory of Lenin's ideas, his predictions of world revolution. We looked at him with love and pleaded with him: "Speak to us some more."

Standing around Trotsky in a solid mass, we suddenly noticed we were pressing him against the brick wall. The danger of an unpleasant incident, it seemed, had developed. Lashevich noticed this first. He, who had been a participant in the storming of the Winter Palace in October 1917 and a commander of our troops in the Siberian theater of war, ordered us in military fashion to form a ring around Trotsky several ranks deep and to hold back the wave of people pressing toward him. A catastrophe was prevented, but people kept crying out, begging Trotsky to say a few more words. Then we lifted him up on our shoulders and he addressed all of us:

"Comrades there is no need for a demonstration. We came here to bid farewell to our comrade. We had no other intentions here. Once again, there is no need for a demonstration. Go back to your homes."

We—more than 10,000 Communists, party activists, electrified by outrage against the anti-Leninist leadership, that little group of usurpers who had taken over the Central Committee apparatus—were waiting for orders from Trotsky for decisive action and we expected decisive orders from Trotsky at that time, but got from him instead an appeal for calm. But none of us had doubts about his correctness. We believed in Trotsky. It had to be that way.

Trotsky was conducted through a narrow corridor of people to the monastery gates, where the car of People's Commissar Beloborodov was waiting for him. When Trotsky drove off, Lashevich told us, "Well, our people have gone, let's go home." We separated, saddened, although in all of our hearts the flame of hope still burned for the victory of the world socialist revolution.

. . . Since that time many years have passed. The land of the Soviets has broken out of capitalist encirclement. Vladimir I. Lenin died prematurely, unable to survive the profound and fatal error made by the thirteenth party conference. This was a political mistake which tragically affected the fate of the majority of Lenin's true collaborators and defenders of his testament.

Trotsky and Stalin

Lenin spoke of them in his testament not accidentally, not as isolated individuals, but as representatives of completely different, opposite, mutually exclusive tendencies in the world revolutionary communist movement. One alternative was that internationalism, world revolution, and international proletarian solidarity would win out. The other alternative was that events would favor the growth of narrow-minded nationalist tendencies in the revolutionary process, a growth which occurred in muffled fashion, muffled by the firing squads of Stalin, and it did so in that way out of iron necessity, because of the influence of the October Revolution. . . . Events favored the growth of "chauvinist riffraff," as Lenin termed them in his last letter on the nationality question and autonomization.

But it must not be forgotten that the symbiosis of nationalism and pseudo-internationalism, such as Stalin tried to implant, was doomed to failure by the ferocious nationalism of Hitlerite fascism, which was smashed to bits by the Soviet people in spite of Stalin's flirtation with the German Nazis.

It is necessary to speak completely openly and precisely about this. The entire prewar policy both internal and external (antirevolutionary and anti-internationalist) placed the Soviet state in a position of political isolation and rendered it defenseless against attack from world imperialism. (On the eve of the war, revolutionary Communist cadres of the Russian Communist Party as well as the Communist parties of bourgeois countries were physically annihilated. Likewise, all the upper military cadres of the Red Army were physically exterminated — from Marshall Tukhachevsky down through every regimental commander.

However the new young cadres of the Red Army, tempered in the fires of World War II, and the revolutionary cadres of the CPSU and the Communist parties of the bourgeois countries of Europe that were involved in the fighting, were forced by the trend of events to take to heart the ideas of Marx and Lenin about revolutionary war against world imperialism.

Above the bayonets of the Soviet Army breaking through into Eastern Europe over the corpses of the overthrown German fascists and their local supporters waved the banner not only of the Soviet Union but of the world socialist revolution. All revolutionary and internationalist figures of the Communist parties of Albania, Bulgaria, Hungary, the GDR, Poland, Czechoslovakia, Rumania, and Yugoslavia led their working class and peasantry in the final battle against the German occupiers and against the national bourgeoisie and established their own Soviet power. [23]

In these historic events Lenin's celebrated thesis to the effect that world war brings with it revolutionary situations was confirmed. "We have entered the epoch of wars and revolutions."

As a result of World War II the Soviet Union escaped permanently from capitalist encirclement, forming around itself — by the force of arms, together with the Communist parties and working classes of the eight bourgeois countries of Eastern Europe — a socialist camp.

With its weapons the Soviet army helped the proletariat of these eight Eastern European countries to take power into their own hands, thus broadening the front of the world revolution and guaranteeing everything necessary for the successful

---

23. [Obviously the memoirist, who had only Soviet newspapers and periodicals as a source, is misinformed about what happened in Eastern Europe at the end of the war. The truth is that Stalin's policy never sought to stir the masses into activity. He only overturned the capitalist regimes in these countries when the United States, through the Marshall Plan, sought to regroup the capitalist forces there against Soviet influence. Later still, in Yugoslavia — where the struggle against the Hitler occupation was carried through until the country's liberation and the overthrow of capitalism — the CP came into conflict with Stalin's policy and went into opposition to the Kremlin from 1948 on.]

building of the material, technical base for socialism and communism in these countries.

This lesson should be taken to heart and understood by certain people who to this day remain under the influence of Stalinist conceptions and are willing to attribute to Stalin certain "merits" according to a scheme drawn up for purposes of self-praise and self-glorification, as was shown by the twentieth party congress. . . .

The victory of socialist revolution in eight capitalist countries of Europe is a revolutionary outcome of World War II. This outcome is a classic example for all Communist parties of the world of how a revolutionary situation in time of war must be used for the victory of socialist revolutions in the remaining parts of the world.

The working class and the Communist parties can study another graphic example from the experience of the last world war: there is no need to give a breathing spell to world imperialism; there is no need to let it make use of the breathing spell to regroup its forces and strengthen its military might for another attack at a later time with greater force against the countries of socialism.

Many people know that at the end of World War II some of our military leaders (Marshal Zhukov and others), as well as the most revolutionary and internationalist individuals, and whole groups, in the CPs of the Soviet Union, Greece, Holland, Belgium, England, France, Italy, and what is now the German Federal Republic, asked the Soviet government not to stop the forces of the Soviet army at the Oder River but to move on and fight their way deep into Western Europe to aid the working class and peasantry of those countries who were rising up to overturn the capitalist structure forever and to establish Soviet power throughout Europe. (To some extent these events recalled 1920 when, on Lenin and Trotsky's orders, our Red Army commanded by Tukhachevsky drove through Poland toward the borders of Spartacist Germany.)

But Stalin opposed this glorious idea, thus extinguishing the dream of the European Communists of establishing Soviet power throughout Europe. The renegades of world communism once again began to play games with the imperialists of America, England, France, and Italy.

But playing games with the enemy never leads to any good.

At Karl Radek's Apartment (December 1927)

We arrived at Radek's on an early December morning. The door was opened by his wife, Roza Radek, a kind and good-hearted woman, whose presence was always warm and enjoyable. After letting us in, she went to wake her husband: "Get up, Karl. The youngsters are here already."

But Karl did not get up. He received us at his bedside. His face looked tired as if he had not slept enough, and his eyes were red and inflamed. As we learned, he had been up all night, having fallen asleep not long before we came. He lit up his beloved pipe and said, smiling, that he had "been on an all-night debauch with the foreign press."

Around his bed, on the floor, a great many papers and magazines were strewn, in all languages of the world. We knew that Radek read and spoke fluently thirteen languages. He was an educated man of the times and was considered very knowledgeable in the field of world literature.

There were always a lot of people around him. They liked him for his sharp wit and lively talent. And his opponents trembled before him. He used to knock them flat with the poison of his sarcasm.

Karl Radek had a well-developed ability to spice up historical anecdotes with erotic puns, sending his listeners into transports of delight. Every witty political anecdote was attributed to him. They never missed their mark and their effects were deadly. For example: "Marx and Engels have issued a declaration renouncing their doctrine and acknowledging the correctness of the general line of the party of Stalin."

Along with the positive qualities of Radek's character, there were certain regrettable traits, which caused chagrin to those who held him in esteem. His much-heralded love affair with the writer Larissa Reissner brought him the bitter disgrace of rejection and the reproaches of conscience. She was the wife of Raskolnikov — a well-known political and military figure of the October Revolution — who at that time was the Soviet ambassador to Afghanistan. She was living there too. She returned to Moscow not at her own wish but under threat of expulsion from the party. Her love affair with an Afghan prince had become notorious around the world and placed the Soviet ambassador to Afghanistan in an awkward position. No sooner had she returned to Moscow than Karl Radek fell in love with her and began to pursue her madly. It became the talk of the town. . . .

She was a beautiful woman and a talented writer. During the civil war she served in the navy as a political commissar, in which capacity she displayed tremendous personal courage. She wrote many stories and short novels about the civil war, characterized by great literary ability and accuracy of description. Especially vivid was her description of the battle of Samara, with Trotsky addressing the troops on the eve of battle: "Here the revolution takes its stand. It will retreat no further."

Larissa made use of her natural gifts quite heedlessly. On one occasion she confessed to Radek that she was madly in love with Trotsky and wanted to have a baby by him. She begged Radek to tell Trotsky about this, as she herself was afraid to confide it to him. At first a terrible jealous scene broke out between them. But then he said it was all the same to him, and promised to fulfill her request.

Larissa Reissner's behavior astonished many people in those years. That was a time when a considerable section of women Communists — veterans of the civil war — were influenced by Aleksandra Kollontai, who propagated the idea of "the love-making of worker bees," that is, the notion that men and women should flit freely "from flower to flower" rejecting any kind of family tie whatever. These were proclaimed "petty bourgeois" and "survivals of private-property relations with respect to women."

Karl Radek idolized Trotsky as only a disciple can adore his teacher and friend. Fearfully, and no doubt with the addition of some half-hearted puns, he told Trotsky of his intimate relations with Larissa Reissner and of her fantasy about bringing into the world a child that would harmoniously combine the beauty and talent of the mother with the intellectual genius of the father, supreme leader of the world revolution. With frozen smile Radek awaited Trotsky's reply.

Radek was wild with joy when he heard Trotsky say: "Calm down, Karl. Tell your beloved that I decline the offer."

A week after this incident, a conference of all military correspondents and writers was held at the Military Revolutionary Council. Larissa Reissner, too, attended. She was quite agitated. She blushed and lowered her eyes when Trotsky came up to her and began a conversation. He spoke with her, as politely as ever, about literature and its importance in the training of Red Army men and about other matters, never referring in any way to the discussion he had had with Radek.

. . . We had come to Radek's to learn the details of what

had happened at the fifteenth party congress. Radek told us
that Zinoviev had been in touch with Ordjonikidze to determine
the exact conditions for the Opposition to be readmitted to the
party.[24] Ordjonikidze had answered Zinoviev in the name of
Stalin and his entire group as follows: "We are the revolutionary center. We demand total capitulation of the Opposition
headed by Trotsky. Only if that happens may the question of
readmitting the Opposition be raised at the congress." This was
Stalin's ultimatum to the Opposition.

A conference of the Opposition's central leadership was hur-
riedly called to discuss this ultimatum. It was held at Piatakov's
apartment. There were about fifty people at the conference — Old
Bolsheviks, leaders of the Opposition. Among them were
Trotsky, Zinoviev, Kamenev, Rakovsky, Muralov, Mrachkovsky, Smilga, Preobrazhensky, I. N. Smirnov, Radek, Piatakov,
Yevdokimov, Zalutsky, Bakaev, and others.

For two days and nights, without rest or sleep, a fierce polemic went on. The Zinoviev group insisted on capitulation
to the fifteenth congress. They did not take into account the
fact that Stalin needed that kind of capitulation in order to
discredit the leaders of the Opposition and lay the basis for
reprisals against them later, according to a stealthy plan that
had been worked out long before. . . .

On the second day of the conference Trotsky spoke: "You
can all go your way. . . . I will remain even if it be alone.
Lenin was not afraid to stand alone. He was always principled.
There can be no lying. There can be no bargaining with ideas.
That is repulsive. It is against honor and conscience." After
Trotsky's intervention the Opposition split into two groups — the
Trotskyists and the Zinovievists.

Two declarations were addressed to the fifteenth congress:
one from the Zinovievists, renouncing the ideas of the Opposition; the other from the Trotskyists, remaining true to their
views and to the proposals laid out in the well-known document
entitled *The Platform of the Left Opposition.* The first declaration was signed by Kamenev, Yevdokimov, and Zalutsky; the
second, by Radek, Piatakov, and Preobrazhensky.

. . . Hardly six months had passed since the closing of the

---

24. [After the fifteenth congress, which voted to expel the Left Oppositionists, the Zinovievists asked for readmission into the party, which
they achieved by disavowing the ideas of the platform they had
presented together with the Trotskyists.]

congress when arrests of Trotskyist Oppositionists began. [25] Karl Radek was the first arrested. He was to be sent off to exile in Siberia. A great many people gathered at the Kazan station to see him off. Everyone wanted to say farewell to this man, one of the most outstanding figures of our generation. He was cheerful and talked a great deal. Even at this fatal moment in his life he did not lose his presence of mind. . . .

Being exiled to Siberia along with Radek was Kasparova, the former wife of Stalin. [26] Only a few of the words that she spoke that day at the station have stuck in my memory: "He is a megalomaniac. . . . He will shed much blood, ours first of all . . . and will destroy the revolution."

Just before the train pulled out Radek whispered in our ears that preparations were being made for the arrest of Trotsky. Thus began the reprisals against the supporters of Lenin's testament, the revolutionists of October. *Lenin* created the Cheka for the struggle against the enemies of the October Revolution. *Stalin* created the OGPU for a struggle against the organizers of October. *Such is the irony of fate.*

---

25. [Arrests actually began a little before the congress. Deportations immediately followed it.]

26. [Vera Kasparova was an Old Bolshevik who was in charge of work among women of the East for the party and for the Comintern's International Women's Secretariat, beginning in 1921. The Secretariat was dissolved in 1926. Kasparova, a leading member of the Left Opposition, was expelled at the fifteenth congress in 1927. Why the memoirist refers to her as a former wife of Stalin is unclear.]

With Nadezhda Konstantinovna Krupskaya (1928)

We stood in the reception room at the Commissariat of Education and asked Krupskaya's technical secretary, Vera Dridzo, to let us in to see Nadezhda Konstantinovna. We told her that we were student representatives from five of the most important higher educational institutions of Moscow — Moscow State University, the State Institute of Journalism, the Communist University for the Toilers of the East, the Plekhanovka, and the Timiriazevka. This had no effect on Vera Dridzo. She eyed us coldly and repeated in a frosty voice, "Impossible, impossible."

The whole appearance of this "secretary" of Krupskaya's and her attitude toward us aroused feelings of repugnance and wariness in us. Looking at her we recalled Kamenev's story about the secretaries recruited by the secret police to "serve" Central Committee members and relatives of Lenin.

We told Dridzo that we wanted to see Krupskaya because she was an Old Bolshevik and a collaborator of Lenin and not because she was chairwoman of the Academic Council of the Commissariat of Education. This had no apparent effect on her. She gave us a standard form to fill out, so that we could state our business. At her direction we put our names, home addresses, the places where we were studying, and what we wanted to speak to Krupskaya about. We put all these things down on the form. Having taken the form from us, Vera Dridzo asked us to come back in three days, and three days later she told us the same thing. We began to suspect a crude deception. Outraged, we threw open the door and walked in on Krupskaya unannounced.

Finding ourselves in a large bare office we saw the legendary co-worker of Lenin sitting at a little desk staring at us with eyes wide open from surprise. We begged her pardon and told her of our dealings with her secretary. Krupskaya was very surprised and embarrassed. "Please don't be angry," she said. "Come closer and tell me what has happened to you."

We told her that we were Moscow student representatives who in the past had been workers on the line and participants in the civil war, and Communists. We did not hide from her the fact that at the present time we had been expelled from the party for adhering to the Opposition. We began to expound our reasons for coming.

Krupskaya listened to us with great attentiveness. She seemed to be studying each of us, separately, searchingly, looking directly into our eyes. And when we had finished a certain part of what we had to say she looked at the door and quietly said, "Who are you for? Trotsky?"

We told her that we were Bolshevik-Leninists and that we defended Lenin's teachings and testament. She was deeply moved. Taking her handkerchief from her pocket, she began to wipe away the tears that were running down her cheeks so that we wouldn't notice. Holding the handkerchief next to her eyes, she listened to us further.

We spoke of the arrests taking place in the country; about the deportation of Karl Radek and Kasparova to Siberia. This she didn't know about and was extremely surprised at our information. And when we told her that there were preparations being made to arrest Trotsky, she replied with a trembling voice, "No, things will not go that far. The party will not permit it."

We wanted to know which side she was on, with us or Stalin. Pressing for a clear reply, we asked, "If it does go that far, if Trotsky is arrested, what attitude will you take?" We looked her in the eye and waited for her answer. Krupskaya was thinking intensely. Her public position required her to weigh every word. It was obvious what an inner struggle was going on within her. We felt sorry for her, but it was not only we who awaited her answer. There were only five of us, but many thousands of student-Communists who had sent us here were waiting for Krupskaya's answer. They too were greatly disturbed by the arrests taking place throughout the country, which foreshadowed unknown turns of fate for the revolution. Krupskaya understood this and sensed that we would not leave without an answer. Looking guardedly out of the corner of her eye toward the door again, she said with a firm voice— it was as though she were unafraid . . . but greatly moved —"Even in prison Trotsky's light will gleam brightly." Then quietly and with sadness in her voice she added, quite out of character from her previously expressed thoughts: "And if they do arrest him I will be the first to bring him parcels in prison."

We thought to ourselves, "No, she does not have the power to forestall prison for Trotsky, no matter how much she wishes that were not so." Our mouths grew dry from an excess of emotion and our hearts beat like hammers. . . .

"She's with us, she's with us," our hearts cried out, "in her

revolutionary, proletarian instincts she's with us." We knew
her good and pure intentions, and no matter how bitter for
us was her reply on the inevitability of prison, we understood
that we could not get any other answer from her in those
surroundings, behind that door.

In taking leave of us she came out from behind her desk
and embraced us all in a motherly way. In her eyes heartfelt sympathy toward us glowed silently and without words,
such that to this day it remains before my eyes.

But when we went out past her secretary Vera Dridzo,[27] we
did not just sense, but plainly saw, how ready she was to
chew our throats out.

With Army Commander Tukhachevsky (the 1920s)

It was not without emotion that I first entered the office of
the Chief of Staff of the Red Army Tukhachevsky. I had in
my hands a decoded telegram from the commander of the
Turkestan military region. There was savage fighting that
year with the counterrevolutionary robber bands in Turkestan
called the *basmachi*. The local bourgeoisie and the Russian
White Guards took advantage of food shortages in the country
and the religious prejudices of the population and led the more
backward sections in armed struggle against Soviet power . . .

I came up to Tukhachevsky and spoke to him. He took
the telegram and had me sit down and wait. I watched him
attentively. His military talents were legendary.

After reading the telegram he went over to the large combat
map on which red and blue little flags were pinned. He took
out several red flags and put blue ones in their place. I watched
his face closely and observed on it the reflection of the inner
labors of mind and will. As he looked at the map his mind
and entire self were for the moment far away on the battlefield
in Turkestan. During such moments he would resolve military
problems in an inspired way. Victory over the enemy was
the product of this exertion of willpower and talent.

I sat without moving. I didn't want to interrupt his train
of thought, the thoughts of Commander Tukhachevsky. When
his work at the map was through he sat down at his desk
and began to write military orders for the commander of the

---

27. Vera Dridzo was arrested in 1937.

Turkestan military region, laying out a new military plan for smashing the basmachi.

Few remember today that in the first months and years of the young Soviet Republic, former officers and generals of the czarist army were in the top leadership of the Red Army and played no little role in saving the Russian Revolution from military defeat. The Soviet Republic was at that time left disarmed by the complete collapse of the old czarist army while the Russian proletariat had not yet built up its own revolutionary army. The working class and the poor peasantry had taken power, arms in hand, and were obliged to hold on to those arms and direct them immediately against the internal counterrevolution and the capitalist encirclement that supported it. Commanders were needed. We didn't have enough of our own. The fronts were many, commanders few. Modern warfare requires precision in the organization of military operations and firm discipline. If the party had not been able at that time to win over certain elements among the officers, and the generals, of the old army, the so-called military specialists, our victory over the enemy in the civil war would have cost the workers and peasants of Russia much more in terms of losses than it actually did.

The White armies entered the field against the disarmed young Soviet Republic in full military preparedness. The Russian bourgeoisie was getting ready to take full revenge on the October Revolution, and it began pulling together regiments of armed White Guards against the revolution in the North, South, East, and West of Russia. Sent hastily to support the White Guard army were troops and technical aid from fourteen imperialist states. A considerable number of former czarist army officers, men of clean conscience, entered into the work of instructing the Red Army men in military discipline and the rules of warfare and led them into battle against domestic and foreign enemies. "When Comrade Trotsky informed me recently that the number of officers of the old army employed by our War Department runs into several tens of thousands, I perceived concretely where the secret of using our enemy lay," said Lenin in 1919 in his pamphlet "The Achievements and Difficulties of the Soviet Government" (*Collected Works,* Vol. 29, p. 71).

In spite of the exceptionally positive role of the military specialists in the Red Army, some people appeared in the party who not only opposed the old officers' serving in the Red

Army, but saw a traitor or enemy spy in every one of them and sowed the seeds of suspicion in the army and among the people toward such commanders. Not only that, but worst of all they brought Trotsky under fire for having supposedly implanted traitors in the Red Army on every front — that is, these veteran military specialists.

Among these slanderers of Trotsky during the civil war were Stalin, Voroshilov, Kuibyshev, Ordjonikidze, Gusev, [28] and others. They poured slander into Lenin's ears against Trotsky in every way, attributing specific failures on the front to the military specialists, who, supposedly, were being backed by Trotsky, while victories on the fronts they attributed to their own ingenious and heroic actions counteracting the "traitorous military specialists."

Naturally not all the military specialists who joined the Red Army were devoted to the cause of defending Soviet power. There were a few cases of betrayal, of hanger-on types coming over to the Red Army, types like the Roshchins, described in Alexei Tolstoi's novel *The Road to Calvary*. (As the story went, these two were later built up as "leaders" of the Red Army and nearly decided the fate of Commissar Chesnokov, the political worker assigned to Kvashin, who was strangled by the Roshchins and whose corpse was thrown into the river.) But the overwhelming majority of military specialists in the Red Army worked for the victory of the proletariat.

Thanks only to Lenin and Trotsky, many military specialists during the civil war were saved from physical reprisals on the part of the group of slanderers and careerists who were trying to undermine Trotsky on the question of the employment of military specialists and to make him appear in Lenin's eyes as a defender of traitors. Fortunately for the Soviet Republic they did not succeed in this. The party was able to save and educate a number of people from among the leading commanders of the Red Army — Tukhachevsky,

---

28. Gusev was the father of E. Drabkina. He himself was shot. His daughter in 1937 was sent to a camp for about twenty years. She is alive now but is persecuted by the censorship. [Elizaveta Drabkina, in her youth, had worked as a secretary for Sverdlov. A work written by her, dealing with Lenin's last struggle, was printed in the Soviet literary magazine *Novy Mir* in 1968 and criticized in other Soviet publications. It was published in French as *Solstice d'hiver.*]

Primakov, Uborevich, S. S. Kamenev, Kork, Levandovsky, Lebedev, Shaposhnikov, Smirnov, Yegorov, Pugachev, and many others. Out of all these military specialists, Tukhachevsky was the most outstanding and the most talented.

M. N. Tukhachevsky was a hard worker. He worked fifteen to seventeen hours every day. He would come into the headquarters in the middle of the night and work until morning. Despite his fame he always remained modest and attentive to his subordinates. He was always calm and collected, both inwardly and to outside appearance. You never saw him with his shirt collar open or leaning back carelessly in his chair.

Once I found him in his office with Commander-in-Chief S. S. Kamenev, Assistant Chief-of-Staff for the Red Army Pugachev, and Chief of Operational Administration Shaposhnikov. They were talking worriedly about the coming meeting with the Commissar of War and Chairman of the Military Revolutionary Council, Comrade Trotsky. The meeting was set for twelve noon.

The commander-in-chief was walking to and fro in Tukhachevsky's office and telling about something in a very agitated way. Shaposhnikov and Pugachev were also uneasy about the coming meeting with Trotsky. Only Chief-of-Staff Tukhachevsky was, as always, calm. In his intelligent blue eyes you could read the thoughts, "I have nothing to worry about; my conscience is clear. Everything is in good shape in the army, the borders are tightly sealed, and the troops are ready for action at a moment's notice."

The military workers at that time knew well that Trotsky loved Tukhachevsky for his great military talent, for his combat experience and creative initiative in battle. His personal charm won the confidence of his subordinates who dealt with him in the course of their work.

Nowadays, many lies are written about the relations between these two great figures of the civil war period and after. These lies began to be written at the time when the order was given to "expose" Trotskyism, which was supposedly trying to substitute itself for Leninism. Surely the reader must be blind not to notice the strained quality, the lack of verisimilitude, in the stories written out of fear, pressure of the Stalinist yoke, concerning Trotsky's role in the revolution and civil war and afterwards. Such stories were written by people like Antonov-Ovseenko, Podvoisky, and M. D. Bonch-Bruevich, who had worked with Trotsky shoulder to shoulder and were under his command in those crucial years. Even Krupskaya's *Rem-*

iniscences of Lenin, written at a time when she was threatened
with expulsion from the party by Stalin and was persecuted
by his secret agents, suffers from the obligatory lies about
Trotsky that it contains, lies written with the aim of gaining
personal security. These lies about the relations between Trotsky
and Tukhachevsky were written because it was impossible
to tell the truth. . . .

. . . Whenever I left Tukhachevsky's office for the night,
he would look at his watch and say "It's already midnight,
time to go."

There is much that has not yet been told about Tukhachevsky's military defeat near Warsaw in 1920. Stalin's negative
role in this defeat remains unclarified to this day.[29] We know
only that Stalin refused to carry out the order of the supreme
commander regarding the transfer of three combat armies,
including the First Cavalry Army, to assist Tukhachevsky.
The secret reasons for Stalin's military sabotage remain un-
explained. When he was sent to the Tsaritsyn region to help
in grain collection he got into the military council of the south-
western front, which was commanded at the time by Yegorov,
and as a member of the military council carried on intrigues
against the high command of the Red Army.[30] It only became

---

29. [In 1920 Tukhachevsky conducted the Red troops against Warsaw. The future Marshal Yegorov advanced toward Lvov. With
Yegorov was Stalin. When it became clear that Tukhachevsky was
menaced on the Vistula by a counterattack, the Moscow command
ordered Yegorov to turn north in order to help Tukhachevsky. But
Stalin feared that Tukhachevsky, after taking Warsaw, would go
on to take Lvov, thus depriving Stalin of the glory of that achievement. Hidden behind Stalin's authority, Yegorov did not fulfill the
order of the General Staff. Only after four days, when the critical
situation of Tukhachevsky became acute, did the armies of Yegorov
turn north. But it was already too late. . . . . In the high councils
of the party and of the army, everyone knew that the person guilty
for the defeat of Tukhachevsky was Stalin.]

30. [During the Russian civil war, the town of Tsaritsyn, which
had a strong tradition of partisan guerrilla warfare, was the headquarters of the Russian Tenth Army, under Voroshilov. Under Stalin's
influence, it became a seat of the "military opposition," which opposed
the use of military specialists from the old czarist army and resisted
the centralization of the Red Army under a unified command. Stalin
used the group of commanders there as a basis for his personal

known afterward, obviously, that the reasons for Stalin's oppositional activity were very deepgoing and involved a kind
of deeply disguised political sabotage. His aim consisted in
discrediting Trotsky and Tukhachevsky and getting them removed from the leadership of the Red Army.

Stalin had no illusions concerning the consequences of defeat
for the Red Army near Warsaw; still he worked toward the
defeat of our troops there in every way. He wanted this for
two reasons: (1) to discredit the military leadership of the
Red Army, primarily Trotsky, Tukhachevsky, and others;
(2) to strike a blow against the world revolution (the second
blow after Brest-Litovsk).

Stalin was an envious and vain person. He envied Lenin's
genius and Trotsky's political and oratorical talent and high
position of authority in the party and the country. Everywhere Trotsky was placed side by side with Lenin and was
considered the first person after Lenin. Stalin envied Tukhachevsky's military talent, and in his gloomy soul he nourished
plans for removing everyone from his path who to any degree
was superior to him or more capable than he was. For this
purpose he was ready to use slander and did not shrink from
the use of poison, the dagger, or the most vile betrayal of
Lenin, of the world revolution, and of internationalism.

The victory of the Red Army at Warsaw would have meant
a still greater authority for his rivals. The establishment of
Soviet power in Poland would have brought the Red Army
to the borders of Germany, which was in ferment. There, under
the pressure of the crisis and defeat in the imperialist war,
a revolutionary situation was developing. The arrival of the
Red Army at Germany's borders in and of itself would have
aided the victory of the proletarian revolution in that country.
The insurgent German proletariat would unquestionably have

---

intrigues and maneuvers, capitalizing on their grudges against the
center of command to accumulate personal loyalties to himself. The
eighth congress of the Russian party in March 1919 rebuffed the
Tsaritsyn group and reaffirmed the military policy that Trotsky,
as head of the Red Army, had been implementing. In 1919, when
the group began disobeying direct orders and endangering the course
of the civil war, Lenin and Trotsky finally had Voroshilov transferred
to the Ukraine, where, again with Stalin behind him, he created
a similar opposition group. After Lenin died, Stalin renamed Tsaritsyn
"Stalingrad."]

been victorious, thus expanding the front of the revolutionary war against world imperialism. This would have meant the realization in practice of Lenin and Trotsky's plan for unleashing the forces of world revolution. [31]

The Russian people always longed not for national isolation, but for general happiness in the world, and for that reason the idea of world revolution hurled forth by Lenin from the top of the armored car at the Finland Station won the people's support and inspired them to struggle for international communism and world revolution. This was reflected in the folk songs of the 1920s: "Give us Warsaw, then Berlin. Look out, Crimea, we've broken in." Or such songs as this: "Irkutsk and Warsaw, Berlin and Kakhovka — these are steps along the great road."

But what did Stalin care about the people's aspirations and dreams? The world revolution didn't coincide with his personal, purely careerist plans. It ruined his game. A national arrangement suited him better, in multinational Russia, where he dreamed of becoming the arbiter of fate, where he did raise himself, higher than Trotsky or Lenin, or the party, or the people, the one and only above all others.

He chose to realize his dream not by igniting the fire of world revolution but by finding every possible way to smother that flame. His whole subsequent activity, all his anti-Leninist actions confirm these views and propositions of the Opposition. Tukhachevsky is but one more illustration of these deeds of Stalin. But the way that the path of Tukhachevsky passed, his life and deeds left vividly marked signposts along the highway of Russian history. These will never be wiped out of the memory of the people.

Tukhachevsky was the first military leader of the October Revolution who, in the Warsaw campaign, under the leadership of Lenin and Trotsky, carried out *the Leninist plan of revolutionary war against world imperialism in the name of the victory of worldwide socialist revolution.* And they are not to blame that the intrigues and crimes of Stalin were so

---

31. [The author seems to be unaware of the differences within the Politbureau regarding the march on Warsaw. Lenin was for it because he thought it would give a boost to the revolution in Poland, as a number of leaders of the Polish CP claimed, while Trotsky, who did not share this conviction, wasn't in favor of the march on Warsaw.]

tragically reflected in the outcome of the battles for the world revolution and in the lives of these great bearers of internationalist ideas. [32]

32. Several days before Marshal Tukhachevsky's arrest the Soviet military postal system delivered him a letter written in a mysterious foreign tongue. In this letter was a Russian translation which said the following: "Pray, my son. Your life on earth is coming to an end. Thus is it written in the book of fortunes told by the stars. Bring your earthly affairs to a close, and get ready for eternal wandering in the other world. Amen." The question must arise: Who wrote this letter? Where was it written? If the letter came from abroad, why didn't the Soviet censorship intercept it? Even greater suspicion is raised by the fact that letters of exactly the same kind were received on the same day by the other military commanders later shot by Stalin along with Tukhachevsky. Reading the text of these peculiar letters, the military leaders expressed alarm. They were too pure in mind and conscience to suspect that the authors of these letters were their own murderers of tomorrow.

Trotsky (Meetings, Arrest, Last Send-Off)

A great end gives rise to great energy.
— Voltaire

I first heard about Trotsky while riding in a horse-drawn streetcar near the Narva gates in Petrograd. This was in March 1917 not long after the overthrow of Czar Nicholas II. [33]

A lot of people were riding in the streetcar: soldiers, workers, and women with their bags, as well as two students of the transportation and engineering school, a deacon in a black cassock, and a postal official with a white armband on his sleeve. The people's militia, established by the Provisional Government in place of the czarist police, which had been broken up, were identified by such white armbands with the red letters NM [Narodnaya Militsiya — People's Militia].

There was a lot of noise in the street car. The women were complaining about the long bread lines and about the high cost of living, blaming the former empress who was a German and her German ministers. The workers and soldiers listened to the women's conversation and disagreed. They considered the capitalists and landowners to blame for the sufferings of Russia. They were the ones who had started the war and sent Russian soldiers to die while their children and wives were left to starve on the home front. A young worker next to me said, "The bourgeoisie got us into the war; it brings them riches but to the workers it's death and starvation. We can't live like this any more."

The young worker's words created a stir in the streetcar. An elderly soldier in grey greatcoat and tall sheepskin hat [papakha] said, "Is this a Christian way to live? For three years I've fed the lice in the trenches, and what have I gotten for it? Nothing. All I have is a small plot of land and I can barely make ends meet. But the landlord has plenty. We work on his land and all he does is rake in the money. We can't live like this any more. No, it's not a Christian way."

In the elderly soldier's words could be heard the age-old

---

33. [Trotsky actually didn't leave New York until March 27, and he didn't arrive back in Russia until May.]

dream of the peasant for land and a decent livelihood. Next to him stood a wounded soldier whose arm hung in a black sling. The women looked at him and sighed deeply. The soldier had a silver cross of St. George the Conqueror on his breast. This was the highest possible award for bravery in battle.

The wounded soldier began telling his comrades about a meeting at the Chinizelli circus the previous day where Trotsky had given a long speech. "Well, brothers, what a talker that Trotsky is. His voice, it rings like a bell. He talked about world socialism . . . where there won't be any rich or poor. He talked about the Provisional Government being a government of the capitalists and landlords. . . . The way they're going is not our way. We ought to build our own socialist government of workers and peasants. Trotsky also said that we should take the factories and the land and give them to the workers and peasants without paying for them and use them for the common good. . . ."

The wounded soldier's story had quite an impact on the passengers. It was as though thunder and lightning had struck out of a clear blue sky. The women gathered around him looking at his silver cross and wounded arm. Someone asked what party Trotsky belonged to. The soldier didn't know. But an old worker in dark glasses sitting nearby came to his rescue. "Trotsky's in the socialist-internationalist party," he said. "In 1905 the workers elected him chairman of the St. Petersburg Soviet of Workers' Deputies. In 1905 Trotsky led the uprising of the Petersburg workers. For that Nicholas II banished him to Siberia for life, but he escaped from Siberia and went abroad. Now he has come back to Petrograd."

The talk grew louder in the streetcar. People were telling each other what the old worker had said. Everyone was deeply moved. The stories about Trotsky and his recent speech pleased everyone. This was the latest word on the revolution. Then the powerful voice of the deacon rang out and everyone fell silent. "Orthodox people," he said, "Trotsky is not a Russian. He's a Jew. He's not of the Christian faith, but of the Jewish. Come to your senses, good Christians. A Christian cannot follow a Jew. The Lord God and his Orthodox Church forbid it." Everyone in the streetcar fell silent and hung their heads. All the passengers were, above all, loyal believers, and they feared the punishment of God for not following God's word, spoken by the priest. These people did not know at that time that the Orthodox Church was living through its last vespers. . . .

In the silence that had fallen, hearts beat anxiously. In the midst of the tense silence and worried thinking, the clear young voice of one of the students rang out. "You're wrong, Father," he said. "A man should be judged not by his nationality and belief in God but by what he sows on earth, whether good or evil. Jesus Christ was also a Jew, but half of humanity now worships him. If Trotsky brings good to the earth, millions of people will follow him."

Everyone breathed a sigh of relief. It was as though a danger had passed to the side. They looked at the student gratefully. He had known how to calm the reproaches of conscience in the souls of his listeners and to resolve the doubts that were disturbing them. This conversation in the horse-drawn car made a deep impression on my young mind and has stayed in my memory the rest of my life. With great joy I realized then that the Russian working people had a brave defender in the person of Trotsky, who was willing to go to his death for the people's good. . . .

* * *

The nature of my work in the headquarters of the Red Army and the Military Revolutionary Council of the Republic required me often to work twenty-four hours a day. Once at midnight Trotsky's secretary Glazman called me to say, "The chairman of the Military Revolutionary Council wants to see you." We code workers were frequently called by Trotsky, Sklyansky, S. S. Kamenev, and Lebedev.

I guessed that a hard night's work lay ahead of me. The way to the Military Revolutionary Council office led past the staff room of the Red Army, down a long, straight corridor in the former Alexandrov military school where the night guards defending the heart and brain of the Red Army were stationed at short intervals from one another.

Glazman met me in the secretariat room of the Council's office and told me that Trotsky was writing a very important order to Tukhachevsky.

I opened the door quietly and entered the office. Trotsky was writing at his desk, which was brightly lit by a lamp with a green shade. I frequently found him in this kind of working arrangement and whenever I did I experienced an inexplicable agitation. There was something remarkable about him, unlike other people. It was an unparalleled, miraculous, natural phenomenon. Everything about him was bright. His gaze transfixed you; you could not turn away from it. The color of his hair was blue-black. His spellbinding voice with its metallic enunciation rang like music. When he gave speeches, the sounds aroused people to great accomplishments, went to the hearts of his listeners and seemed to work on them in mysterious ways, saying "Dare. Struggle. Win." And people dared and struggled and won. They marched into battle not sparing their own lives for the cause of the revolution and for the proletariat.

Trotsky was one of the world's great orators.

I received the order for Tukhachevsky from him. In handing it to me, Trotsky asked in a concerned way how long it would take for the order to reach Tukhachevsky. He was commanding the western military region. I answered two hours. My answer satisfied him and he said, "Thank you; you may go."

The alarming content of the orders aroused a great feeling of responsibility in me. I coded the orders carefully and quickly and then took the coded message to the military telegraph. I didn't leave the telegraph apparatus until the last coded item had been clicked out. The hands of my watch said 2:00 a.m. I called up Glazman and told him that the orders for Tukhachevsky had been sent to Smolensk.

Trotsky was no longer at the Council's office. He had gone over to the Kremlin.

Less than an hour had passed when the telephone rang again. Trotsky's assistant Sklyansky was calling me. He told me that Trotsky had changed his orders for that night, and it was necessary to get in touch with Smolensk immediately by direct wire and prevent those orders from going into effect.

I rushed to the telegraph and got the night code worker at the western military district headquarters and learned from him that the orders had only been half decoded and no one in the headquarters there knew about them yet. I relayed Sklyansky's instructions to him, to have the coded message burned and a form filled out as to its being burned. After that I called Sklyansky and told him of the measures taken. Three short words rang out in the telephone earpiece, "Thank you, comrade."

That was the end of the business with Trotsky's night orders. It was a night full of alarm. Not only did it give me, a rank-and-file worker in the Red Army, no rest; it gave none to the two sentries of the revolution, Trotsky and Sklyansky, as they carefully listened to the pulse of the bourgeois world. What the episode came down to was this: According to information from our agents there was a troop concentration on our western border by one of our hostile neighbors. This information was

double-checked and confirmed. Trotsky's night orders called
for an immediate military alert and preparation for combat.
However, two hours after this information, new information
came from the western border to the effect that the neighboring
country's troops had returned to their original position. Our
hostile neighbor was playing on our nerves. The troop concentration on the border, apparently intended for an attack
on us, was merely a feint.

Having guessed the real intentions of the enemy, our commander reversed the original orders about placing our armed
forces on combat alert. In those warlike days our military
leaders were always in a state of revolutionary vigilance and
readiness for action.

*   *   *

Trotsky had two strong military assistants, Sklyansky and
Glazman. Sklyansky didn't have a special military education.
Before the revolution he had been a military physician. Then
the revolution had come and made him the chief administrator
of the Red Army. In that post he displayed tremendous organizational abilities. As chief administrator he could be compared with Carnot, the great military figure of the Convention
period in the French Revolution.

When Stalin began thinking about undermining Trotsky and
replacing him (he was busy at such work even during the
civil war) he decided first of all to get Trotsky's assistants
out of the way, Sklyansky being his main target. During the
party purge of 1922 Sklyansky was accused of personal "de-
pravity," which made his "further presence in the Red Army
impossible." He was soon removed from the army and sent
to South America as a trade representative, where he died.[34]

At around the same time Trotsky's other assistant, Glazman,
died. There was a campaign against Glazman. They were
pressuring him to give false testimony against Trotsky. But
Glazman was an honorable man and preferred instead to
put a bullet in his temple.

---

34. [When Sklyansky was removed from the war department he was
in fact assigned to economic work. In the summer of 1925 he went
to the United States to buy machinery, and drowned in a lake there
while boating.]

Only during the funeral at the cemetery did we learn from the speeches of Movchin and Ostrovsky about Glazman's nobility of character and his devotion to the revolution. During Trotsky's constant travels on the roads of the civil war Glazman had not only been Trotsky's secretary but his bodyguard. It often happened while traveling that Trotsky's car would come into enemy territory by mistake. Hundreds of bullets would fly at the automobile, any one of which could have killed Trotsky. At such times Glazman would literally cover Trotsky with his own body, ready to sacrifice himself to save Trotsky.

Once, Trotsky's car fell into Makhno territory. [35] Makhno's men surrounded the car instantly and ordered Glazman, Trotsky, and the driver out of the car. At that moment the lives of all three hung by a thread. Rifle barrels waved under their noses. Only a miracle could save them from death.

And a miracle happened. With his fiery eyes gleaming, Trotsky got up on the roof of the car. All the rifles and pistols were aimed at him. With a quick gesture he cut the air with his hand and gave a short fiery speech. The result was amazing. The mutineers cried out "Long Live Trotsky!" They put him up on their shoulders and tossed him about. After that to the last man, they joined the Red Army because of Trotsky.

This seems impossible nowadays, but that's the way it was then.

*   *   *

. . . In the fall of 1926 a meeting was held between representatives of the Moscow student youth and Trotsky. My comrade from the war years, Poznansky, arranged this meeting of Oppositionist students. Poznansky at that time was carrying out the duties of Trotsky's secretary. The meeting took place on Malaya Dmitrovka in the Glavkontseskom building, where the Journalism Institute had previously been located.

Our entire group came to the meeting place well before the appointed hour. In order not to waste the time, Poznansky

---

35. [Nestor Makhno was the leader of small partisan bands of peasants who fought Ukrainian reactionaries and German occupation forces during the Russian civil war. He refused to integrate his forces into the Red Army, and ultimately came into conflict with it. His forces were finally dispersed by the Soviet government.]

regaled us with interesting reminiscences about Trotsky's life. Two of the episodes that were then related have stayed with me ever since.

After the 1923 discussion, Trotsky came down with a throat ailment. The illness had been brought on by nervous exhaustion and threatened not only Trotsky's voice but also his life. An immediate operation was required, but the necessary surgical specialist did not exist in Russia at the time. The Soviet government appealed to Germany for medical assistance. The Social Democratic opportunists were at the head of the government at that time.

The Commissariat of Foreign Affairs got on the telephone with the German minister of foreign affairs, Stresemann, and arranged with him for Trotsky to be sent to Germany immediately for treatment. A gentleman's agreement was made with Stresemann guaranteeing Trotsky's personal safety. Just in case, a group of armed Red soldiers traveled in the car with Trotsky dressed as male nurses. Trotsky was in Germany incognito. No one except Stresemann and the doctor knew that Trotsky, the terror of the world bourgeoisie, was there on German territory.

The throat operation went successfully. Trotsky's life and voice were saved. In vain certain people in the Kremlin had hoped for the operation to turn out fatally. These people were sure that the Germans would kill Trotsky on the operating table. But the Germans turned out to be honorable people. They didn't want the blood of the great revolutionary on their hands and they kept their word of honor about taking care of Trotsky. After Trotsky got better he was transported from Germany to the Caucasus to continue his convalescence. He was living in the Sukhumi region in a railroad car at a junction protected by Red Army men.

One night some armed Georgians attacked Trotsky's car. The attackers began to shoot at the car with dum-dum bullets. Trotsky's guards shot it out all night long, preventing the bandits from reaching the car. Only toward dawn did the shooting die down. There were people killed on both sides but it was not possible to establish the identity of the Georgians who had been killed; there were no documents on their bodies. However, even without documents it was clear where these killers had come from and who had sent them.

At that point the story broke off. Trotsky came in. He shook hands with us and asked us into his office. We sat on soft leather chairs and waited. Only one of us, Vasia A., refused to sit in Trotsky's presence. We tried to persuade him, and even Trotsky's request had no effect. Like a soldier on duty, he stood next to Trotsky for two and a half hours.

The meeting began with the question of the tasks of the Opposition. The following was approximately the sense of the meeting, going by memory: "We must go to the working class and to the working class section of the party. On the international scale our tasks are to gather our forces, to bring together the revolutionary forces in the bourgeois countries. We must aid the international proletariat in preparing armed insurrections in these countries. We do not have the right to let revolutionary situations slip by. Our ultimate goal is the world socialist revolution.

"On the domestic arena we must begin the industrialization of the country at the necessary rate and not at the expense of increased exploitation of the working class but by increasing the taxes on the well-to-do and bourgeois layers in the city and country. They want to tear us away from the working class, but they can do this only with bloodshed. They will arrest us and may even shoot us. It is necessary to think through carefully what such measures by Stalin will mean. The weak ones will leave us. Only the strong will stay with us to the end."

In Trotsky's words there was a note of alarm. Reaction was intensifying in the country. It was coming with the speed of a thundercloud. The Stalinist hierarchs had taken all the key posts in the party and government. They did not want the revolution to be deepened. They did not want it to be extended in the international arena. In all countries of the world at that time there were revolutionary situations, situations favorable to the overthrow of the decayed capitalist governments. But the Stalinists did not understand that the world revolution would not come by itself but had to be organized. Even in the colonial and semicolonial countries, India, China, and others, the insurrection of the oppressed people was ripening. "But there can be no delaying of the world revolution. It must be carried out now while the old experienced generations of Communists are alive, the participants in the October Revolution and civil war. This is necessary not only for the victory of the revolution but for passing on to new generations the Bolshevik-Leninist heritage.

"Our generation has had much revolutionary experience, sufficient for the whole world. Every effort to hold back the progress of the world revolution is collaboration with imperialism in its effort to crush Soviet Russia, and works to the detriment of the revolutionary movement in the bourgeois countries.

"The adherents of national socialism in Russia have placed the people in a position of constant fear of a new war. A condition of militarization is created on Soviet soil which leads to the suppression of democracy in the country and favors the seizure of power by barefaced adventurists; by self-seekers greedy to enrich themselves; by careerists.

"These conditions would inevitably lead to a division of Soviet society into two antagonistic social layers: a materially secure and well-off layer (those who hold power), infected with the 'ideals' of private property accumulation, who will observe the life and customs and culture of the foreign bourgeoisie and copy the negative features of their way of life; and a layer of toiling people who are poorly provided for, spending their lives in constant worry and care over where their next day's bit of black bread is coming from.

"The adherents of national socialism have 'grown weary' of revolution; they want to rest. But only renegades can behave that way, not proletarian revolutionaries; only those who have forgotten Lenin's words that ours is 'an age of wars and revolutions.' The facts of life confirm this and remind us of it every day and every hour."

Someone asked Trotsky at that point, "If Stalin is going to shoot us, he is going to wipe out all the revolutionary cadres. Can we really let him get away with that? Shouldn't we take preventive measures?" This was the most difficult question troubling the Opposition. Thousands of our comrades had asked him this. What was at stake was not only the fate of the Russian revolutionary intelligentsia, which Stalin could physically annihilate, but the fate of the whole Russian people and the October Revolution. The fate of our Opposition of Bolshevik-Leninists also depended on the correct solution to this problem.

Trotsky discussed this question in the circle of his closest cothinkers. In the course of this discussion they analyzed the causes of the collapse and degeneration of many revolutions over many centuries of world history.

Trotsky answered our question along the following lines: "Stalin's move can only be stopped by force," said Trotsky, gesturing with his hands. "But force is not our road. I beg you to remember this well. History will not forgive a nonparty method of solving an internal party problem. If we want to prevent Stalin's move by force, we must pick up arms and begin a civil war. If we shed one drop of blood of our party comrades who have gone astray, the curse of present and future generations will be on our heads."

When Trotsky said this to us, I remembered the tense situation in the country in 1918: the Mensheviks and SRs at that time were attacking Trotsky furiously. They were opposing his appointment to the post of commissar of war, predicting all sorts of terrible things such as: "He'll become a Bonaparte. He'll become a dictator."

Their prophecies were mistaken. Trotsky by his very nature could not become a Bonaparte. He was a fierce opponent of adventures in politics. He always rejected every impure thing that might sully his honor. He was always opposed to tyranny and usurpation.

Trotsky defended the idea of world socialist revolution throughout his life because it was the most humane of concepts and would bring with it the freedom of all the oppressed and enslaved peoples of the world. Trotsky was a morally pure person. He never made use of his power for dubious political ends. In this regard, the matter of the *carte blanche* given to him by Lenin during the civil war is characteristic.

As a sign of special confidence in Trotsky, Lenin as chairman of the Council of People's Commissars gave him a *carte blanche* in 1918. At the bottom of a blank page, Lenin wrote with his own hand, "This order of Comrade Trotsky's I consider correct and I subscribe to it. Signed, V. I. Lenin, Chairman of the Council of People's Commissars."

The story of how this *carte blanche* came to be written is as follows: During the civil war the so-called Military Opposition arose in the Bolshevik Party, headed by Stalin. It opposed the recruitment and employment by the Red Army of officers from the old czarist army. Since Trotsky was bringing these military specialists into the army, slander was spread against him that he was supposedly shooting commissars and putting czarist officers in their places. (They had in mind episodes involving Kuibyshev, Tomsky, Zalutsky, and others.) Lenin did not believe this slander and, as a token of his complete confidence in Trotsky's actions, gave him this blank piece of paper with his signature at the bottom.

In 1927 Trotsky submitted Lenin's *carte blanche*, unused, to the party archives.

No, Trotsky had never used this against his enemies. His moral purity was always of the highest order. With good reason he said to his followers, "It is better to be a martyr than a hangman, better to accept death than dishonor." Trotsky looked into the mirror of history and always shrank from seeing himself there as a tyrant. He repeated this thought to us in meetings in many different ways. He did not wish to cut the knot within the party with a sword offered to him by his military cothinkers. He refused this sword because he respected the judgment of history.

As we were leaving he shook hands with us one by one. It came the turn of our comrade Vasia A. He firmly grasped Trotsky's hand and cried out loudly, "Long live the chief of the world revolution, Comrade Trotsky!" Lev Davidovich looked at him reproachfully and sternly said, "That's not right, comrade, and it shouldn't happen again." This fanatical praise of his personality was repugnant to him.

We went our separate ways homeward in silence. Every one of us was thinking over Trotsky's thoughts to ourselves, trying to impress in our memories which methods are permitted and which are not in a political struggle within the party.

After that meeting I began to learn to my sorrow and distress the ABCs of prison life.

* * *

> *I will not be the last person*
> *on the last Bolshevik barricade.*
> (L. Trotsky)

It was November 1927. The Soviet people anxiously awaited their future. Between Stalin and Trotsky a stern political struggle was going on. The development of further events depended on its outcome.

The struggle was conducted under unequal conditions. On Stalin's side were the press, the party and state apparatus, prisons, and internment camps. On Trotsky's side there were only ideas and truthful words.

In order to draw up the "balance sheet" on the carrying out of Stalin's orders to "unmask" the Opposition and in order to pronounce "sentence" on it after allegedly having "defeated" it, an enlarged plenum of the Central Committee and Central Control Commission was held in the Kremlin. Hypocritically referring to the resolutions of the local party organizations, which had been deprived of any truthful information on the essence of the real differences in the party or on Lenin's last documents or on his testament, and deceiving the party and intimidating it by the expulsion of Trotsky, Zinoviev, and many other Old Bolsheviks from its ranks, the plenum held in the Kremlin celebrated its triumph.

The personal composition of this highest body of the party after the death of Lenin had changed drastically. All the honest and ideologically developed Communists who had taken the leading part in the revolution, the civil war, and the founding of the Communist Party had been severed from it. In their place gradually, underhandedly, Stalin had put people of the second rank of the revolution. These were people of lower ideological development, less convinced, less principled, but on the other hand, more manageable and obedient. . . . Many of them managed to appease their consciences and vote at meetings for things that were repellent to their convictions and beliefs. This was a time when the party and state apparatus was degenerating into all sorts of crooked dealings. Out of fear, these people would vote for any proposal from the general secretary, Stalin.

In those years the authority and importance of the first secretary of the party and of the party committees began to increase inordinately. To aid the first secretaries in the regional and provincial committees and in the Central Committee, special semimilitary groups of Young Communists were formed which carried out any orders given by a first secretary. These groups of so-called "molodchiks" might be sent out to any kind of party meeting, with special instructions — for example, to see to the defeat of any objectionable candidates, to support the creatures of the Stalinist apparatus, and to disrupt any speeches by honest Communists, and so forth.[36] In these strong-armed youngsters, Stalin was selecting reliable cadres of reaction, ready to smother the Russian Revolution and make it purely national, narrow-minded, and Thermidorian.

In his last appearance at the Kremlin, Trotsky read a prepared speech. His friends had warned him ahead of time that many of these molodchiks would be permitted into the plenum hall with orders to disrupt his speech. This was the first time that Trotsky wrote his speech ahead of time.

This is what he said at that time (from memory): "Blinders have been placed over the eyes of the party. The party is feeling its way, not knowing where it is going. Allow it to see for itself where it is being led. . . . The revolution does not stand still. It either goes forward or falls backward. There is no third way. Socialism in one country is national socialism. Such socialism is foreign to Marx and Lenin, who taught us no such thing. . . .With your brakes on, you are slowing down from the international to the national. You consciously and intentionally let revolutionary situations slip by in China, India, and other countries. You did this because you don't believe in the victory of the world revolution, an idea which eternally lives in the hearts of the peoples. . . . For the sake of building national 'socialism,' you have put out the flames of the Russian Revolution, of which there remain only smoking embers. You managed to fit every world event into your national theory. This is a crime against history and the proletariat of all countries. You are betraying the ideas of internationalism and communism. . . . It is twilight for the Russian and world revolutions. . . . You have retreated from Lenin domestically also. The Russian proletariat conquered Soviet power with its blood, and what has it gotten for that? The life of the workers has not improved. You rejected our plan for industrialization of the country, calling us superindustrializers. We proposed that industrialization be carried out at the expense of the wealthy, by increasing taxes on them,

---

36. This practice is now normal and legal.

on the well-to-do sections of the population in both town and country. But you wished to do this at the expense of the physical exhaustion of the working class. Between our plan and yours lies an abyss. . . . Bureaucrats are lording it over the country. They are trampling on revolutionaries, and in condemning them, they say 'take that for 1918.' You select leaders on the principle: 'If you support us, we'll elect you; if you don't, we'll drive you out and throw you in jail.' You are traveling down the dangerous path of degeneration. . . ."

Trotsky spoke rapidly. His voice would die down and then again resound like the clanging of a bell, so that his angry words flew through the hall and confounded the minds of the party functionaries. Like madmen, they would leap from their seats and cry out "Enough! Shut his mouth! Down with him!"

In the hall an unbelievable noise arose and kept growing. The functionaries and molodchiks had gone mad and were banging, pounding, stamping their feet, yelling, and moving their chairs around. And they were creating these disruptions and disturbances in response to signals from the grotesque bullies sitting on the presidium, to their scornful laughs or their grimaces. Struck at their weakest point, the party bureaucrats gathered around Stalin, never suspecting that they would only be his temporary companions — that he would deal with them in their turn. They raised a tremendous commotion, displaying extraordinary zeal. Some began to throw heavy books and objects at Trotsky on the rostrum. From the hall cries could be heard, "Snake! Scum! Worthless trash! Put the snake up against the wall!" Stalin made faces from the platform, and Kuibyshev at his signal whipped up the youngsters and egged them on to disrupt Trotsky's speech.

This was a dramatic hour for the Russian Revolution. Trotsky stood on the platform, calm and stern. In those minutes he reminded one of a captain on a sinking ship. Only, around him it was not the sea that was swirling, but pirates, reptiles, hissing, getting ready to bite the captain, getting ready to kill him, to poison him. In order to keep from hearing this reptile hissing and the savage shrieking coming from the hall, Trotsky concentrated firmly and kept reading his written speech. He was not reading it for the bureaucrats, but for the judgment of history.

Powerless to make Trotsky stop speaking, the leaders of the conference led the stenographer out of the hall before Trotsky had finished reading his speech. With that the outcry against Trotsky grew even greater, going as far as outright calls for violence against him and for killing him. "Beat the snake, beat the snake, beat the snake," chanted the scoundrels.

It was as though they all had gone out of their minds. In some cases uncontrolled anger verging on madness could be seen on their faces; in other cases the eyes were blood red, and ferocious hatred toward the speaker gleamed in them. These were the molodchiks. They rushed at the platform like murderers. They did not get there.

In front of them loomed the giant figure of the commander of the military region of Moscow, the Old Bolshevik, the old Petersburg worker, Nikolai Ivanovich Muralov. He stood with his fists up and waited. The murderers retreated.

That was a gloomy day for the Russian Revolution. On that day the banner of the Russian Communist Party was stained, the banner that had been held high through three Russian revolutions, the banner of the October Revolution. On that day two of the leading figures, Trotsky and Zinoviev, were expelled from the party.

The party and the working class took this reprisal against the leaders of the Communist Party as their own personal tragedy. As a sign of protest many Communists handed in their cards. The party fell silent because of the terror tormenting it. People stopped being themselves any more. They began to think one thing and do another.

Hypocritically calling the recruitment of young, poorly educated people to the party "Leninism," the Stalinist bureaucrats began to make use of these recruits to continue their crimes against the party. These crimes never stopped. It was the dawn of the *Russian Thermidor*. . . .

Early one summer morning in 1928 the Chekists arrested Trotsky.[37] Who could have raised his hand in favor of such a shameful action?

Trotsky was not living in the Kremlin at that time, but in the apartment of his cothinker, Commissar for Internal Affairs of the RSFSR Beloborodov. Trotsky had left the Kremlin with his family shortly after his expulsion from the party.

Beloborodov was the great-grandson of the celebrated Beloborodov who had been executed in Moscow, at Lobnoe Palace, for participating in the Pugachev uprising. Empress

---

37. [Trotsky was actually arrested and deported to Alma Ata in January 1928.]

Catherine II had signed the order for his execution, the great-grandmother of Nicholas II. The great-grandson, Beloborodov had written a death sentence in 1918 in Ekaterinburg [Catherine's city] for Nicholas II, the great-grandson of Catherine.

At Beloborodov's place on Granovsky Street, I saw a rare photo, the arrival of Czar Nicholas II and his family in Ekaterinburg, from Tobolsk, in 1918. Czar Nicholas, with the train on which he had just arrived in the background, stood with his heir, Alexander; the czarina, Alexandra Fyodorovna; their four daughters; and the czar's personal physician. Czar Nicholas was in a military uniform on which could be seen the insignia of a colonel of the Russian army. Standing at military attention, he was saluting the leaders of the Ural-Siberian government, Beloborodov, Mrachkovsky, and Yefimtsev who were standing opposite him in leather jackets with Mausers at their belts. All three men signed the death sentence of Nicholas II. Eighteen years later they were all shot on Stalin's orders.

I have strayed somewhat from my story, but that side note is very persuasive proof of the Thermidor brought about by Stalin's accomplices. Who was it that they killed? Who was it they arrested?

The Chekists, after making a thorough search, told Trotsky that until 7:00 that evening he would be under house arrest and after that he would be deported to the city of Alma Ata. Beloborodov's wife notified me of this by telephone. That was Faina Viktorovna Yablonskaya, a teacher of Russian history at the Journalism Institute and a close friend of Trotsky's wife, Sedova. She accompanied Trotsky's family right to the train itself at Kazan Station. Yablonskaya's life was tragically cut short in 1937 at Rostov-on-Don, where she was shot along with her husband. Yablonskaya asked me to immediately let our comrades know about Trotsky's arrest, so that they could get to the Kazan Station at 7:00 to bid farewell to Trotsky.

At the indicated time 10,000 Communist Oppositionists gathered at the Kazan Station. Every part of the station was filled with people, including the platforms and the tracks. Trotsky's things were piled up by the door, trunks, books, bundles. Here too on a leash was his dapple-grey hunting dog. The train was already under full steam and ready to go. At the end of the train an empty car had been coupled on with the white shades on its windows drawn down. This was for Trotsky and his family.

It was already 7:00 but he had not come yet. We asked the Chekists wandering among us why Trotsky had been delayed, but they said nothing.

All up and down the tracks rallies sprang up. Speakers talked about the conspiracy in the Kremlin against the revolution and the Communist International. Suddenly a great many portraits of Trotsky appeared, pasted up on the railway cars and on the windows of the station.

Time passed but Trotsky did not come. We grew worried. His whole life passed before our eyes. "How dare they raise their hand against Trotsky?" was our troubled thought. There are few great people on the earth who devote their entire lives to the good of humanity. Trotsky was a citizen of the world, the entire world.

At last the engineer appeared on the platform. He looked troubled and was in a hurry to get into the engine. We stopped him and began to question him. He broke away without saying anything. The Chekists ran to his assistance and got him out of our circle.

It was already 11:00 at night. The train gave a whistle and began moving. We didn't know what was going on. Trotsky wasn't there but the train was starting to leave.

Somebody yelled, "They've hidden Trotsky from us in the car!" This cry flashed down the whole platform like lightning. We seized onto the handrails, trying to hold the train. We wanted to see Trotsky. But the train built up speed and threw us off in different directions. People fell and jumped back up and grabbed at the handrails again. The train seemed to be slowing down but that was only how it seemed to us. Many of us ran along the ties after the train, crying out loudly, each in his own way, but everyone with great emotion. Nevertheless, the rumble of the iron wheels drowned out our voices, leaving only a thundering sound like cannon in our ears. . . . This had been a kind of "psychological attack" by Kappel men, in the form of the Stalinist molodchiks, against Chapaev men, in the form of us Bolshevik-Leninists.[38] It was a psy-

---

38. [Vladimir O. Kappel was a White cavalry commander who first came to the fore when he led ruthless raids against the Red Army in the 1918 battle for Kazan. He later became the chief combat general under Admiral Kolchak, ruler of White-controlled Siberia. He died during Kolchak's retreat in 1920. Vasily I. Chapaev was a local Red commander of the Volga region who became a legendary

chological attack by provocateurs which threw the mass of Communists who had gathered there into confusion.

We stopped only when the train had gone out of sight. Everything around was dark and quiet, and the rails gleamed with a cold light. Each of us felt weariness of the body and bitterness of soul. In our sorrow we returned down the railroad ties to the station building. At the entranceway stood a crowd of excited people whom we did not recognize, and they were yelling, "To the Kremlin! To the Kremlin! To the Comintern!"

At first we thought that our "ultralefts" were yelling, having surrendered to feelings of desperation, but looking more closely we saw that the majority of the ultralefts were with our comrades and were categorically opposed to any kind of demonstration. It was provocateurs who were yelling. They were urging us on to demonstrate in the city with the aim of starting a case against us for disturbing the peace and creating disorders.

We should have been ready for that. Stalin's henchmen spread a lot of lies about us in the papers and at meetings and accused us of every mortal sin. We refused to go to the Kremlin or the Comintern and instead, went to our homes, remembering that night for the rest of our lives.

Approaching my home on Malaya Bronnaya, I met an acquaintance. He was a philistine, of which there were many in those days. They kept their noses clean. When it seemed to him that the Opposition was getting the upper hand, he would ingratiate himself with me and butter me up, dropping little phrases of sympathy, having in mind a soft spot for himself someday, with my help. This person was scared now. Looking around from side to side, he came up to me with great caution and whispered, "Don't tempt fate, your game is played out. You better hide yourself somewhere or take off for the countryside. Times are bad. No telling what will happen."

Unfortunately he turned out to be right. Times were bad. All brave and honorable, free-thinking people who expressed their ideas openly about the barbarisms taking place in the party and in the country were removed from their jobs or

---

hero of the civil war. He was killed in action in 1919 on the front east of the Volga and south of the Urals, where Kolchak's troops were often referred to as "Kappel men."]

demoted in rank or sent off to the hinterlands and put on the blacklists that were being prepared for mass repressions.

Arrests of Oppositionists were taking place thoughout the country. Denunciations and slander became an everyday affair. People spied on one another and denounced each other not so much out of loyalty to the "powers that be" as out of fear that if they didn't denounce someone first, they would be denounced or they would be judged and condemned for not having denounced. . . . Many such people were sent off to prison. Such was the situation in the country. Treachery was called patriotism and villainy was called valor. For such qualities, prizes and medals were awarded. People began to be afraid of one another. Fear entered every home. It was dangerous to say hello to the wife of an arrested friend. If someone had denounced you on one day, the next day you were ground into the earth like a worm and the author of the denunciation was rewarded. Then somebody would denounce the informer and he would suffer the same fate. This period is now called "the period of mistrust and suspicion in relations between people."

On the next day Yablonskaya again called me and told me the sad truth about the previous day. It turned out that the day before we had accompanied not Trotsky, but an empty car with the white shades drawn. Stalin was afraid of a large gathering of Oppositionists at the station and ordered the OGPU to postpone the departure until another time. He ordered that the "operation" should take place quietly this time, without advance notification, so that no one would know about it.

They took Trotsky away at 2:00 in the morning after he was already in bed sleeping. They had told him on the previous day that his departuré had been postponed for three days. He believed it and sent his glasses to be fixed. They were his only pair. But they rudely deceived him and he was left without glasses. Seven cars with armed GPU men drove up to the house on Granovsky Street. They were commanded by a specially empowered member of the GPU collegium, Fishkin. Trotsky made a declaration of protest to Fishkin. He demanded the right to speak to Ordjonikidze on the phone. Fishkin answered, "You can't speak with Ordjonikidze, but you may speak to Kuibyshev or Menzhinsky, who are in charge of the operation." "I will not speak with Kuibyshev," Trotsky said. "That traitor should have been shot in 1918 at Samara. . . . I will not speak with Menzhinsky either, because I don't like two-faced people." [39]

Trotsky got up and went into the next room where his wife and son were. The door behind him slammed shut and was locked. Fishkin rushed at the door and began to bang on it with his fists. The door did not open. Then he ordered his GPU men to break it down. They broke down the door and poured into Trotsky's wife's room.

Trotsky sat on the sofa talking with his eldest son. Fishkin, exasperated, rushed up to him and, coming to attention in military manner, said, "Lev Davidovich, I am only a soldier. They ordered me, and I am obliged to carry out my orders. Please understand me. You too were a soldier." Trotsky answered this angrily, "Yes, I was a soldier of the revolution. But you are a soldier of Thermidor."

Fishkin stood there confused and pale. Trotsky's words had struck him like a whip across the face. Collecting his senses, he ordered his GPU men to take Trotsky by the arms and carry him out to the car by force. That was at 5:00 in the morning. The first workers on their way to work were on the street. Sedov, Trotsky's son, appealed to them from the window. He cried out loudly that the Chekists had broken in on Trotsky and were manhandling him. Then they grabbed Sedov by the arms and dragged him down to the car also. Trotsky's wife, Sedova, went down the stairs by herself, supported by Faina Yablonskaya.

The cars rushed off through Moscow at top speed. They got to Kalanchevskaya Square. There were no people there. Armed guards stood everywhere. The car stopped at the Kazan Station. Trotsky was the first to get out of the car. He had no glasses on and no hat. Unable to see anything without his glasses, he started walking away from the station. But the

---

39. Trotsky considered Menzhinsky two-faced, deceitful, and treacherous. "This man belongs to the category of double dealers," Trotsky said of him. Once Menzhinsky came to the Military Revolutionary Council and whispered in a conspiratorial manner to Trotsky, "Lev Davidovich, there's a plot being laid against you. I want to offer you my support." That was in 1923. "I was aware of the plot, whose guiding spirit was Stalin, but I didn't want anything to do with Menzhinsky, whom I did not trust," Trotsky said. [Trotsky relates this incident in *My Life*, pp. 448-50.]

GPU men blocked his way and shoved him back. He again walked forward as though trying to break through the line of soldiers guarding him. Then at a signal from some scum they pushed him from behind and tripped him.

Trotsky fell with all his weight on the rough stone pavement, bloodying his face and hands. It was impossible to look at this mockery without feeling rage. The heart overflowed with blood and cried out to the heavens.

Fishkin ordered Trotsky to be carried bodily, bloody as he was, to the station. On the rails stood a steam engine puffing with a single car behind it with the white shades drawn.

The Verkhne-Uralsk Isolation Prison for Political Offenders (1932-35)

Roza Rozova

I remember a song sung by a remarkable woman some twenty years ago. It was Roza Rozova, a Communist Oppositionist.

Her days as a member of the Communist League of Youth had begun in Kharkov in 1919 when the civil war was raging throughout the country. The Communist Youth were volunteering for front-line duty. Roza Rozova went with them. She traveled many a front-line highway and endured the many discomforts and sufferings of life at the front.

In the battles at Kakhovskaya [against Wrangel] she displayed great courage, for which she was formally commended in a ceremony in front of all the troops. Because of her courage, Roza was brought into the party from the Communist Youth earlier than normal.

In addition to the courage she showed in battle, Roza had the ability to speak convincingly and well. With passionate and well-chosen words she kept up the spirits of the Red Army men and marched with them into battle. Death fortunately passed her by, and she returned uninjured from the front lines of the civil war.

After the war Roza dreamed of studying at a pedagogical institute but in her home town they said to her, "You're still young. You'll have time to get an education, but for now, come, do party work."

For two years she worked in an out-of-the-way place, bringing up the level of the backward inhabitants and drawing them into social and political life. After that she again requested to be sent to the pedagogical institute.

Years passed and she finally completed her final examinations. Roza was ready to become a teacher. But she never succeeded in that.

The fatal year 1927 had arrived. A sharp struggle was going on in the ranks of the party. None of the brave, honest, or thinking Communists stood on the sidelines. Roza defended the ideas of the world proletarian revolution with pure heart and conscience. She joined the Opposition. Thus a new page in her biography began. Roza was immediately expelled from the party and the institute. She was left unemployed, and denied the right to receive a diploma. They refused her the right to work. Her ordeals had brought her to the point of near exhaustion.

Her path in life crossed that of a young man who had also been expelled from the party for belonging to the Opposition. They found that they liked each other a lot and got married, but their happiness did not last long. The husband was arrested and deported to a remote region. Roza waited for his return from exile; but when he returned she was arrested. While Roza was being shipped off to Siberian exile her husband was once again arrested and sent to the Verkhne-Uralsk solitary-confinement prison for political detainees.

In prison, behind bars, time passes very slowly. When you look at the blue sky through the prison window unhappy thoughts come to mind. Roza's husband was finishing his three-year sentence and he wondered to himself, "Where is Roza?" Six years had gone by since they had seen one another, and ahead lay only the unknown.

Going out for the morning exercise walk in the prison yard, he felt sad. He could not throw off a kind of foreboding of imminent disaster. That night a new shipment of women had arrived at the prison. It occurred to him that Roza might be among them. And sure enough when we came out for the morning walk, we saw two new women in prison clothes (sheepskin jackets). One of them suddenly cried out and rushed into our comrade Rozov's arms. It was his wife, Roza Rozova. They stood by the brick wall of the prison embracing and weeping. One could not view without emotion this unhappy pair, so happy for the moment.

Three days later our comrade Rozov was shipped off to exile in a remote region for three more years. Roza remained with us in the prison. From the window of her cell a moving melody often came to our ears, "The Communards are marching; the year is eighteen seventy-one."

To this day that song of the Paris Communards as rendered by the voice of the marvelous Roza Rozova re-echoes in my ears.

Kote Tsintsadze

One spring day in 1933 they brought a new prisoner into our cell — the old Georgian Bolshevik Kote Tsintsadze. He was a celebrated figure, having occupied the post of chairman of the Cheka (and OGPU) of the Georgian Soviet Republic for many years.

The very same day there was an inspection of the prison cells by the "supreme authority" — that was the chief of the prison himself, Biziukov. As he came into our cell he suddenly looked as though he had seen a ghost and exclaimed: "Kote . . . are you here too?" And then with a lowered voice expressing not quite sympathy, not quite reproach, he muttered, "I never thought I'd meet you in prison."

They were old acquaintances. They had worked together in the Georgian Cheka in the struggle against the counter-revolution. Biziukov had been under Tsintsadze and done good work. Later their ways had parted and they had known nothing of one another's subsequent fate.

The former Cheka chairman, Tsintsadze, looked at his former subordinate and said reproachfully: "I'm ashamed of you, Biziukov. You used to be a good Chekist, and now you've become a jailer. Who are you holding? Communists. This is a terrible disgrace for an old Chekist." These were bitter words for Biziukov to hear from his old Communist comrade and chief.

He seemed pitiful in our eyes. In self-justification he appealed to us prisoners to testify to Kote about his treatment of us. We didn't twist things. We said what there was to say about Biziukov. He was one of the few humane wardens. He showed patience toward the prisoners, and who knows what thoughts were churning in his brain? Before Kote's arrival at the prison, his brother — Sandro Tsintsadze — had been confined there. Once, when a shot from a guard's rifle tore open an artery in his throat, Biziukov had saved him from death. Sandro would have bled to death if that humane chief, Biziukov, had not helped him. We told Kote about this and he changed his attitude toward this jailer . . . almost against his will. . . .

There were quite a few like him in those days. That was a long time ago.

From Verkhne-Uralsk prison I was sent to Archangel, and from there they shipped me off to hard labor at Vorkuta. There I unexpectedly met up with Sandro Tsintsadze's wife — Tamara Tsintsadze. She told me of the tragic death of her

husband and of his two brothers, all shot on Stalin's orders
in 1937.

All members of the families of those three brothers were
arrested and shipped off to hard labor or remote exile.

Celebrating the New Year

We greeted the new year, 1934, from prison. A week before
New Year's Day we brewed up some fermented mash, called
brazhka, out of bread and sugar. For two weeks we had saved
up the bread and sugar, bit by bit, out of our prison rations.
We fermented the *brazhka* in a brass teakettle, plugging all
the cracks, holes, and leaks in it with bread dough. We
wrapped the teakettle in old newspaper and hid it under the
floor.

After several days, we took out the teakettle and organized
a collective tasting of *brazhka* (there were ten of us in the
cell). It certainly was deliciously fermented. It made your nose
tingle agreeably. We filled the teakettle with boiling water and
let it cool, and then put it back under the floor.

We were sure that the guards had not noticed our trick.
We figured that the corridor guards had "lost their sense of
smell." And we were extremely surprised once when one of
them suddenly asked us: "Well, how is it? Pretty strong?" It
turned out he was a decent sort—he had known about it and
hadn't reported it. That was a rare thing in those years. Only
an isolated few of the most daring prison overseers, camp
commanders, or sometimes even investigators took such liberties.

On New Year's Eve we asked the guard, who had been
implicated in our "frightful crime" by his "failure to report,"
to knock on our door at 11:30. He knocked and at the same
time handed one of our comrades a telegram from his wife.
She wished her husband, and all of us, Happy New Year.
Electric lights were turned on at night in all the prison cells.
But on that occasion we were allowed to have candlelight.
The telegram stirred us deeply. Each of us thought about
his own wife and family. We longed to forget, to drown our
sorrows. . . .

We dragged the unfortunate teakettle up from under the floor
and set it triumphantly on the table. The oldest among us
was elected official head of the table and we all sat down
around him. The head of the table drew himself up and whispered a parody of a blessing, saying nothing in particular,
then laid out our ten tin cups, prison-issue, and began to fill

them with the thick, strong-smelling *brazhka*. The first toast was to our courageous and long-suffering wives and women comrades, who were sharing our fate. We drank our second toast to the world proletarian revolution. Our third was for our people's freedom and our own liberation from prison.

It was quite late but none of us could sleep. Each thought back over his past life. Our hearts were burdened with trouble and sorrow. It was frightening to look ahead into the future, shrouded as it was in dark banks of clouds. . . .

The Communist Staroselsky

In our cell there were ten prisoners. Among them was a re-markable person — the Communist Staroselsky. He came from a bourgeois background and was ashamed of it. Before the revolution his father had been a prominent Russian banker. But without hesitation Staroselsky had broken with his family and joined the revolution.

He was an educated person and knew three European lan-guages. After the victory of the October Revolution he was asked to work in the Commissariat of Foreign Affairs. He worked honorably and well, and kept the candle burning at both ends.

When he told us about his life we used to listen with bated breath. I will relate one episode that he told us. It was in 1919. The Italian Communist, Bordiga, a member of the Executive Committee of the Comintern, had been sent from Moscow on an illegal mission to Berlin. The Berlin police had picked up his trail and arrested him. . . . Bordiga and the Comintern faced the ominous prospect of a political trial. This was undesirable both for the Comintern and for the Soviet government. The trial might bring out a lot of secret contacts and connections that the Comintern had in Europe and particularly in Germany.

It was necessary to keep the case from coming to trial. The thing to do was simply to get Bordiga out of the German jail. Staroselsky was sent to Berlin on this crucially important mission.

Staroselsky's father was living in Berlin at the time, an emigre from Russia. Being a shrewd financial dealer, he soon established the necessary business connections in bourgeois Germany, was granted credit, and soon prospered as before. Less than a year after he had fled Bolshevik Russia, he had already become a prominent, wealthy magnate of the German capital. He knew that all his property in Russia had been confiscated and that his son was working for the Bolsheviks in positions of responsibility. And suddenly this son appeared at the father's door in Berlin.

At first the father was outraged at his wayward son's behavior, but in the end he did not call the police. Instead he told his son that he could stay three days, and no longer. Making use of his father's money and business connections, Staroselsky soon bribed the right people in the Berlin police establishment and, on the third day of his stay in Berlin, smuggled Bordiga out of jail.

The dangerous mission had been completed. Staroselsky went on to study at the Institute of Red Professors in the history department. After graduating from the Institute he went to France to do research in the primary sources on the Great French Revolution. He spent several years there. When he returned to Russia, he wrote a book entitled *The Ninth of Thermidor*. The events described in the book were very similar to those of 1927 in Soviet Russia. He was soon arrested.

Not long before his arrest he learned of the tragic death of his friend — the Italian Communist party leader Bordiga, who was lured to Moscow from Italy and there shot as a Trotskyist and supporter of the concept of world revolution.[40] A despicable role in sealing Bordiga's fate was played by the Comintern Executive Committee member from Italy, Ercoli,[41] who envied Bordiga's fame and popularity.

Staroselsky had inexhaustible energy. But physically he was a cripple. The nervous strain of the first revolutionary years had undermined his health, and prison added its "contribution." During the hunger strike in our prison in 1934 he suffered paralysis of both arms and legs. He was taken away to the prison hospital, and never came back to us. . . .

---

40. [Bordiga was a long-time ultraleft, not a Trotskyist. He did bloc temporarily with the Left Opposition on some questions in the middle and late 1920s, and was expelled from the Comintern for alleged "Trotskyism." But he soon developed a kind of "state capitalism" theory on the Soviet Union. And far from being killed in Moscow, he survived in Italy at the head of a sectarian group into the post-World War II period.]

41. Ercoli is Maurice Thorez. [Actually Ercoli was Togliatti, and that is what obviously was meant. The confusion is understandable, since Thorez and Togliatti were always coupled in the Kremlin's favorable press about these, its "peaceful coexistence" cothinkers, and the only thing distinguishing the two was that one was French and the other Italian.]

The Communist Pevzner

There was another outstanding Communist in our cell. His name was Pevzner. It was always warm and pleasant to be in his company.

Pevzner was an extremely modest and unassuming person. Although a disabled civil war veteran, he never fell into despondency, nor did he consider himself unlucky. He had lost his right arm from the elbow down. Shrapnel from an exploding shell had torn it off. He never complained and never asked anyone for help. Firm-willed and full of desire for life, he made his left hand do the work of both.

Pevzner was the son-in-law of the OGPU chairman, Yagoda. They had once been close friends and dear relations. However, they now had become ideological foes. Pevzner's wife, the daughter of Yagoda, was also confined in the Verkhne-Uralsk prison. Here she contracted tuberculosis and nearly died. Her father Yagoda knew about his daughter's illness but for a long time he gave her no help. When she began spitting blood, he finally sent his personal airplane and had her transferred to a sanatorium in the Crimea. As before she both loved and hated her father. . . .

She frequently wrote to her husband begging him not to grow tired of her in prison. He was proud of his martyred wife, who had withstood so much suffering. She survived and regained her health. Instead of prison they held her in exile in the Crimea.

The Trial of Zinoviev and Kamenev (1935)

In February 1935, they brought Zinoviev and Kamenev into our cell, from Leningrad. With them were brought many other political activists from the Bolshevik Old Guard, who had been defendants in the trial on the Kirov assassination and had been convicted for allegedly participating in that crime.

Zinoviev looked tired and gaunt as though from severe illness. Only his eyes glistened with that old fire that had set thousands of other eyes aglow not so long before. He was put in our cell on the north side and Kamenev was placed at the opposite end of the prison so that they could not meet. But in every prison the walls part invisibly, and people who are close to each other feel and hear one another. The illegal mail travels around the clock in prison and is delivered immediately. Prison mail hardly ever fails. Kamenev and

Zinoviev constantly communicated, sending each other dozens of letters and notes every day.

We met with Zinoviev twice a day during the exercise walk in the prison yard. We could see Kamenev two hundred yards away. He was very gray but still walked cheerfully. There were always lots of people around him.

On the first day that we met Zinoviev we asked him about Kirov's "assassin" Nikolaev. Did he know him personally? Had Zinoviev really given him instructions to shoot Kirov? "Of course not," exclaimed Zinoviev. "Nikolaev I never knew or saw and now they tell me that he was a member of our Opposition and his wife was supposedly Kirov's secretary. It's possible; but I never ordered anyone to kill Kirov. Stalin himself made up that lie in order to deal with us more easily. The foreign spy agencies killed Kirov or possibly our own secret police on Stalin's orders. . . ."

We believed Zinoviev's words. We understood that he could not be an accomplice to murder. His views, honor, and intelligence all set him against individual terror. Death came to Kirov from the same direction as it had for Frunze. They had both been done away with because they appeared to be rivals for the powerful position of general secretary, the supreme power in the land.

The Leningrad trial had taken place behind closed doors. No outsider was admitted. In the courtroom about five hundred secret policemen in military uniform filled the seats. These were the chiefs of the republic- and province-level administrations of the OGPU, summoned to the trial to familiarize themselves with the new judicial methods for dealing with political opponents. The chairman of the OGPU, Yagoda, was also there. Yagoda had seemed very nervous and kept looking at the door. For some unknown reason the concluding session of the trial, at which the defendants were present, was being delayed. Even the judges did not know the real reason.

Then suddenly Yagoda went over to the door and toward him came an unfamiliar person who seemed like a foreigner of Eastern nationality. No one had ever seen this person before. They guessed that he might have come from the Communist underground in the Orient. Yagoda was extremely courteous toward the guest. He bade him sit in a chair away from the rest of the people. After that, the concluding session of the trial began.

On the bench for the accused sat the Leninist Old Guard, Kamenev, Zalutsky, Yevdokimov, Sarkis, Gessen, Bakaev, Vaganian, and others whose heads had been under the gun many times during the three Russian revolutions. Only the chief defendant was missing from the bench, the paid agent of the OGPU, Nikolaev. This hired killer was too dangerous a witness and he had been quickly gotten out of the way. . . .

Zinoviev stepped forward with his final remarks. He was deeply disturbed and for that reason spoke incoherently. What disturbed him was the mysterious, unknown "guest" who had appeared at the last moment. He recognized this guest as Stalin in disguise. The general secretary, wearing a mask, was looking at Zinoviev the way a boa constrictor looks at its victim. "Why did this frightful person come here?" A thought flashed through his mind, striking him like lightning and throwing off his ability to speak and think clearly. "What brought him here? Mysterious fate draws all murderers to the scene of the crime. . . . He came here to kill."

Zinoviev's spiritual powers could not withstand the nervous tension. He wanted, but could not bring himself, to expose the true assassin of Kirov who at that moment was sitting in the courtroom in greasepaint. Struck by a heart attack, Zinoviev crashed to the floor. The court suspended the session for half an hour. After the break Zinoviev continued his speech as a sinner confessing crimes he had never committed. It was shameful to see Zinoviev in a state of complete spiritual chaos. One did not want to believe that Lenin's collaborator and the president of the Comintern could come to this point of collapse.

The Stalinist judges carried out their black deeds. They broke the will and corroded the soul of one of the most outstanding figures of Russian Bolshevism. Greasepainted, Stalin exulted over the abasement of his political opponent.

Stalin knew that when the Chekists had come to arrest Zinoviev he had cried out with passion, "This is Thermidor. The revolution has perished." Now Stalin laughed at this Russian Robespierre who had been brought down. "I am making world history," thought the murderer Stalin. "Future generations will believe only me as to who occupied which squares on the chessboard of revolution."

After Zinoviev, Kamenev gave his final statement. His speech was restrained and convincing. In this fatal moment he defended the honor.of the Opposition and his human dignity. Kamenev possessed a critical mind, for which Lenin loved him and always kept him close. Kamenev had been Lenin's deputy simultaneously in the Council of People's Commissars and in the STO [the Council for Labor and Defense] and frequently represented him in meetings of the Politbureau.

In his two-hour speech Kamenev spoke along these lines:

"History did not give the French Hebertistes time to think over their mistakes.[42] They perished on the guillotine. History has given us a great deal of time, but we did not make use of it or make the necessary decisions. We are to blame for this." (I am quoting from memory.)

During the break Yagoda came up to Kamenev and asked him to correct the stenogram immediately. Yagoda's haste disturbed the defendants. They concluded that Stalin was hastening to finish with them as soon as possible and wanted to leave a corrected stenogram for history. "They are going to shoot us," thought all the defendants including Kamenev. He began to correct the stenogram but because of his agitated state, his hands trembled. A large ink spot fell and spread over the page of the stenogram which he was correcting.

Kamenev looked at Yagoda embarrassedly and guiltily, though he said nothing. After a short pause Yagoda said to Kamenev, smiling with forced gaiety, "Lev Borisovich, you're not yourself today. It's all right, you can correct it tomorrow." He took back the stenogram and went off.

A spark of hope raced through the ranks of the defendants. "No, they're not going to shoot us." And they did not shoot them, not at that point. They sentenced them to prison terms of various lengths.

They were shot two years later in the bloody year of 1937.

That year Stalin had a lot of "work" to do. He exterminated the entire Old Guard, everyone who knew about the foul ways in which he had gained the enormous power of the general secretariat, all those who knew of the last documents and the testament of Lenin. He left not even the graves of the Old Guard on the earth. He made certain that any recollection of them had disappeared without a trace. He decided to have himself placed in the mausoleum, where he left little room even for Lenin next to his own "greatness." . . .

But he was seriously mistaken.

Even during his lifetime he wrote his own adulterated history, painting it up with false versions and fables about his genius and "farsightedness" and "historical correctness" and the like.

---

42. [Jacques Hebert was a revolutionary French journalist who became the leader of the radical left wing after Marat's death. An alleged attempt of the Hebertists to seize power served as a pretext for their suppression by the propertied middle classes, and Hebert himself was guillotined in 1794.]

High-handedly and complacently he pronounced "truths" which were made the equivalent of historical laws by those who sang his praises. . . . He did not fear the judgment of history. He was sure that no one would dare to judge him. He placed his hopes in his toady supporters, who he thought would prevent any insult or affront to him in death, just as they had during his lifetime.

Again he was seriously mistaken. Once free of him, humanity breathed more freely. But his heralds and disciples of yesterday began pouring upon his head the filthy slops that he had left behind, wading in it and using it to wash themselves free of the blood of the millions who had perished at his hand, as a result of his intrigues and of his toying around with the Nazis.

Having allegedly devoted himself completely to the Russian people, he offered ceremonial toasts to their name, but he was completely alien to them. He did not know their history; and he did not know the true Russian soul.

The Russian people never forgave Boris Godunov for just one *innocent victim*, one *innocent soul.* But the butcher Stalin had hundreds of thousands and millions of such victims. The Russian people and the peoples of the entire Soviet Union will never forgive him these victims.

The Death of Aleksandr Slepkov (1933)

> *Oh, what a lamp of reason has gone out.*
> *Oh, what a heart that now has ceased to beat.*
> (Nekrasov)

Of the educated Russian youth in the first years of Soviet power, Aleksandr Slepkov was the most outstanding. He had a warm heart and a lucid mind. Always principled, he never compromised with his conscience or retreated in the face of falsehood. Even in his student days at the Institute of Red Professors, he engaged in an unequal struggle, on his own, against the Politbureau member Molotov, who rudely insulted Slepkov in the public press. A real fighter for truth, Slepkov dragged Molotov before a party court at the Central Control Commission and there forced him to apologize.

Despite his youth Slepkov was already an important scholar, having devoted himself to work on Russian medieval history. He brought up all his interesting research work in this field for discussion at meetings of historical scholars; there he would test out the worth of his discoveries in sharp disputes with his opponents. His was a creative and imaginative mind, and he

always amazed his listeners by his thoughtful, critical approach
to the material he worked on, applying the viewpoint of historical materialism. He laid down truth in the minds of his
listeners the way a bricklayer lays down bricks for a building.

On one occasion, Slepkov was invited to the home of the
Kamenevs (Lev Borisovich and Olga Davidovna, Trotsky's
sister), where on Saturdays well-known figures of the cultural
world used to gather. Regularly attending these evening gatherings was a remarkable woman — a representative of the prerevolutionary artistic intelligentsia, a certain N. Although in
questions of culture she stood on Soviet positions, she had a
highly critical attitude toward other features of Soviet reality.
She expressed particular dissatisfaction over Soviet youth, considering them "morally crippled" and "half-educated" and therefore "unqualified to receive the torch of Russian culture from
the hands of the older generation."

The Kamenevs argued with her and quickly named off the
many young people of the next generation who might bring
glory to Russian culture. She asked them to show her "just
one truly Russian young person with a bright mind and warm
blood in his veins."

The choice fell on Aleksandr Slepkov as the most outstanding
representative of the Russian national intelligentsia. Slepkov
arrived without ceremony: in a black sateen Russian blouse
(kosovorotka) and plain Russian boots *(sapogi)*. It was as
though his outward appearance symbolized the desperate material need of the Russian people in the period of "war communism," the first years of the revolution, as well as the critical
attitude of the new Russian youth of those days toward superficial glamor and finery.

The conversation between Slepkov and this lady of intellect
lasted two hours. When Slepkov left, she said to Kamenev in
amazement:

"It seems that I've been sleeping all these years, or living
with my eyes shut. But Lord be praised, all is not lost. The
spark of talent in the land of Russia has not died out. That
lad is the hope of Russia. What a brilliant mind he has."

Years passed, and Slepkov became a prominent scholar
and well-known political figure. He was frequently invited to
sessions of the Politbureau, the highest party body, although he
was not a member. On days off, Slepkov, Bukharin, and Maretsky[43] were invited to Stalin's dacha outside the city, where in

---

43. Maretsky is the author of the only biography of N. Bukharin

addition to them the following people were always to be found: Kalinin, Molotov, Rykov, Ordjonikidze, and Kuibyshev. Stalin never invited Zinoviev, Kamenev, or other well-known figures of Jewish nationality to his dacha with the exception of Trotsky, whom he repeatedly invited to come visit. But Trotsky always refused and told Stalin reproachfully that political questions should be settled, not over a glass of wine in domestic surroundings, but at sessions of the Politbureau in the offices of the party's Central Committee.

Stalin was displeased by these reproaches from Trotsky, because they were very much to the point. Political questions continued to be resolved over drinks. These were then brought before the Politbureau only for the sake of information. (Later, this factional antiparty method found its expression in the well-known Septemvirate, which Zinoviev told the party about in 1927 in his open letter. That was being circulated in those days, along with a number of Opposition documents whose publication Stalin did not permit.)

Stalin had a benevolent attitude toward Slepkov. He appreciated the latter's talent, character, and ability. Stalin did not forget Slepkov, even after he was expelled from the party and sent into penal exile at Samara. At the height of the political clashes between Stalin and the Right Opposition, he ordered Slepkov to be brought to the Kremlin. When Slepkov, back from exile, was brought into Stalin's office, the latter deigned to rise and come over to greet Slepkov and embraced him and slapped him on the back. Like an old pal and crony, Stalin — with feigned friendliness — seated Slepkov in an easy chair and questioned him at length about his experience in exile, even reminiscing about his own prerevolutionary exile in the Olonets gubernia, trying in every way to win Slepkov over.

All this was preparatory, introductory, to the real aim Stalin had in mind in holding this meeting: namely, to persuade Slepkov to transfer his allegiance from the Right Opposition to his, Stalin's side. In a blatant and cynical manner Stalin proposed to Slepkov that he break all political ties with N. I. Bukharin and the Right Opposition, and come work for him as a member of his ideological secretariat.

The concepts of honor and conscience were foreign to Stalin. He was distinguished neither by modesty nor by any feeling of respect for others, such as an educated person might have.

---

in the Great Soviet Encyclopedia (first edition).

Insulted by Stalin's crudeness and cynicism, Slepkov — barely managing to keep his temper — asked him: "What do you want me for? You already have Ksenofontov. . . ."[44]

Stalin cursed rudely and then broke out in savage laughter, cracking a nasty joke at Ksenofontov's expense to the effect of his being a "worn-out shoe." He had valued Ksenofontov as long as the latter had been young and at the height of his "creative" powers. . . . But as soon as Ksenofontov's talent began to fade, Stalin pitilessly tossed him aside. Now he needed the talent of Slepkov, which was a brighter talent. Patting Slepkov affectionately on the shoulder, Stalin spoke to him ingratiatingly, with the tone of a "friend" and "wellwisher": "Come on over to my side, won't you?"

Slepkov was necessary to Stalin as someone who would think for him and compose articles for the press and public speeches for him. Later these same writings could be included in Stalin's complete *Collected Works.* Few people know that whole volumes of Stalin's *Collected Works* were not written by him but by his literary secretaries, above all Professor Ksenofontov. By winning over Aleksandr Slepkov, Stalin hoped not only to enrich his "own" *Collected Works* but also to strike a blow at Bukharin, that outstanding scholar and political figure, who had refused to collaborate with Stalin. A betrayal by Slepkov would have hurt Bukharin dreadfully. That was in essence what Stalin was trying to achieve in calling Slepkov to Moscow.

But fortunately that did not happen. Slepkov did not betray his teacher and friend or renounce his own ideas. He told Stalin that if he were to come to work for him, he would despise himself as a traitor for the rest of his life.

After this conversation Slepkov was returned to penal exile at Samara, where he was soon arrested and sentenced to five years' imprisonment. Slepkov was brought to the isolation prison for political offenders in the summer of 1933. With

---

44. Ksenofontov was a Red Professor. He studied at the Institute of Red Professors along with Slepkov and Maretsky. He worked in Stalin's ideological secretariat, helping him in the falsification of the history of the party and civil war, and in distorting Marxism to make it fit with Stalin's pronouncements on questions of economics, linguistics, etc. To his pen belonged all of Stalin's works devoted to the "routing" of the Left and Right Oppositions. He took an active part in creating the cult of Stalin's personality. [Ksenofontov's role as the real author of Stalin's "theoretical" writings against the Left Opposition in 1924-25 (*Foundations of Leninism*) is also brought out in Medvedev, *Let History Judge*, pp. 509-10.]

him was his celebrated friend, Mitya Maretsky, as well as other leading figures of the Right Opposition. They were all important scholars in various fields of learning and constituted a real constellation of talents from the ranks of the Red Professors, having gained special prominence in the struggle against Trotsky. . . .

When Slepkov and Maretsky were brought into our cell, we sincerely rejoiced at the arrival, with them, of news from the outside world, a political breath of fresh air in the isolator. All-out cross-questioning began and the telling of each other's stories, lasting several days on end. We longed for freedom and thirstily absorbed the latest news from the political world.

But the day finally came when the newness of the questioning and recounting was over and we once again became Left Oppositionists, and they Right Oppositionists. We recalled our political differences, which had placed us on different sides in the struggle. They had wanted to extinguish the revolution, while we had wanted to make it burn more fiercely and, with its flame, to light the bonfire of world revolution. We recalled all this even in prison, and between us there arose once again the same old estrangement and veiled animosity. This forced both sides to consider the situation that had arisen. To be in prison — and in the very same cells at that — with one's political opponents is a very difficult thing. We decided not to get into political arguments with the Rights, but they continued to argue with us. And then with undisguised transports of feeling they would sing a tune with the words of Nekrasov:

Is there such a spot under heaven —
the likes of which I've never seen —
where our sower of seed, our preserver,
the muzhik lives unsuffering, serene?
Volga, Volga, even in the gush of springtime,
you don't flood the broad fields the same way
that the vast and great pain of the people
overflows Mother Russia today. . . .

In this Russian national song could be heard a lament for the fate of our peasantry. The Narodniks at one time had sung it, going off to hard labor or to the gallows for the sake of the people. In our day this song could become the hymn of the individual peasant owner alarmed by collectivization. Some of our ultraleft comrades christened it the "Hymn of Thermidor."

In protest against this song we began singing the "Varshavianka" and "Exhausted and fallen in our chains." These songs told of the difficult lot of the working class and of its struggle against its oppressors. Our songs displeased the Rights and became the basis of a scandal and a break in our relations with them.

Making use of our overwhelming numerical advantage in the cells, we applied brute force to the Rights and threw them out of our cells. They began to reproach us, likening our way of dealing with them to Stalin's reprisals against us. We began to feel sorry for them, but the deed had been done.

They stood in the prison corridors, pitiful, humiliated, at a loss — realizing the terrible danger of their situation. Some even wept. The attention of the prison authorities was attracted by all this. In placing the Right Oppositionists in the same cells with the Left, the prison authorities, one must suppose, were guided by "instructions from above": out of this struggle in the prison cells they sought to gain something of use to themselves, through their own network of agents. The prison authorities were supposed to report all "excesses" in the prison to higher bodies. Toward our break with the right wing they adopted an attitude, as it were, of "complete understanding" . . . and no one was punished for the unauthorized action. The Rights were placed in other cells, and Slepkov and Maretsky were even given a separate cell all to themselves.

Now there officially began to be two Communist sectors in the prison — a Left and a Right. Thus ended our brief "friendship," our temporary sharing of common ground with the Right Oppositionists. Our ideological differences with them were so great that not even prison walls and a mutual hatred of the Stalin regime could reconcile us for long. On questions of prison conditions we maintained our former relations with them.

Slepkov was a really good comrade, and everybody liked him. He was so generous it was almost an oddity. He would literally take the shirt off his back and give it to a comrade, and likewise would share his last five kopeks. Slepkov's books traveled around, through all the cells, and his tobacco pouch never stayed home for the evening. His friendship with Mitya Maretsky and Levina was of a kind that is rarely seen. It began when they were Young Communists, when Slepkov was editor-in-chief of *Komsomolskaya Pravda*. The three of them preserved their friendship through the dust and gunpowder of the civil war and brought it with them, unstained, into prison itself. Levina behaved toward them as an older sister toward younger brothers, and they looked out for her as they might for a beloved sister of their own.

In those days of 1933, the Soviet land resembled an enormous concentration camp surrounded by barbed wire, enclosing millions of Russian people.

The central press those days was furiously attacking the leaders of the right wing — Bukharin, Rykov, Tomsky, Slepkov, and Maretsky — ascribing to them all the deadly sins. The Right Opposition was termed a kulak counterrevolution, etc. *Pravda* ran a long article on Slepkov, which told of a secret trip to the Don region made by him in 1930 with the aim of organizing the Don Cossacks for an armed uprising. *Pravda* alleged that even the day of the uprising had been set and that only blind fate had prevented its occurrence. The article made a big stir among us in prison. There was the smell of blood in the air: we could see that once again thousands of innocent Russian people were going to die.

One day, during the morning walk, Slepkov said: "They are preparing harsh measures against us. I am very worried about Nikolai Ivanovich (Bukharin). If they start torturing him, God knows what he'll say against himself. For my own part, I am not afraid."

Slepkov did not appear for the evening walk. Maretsky told us that Slepkov had been writing something all day and would not show it even to him, Maretsky. At midnight we were awakened. Several armed soldiers took up positions outside our doors while others made a thorough search of the cell. They ordered us to stay in bed. In the cell, there were no electric lights on. The only light was from a kerosene lamp on the table. A huge ladder stood in the middle of the room, and on it an electrician was removing an electric cord that extended down to the floor. He put a bulb in a socket in the ceiling and turned on the light.

Immediately after that the section chief came into our cell and asked if we didn't have some of Slepkov's books. We answered no. At this point we all concluded that they were probably taking Slepkov off to Moscow for further investigation, and when the soldiers left we went back to sleep.

In the morning we learned the appalling news: "Last night Slepkov hanged himself with an electric cord, and Mitya Maretsky has disappeared without a trace." The entire prison was shaken. All songs, laughter, games, arguments and discussions stopped for a period of mourning. Grief drove Levina out of her senses.

One more bright star in the Russian political sky was extinguished. People of rare talent were going out of our lives forever.

Urusova on Trial (1935)

Urusova spent her childhood in a little village near the Rosva River in Kaluga province. She did not remember her parents and knew nothing about their lives. Once when she asked her adoptive mother Aksinia about her real parents, she learned to her sorrow that they were no longer alive. Feeling completely orphaned and alone in the world, she nursed a sense of bitterness over her fate. Loneliness drew her close to "Aunt Aksinia," who took the place of parents for her and whom Urusova came to love as her own dear mother.

Aksinia had no children of her own, and she grew attached to Urusova as to her own daughter. Coming from among the poor people of the village, and being illiterate herself, Aksinia used to impress upon the growing girl how difficult it was to live in this world unable to read or write, being one of the "dark people."

The daughter remembered these words. They sank deeply into her consciousness. She studied diligently and with great application, absorbing everything that was taught her in school. When she graduated from the rural high school, Aksinia managed to wangle official permission for her to go to the Moscow Institute of Political Education. Thus Urusova came to be in Moscow. Urusova's successful performance in her studies and friendly, outgoing nature attracted the attention of both students and teachers. In her second year at the Institute she was elected a member of the Communist Youth bureau and became the darling and inspiration of the student youth.

Years went by. Urusova's studies at the institute were drawing to a close. Before her final examinations she was asked where she would like to go to work. She answered that she would like to go to her native region in Kaluga province. . . . She had been getting letters from Aksinia calling her back to her childhood home. With joy in her heart, she was preparing to return.

But fate decreed otherwise: at the student graduation party she caught the eye of Yenukidze, secretary of the Central Executive Committee of the Soviets. Noting her exceptional qualities, he offered her a position in the Kremlin library. Not without hesitation, she agreed to this, accepting what fate had in store for her. She was afraid to refuse such a highly placed personage.

The hustle and bustle in the Kremlin at first enthused Urusova. The Kremlin library had an enormous collection of books of both ancient and modern vintage. She would get together the books requested for use by Stalin and other leading party figures. She was fond of this work, having loved books ever since early childhood, when she used to stay at the school library late into the evening. Her financial situation and living arrangements were excellent. In the special store at the Kremlin, closed to the public, she could get anything she wanted at reasonable prices. She even invited Aksinia to come live with her, but Aksinia refused, saying there was "nothing for her to do in Moscow."

The seventeenth party congress took place before Urusova's eyes. She set up book displays for the delegates, where she met and conversed with them. Not a single cloud obscured her horizon. . . . Tranquility and good humor reigned in her soul, and it was her impression that things were going equally well for everyone and for the country as a whole.

Then suddenly disaster threatened. . . . Everything began to whirl around and go topsy-turvy. . . . Urusova secretly learned that Stalin had been voted down at the party congress. During the secret balloting for the new Central Committee only 100 delegates voted for Stalin and the remaining 1,100 voted against him. At the same time, of all the delegates, *Kirov* was elected unanimously to the Central Committee.45

At that time no one guessed what a fatal role that vote would play in the future of the party and the Soviet people.

Soon after the congress, Stalin's rival, Kirov, was assassinated. With that, the Stalinist terror began. Throughout the country innocent people began to be shot for alleged complicity in the Kirov assassination. On December 6, it was an-

45. [This sensational story hardly seems possible. If Stalin had only received 100 out of 1200 votes in the secret balloting, one way or another his elimination would have been assured. The seventeenth congress was called the "victors' congress" of the Stalinist faction — it had defeated the Left and Right Oppositions and effected some improvement in the standard of living in the country, which had been ravaged by the forced collectivization. A relatively strong current was noted at the congress in favor of a certain liberalization of the regime; Kirov, who supported this position in Leningrad, was particularly acclaimed by the congress. He was supposed to transfer to Moscow following the decisions of the congress. These demonstrations upset Stalin. A short time after the congress, before he could come to Moscow, Kirov was assassinated.]

nounced in all the papers that more than a hundred "terrorists" in Leningrad, Moscow, Minsk, and Kiev had been sentenced and shot. Then on December 22 there was a "clarification": it was not these people, already executed on the basis of certain blacklists, who had murdered Kirov, but alleged "former members of the Zinoviev Opposition" headed by Nikolaev, Kotolynov, and others.

These were the preliminaries to the annihilation of the thousand and more seventeenth congress delegates who had dared to raise their hands against Stalin in the voting. All 1,100 of those delegates had been Old Bolsheviks, active participants in the three Russian revolutions. Led astray by Stalin's factional Septemvirate in 1923-27, they had clearly tried at the seventeenth congress to curb the butcher after all, by their vote against him and for Kirov. They were shot as "enemies of the people."

The overwhelming majority of student Communists at institutes of higher education were expelled from the party and banished to Siberia and Kazakhstan. In Moscow and Leningrad the following were closed down: the State Journalism Institute, the Institute of Red Professors, the Communist Institute for the Toilers of the East, Sverdlov University, Zinoviev University, and others. The country trembled in the throes of bloody terror.

Zinoviev and Kamenev were charged with organizing the Kirov assassination and were arrested. New arrests and shootings were in the making. Each day the papers were filled with slanderous denunciations of Communists, Soviet people, accusing them of being terrorists, wreckers, and enemies of the people. It was not long before these events transformed Urusova completely.

Previously the name Stalin had been connected in her thinking with the entire future of Soviet Russia; now she saw in Stalin a tyrant over Russia and its constituent peoples. More and more often she asked herself these questions: "Do I have the right to ignore the way our people are suffering? No, that right I do not have. If I take no notice of the people's sufferings, if I close my eyes to them, I thereby become an accomplice in the crimes against them myself. It is necessary to struggle against the oppressors of the people. The people's tormentors must be removed. The tyrant must be slain."

Her ideas of killing Stalin matured instantly into a firm decision. But how to bring it about? She had no weapon, and even if she had, she would not have been able to use it. They would never admit her to his presence. "What could she do?" But an inner voice kept pressing her insistently: "The tyrant must be slain. The innocent victims and the very future of Russia demand it."

With the help of friends and with luck she chanced to get hold of some poison in powdered form, which she began to sprinkle on the pages of books ordered for Stalin. This had to be done with caution, in order not to attract the attention of any undercover agents. She was able to sprinkle only a few books with poison before the agent assigned to watch her caught her in the act and arrested her.

The long days and nights stretched out in the solitary cell at Lubyanka. She was questioned uninterruptedly for ten hours a day. The investigators took turns, yelling at her, threatening that she would be shot. But she bore herself with dignity and never flinched.

She told the investigators that she was now ashamed to recall the soft and pleasant life she had had in the Kremlin. She now realized how the Soviet people were suffering, and what a regime of terror this tyrant had imposed upon them. The people cursed Stalin from his prisons. She concluded her statement to the investigators with the following daring and resolute declaration: "I wanted to kill Stalin. I wanted to remove this tyrant. I wanted the people to be able to breathe freely. I do not fear death."

Urusova's outspoken audaciousness drove her investigators, already angry and irritated, into a white-hot fury. They began to ask themselves: "Where did such unbending will come from?" After lengthy consultations, the investigators decided to question the adoptive mother, Aksinia, who was brought from Kaluga for that purpose.

The investigators demanded that Aksinia confess truthfully who Urusova's parents were and where they were at that time. Aksinia held her tongue for twelve days. Then they applied torture, from which she nearly perished. On the thirteenth day Aksinia confessed everything. She stated that Urusova's parents had not been peasants but hereditary nobility. They had not died but had fled abroad in 1917. Her father, Prince Urusov, had been a large landowner in Kaluga province. Besides the estate at Rosva and a mansion in Kaluga, he had had a liquid-starch factory at Ugra. From the time the Urusovs had fled abroad, eighteen years had passed without any word of them. . . .

The investigators were exultant: trapped behind bars, they were holding a Russian Charlotte Corday. With icy scorn the investigators and prosecutor confronted Urusova with Aksinia's confession. The young woman cried out: "Lies! You are trying to discredit me in the eyes of the people. It's slander. I'm not an aristocrat, but a peasant girl and a Young Communist."

They brought Aksinia in for a face-to-face confrontation. Urusova failed to recognize her when Aksinia was led into the room. There stood a bent old woman, gray-headed, with a lifeless, ashen countenance. Nothing remained of Aksinia's former stately, energetic self. On seeing Urusova, Aksinia hung her head and for a long time could not say anything. Then when she had gathered herself together, she said with a great sigh: "Yes, my girl, it's all true. I accepted you from your parents' hands — Prince and Princess Urusov. . . . You were only two at the time. I made a vow to your mother before the icon of the Holy Mother of God. I promised to take care of you until she returned and to keep your princely origins secret. I did not keep my vow. Forgive me for it in the sight of the Lord our God." After this, as they started to take Aksinia out again, she fell on her knees and embraced Urusova's feet. Urusova got her to stand up again and without a word kissed her on the lips. . . .

A new page had been turned in Urusova's life, menacing her like a whip. Now they would try her as a noblewoman and brand her the Charlotte Corday of Russia.

It was nighttime and Urusova could not sleep. Her head ached. Half-forgotten images of her far-off childhood haunted her memory, recollections of a barren knoll near the village by the Rosva River. At this ancient burial mound was the grave, forgotten over time, of Russian warriors who had laid down their lives for their beloved Russia in battle against the Tatars. This forgotten grave always stirred a sense of reproach in her at the nation's forgetfulness of its heroes. . . .

The peephole in the celldoor clicked shut. Urusova got up and began to pace back and forth in the cell. To the rhythm of her steps she whispered, "I must prepare my defense, must prepare my defense."

A closed trial — the Kremlin trial dealing with attempts to assassinate Stalin — got under way in Moscow in the summer of 1935. There were many other Kremlin employees besides Urusova among the defendants: from the kitchen and maintenance crews, the guards, and the educational facilities. Included, too, were Yenukidze, secretary of the Soviet Central Executive Committee; Peters, the Kremlin commandant; and Rosenfeld, head of the Kremlin's cultural and educational facilities. As an alleged accomplice of Rosenfeld's, his brother by birth, L. B. Kamenev, was also brought into the trial.

It lasted ten days. In the course of it many attempts on Stalin's life were revealed. But all the attempts had failed. In her final plea Urusova spoke as follows: "The judges have tried to separate me from the working people of Russia. But they have not succeeded. The fact that I was born to the nobility should not be used to discredit me in the eyes of the people. I was nurtured and raised by a plain peasant woman who became my mother in fact. I was prepared for a life of labor by a Soviet school and the Communist League of Youth. The old world is repulsive to me. I hate oppression and tyranny. That is why I wished to slay the tyrant. I do not fear death. . . . The people will remember me."

Urusova was not shot, because they did not want to make a martyr of her. She was sentenced to ten years in prison. But who can vouch that she was not martyred in prison? Only future generations will be able to tell the truth about the dramatic fate of Urusova, the Young Communist-Princess. The sad fate of this contemporary of ours transcends the ages to echo the sad fate of another woman, an ancestor of Urusova, the heroine Boyarinya Morozova. In his famous painting entitled "Boyarinya Morozova", the painter Surikov portrayed the heroine in chains, alongside her great companion in heroism, Prince Urusov, who perished with her in a sealed monastery.

The seventeenth-century Princess Urusova died for Christianity; the Young Communist-Princess, the twentieth-century Urusova, died for her people's freedom. Although separated by the centuries, they are as one in their nobility of character and readiness to sacrifice themselves.

All that I have described is simply a retelling of a letter from L.B. Kamenev to his colleague G.E. Zinoviev, written after he got back from that trial. The entire prison read Kamenev's letter, including myself. At the Kremlin trial, Kamenev declared the following (almost word-for-word): "This is not a political trial but a criminal trial. I consider my involvement in it juridically unjustifiable. The only thing I have in common with my brother Rosenfeld is that the same mother gave birth to us both. . . ."

Kamenev was sentenced to a total of ten years' imprisonment (counting the Kirov case).

In the Vorkuta Concentration Camps
on the Pechora River (1936-41)

Transport to Vorkuta

It was 1936. In the country, Stalin's punitive detachments were going wild. In place of the butcher Yagoda, came a new butcher — Yezhov.

Two terrifying words hung over the country: Porcupine Gloves.[46] These words meant — terror, lawlessness, torture, death. Throughout the country the party cards of members were being checked. Hundreds of thousands of Communists of Russian and Jewish nationality were expelled from the party. They were accused of sympathizing with the Trotskyist Opposition. Soon after being expelled from the party they were arrested and jailed. The secretaries of the base party organizations played an ugly role in this business. They would draw up blacklists of party members and transmit them to the OGPU. These secretaries sealed the fate of many hundreds of thousands of honest Communists, who were shot or condemned to hard labor or remote exile.

The whole apparatus of the party from top to bottom was obliged to aid the OGPU in carrying out crimes and reprisals against honest Communists. The functionaries of the party apparatus never guessed that in the footsteps of these expelled and arrested Communists, their own turn in prison and camp would come. And how many of them were shot?

In the party, democracy was violated. For twenty years the same posts were held by secretaries of provincial, regional, and local party committees. Thus, for example, at the Molotov auto factory in Gorky the secretary remained unchanged for twenty-five years. This led to his becoming God, czar, and military commander combined, a fountainhead of arbitrariness and lawlessness.

The party apparatus was Stalin's base of support in his struggle against the party, against Lenin's heritage, until the time came when these people in the apparatus had become

---

46. [This is a pun on the name Yezhov and the word *yezh* (porcupine). The idiom "to hold in porcupine gloves" means approximately the same as "to rule with an iron hand," the opposite of "treat with kid gloves."]

dangerous witnesses of his rise, over the corpses of Old Bolsheviks, Communists, and participants in the civil war, to the
position of "genius" and beloved "personality."

Our transport from prison to Archangel took place under
cover of night, conveyed by Chekists with the superior advantage of rifles. We crossed the Dvina in army hydroplanes.
As we disembarked at the marine wharf, a stern command
from the guard rang out: "Sit down or I'll shoot."

It was pouring rain. The angry eyes of Chekists of Tatar
nationality stared at us, over the barrels of rifles aimed in
our direction. We sat in the pouring rain on the wet earth
for a long time. And when the rain stopped, the checking of
our papers began. The convoy guards looked on us as
enemies. They questioned us suspiciously and checked our
answers against the inscriptions on our papers. Then they
began to load us onto a three-tiered steamer. It was at the
dock, ready to go. The Archangel prison guards turned us
over to another convoy, getting a receipt for the whole lot
as you would for a load of cattle.

We took our leave of that northern Russian town with no
regrets. On the steamer there were two thousand of us — Communists condemned for opposition to the Stalin regime. We
were being brought together from various parts of the country,
where until then we had lived in exile. Now exile was ended
and we were being shipped off to hard labor.

Here I met my old friends again — Arais, Robinson, Pol,
Milman, Poznansky, Gamov, Yasha Drapkin, Komonov, Rai-
kin, Pasha Kunina, Grunya Bogatova. They were all old Communists; many of them had helped form the first Bolshevik
cells in the czarist underground and later helped capture the
Winter Palace and the Kremlin; and from 1918 to 1920 they
helped defend Soviet power on the fronts of the civil war.

With us on the steamer was Trotsky's younger son — Sergei
Lvovich Sedov. In the last few years he had been in exile in
Yeniseisk, working at a factory as an engineer. Unlike his
older brother Leon Lvovich, who was like his father in every
way, Sergei was like his mother and like his maternal grandfather, the well-known navigator, Captain Sedov. Sergei had
an open Russian face and light hair. He was a talented mathematician and could have been an important scholar. When
he was taken into the party those who vouched for him
were . . . Bukharin, Stalin, and Ordjonikidze.

In political questions Sergei adhered to the "general line"
of the party. He was not in accord with his father's ideas

and for that reason refused to leave the country with him in 1928.[47] Sergei showed us a letter from his father in Mexico. Trotsky asked Sergei to return to the family and to come to Mexico. In regard to this, Sergei had said to Yagoda: "I am not going anywhere. My homeland is Russia."[48]

On the way to Vorkuta he played chess with us. He seemed unconcerned and there was always a smile on his face. He had no premonition that in a year he would be shipped back to Yeniseisk and shot there.[49] This was not foreseen either by our other comrades, for whom an agonizing death at Vorkuta was

47. [The memoirist is in error here. Sergei Sedov actively avoided politics, unlike Trotsky's three other children. He devoted himself to mathematics and science, and was pursuing a promising career as a lecturer in technical subjects at an institute in Moscow until December 1934. In February 1929, when Stalin had Trotsky deported to Turkey, Sergei chose to remain behind, confident that his well-known abstention from politics would protect him. But Stalin carried his "political struggle" to the point of persecuting the entire families of his opponents.]

48. [Trotsky could not have asked Sergei to "come to Mexico"; by December 1936, when Trotsky first learned that he was going to Mexico, he had lost all contact with his son. From 1929 to December 1934, Sergei had regularly corresponded with his parents. His last letter reached them in the wake of the Kirov assassination. From what has become known (see, for example, Deutscher's *Prophet Outcast*) Sergei was arrested and exiled to the Krasnoyarsk region in 1935 after refusing to sign a statement denouncing his father. He was allowed to work there as an engineer, but around the time of the first Moscow show trial (August 1936) he was arrested again and subsequently shipped to Vorkuta, as the memoirist describes. Sergei first got to know his father's cothinkers only at Vorkuta. He was still uninterested in their politics, but admired their independent spirit and joined their courageous 132-day hunger strike (see below, "Trotskyists at Vorkuta," by M. B.). Sergei was then sent back to Moscow in early 1937, to Lubyanka prison, where he chanced to talk with an old Communist for a few hours. This was Joseph Berger (see note 1 to the introduction). Berger wrote to Sergei's mother, Natalya Sedova, around 1960, to pass a message to her from Sergei. "He wanted his parents to hear about their friends [the heroic strikers of Vorkuta] and of his own change of heart [joining the resistance to the Stalinist jailers]."]

49. [See note 62 below.]

waiting — on the Syr-Yaga, at the brick factories, along the route of transport, in the bathhouse gas chambers . . . in the concentration-camp cemeteries, which dotted the shores of the Usa and Pechora.

We were sailing not far off the deserted shores of the White Sea. From the watery depths emerged strange and wonderful fish and animals which we greeted like new friends. Suddenly an icy wind began to blow on us. The Barents Sea was ahead. Seething waves crashed against the steamer's sides and swept across its decks. Our steamer pitched in every direction, groaning. Icebergs from the Arctic Ocean were heading toward us, threatening to crush our steamer like an eggshell. The alarm sounded on deck. The guards and the ship's command did not wish to perish in the deep and let the ship drift freely before the wind. We were ordered to go down into the hold and wait. . . . In the hold it was dark and stifling: someone began singing a song of Yesenin's about the sorrows of the land of Russia. The ship began to toss. Only a few of the women did not become seasick. Like nurses, they took turns helping, first us convicts, then our tormentors, the guards.

On the next day the sea grew calm and we resumed our course toward Vorkuta. The icebergs had gone and the steamer traveled at full speed. On the deck we found machine guns with their barrels aimed at us. We asked the guards why. They answered that they had feared we would attack them. It turned out that one of our comrades, the Moscow engineer Pertsev, had remarked in the toilet: "Why be afraid of these guards? Let's disarm them and steer the ship to Norway."

In Pertsev's words there was more thoughtless bravado than good sense. He did not realize that seaplanes were secretly accompanying us, keeping watch, and would have bombed the steamer in such a case. The prisoners had no thought of trying to escape and so had not attributed any importance to Pertsev's nonsense and forgot about it. But the guards and Chekists did not forget. They worked up a "case" against Pertsev and not long after, at Vorkuta, he was shot. This was the first bit of our blood spilled at Vorkuta.

We docked at Naryan-Mar. From the dock we could see the long ribbon of the Pechora River. Moored on the Pechora was a little tugboat with five covered barges. We were ordered to get onto those barges, which were then to take us further up the Pechora. These barges in every respect resembled giant gray coffins prepared to carry us off to common graves.

We did not wish to die before our time. People protested and refused to board the barges. The guards yelled at us, threatening reprisals, but we stood fast, demanding a passenger boat. Finally a two-deck passenger steamboat with normal accommodations steamed in to the shore and took us on for Vorkuta.

Along the way we stopped frequently at the docks of numerous campsites, which dotted the shores of the Pechora in those days; we were picking up additional complements of prisoners for transport to Vorkuta.

At Novy Bor, where there was a supply point for the camps at that time, which had been set up by the state farm "Vorkutlag," the escort guards brought on eight women, one of whom turned out to be my wife. Our meeting was completely unexpected and aroused a momentary joy in us, especially because we immediately noticed the anger and vexation of the Chekists and camp guards. They were upset over the negligence that had given us this opportunity to meet. We had not seen one another for four years.

In the distance could be seen our last landing place—the mouth of the Usa River. This was called "Vorkuta Vom." It was the transshipping or reloading point for coal from Vorkuta and the transfer point for numerous shipments of prisoners. From there to the Vorkuta mines ran a single-track railway, sixty kilometers long, built by prisoners in 1931-32 across unexplored tundra, on ground that was perennially frozen.

From there, enormous convoys of prisoners were shipped off to the camps at Vorkuta.

We were received by the camp commission, one of whose members was the prisoner Dr. Gorelik. Seeing Sergei Sedov, he told him about his recent encounter with Trotsky, which had occurred quite unexpectedly in Brussels. Trotsky had flown to the Belgian capital from Turkey, where he was in exile, and given a speech, which made quite a stir, on the cultural revolution.[50]

Our shipment of prisoners was housed in three huge barracks tents; there were six hundred people in each one. Sick people and families were boarded at the outskirts of our transit camp, in wooden shacks. This was the so-called village of "TIT"

---

50. [In exile Trotsky never went to Brussels and never took a plane. He went by boat and train to Copenhagen to speak on the October Revolution there in late 1932 (see *Writings of Leon Trotsky* [*1932*] [Pathfinder Press, 1973]), and this is probably the event the memoirist is referring to.]

where an infirmary was later established for the ill and injured miners from the prison camps. To visit our sick comrades, it was necessary to pass through swampy tundra, jumping from one clump of vegetation to another.

At the deportation point we were greeted by groups of common criminals, convicted for robbery and murder. Seeing our trunks, they said threateningly: "Look at the sitting ducks . . . walking right into our hands today." In the language of these bloodsuckers this meant that today they would filch our things, or simply snatch them out of our hands.

We petitioned the authorities to protect us from these types. But the camp overseer heard us out with a sarcastic smile and refused us any protection whatsoever from the criminals. Later we learned that the prison head relied on these types — common criminals and morals offenders, who were here considered to be "socially close to the working class" — as against the "enemies of the people," Old Bolsheviks, Communists, Soviet people. He made use of those types for reprisals and attacks against the political prisoners. It was from among these "socially close" types that the chiefs, foremen, and "counsellors" of the work crews were appointed.

Thus began our first day of life at hard labor above the Arctic Circle. About this life, the tailor Lyova Dranovsky began to write some very fine and moving poetry one night sitting by the stove in the tent, by the bank of the Vorkuta River; an old Communist, he was shot at Syr-Yaga in 1938.

The first person he read his poetry to then was the duty officer of the tent, Grigory Filippovich Zilberfarb, to whom he dedicated the poem "Duty Officer." Dranovsky's poems became the common property of the whole Vorkuta camp and were set to music, to sad and mournful tunes. The words of one of them are as follows:

Above the Arctic Circle,
far away from all,
night times overhead are
black as lumps of coal.
Wolf voice of the wind
doesn't let you sleep.
Oh, for a ray of light
in all this gloom and grief.
In the murky shadows
something spells our doom.
All of us want to be

alone with our gloom.
Above the Arctic Circle,
my friend, there is no joy.
My tracks are covered over
by savage storms of snow.
So cause yourself no worry,
don't go to any pains,
But if you have a chance to,
remember me, my friend.

Small and delicate in a tattered black robe, hunched over
from the cold, Dranovsky would pace around the tent at night
with a notebook in his bosom and pencil in hand. At times
he would bring out the notebook, jot down something, then
put it back, rushing over to the iron stove to warm his freezing fingers which were in no condition to hold a pencil and
notebook.

One of the most moving things he wrote was "A Farewell."
This was a letter to his wife, full of mental anguish and of
faith that his sacrifice for historical truth, for the world revolution, was not in vain.

Yes, we carried our idea of the world socialist revolution
through great and frightful experiences. But neither the taiga,
nor the tundra, nor our difficult life with its icy breath broke
our will to struggle, to the end, giving up our lives.

Many of us fell in that struggle. But we placed our hopes
in other generations that would come; and they will come,
not only in our country but in all countries of the world, to
carry the torch of world revolution proudly on into every
country of the world without exception, to every people that
lives on our planet.

The "Chekist" Podlesny

Our contingent of prisoners was driven along by a reinforced
convoy of guards. When the guards wanted to rest, they would
order us to sit down right in the snow and not "fidget around."
"No fidgeting" was the most widely used command among our
"vigilant" guards. It meant that you did not dare to move even
one step away from the rest of the prisoners. At night we would
huddle together in cold, uninhabitable quarters, the so-called
transport "stations" that we would come across along the way.

Our bodies ached all over and our legs felt like hunks of
wood from the long, exhausting march. Only toward evening

on the seventh day did we get as far as the women's camp, Kochmes, on the banks of the Usa River.

Here, thanks to the special exertions of the prisoners, virgin soil had been plowed up, the scrub growth of the tundra had been uprooted, and various kinds of turnips were being raised in the open, while other vegetables grew in hotbeds. These were sent to the Vorkuta mines for the free employees (and some got passed along to the convict miners, who suffered from scurvy and other diseases). Here too was a herd of dairy cattle, from which milk and butter were obtained, also for the mines, to feed the military guards and their families, as well as for the free laborers and camp hangers-on. Some of this even got passed on to the hospitals for the miners from the prison camps.

All the most difficult jobs at Kochmes were done by women, of whom there were several thousand. Women were even employed at sawing up timbers lengthways for use in the building of barracks. The heavy labor of ripsawing and of dragging the timbers caused painful hernias and internal bleeding which exhausted the women until they lost all their strength or fainted.

Our contingent of prisoners was driven to Kochmes to build new barracks. They were expecting a new complement of women, new transports of prisoners who were on their way to the camp from the Temnikov camps of Gorky oblast and from other parts of the country.

They bedded us down on the dirt floor of an old cattle-barn and at dawn the straw boss awakened us. "Off to work! Off like a shot!" He repeated this phrase by rote, invariably shouting it at us every morning.

At line-up in the morning the head of the Kochmes camp, Podlesny by name, would show up. His name should have been Podletsny [*podlets* meaning "scoundrel"].

We had heard of Podlesny's savagery long before, at the mines. But what we saw with our own eyes exceeded all expectations. He had a stern face and unblinking eyes. Next to him he always had two Cheka agents, of Tatar nationality, who held two police dogs straining on heavy leashes. The dogs barked furiously at the prisoners, whom they had been trained to hate by the guards. Also standing there was the camp doctor, a prisoner like us. His duty was to care for the sick and, when appropriate, to excuse people from work on account of illness.

In our contingent there were many too ill to go to work, and they asked the doctor if he could look at them or give them something. Podlesny would not let them speak with the doctor. "Fakers! Shirkers!" he shouted, rudely insulting these sick people.

The doctor, frightened by Podlesny's ferocity, found all the sick prisoners "healthy" and turned his back on them. But these people were actually barely able to walk.

Then Podlesny ordered the dogs to be loosed on the sick prisoners. They knocked the people off their feet, into the snow, and began to tear at their clothing and bite them, urged on by their handlers. The prisoners cried out, begging for help, appealing to the guards as though they were human beings, as though trying to elicit a show of humanity from them. But the guards just kept looking at Podlesny with his frightening eyes and his teeth bared like an animal, and dared not drive off the dogs.

The dogs dragged the sick people around and around in the snow to the hoots and catcalls of the common criminals, who mocked these people who were "socially alien" to them. When at last the dogs were called off, the sick were left bleeding and moaning in the snow, only half alive. Podlesny gloated.

This depraved sadist had a favorite activity: visiting the women's barracks late at night. After sneaking up to a woman's cot with stealthy steps, he would rip off her covers, terrifying her out of her sleep and getting a depraved pleasure out of seeing her half naked, frightened, and bewildered.

He did this under the pretext of checking for violations of camp regulations, which prohibited male prisoners from meeting or being intimate with female prisoners. However, despite the strict prohibition even against free laborers consorting or living with women prisoners, this vile individual forced many women to live with him.

If Podlesny ever did happen to discover a man in the women prisoners' barracks, he would make his victim crawl on his knees in front of him right there in the barracks. When he had sated himself with this spectacle of another's debasement, he would pitilessly order the victim to be sent to a cold punishment cell for ten days. All this in spite of the fact that he himself kept more than a few "lovers" from among the women prisoners, making regular slaves of them for a Kochmes harem at the beck and call of his majesty the warden Podlesny.

Among Podlesny's "lovers" was one very beautiful woman who submitted to him only to save her life. He was always terribly jealous of her and caused her much suffering because of that. He even proposed that she marry him after she got out, promising to get divorced from his own wife of that time. But when it came time for this beauty to be released from custody, she chose to go home to her husband, who was also due to be released from prison, having served nearly all of his term.

Podlesny could not endure such a blow to his "dignity." When the moment of parting came, Podlesny, not wishing his "lover" to be separated from him — and so that no other man would ever have her — shot and killed her outright.

Podlesny's "love" for his "fair lady" was not much different from that of the thief Kolka Bazik, a repeated offender imprisoned at the same camp. Bazik bit off his girl friend's nose during their farewell kiss, so that no other man would have her.

In this respect the chief of the camp and the thief-repeater proved indeed to be "socially" and "spiritually" kin.

With a Gag in the Mouth . . . on Orders from Stalin

They brought me into "Adak," the camp's infirmary, barely alive. Penal labor in the Vorkuta mines had worn down my strength and strained my nerves to the breaking point. In Adak they "repaired" us a little, and then sent us back to work in the mines or at the lime mill, fetching limestone or bringing in wood or stoking it into the lime kilns.

In the autumn of 1937 a brigade of prisoners was shipped into Adak from the Adzva-Vom transshipment point to build an infirmary consisting of temporary tents.

The person appointed as brigade chief was Sergeev; the planner was Zubarov; the statistician, Pergament; the supervisor was a certain common criminal named Kornyushin. The superintendent for all construction work in the camp was the lanky Dmitry Platonovich Roze.

The brigade consisted of forty people and was housed in a small tent that barely held them all. The frameworks over which the tents would be stretched had not even been erected when barges of injured prisoners from Vorkuta showed up — old and sick men, mostly Old Bolsheviks physically unsuited for work in the Vorkuta mines.

It was already late autumn. The first bits of ice were already floating down the Usa River when the barges pulled up to the riverbanks at Adak, at the mouth of the Adak River. The sick and injured prisoners were ejected from the barges and left on shore under some small pines, the Vorkuta landscape

changing here from tundra to scrub forest. Some distance
from the infirmary a larger, thicker forest could be seen. It
concealed in its shadows the secrets of events that had gone
on here before our arrival. Older residents told us all sorts
of things about those events. I will not repeat all the things
I heard but did not see myself. I will tell only about how
people died before my eyes, every day, by the dozens, sent
"over the hill," dying in the tents, freezing and crowding around
the iron stoves, dropping from hunger and cold, from dysentery and malnutrition.

I can still see the Old Bolshevik Karnaukov, a railroad
engineer from the Far Eastern provinces, from Irkutsk. He
was found one night on the tent floor, where he had fallen
unconscious, in the dark, never to rise again. On his person
a photograph was found. He had just received it. It showed
his large family — the descendants of many generations of
workers.

Further, I recall the old Communist Mintz moaning in his
death throes, swollen in his pea-jacket scorched by the stove.
I recall the talented aviation designer Barakov; and Tabach-
nik pouring over some weighty scientific tome; and the old-
timers Mikhail Illiaronovich Gelovani, Sysak Oganezovich Muralov, Volobuev, Fadeev. And Edvitia Tsintsadze — a dear
old woman. And many, many other occupants of those tents.

The high rate of illness and death at Adak was caused by
the fact that when the people from Vorkuta arrived, not only
were the tents not ready — so that people caught cold from
sleeping on the frozen ground under the open sky — but also
no food had been provided and there was no kitchen, bakery,
or bathhouse. Out of desperation the starving people pounced
on frostbitten potatoes that were rotting out in the open. Because they were rotten, they caused dysentery and diarrhea
to all who ate them, after which the weaker ones began dying
like flies. In kettles over open fires, a kind of foul-smelling
codfish, some that had gotten frozen and some that had frozen
and thawed, was boiled and then served in this boiled form
right into people's dirty hands. There was no bread. Instead
they boiled lumps of dough in the same kettles over open
fires. One of these, half-wet and boiling hot, would be doled
out to each person to last the whole day. The starving people
would bolt these down greedily and the next moment be clutch-
ing at their stomachs in pain.

The chief doctor at Adak at that time was Doctor Lyov

and the chief cook was Lyov Gerasimovich Paniev. Both being prisoners, they were powerless to combat all that illness and death.

When the Usa froze over, the infirmary and its settlement were cut off from the rest of Vorkuta and from the entire outside world. Left to its own resources, and local bosses, it fell as silent as though—or so it seemed to the doomed inhabitants—a gag had been shoved in its mouth.

Silent death carried off hundreds that first winter. Only the younger and stronger survived. . . . The bloody extermination of Communist Oppositionists and of people who sympathized with them or had come into contact with them to one degree or another went on in 1937-38, not only at Adak but at all the campsites of the Vorkuta-Pechora and Ukhta detention districts.

The tragedy of the people who worked at the brick factory near Vorkuta arouses a feeling of chill horror toward all the butchers who carried out their bloody work at that place. Under the pretext of transporting them to Obdorsk (now Salekhard) the prisoners were led out into the tundra and shot down with machine guns or blown up by explosive charges planted in the snow beside the road.

Hundreds of people were shot this way at Syr-Yaga in 1938. There were cases where some prisoners came through completely unharmed or only lightly wounded. Not suspecting any danger from their own guards, in cases where explosions had gone off, they appealed to them for help, and sought their protection. But the guards replied to these appeals with deadly pistol fire—frequently shooting their wards while looking around in fear at their own superiors who were watching their every move.

The scarce, few witnesses who chanced by some miracle to survive from among those who took part in the annihilation of the old Communists also told us that bathhouses at the brick factory had been rigged up as gas chambers for Oppositionists. Under the pretext of giving them sterilizing baths for hygienic purposes before they were to be shipped off, they herded people into these bathhouses, from which they never returned alive. The corpses were taken out into the tundra and burned. [51]

The extermination of Communist Oppositionists was directed

---

51. What was so new, then, about what Hitler did?

by a duly authorized NKVD man, specially sent from Moscow, a certain Kashketin. He already had acquired experience in butchery, having annihilated more than fifteen thousand Communists at Kolyma before coming to Vorkuta. After completing his bloody butcher's mission, he was recalled to Moscow and shot. A rumor spread around the camp that he had been shot supposedly because the name of Virap Virapovich Virapov had appeared on the list of the executed. Virapov had been a lean and lanky, towheaded Communist with a Mephistophelian profile. He had participated in the hunger strike by the "Orthodox" Oppositionists.[52] (That is what the oldtime Oppositionists called themselves as distinguished from those who in 1929-30 had renounced the Opposition but who nevertheless were not spared by the Stalinist terror in 1936-38).

The truth of the matter is that the executioner's masters in Moscow were trying to cover their tracks by getting rid of witnesses. Under various pretexts all those who had convoyed those executed victims went the same way as Kashketin, being exterminated themselves — both officers and soldiers. The participants in the shootings at Kolyma and Vorkuta and in other parts of Russia were frequently people who believed what their officers told them and for that reason were the most dangerous witnesses of all. But the possibility is not excluded that certain individuals from among those backward types may still be alive and may tell everything that they saw and that they were forced to do on orders from those who intended to execute them in turn. And if such people do not appear, the earth itself will tell about these crimes.[53] And not only the earth. After all, won't the hundreds of cities, industrial sites, factories, and mines that have sprung up in the outlying regions of our country, built by the hands of Communist prisoners and over the corpses of Old Bolsheviks, Soviet people, participants in the October Revolution and civil war — won't these remains tell their story to future generations, even though they have been given names like "Komsomolsk," supposedly

---

52. [References to this 132-day-long strike are found in Solzhenitsyn's book *First Circle.* For a full description of the 1937 strike, see below, "Trotskyists at Vorkuta."]

53. Since Kolyma is located in a region of permanent frost, corpses there are preserved in their entirety.

symbolizing that these are products of the labor of Young Communists (Komsomols)? [54]

The Communist Altman

At Adak in 1938 I met the Communist Abram Altman. He was an Old Bolshevik and an honest and courageous person.

Before his arrest he had lived with his family in Leningrad, where he worked as the director of a plant engaged in military production. After being arrested, he was taken to Moscow and put in Lefortovo prison, where the latest torture techniques were being applied. The investigation of his case was pursued stubbornly over a long period of time. He was accused of secret ties with Trotskyists, and he was asked to reveal their names.

Altman would not name any names. Then they began to torture him: crushing his fingers in a door, and beating him over the head with a club. Still Altman would not talk. They then put him in a wet punishment cell, where there was water up to his knees. He spent three days there without rest or sleep. Still Altman held his tongue. Then they began to beat him on the genitals with a rubber cane. His teeth chattered and the hair stood up on his head from the terrible pain. His genitals became greatly swollen. But he never told them anything. Behind bars he turned gray and went totally blind. Even as a blind man they tried him and sentenced him to ten years at penal labor.

Altman and I were bunkmates in the barracks. On winter evenings he used to tell us about the Bolshevik underground before the revolution and about the tragic days of his imprisonment at Lefortovo.

Sometimes he and I played chess. He was able to picture where the pieces were on the board by memory alone. And who knows what he might have been able to see if he had still had his sight?

Among the Old Bolsheviks there were quite a few like Altman. They went about their creative, narrowly practical work wholeheartedly, without noticing that something improper was

---

54. [The massacre of the "orthodox" Trotskyists at Vorkuta, directed by Kashketin, is also described in "Trotskyists at Vorkuta," below; in Solzhenitsyn's *First Circle;* in Medvedev's *Let History Judge* (p. 281); and in Berger's *Nothing But the Truth.*]

going on behind their backs. Later someone came after them
and dragged them off to prison because they were old Bolshevik-Leninists to the marrow of their bones. But they were
light-minded about the fate of the revolution, even though
they entered into the building of Soviet society, of socialism,
with their sleeves rolled up.

We loved Altman for his iron courage, for his pure and
sensitive heart. About the "ties with Trotskyists" of which he
had been accused, he never said anything; either there had
been no such thing, or else he kept silent about that around
us, fearing the "gag in the mouth."

On Friendship and Villainy

Simonov's poem "On Friendship" and Korneichuk's *Wings*
were the first swallows to fly out of the cage after Stalin's
death.

The theme of friendship in contemporary poetry and drama
is not accidental. It arose again after a long period of hate
and the cult of hatred of humanity brought about by the tyranny of the period of the personality cult. Now the time has
come to again summon Soviet youth to friendship based on
mutual ideas, on struggle and striving for a better future for
all humanity. Legends about people who preserved their friendships intact through all their experiences are being passed
on from one generation to another. Such was the friendship
between Marx and Engels, between Herzen and Ogarev.[55]
Their friendships were strengthened by the idea of fighting
for a common cause.

Such was the friendship between Lenin and Zinoviev. It
lasted all the way to Lenin's death. It did not leave them in
the years of emigration, far from home, nor in their home-

---

55. [Aleksandr Herzen was a Russian revolutionary leader and
writer. After being sent to Siberian exile in 1834 he emigrated from
Russia and lived in Paris, and then England, where he set up the
first free Russian press abroad. In 1855 he published a history of
the revolutionary movement in Russia. He published the journal
Kolokol (The Bell), attacking czarism. Nikolai Ogarev was a revolutionary publicist and poet who joined the revolutionary movement
young and was closely associated with Herzen. He co-edited *Kolokol*
and was an organizer of Land and Freedom, a populist movement,
in the 1860s.]

land in the period of reaction, in the czarist underground. After the July days in 1917 Zinoviev, risking his life, would not abandon his teacher and friend in those dangerous hours and days, but shared his fate in the hut near Petrograd. (With deep regret we recall the serious mistakes of Zinoviev and Kamenev at the time of the October insurrection, when Lenin called them "strikebreakers." And with still greater regret we cannot leave unmentioned their second mistake, disastrous for their own lives, which to a certain degree was the result of their first mistake at the time of the October insurrection — that is, their following Stalin rather than Lenin in 1923, instead of acting on Lenin's advice, in his last letter, to remove Stalin from the post of general secretary. Their strikebreaking in 1917, in which they were associated with Stalin, united them with him in 1923 for a short time, and when they realized their mistake it was already too late.)

The friendship between Zinoviev and Kamenev after Lenin's death was of the same kind. They both died in 1937 as a result of that fatal mistake. They were unable to see Stalin for what he was — an enemy of the idea of world revolution, the idea for which they had always been ready to sacrifice themselves.

Equally sincere and devoted was the friendship between Bukharin and Aleksandr Slepkov. In order not to betray his friend and teacher while being questioned under torture, Slepkov hanged himself with an electric cord in his prison cell.

Equally firm was the friendship between Trotsky and Joffe. They maintained their friendship through prison and exile, without every sullying it. And when danger threatened Trotsky, Joffe committed suicide as a sign of protest.

Such friendship always begins in the years of one's youth and is dedicated to something great, exalted, and purposeful. Such friendship makes one want to bow the head in respect. . . . But not every friendship is able to stand up against adversity. . . . When a reign of terror rages in a country, the time comes when friendships are put to the test.

There was a time when the friendship between the two best-known journalists of the first decade after October, and even of the thirties, Koltsov and Sosnovsky, was much spoken of.

Koltsov treacherously disavowed his friend the moment he was arrested. Moreover, in order to make his disavowal all the more convincing, Koltsov went so far as to insult Sosnovsky's wife. At the Hall of Columns in the House of Soviets in Moscow, Sosnovskaya was collecting donations in support of arrested Soviet writers and journalists. Koltsov refused to help those who had been arrested. When Sosnovskaya told him that this was disgraceful cowardice, he struck her in the face.

That was in 1928. This scandal even became known abroad. Koltsov's action aroused a storm of indignation. The most outrageous thing about it was that he had publicly insulted an older woman, a generous soul who had always welcomed him as her own son.

Koltsov's degraded act aroused revulsion against him. Everyone saw in what he had done a fear for his own well-being, for his own career, for his own skin. In prison, Sosnovsky lost his sanity. He was accused of ties with "international Trotskyism." Ten years later Koltsov was shot, also on charges of ties with Trotskyists, those in Spain.

Incidentally, a careful reading of Koltsov's *Spanish Diaries*, published after his posthumous rehabilitation, makes clear, painful as it is to realize, that Koltsov played a despicable role in the Spanish Civil War as Stalin's special emissary.

Trotsky's influence on the armed forces of the POUM and on the operations of the powerful Anarchist section was at first so great that Stalin, fearing the victory of these elements in the Civil War, took his favorite path of provocation, and aimed at cutting off the elements of the POUM, setting against them the units that followed Dolores Ibarruri and Jose Diaz. Koltsov then went to Spain with the assignment from Stalin to isolate the POUM and reduce its influence in every possible way, dividing the forces fighting against Franco. And he fulfilled this assignment, really going all out, not even hesitating to risk his own life.

One can only explain why Koltsov was shot by the desire to remove a dangerous witness to the real reasons for the defeat of the international brigades in the Spanish Civil War. His diaries should be viewed in quite a critical light now, after the twentieth party congress, when Stalin's true face has begun to be revealed as that of a person endeavoring to destroy everything internationalist in the name of the victory of his *idee fixe*—"socialism in one country."

It is hard to believe that Stalin could have behaved as a political saboteur against the world revolution, beginning even at the time of the civil war, simply out of vanity or hatred and resentment of Lenin, Trotsky, and Tukhachevsky. No, apparently what you had here was an undiscovered, subtle undercover operation, hidden under Jesuitical, hypocritical phrases and carried out by an enemy of communism, an enemy of internationalism, who wormed his way into Lenin's confidence in the first years of the revolutionary underground and in the early years after October. The facts cry out to this effect.

1. The first and most convincing of these was his counteracting of orders from the supreme command of the Red Army to send three armies to the White-Polish front in support of Tukhachevsky. The Red Army's approach toward the borders of Germany at a time of heightened revolutionary ferment among the working masses of the German nation would have been the most suitable moment for utilizing the revolutionary situation in that country to accomplish the socialist revolution and the seizure of power by the proletariat. With his intrigues against Trotsky, Stalin broke the revolutionary spirit of the Red Army soldiers, seized with the enthusiasm expressed in the unanimous and most widespread slogan of those years: "Surrender Warsaw. Then give us Berlin." And in several sections of Germany the workers, feeling the approach of the liberators, seized power. Here is how events unfolded:

In March 1920 the Iron Cross overthrew the Scheidemann government and put Doctor Kapp in charge of a monarchy. On March 20, Kapp renounced his powers under pressure from a railroad workers' strike. In place of Kapp, Von Lutwitz took power, proclaiming himself dictator. At that point Soviet governments were formed in the cities of Chemnitz and Pilsen. In Wilhelm-Hoffen the sailors proclaimed Soviet power. In Upper Bavaria Soviet power was proclaimed on March 17. Under the pressure of the workers' strikes and insurrections, Lutwitz discarded his dictatorial powers and, together with Kapp, fled from Berlin on March 21.

During those days the reactionaries began to put out proclamations calling for pogroms against the Jews and Spartacists. As soon as the defeat outside Warsaw became clear, a coalition government (composed of the Social Democrat traitor Ebert and outright reactionaries) began to disarm the Spartacists, and to suppress the Soviet power the Spartacists had established in a number of German cities.

That is what Stalin's treachery led to: In countermanding orders for the sake of his intrigues against Trotsky, he ruined the plan for an offensive against Warsaw that would bring the Red Army to the borders of insurgent Spartacist Germany.

In spite of the temporary victory of reaction in Germany, that country continued to be a smoldering powderkeg up through 1923. In those years the German Communist Party gained strength and its influence and degree of organization reached a high level. The success of an armed insurrection of the working class in 1923 would have been assured. But unfortunately in 1923 the "general secretary" Stalin appeared on the scene with intrigues of an even more dangerous character, verging on political sabotage against the German revolution.[56] In the ranks of the Comintern confusion and vacillation arose. The leadership of the German Communist Party, as well as the rank and file of the Spartacists and revolutionary workers, were demoralized, which created the conditions in Germany for entrance of the National Socialists onto the political arena.

The revolution in Germany was wrecked. Who wrecked it? Who carried out this political sabotage against the extension of the world revolution? None other than its worst enemy, that most ferocious provocateur.

2. The second proof of Stalin's treachery is his role in Spain. The international brigades, Communists of the whole world, everything that was worthy and profoundly ideological in the ranks of the world's Communist parties, were sent to their destruction in the Spanish Civil War. He secretly indulged in bloodletting in Spain, even at a time when he clearly saw that German fascism was helping Franco in the destruction of the internationalists by means of superior technology — aviation, bombers — at a time when the forces of the Spanish revolution were splintered.

3. Finally, the third proof of treachery is his role in Lenin's death, in isolating him, in opposing Lenin with the aid of temporary accomplices, which disturbed Lenin so that he insisted on Stalin's removal from the leadership of the Central Committee.

History will disclose quite a few more facts about the villainous treachery of this enemy of the revolution, whose methods of self-advancement were provocation, poison, and the dagger. He too had "friendships" with his many temporary accomplices, who never suspected that he would butcher them in the future. They supported him against Lenin and Trotsky and later themselves fell under his cleaver. Stalin's friendship was the friendship of a wolf for lambs. . . .

Our literary artists should also hold up as models for the

---

56. [In 1923 Stalin was a partisan of "applying the brakes" to the German Communists. See his letter to Zinoviev and Kamenev in Trotsky's *Third International After Lenin.*]

edification of the young generation the friendships of women of preceding generations. The wives of the Decembrists offer illustrious examples of such friendship. They continue to stir people's souls to this very day. The subsequent history of humanity presented many other unforgettable women's names: Sofia Perovskaya, Laura Lafargue, Rosa Luxemburg, Nadezhda Krupskaya, and many others.

The tragic decade of the thirties of our century proved to be most abundant in heroic deeds by women in the name of friendship. These years enriched humanity with thousands of examples of women who sacrificed themselves for the sake of revolutionary ideas and friendships devoted to those ideas. The names of these women martyrs are unknown today to the broad masses of the people: only their relatives and close acquaintances know and remember them. But their unusual fates even now disturb the conscience of humanity. They were shot or died under torture. Where they are buried, no one knows. "No mound, no marker with name or date."

Their names some day will be on people's lips. The time will come when prison archives will be unearthed and everyone will know the names of these great martyred heroines.

I will only mention the names of those women Communists who were shot or otherwise perished, those who especially impressed me: There was Pasha Kunina—a woman who had great beauty of soul. She was a Communist and believed in the triumph of the idea of world revolution. Being the wife and friend of Kossior (the elder) she went through the trials of prison, exile, and penal labor with him. In the winter of 1937 she was shot along with her husband at Vorkuta. Another martyred woman was Roza Magidova, the wife and companion of the Communist Mark Simkhovich. She died at hard labor in 1938 in the Kochmes women's camp. Another martyred woman I remember was Grunia Bogatova, wife of the Communist Genkin. She went insane at hard labor at Vorkuta. A fourth who endured great suffering was Liuda Karadzha, companion of the Communist Khotimsky, who was shot in 1938. She came to Vorkuta together with her husband and two sons, who also perished—one at the front and one on the railroad. She was left all alone at Ukhta. The names of Faina Yablonskaya, Roza Radek, Liuba Heifits, Gisia Chusovskaya, Ida Shumskaya, and many others who were shot or died at Vorkuta in the thirties will never be erased from our memories. They were companions and wives of Communists who devoted their lives to the cause of the working class.

Along with those women who perished three names will never be forgotten: Sedova— Trotsky's wife; Lilina— Zinoviev's wife; and Maria Joffe—wife of [Adolph] Joffe. These women are still alive. [57] They have traveled a difficult road, crowded with revolutionary struggles, and have endured inhuman sufferings.

My memory has preserved one other woman martyr whose name has been temporarily blotted out of my memory but whose image remains vivid to this day. I met her at the Verkhne-Uralsk prison in 1935. She was elderly and quite gray. She had been sentenced to ten years for terrorism, something she had not the slightest conception of. She was the victim of a juridical "error" of the type that were being fabricated by the tens of thousands at that time, in order to keep the party and people in fear.

Hers was a heroic story. When still in high school she had joined the Social Revolutionary Party (SRs). She was arrested many times under the czarist autocracy and once she was sentenced to hard labor in Siberia for participating in terrorist activity against the czarist regime. Only the February Revolution freed her from imprisonment.

After the October Revolution she broke with the SR party and gave up political activity for good. She returned to her native town of Voronezh, and went to work as a schoolteacher. The Cheka and OGPU did not bother her. She religiously observed her commitment to abandon all political activity.

Once on the streets of the town she unexpectedly ran into an old friend from the czarist underground whom she had not seen for sixteen years. He was passing through Voronezh, seeking a distant relative in the town. He began to weep from joy at the unexpected meeting. He looked quite ill and kept coughing badly the entire time. He wanted to ask her something but coughed so much that he could not get out a single word. Thus they parted without saying anything of significance to one another.

In parting with him she gave him all the money she had with her — sixty rubles (1934 value). He took the money thankfully. Out of emotion he again began to cough and weep. No more than a week went by from that day when she was visited by night and arrested. During the investigation they asked her:

---

57. These women are all dead now.

"How long have you known this old terrorist whom you gave 600 rubles for terrorist purposes?" She replied that she had known the old man since prerevolutionary days and that she and he had been in the same contingent of prisoners shipped off to hard labor in 1907. To the investigator's question, "What was he sentenced to hard labor for?" she replied: "He was a member of a terrorist detachment of the SR party and brought vengeance down upon the czarist butchers of the Russian people. But he was always pure and honorable. During our transport to hard labor, he was like a brother to me and helped me in time of trouble. That I will never forget as long as I live. . . . And now he is a sick old man, with no job or pension. I gave him sixty rubles because of his poverty, not six hundred for terrorism. What kind of terrorist is he? He left politics in 1918, just as I did. Let me speak with him in person. This is a misunderstanding, it can be cleared up at once."

She was quite excited and believed in the possibility of saving her old friend from disaster. But the investigator responded drily that the old man had been shot the previous day. Hearing the frightful words "has been shot," she broke into sobs and cried out: "What for? Why shoot a poor old man? What did he ever do to you? You are heartless . . . evil . . . people!" The severe investigator simply rang for her to be taken away.

Two months later she was notified of the decision of the OGPU Special Board decreeing ten years imprisonment in her case. This was the price for her friendship. It was imposed by the Stalinist bullies upon all honorable people in the country who valued their friendships and remained unfailingly true to them for decades.

In Prisons and Camps, and at Hard Labor (Notes, Episodes, and Recollections from the Forties and Fifties)

The Chekist from Kaluga

In the Kaluga MGB, he occupied the post of chief of the investigating section. His eyes always had an agitated look about them, like those of a drug addict. His name was Kalyabin.

He asked me once about a letter we had sent to Alma Ata, to Trotsky, and about Trotsky's reply. I did not want a discussion with Kalyabin on this subject and I tried to avoid it. I asked him, "What do you want to know for?"

"For history," he answered with the self-satisfied air of a know-it-all.

"History will be written by historians, not by employees of the MGB investigation section," I said.

Stung to the quick, apparently, he snatched a book out of his desk drawer, the *"Short Course" History of the CPSU*, and cried out: "Here's our history. Right here. It's already been written." He unleashed this tirade standing up, holding the book in the air with his right hand. His eyes gleamed like a maniac's, and his lips were twisted in a vicious sneer.

Unable to restrain myself, I said, "What you have in your hands is not history, but the falsification of history."

Kalyabin looked at me threateningly and shouted in anger: "Don't forget where you are. You're not at your in-law's for tea and cakes." Right after that he nervously hid the book in the desk and pressed a buzzer. In came the orderly and began to lead me out. "Give him two hours in the 'box,'" ordered Kalyabin.

They threw me into the closed wooden closet for two hours, where there was no fresh air, no room to move, and no light. From that day on they began to apply that form of punishment to me. Twice a day I was taken for questioning. Then for a stretch of two weeks instead of being taken for questioning I was just held in the "box." Later I learned that Kalyabin had been away from Kaluga those two weeks. He had been in Moscow, but before leaving he had given instructions that I was to be put in the box each day during those two weeks. Such was the prison official Kalyabin.

At Hard Labor

. . . I am held behind barbed wire, seven layers deep, and behind that obstacle is a high wooden fence with towers manned by soldiers with machine guns and floodlights. Beyond the wooden palisade, guard dogs are leashed to a metal wire that rings the enclosure. We are guarded by dogs like these, too, when we are led out each day to the stone quarries. It is hard labor, forced labor. All our strength is drained by it.

For work at distant locations they take us in trucks holding twenty persons each. We are not allowed to stand in the back of the truck but are forced to sit down on the metal floor. One's entire body aches from sitting and being jarred this way. Shifting one's position is not allowed. They may shoot a person without any warning, for "trying to escape." We gave this kind of trip the name "death on the installment plan."

The prison guards are Kazakhs or Tatars. They are very harsh and brutal, and look upon us as cattle. Identification numbers have been sewn onto our prison clothing. On a square piece of dirty white linen there are five digits, preceded by a letter of the alphabet. These numbers are sewn on one's cap, pea-jacket, quilted jacket, trousers, and work shirt. We are called by these numbers nowadays, rather than by our names. We are poorly fed and consequently are always hungry. We work ten hours a day with no breaks. After work hours we are locked up in the barracks, with its barred windows and bucket-latrine on the inside. This then is the penal-labor prison. That is how modern "socialism in one barracks" looks in Karaganda, at hard labor.

More on Hard Labor

My wife writes me from Siberia that where she is now they use the threat of "the sands," where I am, to frighten the children. And indeed our "Special Camp in the Sands" is a frightful place. The Siberia of old with its forced-labor system pales before the modern version. The air here is polluted by gas, and everything around is blanketed by filthy black coal dust. People's lifespans are short here; they die of black lung disease.

There is no vegetation. In its place there are hundreds of miles of sand. When a windstorm comes up, no one can go outdoors: they might get blown away. Thousands of tiny sand particles work their way into one's eyes and ears and under one's collar until they cover the entire body, like the midges used to at Vorkuta.

Of all the feathered kingdom only the sparrows live here. All the rest of God's winged creatures fly past. "Hither no beast doth wend, nor raven fly. . . ."

A few days ago we learned some disturbing news. On the sealed folders in which our dossiers are kept there had been stamped the terrifying words: "To be opened on notification from Moscow." In each folder an "OSO ruling"[58] had been placed, stating: "Sentenced to death. Execute immediately." On the basis of this sentence we were to be shot in either of two events: (1) in the event of any camp disorders; and (2) in the event of war. It was the chief of the escort troop assigned to us who let us know about this. He told us: "You've been crossed off the list already."

But Lord be praised, the end came all of a sudden for the forced-labor system. Our special sandy hellhole is being abolished; it is being shifted over to the regular penal camp system. The work regime has been greatly relaxed. They began taking the gratings off the windows and the locks off the doors. Yesterday they took the bucket-latrines out of the barracks and left the doors unlocked all night. They have promised to pay for compulsory labor at half the scale. The death camps are passing into oblivion. . . . Moscow Radio reported the execution of Minister of State Security Abakumov. This news stirred feelings of profound gratitude toward the government in the hearts of every prisoner—for punishing crimes against humanity and decency.

A Humorous Incident Recalled (Concerning the Pope)

One of our comrades in the labor camp was a cheerful fellow who had been sentenced for no reason at all to twenty-five years. He appealed his case to every possible authoritative body and received one and the same reply from all: "Justly convicted."

There was nowhere left to appeal; so he wrote a letter to the Pope in Rome. To this letter he attached a note addressed

---

58. Osoboe Soveshchanie (Special Board), a form of "court," or of meting out penalties without benefit of lawyers or witnesses or being open to the public, or any similar "formality."

to the chairman of the Soviet Red Cross, explaining why he had been obliged finally to appeal to the head of the Catholic Church. In this note he said the following: "There is an old saying among the Russian people— If you've no one to complain to, complain to the Pope in Rome."

This amusing business took place two weeks ago. Soon after, the order came from Moscow for the immediate release of our petitioner.

He is undoubtedly home now, sincerely thanking his unexpected savior — the Pope. (Of course, his appeal simply happened to coincide with "the thaw.")

Briussov Alley
(Episodes from the Life of Yesenin)

Among the few humorous events and the many sad ones of our life belong my recollections of Sergei Yesenin. These are little-known episodes from the life of this great national poet of Russia. They took place in 1922-24, when he lived in the apartment of Galina Benislavskaya on Briussov Alley in Moscow. They lived in the apartment house "Pravda," in apartment twenty-six, and I lived next to them in apartment twenty-five. As neighbors we often ran into one another. The following episode remains fresh in my memory.

Yesenin came home once in an inebriated state and got into an argument with the coachman who had driven him. The coachman tried to trick him by asking for the fare a second time. ("You have to pay your fare, mister.") Yesenin was not agreeable to paying twice.

Cursing the coachman as a "thieving swindler," and unable to restrain himself, Yesenin struck him across the back with his walking stick. The coachman dealt him an answering blow — a kick in the chest. The poet was thrown headlong from the carriage and went sprawling into a basement window of the adjacent building. The glass in the window frame shattered and the jagged edges cut Yesenin's face and arms. He lay there, over the windowsill, all bloody and showing no signs of life. All this took place before my very eyes. Besides myself, the elevator operator of the apartment house and several other people were standing there.

We ran over to the poet and helped him up. We could see where tears had come to his eyes. Supporting him by the arms we got him, with great difficulty, to the elevator and took him up to the ninth floor.

Galina Benislavskaya answered the door at apartment twenty-six, and when she saw Yesenin, bloody as he was, she bit her lip in fear. Then with her help we laid him on his bed and went our way. A few minutes later the ambulance arrived and took him off to the Sklifasovsky Institute.

A fatal role in Yesenin's destiny was played by his literary enemies, who called him a "kulak poet" and a "fellow traveler." They accused him of drunkenness, hooliganism, and naturalism. These were, for the most part, people who envied his talent. He was subjected to insults and plain slander at literary evenings and debates organized by his enemies. The derogatory term "Yeseninism" came into fashion, which was supposed to designate a mood of "decadence," enfeebled intellectualism, and so forth.

But it wasn't as if Yesenin had nothing but enemies; there were also many friends and devoted admirers of his talent. Many outstanding figures among the artistic intelligentsia regarded him with great affection — Kachalov, Meyerhold, Marienhof, Zinaida Raikh, and others.

Lev Davidovich Trotsky, too, had warm feelings for Yesenin. As for Yesenin's attitude toward Trotsky, that is indicated by the poet's unpublished letter to Lev Davidovich, written during the latter's "honorary" exile in the Caucasus. I memorized several lines from that letter, and they are as follows:

"Dear Lev Davidovich. Life in Russia has become very bad. The swindlers and cheats have taken over completely. . . . They are living high like the czars used to before. Only for us two, you and me, honest Russian people, there is no way to live in Russia. You they are holding in the Caucasus; me, in a basement cell of a police station. . . ."

Trotsky dedicated a eulogy to Yesenin entitled "On the Death of a Poet," which was published in *Pravda*. In terming Yesenin a "clear-voiced squadron leader of the revolution" Lev Davidovich gave a highly favorable assessment of Yesenin's poetic work. [59]

On Tverskaya Street in Moscow there was an old, favorite haunt of Yesenin's where he would go at times when his spirits were low, to get away from his vicious and envious persecutors. This was the celebrated cafe of the literary set, "The Stable of Pegasus." All the true devotees and admirers of Yesenin's talent would gather there. They would come in the hope of seeing the poet or hearing him read from his latest verses.

When Yesenin would appear at the door of the cafe, thunderous clapping would break out in his honor. He would be lifted up bodily and placed on a table in the center of the cafe.

---

59. [The quoted phrase does not seem to be part of Trotsky's eulogy, which appeared in *Pravda* January 19, 1926. A translation is available in *Leon Trotsky on Literature and Art* (Pathfinder Press, 1970), pp. 162-66. The author of these memoirs does not recall accurately Trotsky's theme in the eulogy. Far from implying that Yesenin was a militant spokesman for the revolution, Trotsky emphasized that though Yesenin was not alien to the revolution, he was no revolutionary.]

In front of the listeners and spectators, the unforgettable figure of the Russian poet rose up, full length, in long-waisted coat and sky-blue blouse, with a tasseled sash around his waist, twisted and tied in the village manner.

And when Yesenin would read his verse, his enraptured listeners would weep. Tears glistened, too, in the eyes of the poet. The poetry reading would go on into the early hours of the morning. Bursts of enthusiasm would alternate with moods of melancholy and vice versa, and so it would go without end. Yesenin's listeners would sit there transfixed.

Not many people in those days guessed that at "The Stable of Pegasus" a new pearl of Russian poetry was being polished — the second since Pushkin.

> I want to be stern and silent,
> I study the stars to learn how;
> If I could be a roadside willow,
> Over slumbering Russia I'd bow.
>
> Deep blue May gives a rumble of summer,
> There's no tinkle of latch from the gate;
> A sticky smell wafts from the wormwood
> And the cherry tree sleeps in white cape.
>
> The packed snow crumbles and breaks underfoot,
> The frozen moon shines from on high;
> I see once again the village's edge
> And through snow, in the window, a light.

MEMOIRS OF
ALEKSANDRA CHUMAKOVA
(Participant in the Civil War
in the Tambov Region, 1919-21)

[These memoirs were included on the same samizdat type-script as those of the anonymous Bolshevik-Leninist. They end very abruptly, indicating that they were not completed.

[Although shorter than the anonymous memoirs, Chumakova's account gives an equally accurate outline of the policy differences involved in the struggle between the Left Opposition, the Stalin center, and the Bukharinist right wing, especially on questions of industrialization and collectivization. On the international context of that struggle, Chumakova, like the anonymous memoirist, is weaker — although her observations on the Spanish Civil War and the Nazi invasion of the Soviet Union are very much to the point. As another first-hand account in samizdat of the truth about the Left Opposition, they are of great value. And they are unique in portraying the special difficulties faced by women Oppositionists, in their own words.

[Chumakova also describes the harsh conditions faced by industrial workers in 1932 and the continued influence of the Left Opposition among them even then. Her account of the May Day 1932 textile workers' demonstration belies the arguments of those who say the Left Opposition was only supported by students and intellectuals. The picture of life among Moscow Oppositionists that emerges is also of great interest.

[The translation is by the editor.]

The Glukhovka Textile Mill (1932)

The Glukhovo plant was the oldest textile mill in Russia. The regular year-round labor force there consisted of several thousand working men and women.

Before the revolution the plant, nicknamed Glukhovka, was famous throughout the land for the revolutionary spirit of its workers, whose working conditions were very bad. In October

1917 the workers of Glukhovka were in the front ranks of those who fought for Soviet power in the town of Bogorodsk, now called Noginsk. Fifteen years had gone by since then but there had been little change in the living conditions at the factory. The old familiar pattern of poverty and gradual exhaustion of the workers was still there.

Here is what happened at Glukhovka in 1932:

That year I was serving as a party worker in the Moscow Committee of the Russian Communist Party. The secretary of the committee was Lazar Kaganovich, who had been assigned to inform the Politbureau about the food situation for the working class in Moscow and the Moscow area.

Kaganovich knew very little about the food situation at the Glukhovka factory. His assistants, Krymsky and Malenkov, knew no more than he. They never went to the factory and their information came from the data provided by the secretary of the factory party committee, which were not very objective.

In reality the dark shadow of starvation hung over the Glukhovka factory. Therefore the decision was made to send a Moscow Committee worker to Glukhovka for an objective investigation of the food situation. The choice fell on me.

When I arrived at the factory I was immediately struck by the horrifying unrelieved poverty of the workers. Gaunt from hunger, they were barely able to get to work and stand up at their machines for the allotted eight hours. Through the streets of the factory settlement wandered the starving, emaciated children of the workers. They gathered around the garbage cans of the factory dining hall and waited for something edible to be thrown out. The textile workers would call their children into the dining halls and share with them the one bowl of soup allowed each worker per day. In the barracks where the workers lived it was crowded and filthy. The workers had inherited these barracks from the former factory owner. There were none of the comforts of home in these barracks. Curtains were hung up to screen one family off from the next. Fifteen years had passed since the conquest of Soviet power (1917-1932) but the living conditions of the workers remained as of old.

Besides the barracks there were also some small houses on the factory grounds; these had been built by the former owner for older workers and for those with large families. In one of these small houses I made the acquaintance of a family of hereditary textile workers.

The head of this household was Nikolai Kolomenkin, a

mechanic at the factory.[60] Sharing his household was his mother, an elderly textile worker who had worked in the factory for forty years. Other than a homemade bed that the whole family slept on and an old table with two benches, there was no furniture. The grown-ups' clothing was old and worn-out, and the children wore the hand-me-downs of their elders. Their school attendance was irregular because of the lack of warm clothing and footwear.

Nikolai Kolomenkin was thirty but he looked like a sick, old man. He was considered the best worker at the factory but earned very little. Wage rates had fallen drastically at the factory in the preceding few years and production norms had risen. All this led to the exhaustion of the workers and the ruining of their physical condition.

Kolomenkin was a Communist. He called himself a Bolshevik-Leninist. He asked me about Lenin's testament and was interested in party matters. He had nothing good to say about Stalin, considering him a bad sort. As I came to find out, the Glukhovka workers had no respect for Stalin. During the 1932 May Day demonstration they had carried portraits of Lenin and Trotsky through the streets of the settlement and had shouted angry phrases against Stalin.

Soon after that, new arrests began at the factory. Many of Kolomenkin's comrades, worker-Communists, were already in prison. What saved Kolemenkin from prison was his children and old mother. "If he is arrested, the whole family will die of starvation," his mother pleaded.

What I had seen at the factory caused me alarm. I could not remain indifferent to the terrible human suffering that this work force of many thousands was experiencing. Immediate government relief was needed — food, clothing, household goods, and other necessities.

I drafted a rough copy of a report to Kaganovich and showed it to several Old Bolsheviks at the factory. They approved the draft of my report and saw a ray of hope that the workers might be saved.

I knew that my proposals would meet with opposition from

---

60. Nikolai Kolomenkin was a worker Communist who was arrested in 1932 as a "Trotskyist-Oppositionist" and imprisoned at the Verkhne-Uralsk isolation prison for political offenders. His subsequent fate is unknown to me.

Krymsky and Malenkov. Even before my trip to Glukhovka they had been weighing a plan to create a secondary industry at the factory. But such a plan could not give the workers immediate, effective relief. It would take two or three years for its results to be felt. And the workers needed immediate assistance in the form of food.

I earnestly hoped that Kaganovich would respond in a positive way to my proposals and make the matter known to the Politbureau. But my report, addressed to Kaganovich, was not destined to arrive where it was intended. On the day of my return to Moscow from Glukhovka, my husband, a Communist, was arrested. During the search of our apartment, the Chekists confiscated, among other things, my report to Kaganovich on the situation at the Glukhovka factory. The report proved distasteful to someone and because of it I was soon removed from my job in the Moscow Committee apparatus.

We Communists of the first decade after October did not delude ourselves with rosy hopes for an immediate, substantial rise in the workers' standard of living. In the wake of the world war of 1914-17 and the civil war of 1918-22, the economy we inherited from the capitalists and landlords of defeated czarism was in ruins, with the NEPmen in the city and the kulaks in the countryside working against its restoration. The party saw the salvation of the working class and of workers' power in speeding up the industrialization of the country.

We could not conceive of a successful advance in the effort to industrialize the country at the appropriate rate without a minimal improvement in the life of the workers and the preservation of the cadres of revolutionary workers.

For that reason thoughtful working class members of the party like Kolomenkin placed a fundamental emphasis on extracting the resources for industrialization from the urban NEPman bourgeoisie and the well-to-do rural kulak layers by imposing harsh taxes on them and even going so far as to confiscate their plundered wealth.

Those views and demands of the conscious vanguard workers were reflected in the ranks of the party by the Communists who advocated fulfillment of Lenin's testament.

The testament dealt not only with the question of removing the careerist and intriguer Stalin from leadership in the Central Committee as its general secretary, but together with Lenin's last letters and articles it constituted a fundamental program for the economic reconstruction of the country (see Lenin's letters and articles entitled "On Cooperation," "On the Workers' and Peasants' Inspection," "On 'Autonomization' and the National Question," and others).

The removal of Stalin from leadership in the party and state as someone who had gathered "enormous power" in his hands and was capable of misusing it to the detriment of the working class and the Communist Party, this was not a "trifle" to Lenin, as he said in his testament.

Stalin, basing himself on the all-powerful state and party officials, and making use of his "enormous power," schemed and intrigued, taking over Lenin's and Trotsky's views and proposals as his own. And so that these would look original, he added a little contribution of his own, primarily as regards the time when they should be implemented. It was as if to say, "When Lenin or his supporters (Trotsky and others) proposed certain plans or timetables for industrialization, their timing was wrong, but when I, Stalin, propose them, the timing is right."

And all along, the timing of our industrialization, the sources used for it, and the rates at which it proceeded determined the main lines of development in the life of our country and in the subsequent battles with world capitalism and domestic capitalist forces.

Does not the limited and backward character of our technology and defense equipment at the time of the Spanish Civil War and later, on the eve of the war with fascist Germany, serve as confirmation of this? After all, would fascist Germany have dared to attack us if we had demonstrated our might in Spain?

It was not accidental that the working class of our Soviet land, having been oriented by the great Lenin toward the accomplishment of the world revolution, instinctively opposed the anti-Leninist intrigues and activities of Stalin.

Stalin called the supporters of Lenin's testament "superindustrializers." He claimed that they advocated breaking the alliance of workers and peasants. They "underestimated" the peasantry. This was so-called "Trotskyism" — the so-called "substitution of Trotskyism for Leninism."

But essentially he equated the peasantry with the kulak. Stalin was supported by those whom he later accused of following the policy of "letting the kulaks grow over into socialism" (Rykov, Tomsky, and others). To a certain extent that fit in with Stalin's ambitious designs. They helped him gloss over and put off resolving the most pressing problems — industrialization and an improvement in the material conditions of the working class that would inevitably have accompanied industrialization.

The time that was thus lost made itself felt throughout the country in those years in the form of universal discontent within the working class. And so it was at the Glukhovo mill as well.

In my report to Kaganovich the minimal possible measures so vitally necessary to improve the workers' conditions were indicated. BUT. . . .

In an OGPU Trap (1932)

Late on the night of September 2, 1932, someone knocked on our door. My husband's call of "Who's there?" was answered by the superintendent of the building. My husband and I thought that the super was probably having family troubles, and so we trustingly opened the door.

Instead of the super, in the corridor we found several armed Chekists, who quickly entered our room. They suggested that my husband get back in bed and not move. One of the Chekists — in plain clothes — showed my husband the search warrant and the warrant for his arrest. The warrant was signed by the chairman of the OGPU, Yagoda. Then a search of the apartment began, which lasted all night. Only after the search were my husband and I able to get up and get dressed.

We were warned that an OGPU control point was being set up in our apartment. No one was allowed to go out and everyone who came to visit us was detained. Clearly the Chekists knew something about my husband and were expecting someone at our apartment. Some agent in the pay of the OGPU, some provocateur, had wormed his way into the circle of my husband's friends and had reported everything about him to the OGPU.

My husband and his friends were Communists. They called themselves Bolshevik-Leninists. They were totally involved in party life, and were deeply concerned for its fate. They spoke out quite openly at party meetings, and it never occurred to anyone that they might be persecuted by the OGPU. They were honest and principled Communists.

At eleven in the morning, my friend Lina Neiman came to see me. A Communist, she had graduated from Moscow University that year and was being sent abroad on an assignment by the Central Committee of the party. Lina had come to say goodbye to me and unexpectedly fell into the OGPU trap. After she had come in and closed the door behind her, the Chekists rushed at her with cries of "Hands up! This is an OGPU control point!"

Lina shuddered with fright and raised her hands. She was searched and her diploma showing that she had graduated from the department of Soviet law at Moscow State University and her passport for travel abroad were both confiscated. Now her trip would never be, and her personal happiness was threatened with grave danger. Crushed and miserable, Lina began to sob.

That evening another friend of mine, also a party member, came to call—Dusya Lebedeva. The Chekists surrounded her at once and took her off into the telephone room. Dusya blabbed freely with them, in a thoughtless way, and, as it turned out, her loose tongue caused her to betray her own friends.

During the three days that the control point was maintained, many different people came to our apartment, upwards of fifty in all. They all had "Hands up!" yelled at them, were searched, and then were placed in various rooms. Some were in the kitchen, some in the bathroom, and some simply in the hallway. The apartment in general was turned into a temporary prison.

Our neighbor Kozharinova, a Young Communist, was allowed to go to the store for groceries. She bought bread and milk not only for the tenants of the apartment but also for all those being detained. She was escorted by a Cheka guard.

Our telephone was also placed under arrest. Whenever it would ring, a Chekist would rush over and answer it, yelling into the mouthpiece: "Yes, yes, he's home. He's taking a bath. Come on over, he'll be out right away." The Chekists were trying to lure all of my husband's friends into their trap. Two of his closest friends fell into this trap—the Communist students Filippov and Abaturov. The search of their persons disclosed Opposition literature, including a letter written by Trotsky from abroad, and addressed to the Russian Communist Opposition.

On the third day of the control point's existence, another close comrade of my husband's, the journalist Kolya Vlasov, was supposed to come see us. My husband was very worried for him, fearing that he too would fall into this trap. But Vlasov did not come, and we breathed a sigh of relief.

After Filippov and Abaturov had been detained, the Chekists phoned in to the Lubyanka. Soon, Senior Investigator Bogen arrived from OGPU headquarters. He was considered the terror of the Trotskyist Opposition. Bogen ordered those under arrest to get dressed and come with him to Butyrka prison.

There was a wave of searches and arrests in Moscow at that time. Many of our friends were taking leave of Moscow forever. Along with my husband, they took Filippov, Abaturov, and my loose-tongued friend Dusya Lebedeva off to prison.

As the last Chekist was leaving our apartment, his way was blocked by those who remained, both those who lived there and those who had been detained. "And what about us," they asked. "Can we go free? Or are you taking us to prison too?" The Chekist answered that they were free. . . . They all fell on their knees with joy and, as with one voice, cried out to him in gratitude, "Thank you, thank you!" All of these people were in the grip of fear, which made them forget their own human dignity and fall down upon their knees.

Two weeks later I learned that Dusya Lebedeva had gone out of her mind in Butyrka prison and that a friend of my husband's, Lazar Ionov, a Moscow University student, had hanged himself with a towel.

How I Was Expelled from the Party (1932)

The arrest of my husband tore the veil of illusion from my eyes. I began to look at the world around me in a new way and understood that I had been deceived by the official press reports on the events of the preceding years. I no longer believed in the infallibility of Stalin or in the so-called treason of the Old Bolsheviks who had "sold themselves to the world bourgeoisie." These lies had a preplanned and bloody purpose to them.

They were arresting the Russian and Jewish intelligentsia, which had borne the burden of the October Revolution and civil war upon its shoulders. The national bias behind these bloody acts of repression was tantamount to a conspiracy against the Russian and Jewish peoples. . . . That's how the situation looked to me even then, at the beginning of the thirties.

After my husband had been taken off to prison, I began to feel as if I was living in a kind of lethargic dream world. Hour after hour I would wander aimlessly through the streets of Moscow. Thus I came, by chance, to the gates of the OGPU inner prison at Lubyanka Square and there I stopped as though bewitched. I had the notion that the gates might open and I might see my husband. I had come up quite close to the gates when suddenly I heard a shout, "No standing here!"

A strange-looking man came walking up to me, looking me very sharply in the eye. I realized that a Chekist, an outside guard of the OGPU prison, stood before me. I turned away from the prison gates and headed off down the sidewalk in the direction of the China Wall. Looking around, I saw the agent, still watching me carefully. I went home late that evening.

My mother informed me that Krymsky of the Moscow Party Committee had called. He had inquired of her about my material situation. Then he had asked about my mood after the arrest of my husband. This was not a display of friendly concern about my fate. No, it was a bit of sly scouting.

My material situation was not good. My husband and I had never saved up for a rainy day; we hadn't expected one to come along. But it had, and it caught me without any means to fall back on. In order to afford food packages for my husband, I had to borrow from the neighbors.

I had to hunt for my husband through all the prisons of Moscow, and everywhere I received the same answer, "No one by that name here." Where was he? I wondered. Surely they wouldn't have shot him. Uncertainty about my husband's fate left me completely prostrate..

At that time, the journalist Kolya Vlasov came to visit me. It was strange to see him free when all his cothinkers were in prison. I was not cheered by his visit, but put on guard. There was something unclean about him that I hadn't noticed before. He did not have a word of sympathy about the arrest of my husband or of his two friends. He was indifferent to their fate. I suddenly realized who he was. Doubting his honesty and sincerity, I had little to say and answered his questions coldly and reluctantly.

Nevertheless, I fell into the snare he had laid for me. He offered me his "services": he would draft a letter of appeal to Kaganovich which I would sign. This later served as the pretext for my arrest. I agreed, not realizing the insidiousness of the offer. This letter, written by Vlasov's hand, is still filed, today, in the dossier on my case. Because of this letter I spent twenty-three years in prison and still have many years to go.

Several days after Vlasov's visit, I was called in to the Moscow Committee. There they told me that a general membership meeting would be held, at which the question of my expulsion from the party would be raised. They would not let me attend the meeting. I stood outside the door and awaited the decision.

Everything that I heard then, through that door, has stayed with me ever since.

Krymsky (section head in the Moscow Committee and secretary of the party cell there): "Expulsion from the party is applicable in her case. This meeting should vote to expel her."

Katya Ashkenadze (head of the women's section of the Moscow Committee): "I know her as a devoted Communist with a high level of theoretical understanding. She was an active participant in the civil war in the Tambov region. We cannot expel her from the party."

Pesina (instructor at the Moscow Committee offices): "Her behavior always struck me as suspicious."

Others: "There is no need to be hasty about expulsions from the party. The case should be looked over carefully first. What does it have to do with the wife, if the husband is arrested? We already had one mistake with Ryutin's wife. . . ."

The general membership meeting voted by a majority against Krymsky's motion to expel me from the party. This infuriated him and he reopened the question, bringing his motion up for a vote a second time, darkly warning the party members this time that I was sure to be arrested in the next few days and if a party card was found in my possession when I was arrested the entire Moscow Committee organization would be punished as a result.

This "background information" quickly sobered everybody up. No one defended me any more. They all silently raised their hands in favor of expulsion.

Only three days went by before I was visited late at night by an unknown woman in a leather coat, accompanied by two soldiers. She showed me the warrant for my arrest and for a search of the apartment.

My mother was with me in the apartment. She fainted from fear. I wanted to help her, but the Chekist shouted at me rudely and forbade me to move. With cold and hostile eyes she looked at us as though we were enemies. She could afford to be indifferent to us. Our fates were sealed.

When the search was completed she rudely ordered me to get dressed. Mama began sobbing and crying out, "What for? My daughter fought for the *revolution. She's a true Communist!*" But my mother's words had no effect on the Chekist. They took hold of me on all sides, propelled me out of the room and into the hallway, then out to the street, put me in a car, and in a minute I was in the inner prison at Lubyanka.

When they transferred me from there to Butyrka, where, at that time, there were nothing but Communists, I first learned of the death of Stalin's wife, Allilueva.

The investigation into my "case" did not last long. The Stalinist satraps quickly arranged an "assignment" for me — three years enforced residence at Samara.

I accepted this as a blow of fate, thinking to myself that it was an "error stemming from our time of troubles."

* * *

I returned to Moscow from Samara in the autumn of 1935. My first exile had seemed to go on forever. I had not been guilty of anything, and therefore I spent those three years hoping to return to Moscow and be restored to the ranks of the party.

Then, there I was in Moscow, sitting in Krymsky's office and saying something like this to him, "You made a mistake in expelling me. That mistake has to be corrected now."

Krymsky looked at me, his eyes shifting. He studied the changes that had taken place in my appearance during those three years. Seeing the gray hairs in my head, he said in a grave and pompous way, "You have grown gray from your sufferings. You will never forgive us for that. We are alien to you now and you to us."

I took my leave, and on the way home I wondered, "Could he be right? Am I now alien to the party?"

But an inner voice whispered to me, "No. The Krymskys are one thing, but the party is another. He is a party bureaucrat who has lost all sense of honor and party consciousness. His important post and personal power have gone to his head. He has lost touch with the people. I will keep fighting to be readmitted to the party."

Arriving home, I found a notice from the police on the table. I had twenty-four hours to leave Moscow. I understood that this was Krymsky's work. He was driving me out of the capital.

With no regrets I moved to a place 101 kilometers from Moscow. Three months later I was rearrested and taken once again to Butyrka prison. On this occasion I was very ill and was placed in the prison hospital. From the hospital I was sent to a cell holding fifty women. That year the prison cells were full to overflowing. The metal cots were there no longer. In their place, double-decker wooden bunks had been installed, and on them the women — all Communists or Young Communists — lay side by side, in rows. In these frightfully crowded and suffocating conditions we slept, jammed against one another. You had to make an announcement in order to turn over. As I was to learn, all of us in that cell had previously been working at jobs in Moscow or studying at schools in the capital.

Anya Khromova (1936)

One day a young schoolgirl who had been arrested was brought into our cell. Her face was the small, sweet face of a child and her hair was held back in two short braids. She was fifteen, and her name was Anya Khromova. For a long time she watched and listened to us carefully without entering into the conversation. But when she had gotten to know us, she told us the story of her life.

Anya had no father, and her mother worked as a conductor on long-distance trains and was nearly always away from home. Anya spent her vacation before her last year of school on a collective farm, where she lived with her grandmother and grandfather. Life on the kolkhoz was very hard that year. The kolkhoz members were being paid next to nothing for their work days, and the peasants were starving and dying from hunger. Her grandmother and grandfather were also suffering from lack of food and had fallen seriously ill.

Previously in that village — the old folks told Anya — there had been plenty of everything. Life had been busy and joyful. But now, all of a sudden, everything had gone bad, as though a terrible plague had struck. No songs were to be heard, nor young maids' laughter. It was like a cemetery around there. All the young people had moved to the city. Only children and old people remained in the village.

Upon returning to Moscow after her stay at the collective farm, Anya wrote a letter to Stalin in verses that described the miserable life in the collectivized village of Russia.

Anya hoped that Stalin would aid the starving kolkhoz and save her grandmother and grandfather from death by starvation. But she was mistaken. Her verse letter was not to Stalin's liking, and he ordered the OGPU to call Anya to account severely.

Soon the dread figure of an OGPU investigator arrived at her school and began an investigation. The director of the school, the teachers, the maintenance people, and even some of the students were all questioned. All those who were questioned liked Anya very much and spoke of her with affection. She was a very intelligent and talented young woman. She was an attentive observer of natural phenomena and of human life and she put down what she saw in vivid images, embodied in both prose and poetry.

No one had anything bad to say about her. They all spoke well of her. But the OGPU investigator was a crusty sort. He found it hard to accept favorable testimony about anyone. He did not believe the testimony of the people at the school. He had his own professional opinion, worked out over many years as an investigator and based on suspicion and mistrust of people. He was certain that the verse letter to Stalin about the collective farms had not been written by Anya but by someone else who was hiding behind the skirts of a schoolgirl. He arrested Anya and took her off to jail, straight from school. The entire school wept, bidding Anya Khromova farewell. But even as she sat, huddled in a corner of the car, she was already whispering new verses to herself.

A few days later Anya was called for questioning. The investigator had decided to expose her "alleged literary talent" and to make her tell the name of the real authors of the letter to Stalin. He felt certain that the author of the letter was some hardened enemy of Soviet power, one who was not going to get away.

When Anya was brought into his office, he gave her pen and paper and proposed that she create a literary work in verse about the women with whom she shared her cell.

The investigator left the room, saying he would return in two hours. Left to herself, Anya fell into thought. She began to call to mind the faces of her bunkmates and selected the most striking images to show how their life in prison had become one of unbearable suffering and torment. Among those sharing our cell at that time were the following:

1. Masha Joffe, daughter of the famous Soviet diplomat, A. A. Joffe.

2. Elena Barbina, wife of an official in the Moscow Soviet.

3. A large group of Young Communist women guides at the Gorky Park for Rest and Recreation, who were accused of wishing to emigrate to England. (That summer the British writer George Bernard Shaw had visited Moscow.)

4. Kabakova, wife of the first secretary of the Sverdlovsk Regional Committee of the party.

After two hours the investigator came back and took the

filled-in sheets of paper from Anya. With great irritation, but with eager absorption as well, he pored over the rhythmic phrases of her marvelous poetry. He was overcome with anger, irritation, and chagrin. There in his hands he held a literary work of talent, from whose pages the voice of anguished womanhood cried out, calling for help to the innocent arrested women whose lives were being destroyed in prison.

With great poetic power Anya described one of her bunkmates in prison who had been taken away from her own nursing child by the Chekists when they arrested her. Her breasts became painfully swollen from the sudden interruption in nursing, and the inflamed nipples cracked and bled. The unfortunate mother tossed and turned on her bunk, groaning and cursing her fate as a woman and mother.

The investigator no longer had any doubts. He had tested Anya Khromova's literary talent. He no longer suspected someone else of having written the letter to Stalin. Her fate was now sealed. She was sentenced to penal exile in Siberia. In parting she asked us, "Is it true that Dostoevsky and Ryleev spent time in prison?" We told her it was true. "Then," she said, "I no longer fear for my future."

After the prison gates had closed behind her, it was a long time before any of us could speak. Subdued by what had happened we held our tongues. But in our thoughts we all marveled at this amazing young woman, marked by the hand of fate, and gifted with the mind and talent of a poet. Anya had the soul of an artist. The spark of inspiration burned in her. "Unless Siberia extinguishes that spark, the Russian people will yet hear from another inspired lyric voice." Such were our thoughts.

But where is she now?

Nadezhda Kamenskaya (1932-41)

Today is the day of Faith and Hope. These names are dear to humanity because everyone has faith in or hope for something. Without faith or hope this life on earth would be colorless, bereft of spirit or light. Today I recall a woman who had the modest gaze of a madonna. Her name was Nadezhda (Hope).

I am speaking of our dear Nadezhda Petrovna Kamenskaya. If fate were to fling open the door to freedom for me, I would find Nadezhda Kamenskaya and fall at her feet. She was my woe-ridden mother's dearest friend. When my husband and I were arrested, our neighbors on Malaya Bronnaya Street all suddenly turned their backs on us. They heaped a mountain of lies on us for my mother to hear, which intensified my mother's misery more than ever. Nadezhda Petrovna was the only one who did not believe these fairy tales in which we were depicted as having committed "crimes against the state." She continued to be friendly toward us as she had been for years and she lent my mother a helping hand.

Through the long years of our imprisonment she gave mother both moral and material support. Nadezhda Petrovna Kamenskaya had a noble heart and a pure sense of decency.

Lilya Kostina (1949)

Today is the anniversary of the day my husband was arrested. (How many such anniversaries there have been! And all because of his "sins" of the 1920s.) (This took place in Vorotynsk in September 1949.)

Beginning a search of our apartment, an MGB major asked my husband, "Have you got any guns?"

"No," answered my husband, "I have no gun."

"And if we find one, what then?" retorted the major.

"You can't find what isn't there," my husband answered.

The MGB man took all the documents belonging to my husband, including even an old notebook from his student days in the twenties. My husband's protests were answered by the major's coldly meaningful remark, "You won't be needing this any more." The threatening tone of his words was plain to hear.

Then came the moment of parting. I couldn't bear it and broke down in sobs. After my husband had been taken off, it was as silent in the house as if someone had died. Thrown across the bed were my husband's greatcoat and belt, which they would not let him take with him.

When I had come here I had hoped to find a quiet harbor from the storms of life. But now the moorings had been severed and nothing but endless torment and suffering lay ahead. How could I go on?

Oh, my dear country. When will you be freed from torment? When will you take your destiny into your own hands?

I recalled the words of the poet:

> The people groaned in misery
> And the land awaited someone's coming.

I was terribly afraid they might kill my husband while he

was in Kaluga prison. This thought kept nagging me and gave me no rest.

Outside an autumn rain was falling and spattered against the windowpanes. Dusk crept up unnoticed. The room grew cold and somehow strange. Suddenly someone knocked on the door. I shuddered. "Is it friend or foe?" I wondered. When I opened the door, I found a young woman wrapped in a shawl. She whispered in a low voice, "It's me, Lilya."

At once my heart felt lighter. It was our dear Lilya Kostina, a Vorotynsk teacher. She had come to me, heeding the call of her heart, letting nothing stand in her way, neither the lateness of the hour nor the rain nor the consequences she risked in visiting me, the wife of an "enemy of the people."

Like a true friend Lilya had come to help ease my suffering with a kind word. She told me that the Vorotynsk collective farmers would come to my husband's defense because he had done them so much good. His work as a teacher and in reforestation would never be forgotten in Vorotynsk. Twice he had fought for his country, in the civil war and in the Great Patriotic War. He had been wounded and suffered shellshock. These are things that must never be forgotten. That is what Lilya Kostina said.

These warm, kind words about my unfortunate husband were like balm on the wounds inflicted on my soul in moments of trouble. Lilya Kostina was a noble person. She had a kind heart and a courageous spirit. She did not turn her back on me in time of need, and she scorned the "general opinion" that the cowards and scoundrels were trying to create about me.

Lilya's behavior deserves to be described as a model of courage and sensibilities worthy of Soviet people; when fear reigned all around, she found a way to help another human being with a kind word.

And how pitiful and petty by comparison the character of our good "friend" Vasily Ivanovich Soprokin seems. He was the director of the Vorotynsk secondary school, who after the arrest of my husband (who he had told everyone was his "best friend"), was afraid even to greet me on the street.

Before 1917 he had lived in the village of Kumovskoe in the Babynin region of Kaluga oblast. He had been a kulak and village notable, owning woodland, meadowland, croplands, brick buildings, and racehorses. He was a coward and an adventurist. Through lies and slanders and running down other people he had worked his way into the confidence of the Stalinist MGB.

People like this were avoided like the plague by those un-forgettable people, so dear to us, like Elena Konstantinovna Kostina, to whom we pay all due respects.

Lieutenant Colonel Kalyabin (1949)

After my husband was arrested in 1949 I went to Kaluga to see Lieutenant Colonel Kalyabin. At that time he held the post of head of the investigation department of the Kaluga MGB.

I told him that my life at Vorotynsk had become unbearable after my husband's arrest. They would not let me leave the town but would not give me a job there either. "Remove the stigma of an ex-convict from me or else arrest me again," I told him, in my state of depression and desperation.

"Clear your record I cannot do," he answered with a feigned smile; "as for arresting you, there's no reason to . . . for now."

Only three days had passed after this conversation with Kalyabin when, late at night, an MGB major from Kaluga came for me in a car. Pulling the warrant for my arrest out of his overcoat pocket he smiled at me like Kalyabin had and said in his repulsive way: "Didn't you ask to be arrested?"

Thus by Kalyabin's evil whim, I once again found myself in exile (this time in Siberia) for no other "crime" than having been married to my husband. Moreover, Kalyabin knew very well that my husband and I had had the chance to live to-gether for only four years, the remaining sixteen years of our marriage we had spent apart, thanks to the efforts of the Kalya-bins of all kinds. . . .

TROTSKYISTS AT VORKUTA
An Eyewitness Report
by M.B.

[News about the fate of the Left Oppositionists in and after the mass purges of 1936-38 began to trickle out of the Soviet Union after Stalin's death. The following article, signed only "M. B.," appeared in the October-November 1961 issue of the emigre publication of the Russian Mensheviks, *Sotsialistichesky vestnik* (Socialist Messenger), formerly based in New York and now defunct.

[The article was translated and printed in the Summer 1963 *International Socialist Review* and is reprinted by permission.]

During the middle and at the end of the 1930s, the Trotskyists formed a quite disparate group at Vorkuta; one part of them kept its old name of "Bolshevik-Leninists." There were almost 500 at the mine, close to 1,000 at the camp of Ukhta-Pechora, and certainly several thousands altogether around the Pechora district.

The Orthodox Trotskyists were determined to remain faithful to the end to their platform and their leaders. In 1927, following the resolutions of the fifteenth congress of the party, they were excluded from the Communist Party and, at the same time, arrested. From then on, even though they were in prison, they continued to consider themselves Communists; as for Stalin and his supporters, "the apparatus men," they were characterized as renegades from communism.

Among these "Trotskyists" were also found people who had never formally belonged to the CP and did not join the Left Opposition, but who tied their own fate with it to the very end — even when the struggle of the Opposition was most acute.

In addition to these genuine Trotskyists, there were in the camps of Vorkuta and elsewhere more than 100,000 prisoners who, members of the party and the youth, had adhered to the Trotskyist Opposition and then at different times and for diverse reasons (of which the principal were, evidently, repressions, unemployment, persecutions, exclusion from schools and university facilities, etc.) were forced to "recant their errors" and withdraw from the Opposition.

206

The Orthodox Trotskyists arrived at the mine during the summer of 1936 and lived in a compact mass in two large barracks. They categorically refused to work in the pits; they worked only on the surface, and for only eight hours, not the ten or twelve required by the regulations, as the other prisoners were forced to do. They did so on their own authority, in an organized manner, openly flouting the camp regulations. In the main they had already served nearly ten years in deportation.

In the beginning, they were sent into political isolators and then afterwards exiled to Solovka; finally, they arrived at Vorkuta. The Trotskyists formed the only group of political prisoners who openly criticized the Stalinist "general line" and offered organized resistance to the jailers.

Nevertheless, there were significant divergences within this group. Some considered themselves disciples of Timothy Sapronov (ex-secretary of the Supreme Soviet) and insisted on being called "Sapronovists" or "Democratic Centralists." They claimed to be more to the left than the Trotskyists and thought that the Stalinist dictatorship had already reached the stage of bourgeois degeneration by the end of the 1920s, and that the rapprochement of Hitler and Stalin was very probable. Nevertheless, in the event of war, the "Sapronovists" declared themselves for the defense of the USSR.

Among the "Trotskyists" were also found partisans of the "Right Wing," that is to say of Rykov and of Bukharin, as well as followers of Shliapnikov and of his "Workers' Opposition" platform.

But the great majority of the group was made up of authentic Trotskyists, supporters of L. D. Trotsky. They openly defended the so-called Clemenceau thesis: "the enemy is in our country. It is first necessary to get rid of the reactionary government of Stalin and only after that to organize the defense of the country against external enemies."[61]

61. [The author of the article distorts Trotskyist thought on this question. The "Clemenceau thesis" enunciated in 1926-27, when the Opposition was still in the Bolshevik Party, meant that they did not renounce the struggle to change the line of the party and the state in time of war. In an article dated September 25, 1939, anticipating the war between the USSR and Nazism, Trotsky wrote: "While arms in hand they deal blows to Hitler, the Bolshevik-Leninists will at the same time conduct revolutionary propaganda against

In spite of their differences, all of these groups at the mine
lived in a friendly enough fashion under one common denominator, "the Trotskyists." Their leaders were Socrates Gevorkian, Vladimir Ivanov, Melnais, V. V. Kossior and Trotsky's ex-secretary, Poznansky.

Gevorkian was a calm man, very balanced, reasonable, full
of good sense. He spoke without hurry, weighing his words,
without any affectation or theatrical gestures. Up to the time
of his arrest, he had worked as an expert for the Russian
Association of the Centers of Scientific Research of the Institute
of Human Sciences. He was an Armenian, and, at this time,
was at least forty. His younger brother was imprisoned with
him.

Melnais, a Lett, was a little younger than Gevorkian. After
having been a member of the Central Committee of the Young
Communists, he studied at the Faculty of Physics and Mathematics of the University of Moscow, where, in 1925-27, he
headed a very important group (several hundred people) of
Opposition students. At university meetings, when Melnais in-
tervened, the Stalinists stirred up a storm of hues and cries,
preventing him from speaking. But obstinately, doggedly, Melnais waited; when the howlers were out of breath, exhausted
and silent, the chairman of the meeting rang the bell and told
him, "Your time is up!"

Melnais replied, "Excuse me, that was your time. You have
conducted yourselves like devils and you have screamed; I
have been silent. Now, it is my turn to speak." He then spoke
to the audience.

At the end of 1927, Melnais was one of the first members
of the Opposition at the university to be arrested. His arrest
provoked an explosion of indignation among the students.
The revolting details of the arrest were repeated in the corridors and classrooms of the university. Melnais was married
and lived in a private apartment. His wife, also a student,
was pregnant. During the night, her labor pains started. Having phoned for an ambulance, Melnais nervously paced to
and fro in the apartment, waiting for the doctor. Hearing
the doorbell ring, he eagerly opened the door and let in three
people dressed in civilian clothes. "This way please, my wife
is really in pain," he said, showing the way.

Stalin, preparing his overthrow at the next and perhaps very near
stage" (see "The USSR in War," in Trotsky's *In Defense of Marxism*
[Pathfinder Press, 1973]).]

"Just one minute!" one of the men stopped him. "For the moment we are not interested in your wife, but in you," and he showed him a warrant for his arrest. The doctor and ambulance men arrived very soon; Melnais's wife was taken to the hospital . . . and he to the Lubyanka prison.

Melnais had been imprisoned ever since. In political isolators and in exile, he spent a lot of time working on economic problems and soon turned out to be an eminent and talented economist.

Vladimir Ivanov was a hearty man, with the round and full face of a successful merchant, with a big black mustache and intelligent grey eyes. In spite of his fifty years, one sensed in him a strong will and the strength of a bear. An Old Bolshevik and member of the Central Committee, Ivanov, until his arrest, directed the Chinese Eastern Railroad. He, as well as his wife, had belonged to the "Democratic Centralist" group and were among the supporters of Sapronov. When the fifteenth congress decided that belonging to the Opposition and to the party was incompatible, Ivanov quit the ranks of the Opposition, but this did not save him; he was arrested after the assassination of Kirov.

At the camp, he was in charge of the narrow railroad that linked the mine of Vorkuta to the Usa River. In 1936, following directives from headquarters, the NKVD of the camp concocted a charge accusing Ivanov of sabotage of this laughingstock of a railroad, sixty kilometers long. A special jury of the high tribunal of the Autonomous Soviet Republic of Komi came to the camp. In secret session, after having read the indictment, they said to Ivanov: "What can you say to justify yourself?"

"You have your orders," he replied. "You are assigned to carry out all the necessary formalities and to enforce them in a cowardly way with the death penalty. You are forced to do this. You know as well as I that these accusations are manufactured from whole cloth, and have been prepared by compliant Stalinist police functionaries. So, don't complicate your job; do your business. As for me, I refuse to participate in your juridicial comedy." Then he said, pointing a finger at three false witnesses taken from among the common criminals: "Why don't you ask them? In return for a package of *makhorka* [tobacco] they will not only tell you that I am a saboteur, but also a cousin of the Mikado."

The tribunal could get no more out of him; they could only interrogate the handpicked "witnesses." The examination at the hearing was cut short. On the other hand, the deliberation of the jury lasted a very long time. First a telephone call, then a long wait for the answer, and finally, the sentence was pronounced: "Deserves the highest penalty; but taking into account this . . . and that . . . sentence is commuted to ten years' imprisonment at hard labor." And with shifting eyes, not daring to look at Ivanov, the members of the jury quickly collected their papers and departed trembling. The false witnesses approached Ivanov, seeking to justify themselves. "Get out of my way, you dirty swine!" he roared, and returned to his barracks.

Kossior was a middle-aged man, very short (almost a dwarf), with a large head. Before his arrest, he occupied a leading post in the management of the petroleum industry. His brother, Stanislas Kossior, then sat on the Politbureau, and, at the same time, was secretary of the Central Committee of the Ukranian Communist Party. (He was later liquidated by Stalin. His case was mentioned by Khrushchev in his report to the twentieth congress.) In the camp, V. V. Kossior worked in the boiler room, carrying coal in a wheelbarrow to keep the boiler going. Also at the camp were both his wives, the first, a Ukranian from whom he was divorced, and the second, a Russian whom he had married in exile.

Poznansky, a handsome well-built man about thirty-five to thirty-eight years old, was deeply interested in music and chess. Trotsky's second secretary, Grigoryev, was also at Pechora.

In the autumn of 1936, soon after the frame-up trials against the leaders of the Opposition, Zinoviev, Kamenev, and the others, the entire group of "Orthodox" Trotskyists at the mine got together to confer with one another.

Opening the meeting, Gevorkian addressed those present: "Comrades! Before beginning our meeting, I ask you to honor the memory of our comrades, guides, and leaders who have died as martyrs at the hands of the Stalinist traitors to the revolution."

The entire assembly stood up. Then, in a brief and very trenchant speech, Gevorkian explained that it was necessary to examine and resolve the key problem: what should be done and how should they conduct themselves from now on.

"It is now evident that the group of Stalinist adventurers have completed their counterrevolutionary coup d'etat in our country. All the progressive conquests of our revolution are in mortal danger. Not twilight shadows, but those of deep black night envelop our country. No Cavaignac spilled as much working class blood as has Stalin. Physically annihilating all the opposition groups within the party, he aims at total personal dictatorship. The party and the whole people are subjected to surveillance and to summary justice by the police apparatus. The predictions and the direst fears of our Opposition are fully confirmed. The nation slides irresistibly into the Thermidorian swamp. This is the triumph of the centrist petty-bourgeois forces, of which Stalin is the interpreter, the spokesman, and the apostle.

"No compromise is possible with the Stalinist traitors and hangmen of the revolution. Remaining proletarian revolutionaries to the very end, we should not entertain any illusion about the fate awaiting us. But before destroying us, Stalin will try to humiliate us as much as he can. By throwing political prisoners in with common criminals, he strives to scatter us among the criminals and to incite them against us. We are left with only one means of struggle in this unequal battle: the hunger strike. With a group of comrades, we have already drawn up a list of our demands of which many of you are already informed. Therefore, I now propose to you that we discuss them together and make a decision."

The meeting lasted only a short time; the question of the hunger strike and of concrete demands had already been debated for some months by the Trotskyists. Some Trotskyist groups in other camps (Usa station, Chib-Yu, Kochmes, etc.) had also been discussing the matter and had sent their agreement to support the demands and to participate in the hunger strike. These demands were ratified unanimously by those present. They stipulated:

1. Abrogation of the illegal decision of the NKVD, concerning the transfer of all Trotskyists from administrative camps to concentration camps. Affairs relating to political opposition to the regime must not be judged by special NKVD tribunals, but in public juridical assemblies.

2. The work day in the camp must not exceed eight hours.

3. The food quota of the prisoners should not depend on their norm of output. A cash bonus, not the food ration, should be used as a production incentive.

4. Separation, at work as well as in the barracks, of political prisoners and common criminals.

5. The old, the ill, and women political prisoners should be moved from the polar camps to camps where the climatic conditions were more favorable.

It was recommended, at the time of the meeting, that the sick, the invalids, and the old should not participate in the hunger strike; however, all those in question energetically rejected this proposal.

The meeting did not decide the day on which the hunger strike should begin; a five-member directorate, headed by Gevorkian, was delegated to inform the other Trotskyist groups spread over the immense territory containing the camps of Ukhta-Pechora.

Three weeks later, October 27, 1936, the massive hunger strike of the political prisoners began, a strike without precedent and a model under Soviet camp conditions. In the morning, at reveille, in almost every barrack, prisoners announced themselves on strike. The barracks occupied by the Trotskyists participated 100 percent in the movement. Even the orderlies struck. Close to 1,000 prisoners, of whom half worked in the mine, participated in this tragedy, which lasted more than four months.

The first two days, the strikers stayed in their usual places. Then the camp administration busied itself in isolating them from the rest of the prisoners, concerned lest the latter followed their example. In the tundra, forty kilometers from the mine, on the banks of the Syr-Yaga River, there were primitive half-demolished barracks, which previously had been used during the preliminary boring of the mines. In great haste, these barracks were put into makeshift condition; a call was sent out to the inhabitants of the region, who, with their teams of reindeer, transported the hunger strikers there, where they soon numbered about six hundred. The others were brought together not far from Chib-Yu.

After having isolated the strikers, the GPU took measures to prevent the movement from spreading in the country and from becoming known outside the frontiers. The prisoners were deprived of the right of corresponding with their families; the salaried employees of the camp lost their holidays and their right to leave. Attempts were made to incite the other prisoners against the strikers. At the mine there were food reserves beyond what was required to sustain those who worked in the pits; the camp administration contended that it had to use up its large reserves of fat and sugar, intended for the underground workers, for artificial feeding of the Trotskyists.

At the end of the first month of the strike, one of the participants died of exhaustion; two others died during the third month. The same month, two strikers, non-Orthodox Trotskyists, voluntarily gave up striking. Finally, just a few days before the end of the strike, still another striker died.

Having begun the end of October 1936, the hunger strike lasted 132 days, ending in March 1937. It culminated with the complete victory of the strikers who received a radiogram from the headquarters of the NKVD, drawn up in these words: "Inform the hunger strikers held in the Vorkuta mines that all their demands will be satisfied."

The Trotskyists were then taken back to the mine, received food reserved for the sick and, after a period of time, they went back to work, but only above ground; certain of them worked in the office of the director of the mine, in the capacity of paid workers, bookkeepers, economists, etc. Their work day did not exceed eight hours; their food ration was not based on their production norm.

But little by little the other prisoners' interest in the strikers began to diminish. Everyone's interest was now focused on the new trial at Moscow, which was being broadcast by radio; besides, new prisoners began arriving at the end of June. Their stories described mass arrests, outrages, executions without trial behind the walls of the NKVD, and this all over the country. At the beginning, no one wanted to believe this, particularly since the new arrivals spoke unwillingly and rather enigmatically. But little by little, the bonds between them became tighter and the conversations franker. Without letup, new prisoners arrived from Russia; old friends and acquaintances discovered each other: it no longer was possible not to believe the stories.

In spite of these obvious facts, a certain number of prisoners waited with impatience for the autumn of 1937 and the twentieth anniversary of the October Revolution; they hoped, on this occasion as in 1927, that the government would declare a large-scale amnesty, particularly since a little while earlier the very promising "Stalinist Constitution" had been adopted. But the autumn brought bitter disillusions.

The harsh regime of the camps grew abruptly worse. The sergeants and their assistants in maintaining order — common criminals — having received new orders from the camp director, armed themselves with clubs and pitilessly beat the prisoners. The guards, the watchmen close to the barracks, tormented the prisoners. To amuse themselves during the night they fired on those who went to the toilets. Or else, giving the order "*On your bellies,*" they forced the prisoners to stretch out, naked, for hours on the snow. Soon there were massive arrests. Almost every night, GPU agents appeared in the barracks, called out certain names and led away those called.

Certain Trotskyists, including Vladimir Ivanov, Kossior, and Trotsky's son, Sergei Sedov, a modest and likeable youth, who had imprudently refused to follow his parents into exile in 1928, were taken in a special convoy to Moscow. We can only believe that Stalin was not satisfied simply to hurl them into the tundra; his sadistic nature thirsted not only for blood; he wished first to immeasurably humiliate them and torture them, coercing them into false self-accusations. Ivanov and Kossior disappeared without trace behind the walls of the Lubyanka prison. As for Sergei Sedov, after a "treatment" at the Lubyanka he was "tried" at Sverdlovsk, where he had worked as an engineer at the electric station; according to the newspaper stories, "he recalled having devoted himself to acts of sabotage" and other "crimes," for which he was condemned to be shot. [62]

Toward the end of the autumn, about 1,200 prisoners found themselves in the old brick field; at least half of these were Trotskyists. They were all lodged in four barracks; their food ration was 400 grams of bread a day and not every day. The barracks were surrounded by a barbed wire fence. Nearly a hundred freshly recruited guards, supplied with automatic arms, watched the prisoners day and night.

The prisoners arrested at the mine, at Usa and in other nearby camps were taken to an old brickyard. Those arrested in more distant camps—at Pechora, Izhma, Kozhma, Chib-Yu, etc.—were kept near Chib-Yu.

The whole winter of 1937-38 some prisoners, encamped in barracks at the brickyard, starved and waited for a decision regarding their fate. Finally, in March, three NKVD officers,

---

62. [Sergei Sedov is one of the innumerable victims of the Stalin purges about whose death no official information is available, even thirty-five years afterward. Nearly all unofficial reports say he was shot in 1937, but there is disagreement about the place and circumstances. The author of the "Memoirs" heard he was shot at Yeniseisk, a town in the Krasnoyarsk region where many Trotskyists were exiled in the thirties. M.B.'s report here is surely wrong. The official Soviet press, in February 1937, reported that Sergei had been arrested in Krasnoyarsk (not specifying when) on charges of "poisoning workers' at the plant where he was employed—"on orders from his father." M.B. may have based his assertion about a trial and apparent confession by Sergei on some version of those "newspaper stories."]

with Kashketin at their head, arrived by plane at Vorkuta, coming from Moscow. They came to the brickyard to interrogate the prisoners. Thirty to forty were called each day, superficially questioned five to ten minutes each, rudely insulted, forced to listen to vile name-calling and obscenities. Some were greeted with punches in the face; Lt. Kashketin himself several times beat up one of them, the Old Bolshevik Virap Virapov, a former member of the Central Committee of Armenia.

At the end of March, a list of twenty-five was announced, among them Gevorkian, Virapov, Slavin, etc. . . . To each was delivered a kilo of bread and orders to prepare himself for a new convoy. After fond farewells to their friends, they left the barracks, and the convoy departed. Fifteen or twenty minutes later, not far away, about half a kilometer, on the steep bank of the little river Verkhnyaya Vorkuta (Upper Vorkuta), an abrupt volley resounded, followed by isolated and disorderly shots; then all grew quiet again. Soon, the convoy's escort passed back near the barracks. And it was clear to all in what sort of convoy the prisoners had been sent.

Two days later, there was a new call, this time of forty names. Once more there was a ration of bread. Some, out of exhaustion, could no longer move; they were promised a ride in a cart. Holding their breath, the prisoners remaining in the barracks heard the grating of the snow under the feet of the departing convoy. For a long time there was no sound; but all, on the watch, still listened. Nearly an hour passed in this way. Then, again, shots resounded in the tundra; this time, they came from much further away, in the direction of the narrow railway which passed three kilometers from the brickyard. The second "convoy" definitely convinced those remaining behind that they had been irremediably condemned.

The executions in the tundra lasted the whole month of April and part of May. Usually one day out of two, or one day out of three, thirty to forty prisoners were called. It is characteristic to note that each time, some common criminals, repeaters, were included. In order to terrorize the prisoners, the GPU, from time to time, made publicly known by means of local radio, the list of those shot. Usually broadcasts began as follows: "For counterrevolutionary agitation, sabotage, brigandage in the camps, refusal to work, attempts to escape, the following have been shot . . ." followed by a list of names of some political prisoners mixed with a group of common criminals.

One time, a group of nearly a hundred, composed mainly of Trotskyists, was led away to be shot. As they marched away, the condemned sang the "Internationale," joined by the voices of hundreds of prisoners remaining in camp.

At the beginning of May, a group of women were shot. Among them were the Ukranian Communist, Chumskaya, the wife of I. N. Smirnov, a Bolshevik since 1898 and ex-peoples' commissar; (Olga, the daughter of Smirnov, a young girl, apolitical, passionately fond of music, had been shot a year before in Moscow); the wives of Kossior, of Melnais, etc. . . . one of these women had to walk on crutches. At the time of execution of a male prisoner, his imprisoned wife was automatically liable to capital punishment; and when it was a question of well-known members of the Opposition, this applied equally to any of his children over the age of twelve.

In May, when hardly a hundred prisoners remained, the executions were interrupted. Two weeks passed quietly; then all the prisoners were led in a convoy to the mine. There it was learned that Yezhov had been dismissed, and that his place had been taken by Beria. . . .

Among the survivors of the old brickyard, several Orthodox Trotskyists found that they had escaped execution. One of these, the engineer R., was very close to Gevorkian and was one of the five leaders who had organized the great hunger strike. At the mine, it was said that R. had saved his life at the cost of treason to his comrades; these suspicions were probably well founded since after the executions, R. enjoyed the confidence of the camp administration and rose to the rank of a director.

VORKUTA (1950-53):
Oppositional Currents and the Mine Strikes
by Brigitte Gerland

[The author of the following account is a German writer who joined the Communist Party in East Germany but quickly became disillusioned with Stalinism, was arrested by Moscow's secret political police, and sentenced to fifteen years' imprisonment on the trumped-up charge of being a "British spy." She was released in Malenkov's general amnesty of December 1953, after spending some eight years in Stalin's prisons and camps, six of them in the Arctic Circle. The strike she describes was part of a strike wave that engulfed the camp complexes up to the time of the twentieth congress in February 1956, and certainly played no small role in the decision to dismantle much of the camp apparatus at that time.

[Gerland is also the author of a book about the Vorkuta camps, *Die Holle ist Ganz Anders* (Steingruben: Stuttgart, 1955). The present account was translated for the American socialist weekly *The Militant,* where it was serialized between January 17 and March 7, 1955. The following excerpts are reprinted by permission.]

In 1939, at a time when Stalin and Hitler agreed to divide Eastern Europe between them, the Soviet army entered Volhynia, Galicia, Bukovina, and Bessarabia. Beginning thus with the two Polish provinces, Volhynia and Galicia, and the two Rumanian provinces, the Soviet Republic of West Ukraine came into being; and the curtain rose on a new act of the Ukrainian drama, the most tragic and bloody in history.

It would go far beyond the scope of a newspaper article to enter into details about the many wars, uprisings, and desperate conspiracies which comprise West Ukraine's past. Suffice it to recall here that fifteen million Ukrainians of Poland, Rumania, and Czechoslovakia were always an exploited minor-

ity, without any social and economic rights within these capitalist states. Whenever they fought for the most elementary rights,
they invariably suffered every sort of persecution.

This is why the poor Ukrainian peasants, who had never
submitted without gritting their teeth to their enemies and oppressors, the Polish and Rumanian nobles and landlords
("Pans" and "Domnuls" respectively), greeted the Soviet soldiers
as liberators, showering them with garlands of flowers and
treating them with food and vodka. But the first flush of enthusiasm was soon dissipated.

Instead of the division of big estates hoped for by the
Ukrainians, who owned only tiny landstrips, they were faced
with forced collectivization. This collectivization was carried
out—without any ideological preparation—by incapable and
ignorant bureaucrats, unable to provide the necessary technical
and organizational premises for the collective farms then created
overnight. The population reacted with unexpected violence to
these measures. Buildings were burned down, the torch was set
to crops, cattle were slaughtered, and the peasants took to the
impassable swampy forests of the old Russo-Polish frontier.

That is how the partisan movement was born in the West
Ukraine, which to this day keeps the Soviet army busy. After
a few embarrassed attempts to report the story of "kulak" sabotage, the Stalinist bureaucrats drew a curtain of silence around
the fierce resistance of a sister people, disappointed in their
liberation.

As the struggle against collectivization, enforced with feverish
haste, grew more and more desperate, the bureaucracy resorted
to ever harsher methods to extend its power over the newly
conquered lands. Finally they resorted to deportations to the
Siberian taiga on a big scale. Entire villages were uprooted,
insofar, that is, as it was possible to round up the inhabitants.
In most cases only the grandparents, the sick, and the newly
born could be found; every able-bodied individual had already
left to join the partisans.

Into this atmosphere, amid the blood-red glare of burning
huts, the Germans launched their invasion, after Hitler had
torn up the friendship pact with Stalin like a scrap of paper.
The Ukrainian peasants left their forest hideouts to greet the
new liberators, omitting this time the flowers, not to mention
the food and vodka. But once again, full of hope, they expected, no longer the division of big estates, but the dismem-
berment of the hastily formed collectives that lacked machines,
cattle, and above all workers.

But they awaited with an even greater impatience the formation of an independent Ukrainian state, which the Germans had promised in return for economic assistance. To their disappointment this state was never created; on the contrary, the comrades and allies found themselves suddenly branded as "sub-human Orientals," fit only to eke out a miserable slave existence in the factories of the Master Nation conducting a victorious war. An era opened up of arrests, concentration camps, and forced labor on the territories of the German state.

All those who were able once again took to the forests, taking along some of the youth who had no desire to choose between the Ukrainian SS (storm troopers) and the German labor camps.

The struggle continued; all that changed was the face of the enemy, while the Polish and Rumanian oppressors had now become allies. Nevertheless the collapse of Germany once more rekindled hopes for an independent West Ukrainian state. The peasants were convinced that the Western powers would keep the promises they made over the radio and through their secret emissaries; and that, at long last, the eternal minority would become a nation.

But nothing came of it. The victorious Soviet army made its second entry. This time no one met them with flowers, and it wasn't just because the tanks and armored cars had destroyed everything. For the West Ukrainians liberated from "the yoke," the war was not over. The partisans had suffered great losses, but meanwhile new generations had grown up and the disintegrating German army left behind large stocks of weapons and munitions. At least the problem of arms seemed solved for a number of years.

Soviet soldiers now swarmed in the West Ukrainian villages, just as previously did the German soldiers. But the peasants continued to live as before in the holes they had dug amid the vast marshes, having forever discarded the plow in exchange for a rifle. For them there was no road back. To surrender meant a twenty-five year term in the camps. So they preferred a hopeless struggle for freedom. Their women came along and gave birth to their babies on the rotting leaves in the marshes. At night the grandparents brought milk and bread until they, too, were caught by the soldiers and sent to the North Pole or the remotest corners of Asia.

Year after year this whole people was engaged in desperate combat; even the children participated, serving as scouts and messengers. They were likewise arrested, clapped in prison, and later sent to a camp. Bridges were blown up, warehouses pillaged, munition depots raided by surprise, small groups of

soldiers killed in ambush. The enemy took revenge by burning half-abandoned and half-ruined villages, and by deport-
ing the inhabitants — at any rate, those unable to hide. New
punitive expeditions were sent without cease, only to get lost
in most cases in the merciless countryside before attaining
their goal. From time to time a "nest of bandits" is uncovered —
those who do not fall in battle are shipped to Siberia for life.

So the insoluble tragedy goes on and on, simply because
several million Ukrainians refuse at any price to become collective-farm workers and prefer to remain independent peasants.
Are they backward, incorrigible petty bourgeois? Perhaps so.
But the punitive expeditions, arrests of hostages, burning of
villages — are these the just and correct methods for "converting"
them? It is hard to answer such a question in the affirmative.
The right of nations to self-determination was ever a part of the
Bolshevik program. The bureaucratic epigones try to get
around this by claiming that West Ukraine is merely an
appendage to East Ukraine. But one might with equal justification claim that Holland, or the Flemish sector of Belgium
are a part of Germany, or that Normandy and Brittany are
part of England.

As late as summer 1953 the Soviet government had still
not succeeded in establishing tranquillity and order in the
Ukraine, not even the peace of the cemetery. Each month new
victims of endless waves of arrest and of unending punitive expeditions keep arriving in the camps. Despite this, despite huge
losses, not from battles alone but also from cold, hunger and
disease, the partisan movement has not been wiped out.

*   *   *

The Ukrainian guerrillas, in their stubborn resistance, have no
precise ideas about the future state for which they are waging
so bitter a struggle. They ought to have independence, and
the interests of the small peasant should be protected — these
are their sole watchwords. They do not worry about the form
of government. Ideologies, doctrines, questions of party policy
scarcely interest them. They regard Russians as their most
dangerous enemies.

In their eyes all Russians are Communists and therefore
especially hateful. Communism to them means — expropriations
and forced collectivization accompanied by chaos and anarchy.

In camps where West Ukrainians play an important role by
force of numbers, they live of their own choice apart from the
Russian prisoners, whom they regard as enemies. This was

one of the most difficult problems which confronted the Communist resistance groups seeking to organize a common struggle of all the prisoners against the Soviet bureaucracy. The difficulty lay in establishing contact with the West Ukrainians, because they looked upon other nationals as spies and because they refused to engage in political discussions. Besides, they held that all resistance in the camp was void of meaning, because of their fanatic clinging to the notion that a war would set them free in the near future.

This terrible illusion was quite understandable. Burned by bitter experience, they saw too clearly to believe in a reform of the Soviet bureaucracy; while hope in a political revolution by the Soviet people, which would bring them freedom as well, was completely beyond their comprehension. Their political activity was thus limited to reading newspapers, listening to the radio, and concluding from every bit of news that the Americans were already marching against the East. And anyone who dared to contradict them was treated as a Communist, if they didn't disdain to reply altogether.

One question, however, did provoke almost daily heated discussions, which sometimes led to fist fights. Should the norms be fulfilled or should all the prisoners resort to passive resistance on every occasion? The West Ukrainians sabotaged openly the program formulated and urged by members of the Communist resistance movement. This program was: work as little as possible; organize "Do Virtually Nothing" groups. Despite their guerrilla past, these former partisans took the view that only utter submission could ease their lot and assure their survival, until the day when the Western powers brought them liberty, so anxiously awaited.

Hard reality kept proving the contrary. Because the camp administration was interested exclusively in maintaining order behind the barbed wire fences, it loaded extra work upon those who were passive or unprotesting; but it yielded to all energetic pressures so long as these remained within reasonable limits.

The Vorkuta strike was decided and organized against the wishes of the Ukrainians who, in many instances, comprised half of the prisoners. And it was only toward the very last moments that among most of them the feeling of solidarity of the oppressed, against the common enemy hated by all, was finally awakened. In common action one saw tumbling down the barriers of blind nationalist sentiments, of prejudice and bitterness which they had erected between themselves and their only allies.

Rise of the Anti-Stalinist Youth Opposition

I begin this article with a quotation from the first manifesto issued by the Communist resistance group which calls itself by the significant name of "Istinny Trud Lenina" (ITL, or Lenin's True Works). My purpose is to demonstrate by means of this document, how this group aspires to continue the line of Bolshevism.

"What are the aims of the Communist resistance movement in the USSR? They are:

"To wage a struggle against the system of government which rests on the bureaucracy and the army and which can be eliminated only by a political revolution.

"To install full democracy in the shape of a workers' and peasants' soviet government, the first stage toward the classless society.

"The foundations of a socialist soviet republic are necessarily constituted by the soviets of industrial plants and of collective farms, which exercise legislative, executive, and judicial powers; and which are elected by all the toilers, workers and peasants, through universal suffrage and the secret ballot. In cases of proven incompetence, any member of the soviet is subject to recall through the same electoral procedure; and the term in office is not fixed in advance by a given legislative period.

"Each industrial plant belongs to the union of its particular branch of industry, which is headed by the union soviet. It is elected by the soviets of all the plants in that union. The union soviets together then elect the supreme workers' soviet in which the highest legislative and executive authority resides.

"The collective farms, on the other hand, are joined together by districts; and the peasant soviets, elected by each cooperative, elect district soviets, which, in turn, elect the supreme peasants' soviet in which, jointly with the supreme workers' soviet, the highest powers reside.

"Professional bureaucrats must be replaced by workers' and peasants' committees which carry out all the administrative, economic, and social tasks required for the maintenance and growth of the collective society.

"The permanent standing army with its corps of career officers must make way for a workers' and peasants' militia, whose only superiors shall be soldiers' soviets elected by the armed forces.

"To attain these objectives, it is necessary to sweep away

the monstrous oligarchy of all-powerful bureaucrats and ambitious militarists whose sole interest is to exploit the Soviet people and expropriate them of all political rights in order thus to remain in power. Only their overthrow will clear the road to communism."

This manifesto was drawn up in 1948 by a dozen Moscow students, and then reproduced and circulated secretly at the university. The young Leninists had no contact of any kind with the old Opposition because all of the old Oppositionists had been liquidated by Stalin and his henchmen. The theses of these young Leninists attracted so many students to them that in a few months the ITL already counted hundreds of members and had adherents not only in Moscow but also in the universities of Leningrad, Kiev, and Odessa.

Despite the jeopardy to their lives and livelihoods at so early an age and so definitively, the youth who rallied to this underground organization saw their main enemy not in Stalin, as a personality, but in the bureaucratic, totalitarian system he incarnated. When the dictator, after his long reign, finally died, an event no one regretted, they likewise harbored no illusions concerning his possible successors. They expected nothing from the much ballyhooed "liberalization," since it could not, in the existing circumstances, signify anything else but a move to the right and a further aggravation of the already intolerable social contradictions.

From the very start of Malenkov's reign, the Communist students made it clear that broad layers of the ruling bureaucracy would work, might and main, to consolidate their political power on the economic plane; that is to say they would readily promote private capitalist tendencies, in order, with their aid, to transform themselves from more or less dependent, state-employed persons into independent proprietors; and in this way, convert the unstable layer of exploiters to which they belonged into a ruling class resting economically upon private property relations.

From this standpoint—the only one possible under the Malenkov regime—liberalization and reform meant a threat to the socialist economy and to the Soviet proletariat bound up with this economy, rather than any improvement in the lot of the Soviet toilers as a whole.

No member of the resistance movement would entertain even for a moment the illusion that the new ruling clique would go so far in its "liberalization" as to allow the opposition a chance to express itself, because any such tolerance would spell suicide for the ruling layer; that was something even the most extreme optimist had to discount.

Among the basic tenets held by the Leninist students is this, that the transition to communism can be achieved only by the working classes of all countries, acting in common, in a revolution embracing the whole world. That is why they categorically condemned the Stalinist policy of nationalistic expansion.

Opposition members condemned all the annexations by the Soviet Union perpetrated after the war, because these annexations run counter to the principle of national self-determination so passionately defended by Lenin. They criticized Soviet policy in the buffer countries and East Germany as incompatible with Marxist perspectives. In all their discussions they underscored that if this policy could not be termed imperialist it was solely owing to the fact that there were no private capitalist forces inside the Soviet Union which would lead to the policy of investments in the conquered countries; but in the systematic exploitation of the "native" proletariat of these countries, it was in no way different from imperialist colonialism.

This movement, which lives in illegality and is organized into tiny groups, obviously does not possess a complete program; and there are many lapses in its definition of strategy and tactics. On important points there is a certain vagueness. For example, the Stalinist system is often characterized as state capitalism, despite the numerous clarifications Lenin has made on this subject. But incredible as it may seem, the members of this underground organization have had the opportunity to discuss their program among a rather wide audience, prior to their arrival in camp.

The groups are made up of circles of three to four individuals, linked with one another by liaison agents in order to coordinate propaganda work within the narrow limits imposed. Each circle carries out a different task. One writes leaflets; another operates mimeograph machines obtained with the greatest of difficulties and hidden away in a garret of a love-nest bungalow; a third seeks out the best ways and means of getting propaganda material into the hands of prospective readers.

In addition to written propaganda, and with a view toward recruitment, there is oral propaganda by means of discussion groups, or "flying squadrons" who make their appearance anywhere an opportunity offers for intervening in a political discussion and giving it an orientation.

Naturally, this subversive activity, mounting from month to month, could not long escape the notice of secret-police spies. Nevertheless, "Istinny Trud Lenina" succeeded for almost two years in remaining undiscovered while working in the very centers of intellectual life, and even establishing contacts, quite limited to be sure, with the workers in big city factories.

It was at this stage that the underground organization suffered its first serious blow. In a single night, entirely unexpectedly, hundreds of its members were arrested and condemned to twenty-five-year terms at hard labor, in trials held behind closed doors. But news of the dramatic scenes at these trials nevertheless traveled from ear to ear through the whole of Moscow.

The will of the defendants to struggle for their political aims was not broken by the long journey to the forced-labor camps of Siberia and the Arctic regions. In camp they came in contact with other oppositional groups, of whose existence they had been previously entirely unaware. They found allies and the opportunity for political activity among layers of the population to whom they had no access with their propaganda while they were at liberty.

In the days when the mass arrests had virtually wiped out the Leninist group, there arose, also at Moscow, a second underground student organization, which likewise claimed adherence to Marxism but represented anarcho-syndicalist tendencies. Its slogan was "Soviets But No Party." It saw the root of all evils in the bureaucratic degeneration of the Bolshevik Party; and regarded the party itself as the breeding center from which the official oligarchy grew and spread like a blight over the entire state apparatus. ITL members, on the contrary, always held the position that the world revolution was impossible without a world Communist party, leading the proletariat in the struggle.

Another point of difference was the opposition of the anarchists to any centralization of state direction; and in their program for a trade union government, set up in soviets and coordinated by committees of deputies. To defend the interests of the peasant population, they proposed to form unions of agricultural workers, corresponding in structure to the industrial unions; in this way they believed they could eliminate the political and economic differences between the village and the city.

In the camps, where members of the anarchist group soon made their appearance, the two resistance groups, despite heated theoretical disputes, merged so swiftly that within a few years there was, in effect, only a unified organization, with factions in it.

The most heated discussions occurred over the issue which might roughly be formulated as "War or Revolution?" At the bottom of this interminable dispute was the following problem: Upon leaving the camps, and counting upon the support of millions of political and ordinary prisoners, how best and most effectively to fight the Stalinist regime? The possibilities and perspectives of strikes and uprisings were topics of endless discussion. In these discussions, a differentiation took place.

Some young oppositionists held the view that any large-scale undertaking was out of the question until after the eruption of a decisive military conflict between the East and the West. In this attitude there lurked dangerous illusions about the United States, in which many Marxists and active members of the Leninist and anarchist groups pinned their hopes, to a surprising degree. They were sincerely convinced that the Western capitalist states would agree, after crushing the expanding, totalitarian system of the Stalinist bureaucracy, to effect an acceptable compromise with a Socialist Soviet Republic, and to accept the pre-1939 frontiers.

These erroneous views held by members of the vanguard are obviously to be explained only by their ignorance of the overall political situation and by their decades of isolation from the world labor movement. However, notwithstanding these regrettable and understandable errors, there existed groups capable of giving a clear analysis and an accurate evaluation of the role of the imperialist bloc in a future war.

For a long time they remained in a minority, but the political evolution of recent years kept confirming their views, and events came to their assistance. After Stalin died, they formulated the thesis of an "era of peaceful coexistence between Malenkov and Eisenhower at the expense of the working class," and the "pro-American" comrades came to regard this thesis with fewer and fewer doubts. Thus it was that one of the last leaflets to come into my hands prior to my departure to the West contained the following passage:

"The international bourgeoisie will far more easily reach an agreement with the Kremlin bureaucracy to oppress the workers and crush their revolution with the Kremlin's cooperation, than it would agree to get along with a Communist Soviet state, ready to fight unsparingly for the oppressed and the exploited of all the nationalities. Our only hope lies in the revolution."

How the Great Vorkuta Strike Was Prepared

The idea of a mass strike of forced laborers was popularized in the camp by the Leninist students. No one could keep this idea from spreading, although it was more dangerous than a time-bomb.

Spontaneous strikes, even mutinies, used to crop up everywhere, in one camp or another. These were simply episodic acts of desperation touched off by particularly bad material conditions. They were no more than flash fires which could be extinguished by isolating the more energetic leaders.

The Leninists knew that only a strike which embraced at least an entire forced-labor area that was important economically, such as Vorkuta, stood any chance of success. And so they undertook, systematically and patiently, to forge contacts between all the camps in the city of Vorkuta as well as in the Vorkuta district itself.

The problem of contacts did not present a major difficulty because the MVD, anxious to head off any revolt, had prudently dispersed the "student troublemakers" throughout the entire area; so that in each camp there was at least one small group of three or four. It is also worth noting that prisoners in large numbers were constantly being shifted from one camp to another, as much for reasons of economy as for the sake of dispersing troublesome elements — all of this facilitated contact work.

In addition, the superintendents of work in the bigger construction yards, railroads, and the like, could not avoid bringing together workers from different camps. This invariably furnished new opportunities for getting together, making future appointments, and even afforded the possibility for summing up the overall situation in detail.

A lively correspondence, in secret code, was carried on even with the smallest camps, situated on the shores of the Arctic Ocean, or deep in the tundras. Free laborers, who gladly seized the occasion to hit back at the bureaucracy, and even soldiers, served as couriers.

In this way, three years before the strike, the conditions were prepared which were to make possible the organization of the strike with surprising rapidity, considering that the fifty camps of the area are spread over hundreds of miles. The immediate problem, however, was not that of strike organization and strike tactics, but something more pressing: how to drive home to some 250,000 forced laborers that they could better their lot, and perhaps even gain their freedom, only by acting in concert, only by organizing a powerful action of solidarity?

For a long time this seemed virtually unattainable. The only firm supporters of the strike were to be found among the *blatni* (Soviet outlaws) and the *monashki* (religious sects). In 1949 the Leninists and the *blatni* tried to organize a strike in one of Vorkuta's most important coal pits; but the strike met with no response among the mass of forced laborers, and therefore soon petered out. Several weeks later, the minister of state security ordered the political prisoners to be separated from the ordinary convicts; because, in the light of that first experience, he expected no good to result from the alliance between the Leninist students and the *blatni*.

Vorkuta was made by decree an area of "special regime camps," and the vacancies left by the departure of ordinary prisoners were filled mainly by natives of the newly constituted Soviet Republics of West Ukraine, Lithuania, Latvia, and Estonia.

This shift did not help the oppositional movement, since the "national groups," as they were generally called, held aloof from any united fronts, not only with Communists, but with any Russians whatsoever. A highly perplexing situation came about.

The deeply religious *monashki* made a bloc with the Leninists and the atheistic anarchists, but they found it impossible to come to an understanding about their beliefs and their opposition to the MVD administration with the Orthodox Catholics from the Ukraine, for whom religion also is of paramount importance.

The Ukrainian nationalists not only displayed a total lack of political solidarity, but their blind zeal on the job acted greatly to aggravate living conditions in the camps. The Marxist students and the *monashki* Christians had jointly elaborated, in considerable detail, the tactic for applying a program of passive resistance. This program was accepted by the mass of prisoners, virtually all of whom had ties, more or less close, with one of the underground groups. Meanwhile the *"zapadniki"* (West Ukrainians, Latvians, etc.) did everything in their power to fulfill their work quotas.

They regarded as dangerous every attempt to organize passive resistance on a large scale, going so far as to reject it as a provocation, and they sabotaged it every way they could. This frequently led to bitter fights.

In each camp there thus hardened a Russian bloc, headed by the Marxists and the *monashki*, as against a bloc of West

Ukrainians and Baltic nationalities, led by their most influential guerrilla leaders. Depending on their political views or personal leanings, members of other nationalities adhered to either of these two groups, engaged in fierce, mutual rivalry. The bureaucracy derived much satisfaction from the situation, and spared no effort to sharpen the conflict. The Marxists and the *monashki* made repeated attempts to bridge the gap to the other side; but it took years and exceptional events, before this bridge finally spanned the gap.

The struggle often took on acute forms, because in everything that involved outside work the central issue became solidarity in resisting the methods of unbridled exploitation. It was not just an ideological clash. The alternative was either to give in, to become degraded to the animal level of existence, and to die a slow death, or to unite and to organize constantly better ways of putting up a common resistance, not only thereby to improve daily living conditions, but also with a view to the coming revolutionary combat with the bureaucracy.

But how was the problem posed in practice? The prisoners had only one avenue of exerting any meaningful influence on working conditions, namely, by becoming leaders of brigades (work squads).

The forced laborers were hired out to nearby plants in brigades or squads of thirty on the average, and the brigade leader was responsible for assigning jobs, seeing that the work was done and the norms (work quotas) filled. In actual practice, his powers were much broader, because the free foreman seldom put in an appearance except to fill out the necessary papers, after the work was finished. How a brigade met its quotas was almost always left to the discretion of the brigade leader. He had to be ingenious enough to obtain 100 percent fulfillment — on paper. That sufficed. There was no other effective control.

Unfailingly even the most indifferent foreman quickly learned that the Ukrainian brigade leaders obtained results far superior to the Russian and not with just pen and ink. Plant superintendents were likewise quick to ask only for the *zapadniki* as work-squad leaders. The camp chiefs, among whom there was bitter rivalry, and who often found themselves unable to dispose of their workers, gave in to the foremen and the superintendents and began to select exclusively Ukrainian and Baltic brigade leaders.

This was vigorously opposed by the Russian prisoners, organized and unorganized alike! And it led to a miniature war which dragged on and on, quite costly in both time and forces;

harmful to the growth of the resistance movement, but unavoidable.

A few months before Stalin died, this problem was unexpectedly solved. An MGB (Ministry of State Security) ukase instructed camp chiefs that at least 80 percent of the brigade leaders must be Russians, and no more than 20 percent "aliens" (Ukrainians, Balts, and other nationalities). This measure was intended to appease the Russians who were the source of all forms of resistance. Instead it served to strengthen the revolutionary elements. For, by complying, the camp chiefs had to appoint a large number of Marxist students and sympathizers as brigade leaders. This circumstance played a major role in the outbreak of the Vorkuta general strike.

But the decisive premises for the strike took shape with Stalin's death as the starting point. The despot's death brought with it no modification in the living conditions of the prisoners. Nevertheless, they did derive from it a great moral boost which manifested itself everywhere by stepped-up activity. Many prisoners nursed hopes of an early amnesty which, rumor had it, had been blocked all this while by Stalin. But this illusion burst like a bubble when early in May 1953, the highest MVD functionary at Vorkuta, General Derevyanko, announced that political prisoners should not count on amnesty, since their liberation would jeopardize state security.

This news came as a shock to all those who imagined that with the disappearance of Stalin would also go the terror of the Stalinist epoch. In this way even the most docile elements, who up till then had been straddling the fence, oriented toward energetic action.

But action meant strike action; no other way of protest was available. And so, by the end of May 1953 committees for preparing the strike were set up in several places. To these committees Leninists, anarchists, *monashki*, as well as unorganized elements were elected. For here, participation had been opened to those who were unaffiliated with any underground movement.

The Balto-Ukrainian groups, around whom had rallied all the anxiety-ridden, wavering, or despairing elements during those decisive weeks, flatly rejected the very idea of a strike. "We shall be shot, and nothing more will come of it," they argued. "And why should we, like fools, allow ourselves to be wiped out at five minutes to twelve?" By these words they expressed their conviction that now, with the last great "Bolshevik" dead, war was imminent.

Great Labor Camp Strike at Vorkuta

When Beria fell unexpectedly from the pinnacle of power into the bottomless pit, the scale swung decisively in favor of those prisoners who were ready for action. Everybody took it for granted that Beria's downfall caused great disarray in the ranks of the political police. Most prisoners even looked forward to a whole series of palace overturns, hoping that the bureaucratic oligarchs would devour one another, a hope which was, unfortunately, not realized in life.

It is easy, after the event, to see how exaggerated was the optimism evoked by Beria's fall, but at the time none could have foretold the consequences; and the event itself came as a powerful stimulus to the march of events at Vorkuta.

Many who had opposed the movement until then, particularly among the *zapadniki*, now realized that the hour for action was at hand. They started joining the strike committees, as yet, to be sure, only in the camps under the leadership of the Marxists and the *monashki.* So tense became the atmosphere that everyone was electrified. Committees of Pits No. 1 and No. 7, where the Leninists and the anarchists exercised the strongest influence, decided — with the unanimous support of forced laborers at these camps, totaling some 6,000 — to strike until the government agreed to dissolve the camps and grant to all prisoners the status of free colonists. That is to say, to treat them as free laborers, and to sign three-to-five year contracts with them.

This compromise program of action was needed to win over those prisoners who still hesitated and who would have never accepted the slogan of a strike for unconditional liberation. Work was to stop on the evening of July 20, but that same morning the Pit No. 1 strike committee, recognized by the forced laborers of Vorkuta region as the central leadership of the strike, was arrested. This was done by deploying large contingents of troops who surrounded the pit suddenly and who withdrew just as suddenly two hours later, taking their prisoners along to the Vorkuta penitentiary. They were kept there for a few days and then removed to Moscow. The prisoners of Pit No. 1, however, quickly overcame their initial consternation; they elected a new strike committee. The military operation carried out by the authorities merely postponed the strike for a space of twelve hours.

In the early hours of July 21 the escorting guards stood waiting with their watch-dogs alongside the high fence gates, but there was no movement of any kind, absolutely nothing, inside the concentration city. The prisoners sat silently in their barracks, without the remotest intention of starting work. At first, the sentries on duty made their appearance to urge the recalcitrants to line up at the camp gates. And in their wake came a few officers of the camp administration and, finally, the camp chief himself. But their efforts availed nothing, except a declaration to the effect that the strikers would not present their demands to any person other than the commandant of all the Vorkuta camps, General Derevyanko.

This dignitary put in his appearance two days later, only after ten pits inside the city and on the outskirts joined the strike (involving by then some 30,000). After the strike committee delegates put forward their demands, the general made a long speech, larded with vague promises and threats which were not so vague. But he was butting his head against a wall of hostile silence. For one week this feat of oratory remained the sole reaction of the MVD.

There was an unheard-of confusion at Vorkuta's central administration offices; the telephone lines to Moscow kept buzzing, but the replies that Moscow gave them were worthy of the Delphic oracle. No clear-cut directives. The local authorities dared not act, because one thing was self-evident: Moscow wanted no scandals, no calamities, no bloody repressions. And so they waited.

Each day at the hour for changing work shifts, an officer was sent into the barracks by the camp chiefs to inquire politely whether anybody wished to go to work. No one did. Apart from that, the prisoners were left in peace.

To display its generosity the administration announced that it would continue to provide food for the strikers so long as provisions lasted. As for bringing in new provisions, this was absolutely out of the question, because the financial losses suffered on account of the strike had put the administration into the red for months to come.

The strikers did not waste their time. The requisitioned all the available stocks of paper in order to run off many thousand copies of a leaflet. The text follows:

"Fellow prisoners, you have nothing to lose but your chains!

"Don't expect to gain your freedom through anyone's efforts but your own. No one will help you; no one will save you; only you yourselves can change your lot.

"Down tools! The strike is our only weapon!"

It proved possible to spread these leaflets every place where forced laborers were not yet on strike. And this was accomplished in the main thanks to the aid of soldiers who sympathized with the strikers and therefore incurred the risk of maintaining the contacts which had been broken by the work stoppage. As a result, within ten days, twenty big pits inside the city and its environs were shut down tight.

Only then did Moscow stir into action. Hastily withdrawn were the Russian and Ukrainian troops who had established close ties with the prisoners during their long stay at Vorkuta, and who felt much closer to those whom they guarded than to those who ordered them about. They were replaced by new regiments composed largely of soldiers from Far East tribes, who often spoke no Russian and were thus unable to communicate with the prisoners.

The steady buildup of heavily armed troops did not at all succeed in intimidating the strikers. Only here and there was a voice raised to suggest: "We might as well give up."

In the first days of August, when the strike reached its peak and when even some among the MVD officers were sure the prisoners had carried the day, the state prosecutor, with his retinue of generals, landed at the tiny Vorkuta airfield. He set up his headquarters in the city for several days, in order, he declared, to negotiate and reach a worthwhile agreement.

In an imposing briefcase he had brought with him a number of concessions which were promptly broadcast through all the camps:

1) Every prisoner in special "government camps" is granted permission, effective immediately, to write letters home twice a month, instead of twice a year;

2) each prisoner may receive, once a year, a visit from his family;

3) identification numbers shall be removed at once from trousers and jackets;

4) iron bars shall be removed from barracks windows.

These concessions, however, left the strikers cold. In an open letter to the state prosecutor, the strike leadership gave its answer:

"We are proud of our identification numbers, because they publicly distinguish us from common criminals and thieves; and that is why we have no desire to do away with them.

"Our families will not be able to visit us, not even with the kind permission of the MVD, because they haven't enough money to buy railroad tickets for trips of 4,000 miles and more.

"Writing letters is a superfluous occupation for those who are dead, and that's what we are, condemned to stay here for twenty-five years. We can do without writing letters unless we are granted through revised regulations, the possibility of returning to our families in the not too distant future."

But the state prosecutor chose to ignore this open letter; and General Derevyanko traveled from camp to camp promising better food, higher pay, shorter work shifts. His skill of persuasion had some effect on weaker and less politically active elements; but the influence of the strike committee remained much stronger than capitulationist moods. The comrade state prosecutor knew it as well as everybody else at Vorkuta. And he also knew that a forceful measure taken against the "ringleaders" would touch off a revolt of despair, a truly sanguinary calamity which was to be avoided at all costs.

He then resorted to a ruse. Members of the strike committee and of the central strike leadership were politely invited to an interview at the headquarters, an invitation they naturally accepted. They were cordially met at the camp gate by orderlies, who accompanied them to the city; but not a single one of them returned from this talk.

That was how matters stood, when I was, without any advance notice, hurried off to an unknown destination. This journey, which was to end in my being set free several months later, kept me from witnessing the end of the Vorkuta strike. But I did learn from German prisoners, released a few weeks later, that some pits stayed out on strike until November, for more than three months, that is.

They finally returned to work only because the supply of food and, what is even more vital in polar regions, the supplies of coal gave out. Assuredly, they had not attained their goal — not yet.

But the material improvements to which the MVD was forced to agree under the strike pressure proved to be considerable. And more important by far: although there were many signs of exhaustion, there was not a hint of discouragement or demoralization.

The forced laborers were worn down, but they did not succumb in despair. Their aim was to rally new forces; they wished to draw carefully the lessons from their experiences in order to make better use of them in the future — and they were resolved to continue the struggle.

ON THE MULTIPARTY SYSTEM

[From *Kolokol*, organ of the Union of Communards, no. 4, May 1965. The Union of Communards was a neo-Bolshevik youth group, based in Leningrad. Its newspaper bore the epigraph "From the dictatorship of the bureaucracy to the dictatorship of the proletariat" on its masthead. Four issues came out before the group, numbering as many as 250 members, was broken up by the secret police not long after this May issue began to circulate. Contemporary accounts of the trials of the Communards in early 1966 may be found in *The Militant* and in *World Outlook,* the predecessor of *Intercontinental Press.* Especially frank was the testimony of a young woman Communard when the judge asked what their program would be if they had power: she responded "First, we would send you out to work." Valery Ronkin and Sergei Khakhaev, charged as the leaders of the group, were each sentenced to seven years imprisonment and three in exile. Ronkin went on to play a role in the protest movement that developed among Soviet political prisoners, especially after 1967. He is one of the signers, along with Sergei Moshkov (another Communard), of the "Appeal to the Supreme Soviet," by six political prisoners, elsewhere in this volume. Prominent opposition activists Yuri Galanskov and Anatoly Marchenko have both written favorably about Ronkin and Khakhaev, who were sent to places of exile in 1972, according to the *Chronicle,* after the expiration of their terms in labor camp.

[The translation for this volume is by Marilyn Vogt.]

An analysis of the superstructure of the bureaucratic states, both those belonging to the socialist camp and those outside it (Algeria, the UAR), shows that one feature is peculiar to all of them — the absence of a legal political opposition, and the absence of opposition parties.

Although in such countries as the GDR, Poland, Czechoslovakia, Bulgaria, and even the Chinese People's Republic a multiparty system does formally exist, all the parties in these countries are united in a bloc. They all recognize the leading role of the Communist Party, refrain from any criticism of it, and in elections put forward a joint slate of candidates. They divide up the seats in parliament and in local councils according to an agreement among these parties' leaders; but in essence the leadership of the Communist Party gives the other parties whatever number of seats it considers necessary. The number of members in these parties is also regulated by the higher-ups of the Communist Party.

Under these conditions, the "multiparty system," which remains as a legacy of capitalism and which is retained by the bureaucracy in order to deceive the masses, is transformed into a fiction and in essence becomes no less a one-party system than that which exists in the USSR.

What is the source of this partiality on the part of bureaucracy for a one-party system? The main determining factor is the new position the bureaucratic class finds itself in. Under capitalism, power actually lies in the hands of the capitalist class. The reshuffling of government officials at the top level, like that which takes place in the United States when there is a change of administration between Republicans and Democrats, does not in general affect the interests of the capitalist class. Under a bureaucracy, the real power lies directly in the hands of the bureaucrats themselves and they are not the least bit interested in separating themselves from power or from the privileges associated with it. And it is for just this reason that a bureaucracy makes use of a one-party system. The experience with the fascist states showed, however, that the one-party system opens the way for despotism. Even in many Western Communist parties, voices are heard favoring a genuine multiparty system as the only guarantee against the personality cult (see for example *World Marxist Review: Problems of Peace and Socialism*, No. 9, 1963, the speech by P. Togliatti at a plenum of the Italian Communist Party).

Even in our country, many people are beginning to realize that the presence of a legal opposition party, even if it did not undermine bureaucratism, could at any rate seriously restrict the bureaucracy's despotic rule and subject it to more control. In this regard, the ideologues of bureaucratism are trying somehow or other to justify this discredited system and to portray it as the most highly perfected political mechanism.

Let us analyze their reasoning. As their basic theoretical

argument, they refer to the fact that since the party is the vanguard, the most advanced section, of the working class, to create various parties would mean fragmenting the strength of that vanguard. This argument would be justified if there actually were criteria that would permit a given class to evaluate which of its representatives embodied progressive ideas and which did not. The facts show, however, that all politically active representatives of a class, of the proletariat, for example, no matter what party they might belong to — be it Communist, anarchist, or Social Democratic — consider the ideas of their own party to be the most advanced. The class as a whole, however, judges the parties from another point of view and expresses its solidarity with this or that party by lending it more or less energetic support in its struggles against other parties. In addition, it should be noted that the class composition of a party is very often different than its class character. In many bourgeois parties, actual members of the bourgeoisie by no means constitute the majority, although the party is no less a bourgeois party because of this fact. From this we can see that a party is not the vanguard of a class, but rather an instrument of it in political struggle. The experience of history shows that it is advantageous to all classes (except the bureaucracy) to have several such instruments. If they do, they can exercise a definite pressure on parties acting in their name, by their support for it or indifference to it. In a one-party system, on the contrary, the party always gets out of the control of its class.

As a second argument, the proponents of the one-party system point to the fact that the goals of all of our society are one and the same. Even if such unity existed — and under bureaucratism it does not — it would by no means lead logically to a one-party system. Different parties do not necessarily have to pursue different goals. They may strive for the same goal but propose different paths for its realization (as in the case of the Republicans and Democrats in the United States). The class or society will select the ways most suitable to it. After all, no matter what solution a party — or, more precisely, the party's leaders — may propose to a given problem, it can always turn out to be mistaken, even if these leaders had the best of intentions. But since under a one-party system the person who made the mistakes does not usually have to pay for them, the general line of the party consists basically of correcting one mistake after another. We are not even talking about the leaders' intentional disregard for the will of the workers, something that occurs with still greater frequency.

One could object that in order to have a choice of several different ways, it would be enough to extend internal party democracy and allow the existence of various factions within the framework of one party. But in that case one of two things will happen: either the members of the different factions will be brought under overall party discipline, in which case the minority faction will inevitably be dissolved as inconvenient for the party majority; or there will be no general party discipline and the factions in point of fact will be transformed into distinct parties which are united only by a common name. But here we are getting into a discussion about *form*, and not content.

The third argument in favor of a one-party system boils down to one of frightening people with the specter of anarchy and disorder. If one is consistent in this line of reasoning, one must grant that only the ruling clique has the right to influence the country's state of affairs and that the masses do not even have the right to express their attitude toward government measures. From this point of view, any form of democracy is harmful and impossible. However, opposition parties have existed and do exist in many countries, and although they have often succeeded in toppling the government, they have nowhere been obstacles to the normal economic development of a country and have never plunged a country into chaos. (In cases where party strife has led to political instability — as, for example, in France in 1947-48 — this was provoked not by the multiparty system but by the acuteness of the class struggle.)

In contrast to that, the single-party system has inevitably led to the de facto abolition of basic democratic freedoms and has made possible wholesale repression, violations of legality, and closed mass trials in which the verdicts were handed down on the basis of denunciations and confessions obtained through torture. This system has been able to transform our country into a concentration camp of immense proportions.

Moreover, the party leaders, declaring themselves the indisputable authorities in all areas of human creativity, have brought great harm to the development of Soviet science and art. The attack on cybernetics, the persecution of those with progressive views in the fields of biology and chemistry, the crude administrative pressure applied to writers and artists —

which occurred in the recent past—call to mind the darkest times of the Middle Ages. In making such vileness possible, the one-party system has not saved the nation from upheavals and dislocations, and the general line of the party has long since become the target of the witticisms and mockery of all Soviet citizens. Of course, it is possible that under a multiparty system one or another demagogue could entice a certain part of the populace "in a false direction." The one-party system, however, makes it possible to force an entire people to go "in a false direction" under KGB surveillance and the threat of repression.

The arguments in defense of a one-party system do not withstand any sort of criticism, and they run counter to the Marxist conception of a socialist society. The members of the Union of Communards must clearly explain that a genuine democratization of the bureaucratic regime is impossible without the existence of a legal opposition; that is, without a multiparty system in one form or another.

Volgin

WHO KILLED TROTSKY?
by E.M.

[This article originally appeared in early 1966, in the samizdat publication *Notebooks of Social Democracy (Tetradi Sotsial-Demokratii)*. We reprint it not only to illustrate the interest young Soviet "cultural" rebels have shown in the Bolshevik leader but also to demonstrate the prevailing confusion and lack of accurate information in the Soviet Union about one of the founders of the revolutionary republic — even among those sympathetic to him. The confusion of information about Trotsky's ideas and activities — especially about the period after his expulsion from the USSR — can also be seen in Medvedev's *Let History Judge* and of course in the memoirs of the former Bolshevik-Leninist and Chumakova in this volume. The blame for this lack of clarity naturally does not lie with the individual authors but with the bureaucracy, which for years has banned any but the most falsified and discrediting news about Trotsky or Trotskyism from being printed. Nevertheless it is clear from this essay that more is known today about this subject than the bureaucracy would like.

[The translation, from the French volume *Samizdat I* (Paris: La Verite, 1969), is by the editor.]

On September 12, 1965, *Pravda* published a defamatory allusion to Trotsky. Several days later, the army newspaper *Krasnaya Zvezda* [Red Star] did the same thing. One can only ask why? Why does the word "Trotskyist" ring in so many people's ears as a synonym for opportunism and treason? Why wasn't Trotsky, a true comrade to V. I. Lenin, rehabilitated either after 1956 or after 1961?

A professional revolutionary and conspirator, Lev Davidovich Bronstein (Trotsky's real name) joined the Social Democratic movement when he was still quite young. He is now accused of factionalism. Yes, Trotsky was a factionalist — just like the August bloc[63] and the "Mezhrayontsy." Other figures of the Russian Social Democratic Party also belonged to factions: Lunacharsky, Uritsky, Volodarsky, Bubnov, Rykov, Vorovsky, Dzerzhinsky — all persons whom no one accuses of all the mortal sins, in fact quite the contrary.

L. D. Trotsky was one of the leaders of the October Revolution in Petrograd. John Reed, who later founded the U. S. Communist Party, wrote at the time that the October Revolution was Lenin and Trotsky's revolution (certainly not Lenin and Stalin's). Trotsky was chairman of the Petrograd Soviet of Workers' and Soldiers' Deputies; after the second congress of Soviets, he became people's commissar for foreign affairs and then people's commissar for defense and for the navy. He founded the Red Army and encouraged the appearance of young Red commanders, including Tukhachevsky.

In 1924 Trotsky abandoned the struggle for power; but this did not diminish Stalin's enmity toward him. An extremely intellectual man, an eloquent speaker, and an outstanding publicist, Trotsky aroused the unrelenting animosity of the crafty Georgian. In addition to personal dislikes, serious political differences existed between them. Trotsky supported the theory of *permanent revolution* — first the world revolution and only afterwards the construction of socialism.[64] Stalin, on the other hand, without rejecting proletarian internationalism, gave priority to the theory of *socialism in one country.* Even former comrades of Trotsky supported the latter theory, since Stalin's plan was based on state interests, while Trotsky's program

---

63. [A bloc of Mensheviks, ultraleft Bolsheviks, the Jewish Bund, and Trotsky's group, formed in August 1912 at a conference of Russian Social Democrats held in Vienna, which Lenin and his followers refused to attend. The purpose of this conference had been to attempt to restore unity to the Russian Social Democracy. Trotsky's later evaluation of the August bloc is in *In Defense of Marxism* (Pathfinder Press, 1973), p. 141.]

64. [For a more correct statement of Trotsky's theory of permanent revolution, see note 6. Both Trotsky and Lenin, far from counterposing the world revolution to building socialism in Russia, saw the world revolution as the chief hope for the backward and isolated Russian workers' state. It was precisely in order to rationalize the abandonment of proletarian internationalism that Stalin adopted the theory of socialism in one country.]

was forever changing and seemed to have no future. Thus
Trotsky was replaced.

Trotsky himself was a remarkable personality, but at the
same time he was extremely contradictory and changeable.

He expressed opinions on every aspect of every problem,
combining a profoundly democratic spirit with a highhanded
manner. After innumerable debates and intrigues, Trotsky was
expelled from the party and within two years, in 1929, left
his homeland. [65] . . .

Trotsky engaged in feverish activity to organize his supporters, first in Turkey, and later in France, Norway, and
Mexico. In 1933 he succeeded in creating the Fourth International through a conference of all Trotskyist parties. [66]
Trotsky's authority was so great that the International Zionist
Committee in Paris (to which Rothschild, Leon Blum, Marshall,
and others belonged) asked him to join their ranks. Trotsky
refused on the grounds that his cause was international. But he
wished them success in their struggle to create an Israeli Republic. [67]

Trotsky's activities never ceased to alarm Stalin. Near the
end of the 1930s, when the professional revolutionaries and
conspirators were being ousted from responsible positions and
replaced by professional bureaucrats and apparatchiks, Stalin
was afraid that Trotsky would seize the opportunity to increase his activities in the Soviet Union. So Stalin ordered
Trotsky's death. Shortly before his death, the exiled Trotsky
wrote "Once again fate has granted me a delay. But I know
that this delay will be short-lived."

---

65. [In fact, Trotsky was expelled from the Soviet Union and exiled
to Turkey with his family in February 1929.]

66. [Trotsky and his cothinkers first called for the formation of a
Fourth International in 1933, but it was not actually founded until
1938. In 1933 Hitler took power in Germany; the German CP capitulated without a struggle, and the Comintern refused even to evaluate
the defeat. The militants of the International Left Opposition, till
then a faction in the Communist International, concluded that the
Comintern was dead as a revolutionary organization and that a
new, revolutionary international was necessary.]

67. [This story is not true. For Trotsky's actual position on the
creation of an Israeli Republic, see *Leon Trotsky on the Jewish Question* (Pathfinder Press, 1970).]

An undercover NKVD agent, the Spaniard Ramon del Rio Mercader, was sent to Mexico to carry out the sentence pronounced in absentia. It was quite difficult to break into Trotsky's circle of friends, which included such high personages as the former president of Mexico, General Lazaro Cardenas. [68]

Nevertheless, Mercader, using the pseudonym of Jacson and pretending to be a "representative" of the Spanish Republicans, managed to gain admittance to Trotsky's home on May 28, 1940. He paid another visit on June 12. Then Mercader-Jacson coordinated his criminal plans with the NKVD. He visited Trotsky again, but unforeseen circumstances prevented him from carrying out Stalin's command at the appointed hour.

Finally, on August 20, 1940, using the pretext that he wanted to show him an article, Mercader visited Trotsky once again. Two "accomplices" also entered Trotsky's office. [69] Three or four minutes later, Trotsky's wife heard a heart-rending cry. She ran into the office. . . .

Trotsky was lying near the door, his skull crushed. "What has happened?" she cried.

"Jacson," Trotsky replied, uttering this word as if to say 'It has happened,' his wife wrote in her memoirs. A huge funeral service was arranged for Trotsky, but on the eve of the funeral a fire broke out in the house, and only his bones could be buried. [70]

Mercader withheld his name and his motives for the murder for a long time. In court he professed that "Trotsky destroyed my personal life." With the passion natural to all Spaniards, he claimed that Trotsky had seduced his fiancee, who was Trotsky's personal secretary.

It should be noted that according to the criminal plan, Mercader was supposed to leave the house calmly after the murder and go around the corner, where a car was waiting with his

---

68. [Trotsky's relations with Cardenas were limited to Cardenas's offering Trotsky political asylum in Mexico. The two men never met.]

69. [Actually, Jacson was alone with Trotsky when he struck the fatal blow.]

70. [This story is not true. Trotsky's body was cremated as planned, after a funeral procession through Mexico City, during which tens of thousands of Mexican workers and peasants turned out to pay their respects to the great Russian revolutionary.]

wife and mother. This car was to take the "holy family" to a nearby port, where a Soviet ship was to sail in half an hour.

In 1942, a Mexican court condemned Mercader to twenty years' imprisonment. Since 1960 he has been living near Prague. Incidentally, Stalin awarded him a medal and the title "Hero of the Soviet Union" as early as 1940.

A great politician, erudite and brilliant, L. D. Trotsky has not ceased to attract the attention of many people who have a lively interest in finding out the truth about him. Even today he has his supporters in many countries, who call themselves "Bolshevik-Leninists." The political influence of the Trotskyists is insignificant, but a number have succeeded in becoming intimate with various leaders; thus, Raptis — general secretary of the Fourth International — was an adviser to former Algerian president Ben Bella.[71]

"Trotsky never ordered the derailing of trains," wrote F. F. Raskolnikov to Stalin in 1939.[72] "You know that I have

---

71. [Michel Raptis, better known by his pen name, Michel Pablo, was secretary of the Fourth International and a leading figure in it from the mid 1940s to the early 1960s. Early in the fifties, when the Cold War began, he called for the Trotskyist parties to enter the mass Stalinist and Social Democratic parties; the rationale was the imminence of World War III and the belief that under conditions of war, revolutionary wings would develop in these parties that could be won to Trotskyism. He also viewed degenerated and deformed workers' states like those in the Soviet Union and Eastern Europe as inevitable features of a long period of postcapitalist development. Pablo's policies provoked disagreement and a split in the world Trotskyist movement in the early 1950s which was only healed at the reunification congress in 1963. Pablo was not an adviser to Ben Bella but he did serve as a technician in the agrarian reform undertaken by the Ben Bella government in 1962-64. (Earlier he had been jailed by the Dutch government for his work in support of the Algerian revolution against French imperialism.) He developed serious political differences with the reunified Fourth International and broke from it in 1965. He continues to lead a small movement in several European countries.]

72. [Fyodor Raskolnikov had been vice-chairman of the Kronstadt Soviet in 1917, commander of the Baltic fleet, and ambassador to Afghanistan, Estonia, Denmark, and Bulgaria. From 1923 to 1938 he was a firm supporter of Stalin. In April 1938 he was summoned

never been a Trotskyist. On the contrary, in the press and at mass meetings I struggled against all the oppositions on the ideological plane. Even today, I disapprove of Trotsky's political position, his program and tactics. But I consider him an honest revolutionary. I do not believe, and I never will believe, that he was involved in 'collusion' with Hitler and Hess," he continued.

All Communists and Leninists, all allies of socialist democracy, all citizens with a democratic spirit agree with Raskolnikov's statement, as do all people who want the truth to be known.

Long live historical truth! Down with the falsification of history!

---

back to Moscow because his historical reminiscences of the October Revolution had brought him the label of "enemy of the people." He fled to France, where he wrote a letter to Stalin on August 17, 1939, just a few days before the Stalin-Hitler Pact. He died a few weeks later under suspicious circumstances, probably assassinated by the GPU.

The Raskolnikov letter expresses the revulsion against Stalinism by thousands of Bolsheviks who had believed that by supporting Stalin against the Left Opposition they were defending Lenin's heritage, and subsequently found themselves sucked into a terror they were unable to stop. Excerpts of the letter were published in an article about it in the Soviet magazine *Problems of CPSU History,* in December 1963. Today it is widely circulated in samizdat.]

BALLAD OF DISBELIEF
by Vadim Delone

[Born in 1947, Vadim Delone was a codefendant in the 1967
trial of Vladimir Bukovsky; while on probation he was arrested for participating in the August 25, 1968, demonstration
in Red Square against the invasion of Czechoslovakia, for
which he was tried and sentenced to penal exile with the others.
Delone symbolizes the link between the young literary opposition and the older generation of anti-Stalinists that was welded
into the current protest movement in the late sixties.

[The following is an excerpt from his poem dealing with
the question of the Stalin era and dedicated to the twenty-third
congress (1966), which, despite popular sentiment, marked
a step toward rehabilitating Stalin. The veiled references to
the civil war commander (Trotsky), and to Kamenev and
Zinoviev, show once again the curiosity and receptivity of
the young dissenters toward the revolutionary tradition.

[The translation for this volume is by the editor.]

We are seeking, but still have found nothing.
Seeking? Or losing, more likely!
In the same way, idea-free fighters
Set forth once on untraveled highways.

We remember. We have not forgotten
How those other fighters set out
For distant predawn destinations,
How they fell and again rose to fight.

They were paid for their efforts and exploits
Soon enough — paid off in lead.
Instead of the daybreak, dark rumors
Spread over the Russian land:

Death to Lenin's deputy chairman![73]
Death to the Comintern's head![74]
The captain and chief of victory
In the civil war merely betrayed.[75]

And the testament written by Lenin—
They paid it no heed, shall we say?
It was simply a clash over power?
Well, things often happen that way.

* * *

But later it got much more ugly:
Dark folds over daybreak are drawn,
And ideas are just short of fascist . . .
A congress?—Shoot two-thirds of them! . . .

---

73. [A reference to L.B. Kamenev.]

74. [Apparently refers to G.E. Zinoviev, who headed the Comintern under Lenin. It may also refer to Bukharin, who as Stalin's ally headed the Comintern from 1926 to 1929.

75. [A reference to Trotsky.]

FORTY-THREE CHILDREN
OF MURDERED BOLSHEVIKS
PROTEST REHABILITATION OF STALIN

[The celebrated "de-Stalinization" campaign came abruptly to a halt in the mid-sixties, and Stalin's heirs began quietly and deliberately to resurrect Stalin's image throughout the country. In this letter, children and grandchildren of Bolsheviks who were liquidated by Stalin during the purges of the thirties register their protest against his rehabilitation. By their names and by their actions, they represent a direct link with the Bolshevik heritage of the past.

[This translation is from the Summer 1970 *Fourth International* (London).]

September 24, 1967

To the Central Committee of the Communist Party of the USSR on behalf of the surviving children of the innocent Communist victims of Stalin.

Today, in speeches, in the press, on television, the "merits" of Stalin are praised. This is a political revision of the decisions of the twentieth and twenty-second congresses of the CPSU.

This troubles us deeply. And not only because our parents and ourselves were, like millions of others, victims of the criminal machine of Stalin. It saddens us to think that the betrayed masses were forced to consent to this arbitrary despotism.

This must not be repeated. The rebirth of the past brings Communist ideas into question, discredits our system, and legalizes the assassination of millions of innocent people. All the attempts to whitewash the black deeds of Stalin carry the danger of a repetition of the hideous tragedy that struck our party, our entire people, and the whole Communist movement.

The tragedy of the Chinese events obliges all of us to outline necessary safeguards to prevent a repetition of similar catastrophes. Only by revealing totally the crimes of Stalin and his supporters can we generate the movement, consciousness, and indignation in all of society needed to destroy all the results of the Stalin cult and make the return of new cults and new despotisms impossible.

How can one praise Stalin after all that our people and the international Communist movement have suffered because of him? This adulatory praise shackles our movement, weakens our ranks, destroys our power, and makes the triumph of communism impossible.

We must celebrate the fiftieth anniversary of the great October Revolution under the banners of the party, bearing like a torch the immortal name of Lenin, the greatest democracy, collective control of society by society itself.

To unfurl these banners is the best homage we can pay to the men crushed by the diabolical cult of the individual. On some of them today there is still an unjustified stigma. Others are doomed to oblivion. History will bring them back into the heart of the party, into the heart of the people.

The monument to the victims of Stalin's despotism, promised by the twenty-second congress of the party, must be erected to mark the existence of the Soviet state for fifty years. In these days of celebration, those who fought for a worldwide October will be with us. Their number cannot be counted: from the eminent leaders of the party to the soldiers in the ranks of the revolution. There is no place for the name of the despot on the banners of the party.

We ask you to take notice of all that is written here and to see our letter as part of the struggle for communism. We hope this letter will prevent an irreparable error.

Letter signed by:

Pyotr Yakir, son of I. E. Yakir
L. Petrovsky, son of P. G. Petrovsky and grandson of G. I. Petrovsky
A. Boki, daughter of G. I. Boki
A. Antonov-Ovseenko, son of V. A. Antonov-Ovseenko
G. Troitskaya, daughter of Livshits
G. Akulov, son of I. A. Akulov
S. V. Stanakova (Osinskaya-Obolevskaya), daughter of Communists
G. Poleshchuk, daughter of N. I. Muralov
Yu. Zhivliuk, son of Communists
V. Terlin, daughter of M. S. Gorb
Z. Serebryakova, daughter of Serebryakova

The serious crimes of Stalin make all positive judgment of his activity immoral. I am signing precisely this point:

Yu. Aikhenwald, son of a Communist

S. Fedorova, daughter of G. F. Fedorova

J. Kriapiviansky, son of N. G. Kriapiviansky

V. Schmidt, son of V. V. Schmidt

Yu. Larin (Bukharin), son of N. I. Bukharin and grandson of Yuri Larin

S. K. Radek, daughter of Karl Radek

A. Vseviatskaya, daughter of Communists

A. Gastev, son of A. Gastev

Larisa Bogoraz, daughter of a Communist

I. Yakir, granddaughter of I. E. Yakir and daughter of P. I. Yakir

N. Nechinshchikov, son of a Communist

N. N. Popov, son of N. Popov

N. N. Demchenko, son of N. Demchenko

It is impossible to forget and to justify the crimes of Stalin in the name of any of his "services."

V. Shvartstein, son of a Communist

I. Piatnitsky, son of I. A. Piatnitsky

T. Baeva, daughter of a Communist

R. Yanson, daughter of a Communist

Yu. Sapronov, son of T. V. Sapronov

K. Zonberg, son of a Communist

Yu. N. Vavilov, son of the academician Nikolai Vavilov, president of the Vaskhnil [the Lenin Memorial All-Union Academy of Agricultural Sciences]

V. Blumfeld (Svichis), son of a Communist

M. Ivanov (Kalinin), grandson of M. I. Kalinin

I. A. Shliapnikova, daughter of the friend of Lenin, A. Shliapnikov

V. Yenukidze, in the name of eight people in the Bolshevik family of A. and T. Yenukidze, crushed by Stalin

Aria Reingoldovna Dimze-Berzin, daughter of R. I. Berzin

T. Smilga-Poluian, daughter of Communists

L. Zavadsky, son of a Communist

Yu. Kim, son of a Communist

S. Genkin, son of a Communist

K. Beletsky (Usievich), son of a Communist and nephew of G. A. Usievich

A. A. Berzin, grandson of R. I. Berzin

S. Svetlov, son of a Communist

Part II:

Grigorenko, Kosterin, and the Left Wing of the Movement 1966-69

Former Major General Pyotr Grigorenko (left) and former collective-farm chairman Ivan Yakhimovich in front of the Czechoslovak Embassy in Moscow in July 1968. They delivered a message of solidarity with the Prague Spring, expressing the views of a group of dissident Soviet Communists.

Outside view of "special" psychiatric hospital in Chernyakhovsk, where Grigorenko was held 1969-73. Formerly a Prussian prison.

PREFACE

One of the most significant figures of the post-Stalin opposition movement is former Major General Pyotr Grigorenko, a dissident Communist who has sought, with others of like views, to make a real return to Leninism as the solution to the problems facing the Soviet Union. Because of his political views and the strong influence he and his cothinkers have had within dissident circles, the Brezhnev bureaucrats have confined him since 1969, first in a "special" psychiatric hospital in Chernyakhovsk, and then in a "general" one near Moscow.

It is one of the major tasks of progressive-minded persons and defenders of democratic rights in general, especially those who consider themselves part of the revolutionary left, to wage a campaign to free this 67-year-old fighter from certain death. He is constantly exposed to the refined cruelty and harsh conditions of imprisonment in a madhouse cell, where he is allowed neither pencil nor paper, and, although perfectly sane, is forced to live among the insane, under guard by the secret police.

His case above all illustrates the cynical mockery of recent statements in the Soviet press denying that the regime uses "psychiatric" reprisals against political opponents.

A look at Grigorenko's background and involvement in the protest movement of the 1960s tells a lot about the evolution of Soviet society in general, how neo-Leninist opposition develops, and the kind of positive alternative it represents.

Zinaida Grigorenko gave the following biographical account of her husband's life in February 1971 in an appeal to the World Federation of Mental Health to help free her husband from the abuse of "psychiatric" methods by the regime.

"Pyotr Grigorenko was born in 1907 in the village of Borisovka, Zaporizhka region [Ukrainian Republic]. He began to work at fifteen years of age, as a metal worker at a depot. Simultaneously, he completed workers' high school. He was the first Komsomol member of his village. He became a mem-

ber of the Soviet Communist Party at the age of twenty. Graduated from two academies: the Kuibyshev Academy of Military
Engineering and the General Staff Academy [around 1938].
[The psychiatrists' Report No. 40 indicates that he also studied
at the Kharkov Technical Institute, 1929-31; then being "mobilized" by the party Central Committee to go to the engineering academy.] He is a veteran of the Khalkin-gol campaign
[against Japan] and of the Great Patriotic War. He was twice
wounded. He has six decorations, including the Order of Lenin,
and six medals. His military rank is that of major general;
he is a Master of Military Sciences and has more than seventy
learned works to his name."

At the time of the Nazi invasion of June 1941, followed by
two years of disastrous setbacks which came close to causing
the defeat of the Soviet armed forces, Grigorenko wrote and
spoke critically of the Stalin leadership's blunders and lack
of preparation for war. He was reprimanded, but because of
the crying need for every capable military person against
the invaders he was not removed from his post nor expelled
from the party. At the end of the war and in the immediate
postwar period many such critics of Stalin's military policy
were indeed arrested and sent to labor camps.

Grigorenko had apparently never been a mere hand-raiser
in the party (although he never joined any of the oppositions).
The psychiatric reports made on him after his arrest in 1969
give fleeting glimpses of his critical bent: At the engineering
academy in the early thirties, says one, "he was always active,
took part in various discussions, fought against 'slackness,'
and for clarification of certain theoretical questions he applied
directly to the Central Committee." What these questions were
and how the Central Committee answered them, if at all, are
not indicated.

It is worth pausing to consider the political situation in the
Communist Party at the time Grigorenko joined it in the early
thirties when his critical and theoretical inclinations first showed.
The Left Opposition was expelled in the year he joined, 1927,
and although, in Kharkov, he probably got no clear idea of
the issues in the struggle between the Left, the Right, and the
Stalinist Center, the echoes of the ideas then being debated
may have reached him indirectly. The period 1928-30 saw
the turn to forced collectivization and a five-year plan of industrialization to be completed in four years, and the ouster
of the Bukharinist right wing. And at the same time the surviving Left Opposition was repressed even further, although

it continued its struggle to reach the party rank-and-file with its ideas by methods similar to samizdat. A great deal of ferment existed in the party in the early thirties, especially after the terrible famine and economic disorganization. In spite of the atmosphere of repression, this ferment reached all the way into the upper levels of the party and government apparatus. That was Stalin's main reason for setting up the Kirov assassination of late 1934 and beginning the massive terror of the purges, which culminated in the killing of hundreds of thousands in 1936-38.

Grigorenko's critical bent was expressed again in the first years of the war. He apparently did not develop his criticisms into a general challenge of the bureaucratic system at that time, but pursued a successful military career after the war, from which he emerged with the rank of colonel. As he told a Western reporter in 1968, "I honestly defended the Stalin regime. I believed."

"After the war, he worked in the Frunze Military Academy as a senior lecturer. In 1949 he defended his thesis for a master's degree, but *his defense was held up because of his criticisms of some long-established principles.*" (Report made by Tashkent psychiatrists; emphasis added.) After Stalin's death, Grigorenko was promoted to major general, in 1956, and was appointed head of the department of military administration in 1959.

It is a measure of the crisis faced by Soviet society and of the political ferment that has developed there that a successful figure with a responsible position like this in the government apparatus should have developed as deep-going differences as Grigorenko has.

"The twentieth congress caused him to ponder a great deal on the significance of Stalin as a personality and he came to the conclusion that it was not Stalin who was guilty of everything — *but the system which produced him.*" (Emphasis added.)

Grigorenko told a Western reporter about what he jokingly described as his "first performance." It was a speech to a borough party conference in Moscow in September 1961. Grigorenko declared that the Stalin "personality cult" had not been an accident, that a Khrushchev cult had started, that similar regimes existed in other countries where Stalinist parties had power, and that the entire system had to be changed in order to prevent such developments.

The audience had applauded enthusiastically, but the next

morning Grigorenko's superiors at the Frunze Military Academy called him in, canceled his scheduled lectures, and dismissed him from the faculty. A motion to reprimand him was placed before his local party organization. In response, Grigorenko circulated an open letter to Moscow voters in which he denounced the "restrictions on freedom" and criticized the "unreasonable and often harmful activities of Khrushchev and his team."

After this speech he was dismissed from his post. He protested this reprisal in vain, and in 1962 was transferred to the Pacific Maritime province as head of the operations section of the army there. But his eyes had been opened. The Tashkent psychiatric report describes his further political development.

"He decided to struggle against the existing order, to 'conduct an explanation of Leninist tenets among the people, and to spread Leninist principles.' He began to prepare leaflets and to duplicate them on a typewriter. The leaflets issued from a self-styled Union of Struggle for the Revival of Leninism. He involved his sons and nephew in the preparation of the leaflets."

Grigorenko founded his Union of Struggle for the Revival of Leninism in the fall of 1963. The group studied Lenin's *State and Revolution*. Some of the leaflets they distributed were about the repression of mass protests in Tbilisi, Novocherkassk, and Temir-Tau. One of these leaflets was entitled "Why There Is No Bread." Some official told Grigorenko at a later date that this leaflet had said the same thing Brezhnev did at the Central Committee plenum of October 1964 where Khrushchev was ousted, indicating that the mass discontent in the country had more to do with Khrushchev's removal than might have been supposed.

For his oppositional activities, Grigorenko was arrested in Moscow in February 1964 and charged under Article 70 of the Russian Republic's Criminal Code (against "anti-Soviet propaganda and agitation"). To avoid an open trial, the bureaucrats had their special Serbsky Institute psychiatrists do a KGB-dictated "diagnosis" of the dissident general in April 1964. (His 1969 confinement, then, was a repeat performance.) They found that he was "mentally ill," in part because he had "reformist ideas, in particular for the reorganization of the state apparatus, linked with an overestimation of his own personality [and] messianic ideas." Even worse he "reacted in an uncritical manner to the objections of those conversing with him," namely, the KGB doctors.

In August 1964 — by direct order of Khrushchev, according
to one report — Grigorenko was demoted to the rank of private,
his pension was reduced accordingly, and he was expelled
from the party.

A few months later, Khrushchev himself was removed as
head of the party and government. The new Brezhnev-Kosygin
regime took a number of measures at first to gain popularity
at the expense of their widely hated predecessor. Apparently
this included freeing the dissident general — for the time.

"On May 23, 1965, he was discharged," Zinaida Grigorenko
relates. "A war invalid, . . . he earned his living with work
by the day as a loader. On December 29, 1965, he was removed from the category of mental invalid by a decision of
the Expert Medical Commission for Labor Matters." He was
even trusted so far as to lead classes in politics on the job
as a propagandist in Moscow Construction Bureau No. 20.

During this period Grigorenko decided at first to refrain
from oppositional activity. The Tashkent report, No. 40, states
that his first encounter with the Serbsky Institute forced him
to rethink his tactics. When first interned in the Institute, he
had protested and engaged in a hunger strike, but to no avail.
"Subsequently he became calmer, read a great deal, *saw his
mission to lie in the struggle for the revival of Leninist ideas,
for the creation of 'a generation of new revolutionaries.'* He
considered his work, for the present, to have borne no fruit,
but that it was not useless: the struggle was just, and the path
he had chosen the only correct one. He was intending to use
his trial as a platform for a speech. . . . [His self-]criticism
of his . . . illegal acts was insufficient. He agreed that he had
'behaved foolishly,' and 'had caused trouble for his family,'
but in essence he remained convinced that the political and
economic course followed was correct." (Tashkent report.)

Grigorenko decided, after being freed in May 1965, to concentrate on "scholarly work." To him, this meant writing an
uncensored account of the disastrous initial phase of the war
with Nazi Germany. He was preparing such an account in
detail in 1965 and early 1966, based on notes he himself
had made in the early months of the war (the kind of criticisms for which he had then been reprimanded) and on published and unpublished records by other Soviet citizens.

(His uncompleted work on this subject was confiscated from
him by the KGB on November 19, 1969, but not before the
partial fruits of this labor had become known. In late 1965,
a book was officially published in Moscow by the title *June
21, 1941*. Its author, the previously unknown historian A.

M. Nekrich, compiled a rather modest amount of information demonstrating Stalin's failure to prepare for the Nazi attack or to deal with it effectively in the first days of the war. The publication of the book began a hot controversy over Stalin's role in the war and reopened many questions concerning foreign and domestic policy in general. This controversy was expressed especially at a discussion of the Nekrich book held by historians and military personnel at the Institute of Marxism-Leninism around February 1966. A stenogram of that wide-ranging discussion began to circulate in samizdat. A translation in English may be found in *World Outlook,* former name of *Intercontinental Press,* November 11, 1966.)

In 1967, Nekrich, the author of the controversial book, was expelled from the party and the book withdrawn from circulation. The magazine of the Marxism-Leninism Institute, *Problems of CPSU History* (September 1967), ran a denunciation of the ideas in Nekrich's book, indirectly rehabilitating Stalin as a "military leader." This was all part of the general counter-reform developed by the Brezhnev-Kosygin regime in 1966.

Grigorenko wrote a reply to the magazine, which it of course did not publish. That reply began to circulate in samizdat. Based on the material Grigorenko had been preparing, his letter documented Stalin's military misleadership in considerable detail. And it went much further than Nekrich, who in Grigorenko's words had only "raised the edge of the curtain" on the real military disaster the Stalin clique had caused. Thus, although Grigorenko never completed his "scholarly work," it has survived in the form of his lengthy 1967 letter. The major factual parts of that document are available in English in *Intercontinental Press,* November 10, 1969.

Grigorenko stayed out of political activity for most of the first year after his release in April 1965, working on his materials about the war. But he continued to follow the political evolution of the regime. Late 1965 and early 1966 was a period of considerable ferment, as politicized elements watched the new regime to see which way it would move on democratization and "de-Stalinization." In Leningrad the clandestine Union of Communards, in its samizdat magazine *Kolokol,* criticized Brezhnev's May 1965 speech mentioning Stalin favorably. It was hit by arrests soon after. In Moscow, young literary rebels put out a samizdat journal called *Notebooks of Social Democracy,* which among other things wrote an answer to attacks on Trotsky in *Pravda* and in the official army newspaper *Red Star* of September 1965. Also in September 1965 samizdat authors Andrei Sinyavsky and Yuli Daniel were arrested. A wave of arrests swept Ukrainian dissident circles which were increasingly critical of the regime's Russification policies. In early 1966 the arrested leaders of the Union of Communards were tried and sentenced in Leningrad. The trial of Sinyavsky and Daniel in February 1966 produced a storm of protest among Western Communists and significant protest within the Soviet intellectual establishment itself. On the eve of the twenty-third Congress of the CPSU (March 1966) rumors spread that Stalin would be officially rehabilitated. A group of Old Bolsheviks and young dissenters gathered in Red Square for a protest demonstration. Earlier, on December 5, 1965, the first Constitution Day demonstration was held in Red Square, an annual protest action that continued through 1973. The demands of the Constitution Day demonstrators are freedom for political prisoners and enforcement of the civil rights guaranteed in the Soviet Constitution.

Grigorenko did not remain aloof from this stir of activity. But his participation took a new form — open, public protest demanding the rights promised by the constitution, instead of a semi-clandestine organization and "illegal" leaflets. It was also in late 1965 or early 1966 that he met the writer Aleksei Kosterin, a Bolshevik since 1916. Kosterin had survived seventeen years in Stalin's camps (1938-1955). Upon his release, he had undertaken revolutionary anti-Stalinist activity and become a major influence in dissident circles in Moscow. Grigorenko said of his three-year political alliance with Kosterin, at the funeral of the latter in November 1969, that Kosterin had turned him from simply a rebel into a dedicated lifelong fighter against the bureaucratic machine.

It is unclear whether Kosterin or Grigorenko were directly familiar with the ideas of the Left Opposition, which were still alive in the Communist Party in the early thirties. They have called for the rehabilitation of Bukharin, Zinoviev, Kamenev, Rykov, "and others." And some of Grigorenko's terminology directly echoes concepts held by the Left Opposition. For example, he explicitly refers to the top bureaucracy as a *caste* and states that even after the denunciation of Stalin's cult, there remained *Bonapartist methods of work* in the party. Regardless of whether Left Opposition influences, conscious or not, are reflected in this grouping, the central orientation of Grigorenko, Kosterin, and their friends is the same as that of revolutionary socialism: the example Lenin set in the struggle against bureaucratism. As Grigorenko put it, the Czechoslovak path was "the one we should be following—in other words, democratization and socialism, for there can be no socialism without democracy."

Roy Medvedev, in his book *On Socialist Democracy,* expresses strong disagreements with Grigorenko's ideas. He likens them to what he calls the "anarcho-Communism of 1918-20," but does not make clear if he distinguishes the Leninism of those first years of the revolution from "anarcho-Communism." In particular Medvedev was bothered by Grigorenko's call for the immediate abolition of various bureaucratic government agencies and organizations and their replacement by social control, placing management of the economy directly in the hands of the workers and technicians.

Despite his disagreements with these ideas, Medvedev acknowledges that Grigorenko and his cothinkers were the main influence in the group of radical democratic protestors who came to the fore in the period after the Sinyavsky-Daniel trial.

The kind of influence the Grigorenko-Kosterin alliance subsequently exerted upon hundreds of dissidents can be seen from the documents in this collection. They were able to attract the best rebels, such as the young Latvian collective farm chairman Ivan Yakhimovich, to a serious Leninist approach to the struggle.

The historic place of the oppositional elements that have developed in the Soviet Union, for all their disparateness and loose organization, was described rather aptly by Andrei Amalrik, "You must keep in mind that it is the first opposition of any kind, outside the inner circle of the party, since Stalin triumphed over Trotsky."

Grigorenko himself was clearly aware of the potential significance of their work. "Isn't it true," he asked, "that Lenin, together with a small group of intellectuals, helped make our revolution? That's why it is possible that a small group could help make another revolution someday."

WHY I WILL NOT VOTE FOR KOSYGIN
A Letter to Moscow Electors
by Pyotr Grigorenko

[The following open letter is one of the first documents Grigorenko issued when he resumed political activity after his first confinement in a psychiatric prison hospital. It calls on voters not to vote for Kosygin, and denounces both Khrushchev and the supposedly "liberal" Kosygin as equally complicit in the crimes of Stalin and as products of the Stalinist bureaucratic machine. It reflects the new basis Grigorenko chose for his work at this time: not underground leaflets and conspiratorial organization, but open, public protest asserting the democratic rights granted on paper in the Soviet constitution.

[The English translation is from the June 3, 1966, *Bulletin*.]

Aleksei Kosygin was part of Stalin's government. Then, at Khrushchev's side he occupied the post of first vice-president of the Council of Ministers. He therefore shares responsibility for the activities and mistakes of these two governments.

We can allow such deeds to sink into oblivion and be forgotten when it is clear that the implicated man has become conscious of his errors and does not intend to repeat them.

Unhappily this is not true in Aleksei Kosygin's case. He remains the disciple of Stalin and Khrushchev precisely in the area in which the old leaders failed most seriously: respect for socialist law. Indeed, Kosygin does not think Soviet law concerns him.

I will give several examples of this. From 1961 I spoke out against the unreasonable and often damaging activities of Khrushchev and his gang. From that time I became the victim of unlawful reprisals, and on February 2, 1964, I was arrested. I won't discuss the legality or illegality of this arrest here; neither will I dwell on the way the law was twisted in the course of the investigation and judiciary debates. I will only point out that an appearance of legality was given to the verdict when, on July 17, 1964, the military collegium of the Supreme Court of the USSR aligned itself with expert opinion on my psychological irresponsibility, shelved my case and decided that I must undergo treatment.

According to the law, the shelving of a case is as good as an acquittal. But the authorities did not look at it this way and from the time of the pronouncement of the verdict I was subjected to harsh administrative reprisals.

Shut up in the psychiatric hospital adjoining the prison, I learned by hearsay that by decision of the Council of Ministers, I had been reduced from general to second-class soldier, then struck off the army lists and deprived of all my pension rights. I never received official confirmation of this news at the time, but everything led me to believe that such a decision had been made at the insistence of Khrushchev. The illegality of such proceedings is so flagrant that the government, without wanting to rescind the decision, prefers to keep quiet about it. This is no doubt because of the absurd idea that nothing should "tarnish the honor of the uniform."

But even though I wasn't officially informed of the sanctions against me, I suffered their consequences. From the day of my arrest I haven't received a kopek. Nevertheless, according to the law I should receive the pay due to me up to the day I was struck off the army list, not to mention the service pay.

I was refused the pension legally due to me. I received no document attesting that I'd left the military, and deprived of such a document I could not find work. Accordingly, my family, which includes two invalids, and I were condemned to need.

As I could not accept such arbitrary action I protested as soon as I regained my freedom. At the end of December 1965, almost two years after my arrest and after long months of waiting, I received a pension book in the mail indicating that I would be paid a third of the sum the law gives me a right to.

I therefore protested again. In February 1966, after a long silence, I was answered with the threat of depriving me of my pension, sending me out of Moscow, and shutting me up in a psychiatric hospital for a second time.

Faced with these threats, I wrote directly to Kosygin. I asked him in my letter to tell me at least if the Council of Ministers had actually decided upon my dismissal from the army. The head of the government didn't answer me. I concluded from this that he himself was an accomplice in this arbitrary action against me and that he was perfectly aware of the threats of which I was the object.

A man guilty of such conduct does not deserve the confidence of the electors. Therefore I will vote against Kosygin and I call on the electors to do the same.

PERSECUTION OF YOUNG DISSENTERS IS ADVENTURISM

by Ivan Yakhimovich

[This January 1968 letter was sent by a young collective-farm chairman in Latvia to the Central Committee of the CPSU. It was addressed to Central Committee secretary Mikhail Suslov, considered by many the main inspirer of the campaign begun in 1965 to stop samizdat and frighten increasingly dissident Soviet citizens back into silence and conformity.

[The occasion for the letter was a trial held January 8-12, 1968, in Moscow, that has become famous as "the Trial of the Four," a landmark of the Soviet democratic movement. The defendants were tried for "anti-Soviet agitation and propaganda" in connection with their exposure — through samizdat materials — of the 1966 frame-up trial of Soviet writers Andrei Sinyavsky and Yuli Daniel. The trial of the young dissenters — Aleksandr Ginzburg, Yuri Galanskov, Vera Lashkova, and Aleksei Dobrovolsky — triggered a remarkable outburst of protest. More than 700 Soviet citizens signed their names to statements protesting the trial. Many were collective letters, some with more than a hundred names — actions unprecedented under Soviet conditions since the twenties.

[Out of this wave of protest, which continued for several months, emerged the *Chronicle of Current Events*, its first issue (April 1968) almost entirely devoted to the Trial of the Four. The *Chronicle* was the clearest expression of the fact that the trial had brought a general ferment to a head. Scattered individuals and groups fighting for democratic rights in different parts of the country now began to communicate with and defend one another, to grope toward more organized efforts.

[Yakhimovich's case illustrates this process. His letter to Suslov was written in response to the "Appeal to World Public Opinion" issued at the beginning of the Trial of the Four by Pavel Litvinov, grandson of former Soviet Foreign Minister

263

Maxim Litvinov, and by Larisa Bogoraz-Brukhman, who had never stopped fighting the arbitrary conviction of her husband, the writer Yuli Daniel, in 1966. Litvinov and Bogoraz called for public condemnation of the trial.

[Like dozens and dozens of letters in response to this appeal, from many different regions, Yakhimovich's letter began to circulate among dissidents. His letter was especially impressive because he had been singled out for praise by the Soviet youth paper *Komsomolskaya Pravda* in October 1964 as the model of a selfless, dedicated Young Communist and effective farm director.

[Yakhimovich's letter of January 1968 soon brought him a new kind of fame—a visit by the KGB, who informed him that the Litvinov-Bogoraz appeal was not genuine, but a trick of bourgeois propaganda. He did not take their word, but traveled to Moscow to find out for himself from Litvinov and Bogoraz. While there, he met Grigorenko and Kosterin and soon became part of their dissident circle, and of the "democratic movement" as a whole. (Detailed biographical information on Yakhimovich is contained in Grigorenko's article "My Friend and Comrade, Ivan Yakhimovich," in this volume.)

[The translation is from the March 29, 1968, *Intercontinental Press*, and is reprinted by permission.]

I do not have sufficient information to judge the degree of guilt of those persons subject to repression, but of one thing I am firmly convinced and one thing I know—the type of trial that took place in the Moscow City Court January 8-12, 1968, is causing enormous damage to our party and to the cause of communism, both in our country and elsewhere.

We celebrated the glorious anniversary [of the October Revolution], we pride ourselves on our achievements in economic and scientific techniques, and we ourselves, at the very time the United Nations declared 1968 the Year of the Defense of the Rights of Man, are handing the enemies of communism trump cards to be used against us. It is absurd!

We were naked, hungry, indigent, but we won, because we placed in the foreground the liberation of man from injustice, outrage, lack of rights, etc., and we can lose everything, despite our rockets and hydrogen bombs, if we forget the origins of the great October socialist revolution.

From the time of Radishchev the trials of writers have always been an abomination in the eyes of progressive, thinking people. What were our homegrown leaders thinking of when they shut Solzhenitsyn's mouth, made a fool of the poet Voznesensky, "punished" Sinyavsky and Daniel with forced labor, and involved the KGB in spectacles with "foreign enemies"? [76]

One must not subvert the confidence of the masses in the party; one must not speculate with the honor of the state, even if a certain leader wants to end samizdat.

Samizdat can be destroyed only by one means: the development of democratic rights, not their violation; observation of the constitution, not its violation; the realization in practice of the Declaration of Human Rights, since Vyshinsky signed it in the name of our state, not by ignoring it.

Incidentally, it appears that Articles 18 and 19 of the Declaration read: "Everyone has the right to freedom of thought, conscience, and religion. . . . Everyone has the right to freedom of opinion and expression; this right includes freedom to hold opinions without interference and to seek, receive, and impart information and ideas through any media and regardless of frontiers."

You know Article 125 of our constitution perfectly well; I shall not quote it. I only want to recall the thought of V. I. Lenin to the effect that "we need full and true information, and truth should not depend upon the question of whom it should serve." (*Collected Works*, fifth Russian ed., 1965, Vol. 54, p. 446.)

I believe that the persecution of young dissenters in a country where more than 50 percent of the population is younger than thirty years of age is an extremely dangerous line—adventurism. It is not toadies, not a public of yes-men (O Lord, how they have multiplied!), not mama's boys who will determine the future, but rather those very rebels, as the most energetic, brave, and high-principled members of our young generation.

It is stupid to see in them the enemies of Soviet power, and more than stupid to let them rot in prisons and make mock of them. For the party, such a line is equivalent to self-strangulation. Too bad for us if we are not capable of reaching an

---

76. [Aleksandr Radishchev, the "first Russian radical," was an early progressive thinker and writer who was sent to Siberia for criticisms of serfdom and absolutism expressed in his book *A Journey from St. Petersburg to Moscow* (1790).]

understanding with these young people. They will create, inevitably they will create, a new party. Ideas cannot be murdered with bullets, prisons, or exile. He who does not understand this is no politician, no Marxist.

You, of course, remember the "Testament of Palmiro Togliatti." I have in mind this part of it:

"A general impression has been created of foot dragging and opposition in the matter of a return to Leninist norms, which would insure both within the party and outside it more freedom of utterance and discussion on questions of culture, art, and politics as well.

"It is difficult for us to explain to ourselves this foot dragging and this opposition, particularly in view of contemporary conditions, when the capitalist encirclement no longer exists and economic construction has attained grandiose successes.

"We have always proceeded from the thought that socialism is a system in which there exists the broadest freedom for the workers who participate in the cause, who participate in an organized way in the leadership of social life as a whole" (*Pravda*, September 10, 1964).

Who benefits from a policy of foot dragging and opposition? Only overt or covert Stalinists, political bankrupts. Remember: Leninism — yes! Stalinism — no! The twentieth congress of the party did its work. The genie is at large and cannot be confined again! By no forces and nobody!

We are on the eve of the fiftieth anniversary of the Soviet army [February 23, 1968]. We are on the eve of the consultative meeting of the fraternal Communist parties [in Budapest]. Do not complicate your work for yourselves, do not darken the atmosphere in the country.

On the contrary, Comrade Podgorny could amnesty Sinyavsky, Daniel, Bukovsky, and order a review of the case of A. Ginzburg and others. [77] The Moscow City Court, in this last case, permitted the grossest violations of legal procedure. Prose-

---

77. [Vladimir Bukovsky was committed to a psychiatric prison in 1965 for organizing a demonstration against the arrest of Sinyavsky and Daniel. He was sentenced in September 1967 to three years in a labor camp for organizing a demonstration against the arrests of Galanskov and Ginzburg in January 1967. He was released in January 1970 and documented the abuse of psychiatric treatment of political dissidents. He was arrested again in March 1971 and sentenced to seven years in prison and five in exile.]

cutor Terekhov; Judge Mironov; the commandant of the court, Tsirkunenko, should be punished in the appropriate fashion, primarily for acting like idiots and abusing their power.

One cannot achieve legality by violating the laws. We will never permit anyone to prostitute our Soviet courts, our laws, and our rights. They should be thrown out with a vengeance, for they are doing Soviet power more harm than all your NTS's [Narodno-Trudovoi Soyuz — People's Labor Alliance, a right-wing Russian emigre group], BBC's, and Radio Liberty's taken all together.

Let *Novy Mir* again print the works of A. Solzhenitsyn. Let G. Serebryakova publish her *Sandstorm* in the USSR and E. Ginzburg her *Journey into the Whirlwind*. Anyway, they are known and read; it's no secret.

I live in the provinces where, for every electrified home, there are ten unelectrified, where in the winter the buses can't get through, and the mail is late by whole weeks. If information has reached us on a broad scale, you can well imagine what you have done, what kind of seeds you have sown throughout the country. Have the courage to correct the mistakes that have been made, before the workers and peasants take a hand in this affair.

I don't want this letter to be passed over in silence, for the cause of the party cannot be a private cause, a personal cause, and, even less, a second-rate cause.

I consider it the duty of a Communist to warn the Central Committee of the party and I insist that all the members of the Central Committee of the Communist Party of the Soviet Union be acquainted with the contents of this letter.

The letter is addressed to Comrade Suslov with this in view.

With Communist greetings!

THE THERMIDORIANS
FEAR THE TRUTH
by Leonid Plyushch

[Another example of the surge of protest over the Trial of
the Four is this letter to the editors of *Komsomolskaya Pravda*
from Kiev mathematician Leonid Plvushch. born in 1939. As
in the case of Yakhimovich, Plyushch represents the tendency
for struggles in scattered parts of the country to draw together.
For not only is he concerned about the general struggle for
democratic rights (he becomes a founding member of the Initiative Group for the Defense of Civil Rights in the USSR in
May 1969); he also makes clear his concern for the national
struggle of his homeland, Ukraine. He was one of those, he
points out, who attended trials of Ukrainian cultural activists
in 1965-66.

[Several details in this letter suggest that Plyushch has had
contact with non-Stalinists or anti-Stalinists of the older generation: his use of the concept Thermidor, his reference to certain
facts and personalities in Soviet history, and — outside this
letter — his association with dissident Communists like Grigorenko in several other protest statements of 1968-1969.

[A highly trained specialist, Plyushch was fired from his
job at the Cybernetics Institute in Kiev because of the present
letter. Finally finding employment as a bookbinder he was
fired again when he became active with the Initiative Group.
He remained without work, through the wish of the authorities, although he had a wife and two children, until January
1972 when he was arrested. In January 1973 he was sent to
a prison psychiatric hospital. The KGB's psychiatric specialist
Dr. D. R. Lunts diagnosed his ailment as "creeping schizophrenia with messianic and reformist ideas." The investigator
in his case was heard to remark: "Plyushch is just as crazy
as Grigorenko."

[The translation for this volume is by the editor.]

March 1968

I have before me your paper of January 28 of this year, and the letter by Aleksandr Ginzburg's mother protesting against what she calls the slanderous article published in that issue. How many times have we seen the censored press "wagging its tail like a dog" (as Marx put it) and on the other hand the uncensored samizdat. And that poses the problem: which to believe? It is difficult to verify the facts directly. How would one get access to the materials on the trial of Ginzburg and Galanskov? There is only one thing to do: proceed by indirect verification. I shall try to explain to you why I do not believe the official version, in this particular case.

Argument One

Our press has not inspired any confidence for a long time. We have seen noisy, bludgeoning articles about "enemies of the people" alternate with quiet little items about "unjustly victimized heroes of the revolution and the civil war"; fanfares about the flourishing of the villages — and shameful stories of the millions of peasants who starved to death in the *artificial famine* of the thirties in the Ukraine (this, in any case, is how the hero of the revolution and the civil war, Admiral Fyodor Raskolnikov, viewed the situation); portraits of the "Gestapo agent" Tito — and the furtive apologies to the Yugoslav Communist Party; the persecution of Pasternak, which hastened his death; the ridiculous frenzy during the campaign against culture in 1963; the worship of "our dear" N. S. Khrushchev — the current favorite — and then the small doses of poisonous hints in the form of allusions to voluntarism, lack of culture, etc.; the lies about the "anti-Semite" Sinyavsky, who supposedly detested even Chekhov (I have read his "Graphomaniacs" and I am personally convinced of the falseness of the attacks against the author); the foul lies in the journal *Perets*, about one of the best of the Ukrainian critics, Dzyuba. Even when our press states truthful thoughts, it does it in such an unworthy way that it discredits the ideas themselves (for example, the "unilateral polemic" with Steinbeck).

It is a deluge of lies, both exposed and unexposed: tyrants and flunkeys are lauded and our finest people are covered with filth; history is falsified (for example, the "miraculous" transformation of Bogdan Khmelnitsky from a traitor to the Ukrainian people — see the prewar edition of the *Great Soviet Encyclopedia* — into a hero of the same people); and so on.

This deluge of lies, which began in the late twenties, never entirely disappeared, even during the "thaw," from the twentieth to the twenty-second party congress, or a little beyond, when Khrushchev was doing balancing tricks with half-truths.

As opposed to this deluge there is samizdat.

Is it reasonable to believe the letter by Ginzburg's mother, the "Appeal to World Public Opinion," by L. Bogoraz and P. Litvinov, the "Appeal to Public Figures in Science, Culture, and the Arts," by Gabai, Kim, and Yakir? (Yakir is the son of the famous army commander who was tortured in Stalin's prisons and slandered by this very same press.)[78] I think it is.

Or are they, too, "insufficiently well informed" and "led into error by bourgeois propaganda"? Or in the pay of the NTS, the CIA, the BBC, and the Voice of America? I hope you will not peddle such stupidities.

If they were lying, the KGB and its affiliates would bring libel suits against them, with the greatest pleasure, and there would no longer be the need for special laws, like the infamous Article 190 of the Russian Penal Code. And anyway courage cannot be bought.

Argument Two

If the trial of Ginzburg and his friends had been legal, there would have been no fear of making it public. Ovcharenko states, it's true, that "representatives of enterprises and organizations with which the defendants had been connected at various times" attended the trial. But Litvinov and Yakir assert that they were stooges. I believe them, and not Ovcharenko, because I saw with my own eyes a similar trial, of so-called "Ukrainian nationalists," in 1965, and listened to the fantastically stupid explanations by the magistrates regarding the "public but not public" nature of the trial.

---

78. [The appeal by Gabai, Kim, and Yakir was issued in January 1968 to protest the Trial of the Four and other political trials and the trend toward the rehabilitation of Stalin. (The three mentioned, incidentally, the continued failure to rehabilitate Trotsky.)

Ilya Gabai, a Crimean Tatar, born in 1936, was a young rebel poet who became active in the "democratic movement." Yuli Kim, also born in 1936, like Gabai worked as a teacher. He was popular as a balladeer, a singer of unofficial protest songs. Pyotr Yakir is the well-known former activist in the protest movement, son of General Iona Yakir, who was shot in Stalin's 1937 purge of the Red Army's top commanders.]

If the trial had been legal, *Komsomolskaya Pravda* would have published the letter from Ginzburg's mother; and in public, citing the facts—facts admitted by Yakir or Litvinov (no one would dare to deny facts like search reports and trial records)—it would have proved that the author of the letter was wrong.

But, alas!—the times are gone when the Bolsheviks proudly proclaimed: "We don't fear the truth, for the truth works for us!" Their illegitimate heirs (the legitimate ones were exterminated in Stalin's prisons by Beria), the Thermidorians of October, are afraid of the truth. All they are capable of is stereotypes and distorted quotations, served up at random.

But only the truth could have convinced the public opinion both of the world and of our country that the trial was legal and just. The times are gone when the naive Feuchtwanger could persuade himself—at the trial of Radek, Piatakov, Sokolnikov, and the others—to place faith in the comedy (he could never forgive himself for this).

The falsehood of the article is obvious even to the eye that has not been instructed by past experience. The paper claims that Ginzburg and Galanskov were "paid agents of the NTS," and that they were involved in a dark conspiracy, as befits agents of an anti-Soviet organization. But the same paper, in the same article, explains that their "works" appeared abroad *under their own names.* And the conspiracy? Is this conceivable? After forty years of Thermidor, they should at least have learned how to lie.

Among those who "swallowed the bait" of bourgeois propaganda and signed the "telegram of the fifteen" to Litvinov and Bogoraz-Daniel, Ovcharenko could not bring himself to name Bertrand Russell (the personified conscience of Europe), Igor Stravinsky, etc. But he was not afraid to distort Yu. Galanskov's final statement, in which he explained that fame meant nothing to him.

It seems that Ovcharenko speaks the truth only once. "These names mean absolutely nothing to the Soviet people." In the same way, a few years ago, the name Bulgakov meant nothing to young readers, and even today the name Ivanov-Razumnik and many others mean nothing to them. I pity those readers who do not know that the great Russian writer Solzhenitsyn is living and writing in the land of Russia, the author of the novels *Cancer Ward* and *The First Circle,* and the plays *Candle in the Wind* and *The Tenderfoot and the Tramp.* I pity the people who signed the letters that appeared in *Komsomol-*

skaya Pravda on February 28 of this year. They just haven't understood anything. Perhaps they will be ashamed later on, just as those who went along with the crowd and "indignantly" demanded death for Lenin's comrades are ashamed today. For they are not all in the ranks of the Black Hundreds; rather, they are descendants of the old woman who added her sticks to the bonfire of Jan Hus. May God cure them of this "saintly simplicity." Then there will be no more bonfires. . . .

I pity those who do not know and do not want to know what has happened and is happening in their land. Raskolnikov wrote in his letter to Stalin that people would judge him for everything he had done for our revolution. I hope that the time will come when Stalin and his lackeys will be judged according to the laws of our country, and not by trampling them underfoot. You, the editors of *Komsomolskaya Pravda,* will be judged like all the falsifiers, according to the laws of honor. Under those laws you have already earned the contempt of all honest people, as the lackeys and false witnesses of our day.

WE KNOW MANY COMMUNISTS HAVE
EXPRESSED DISAPPROVAL

[The following document, dated February 24, 1968, was regarded as a major development by Soviet dissidents. In it, protesters from varied backgrounds with different points of view joined together to make a united appeal to the consultative conference of Communist parties in Budapest, Feb. 26-March 5, 1968. The purpose of the conference was to convene a larger one where, Moscow hoped, the Chinese would be condemned; the larger one was finally held in Moscow in June 1969, and Soviet protesters again appealed to the body (see below, "Appeal to World Communist Conference in Moscow").

[A few words on the signers of the present document. Litvinov and Bogoraz had already become prominent in the wave of protest over the Trial of the Four, which they helped to set off with their "Appeal to World Public Opinion," described above in the preface to "Persecution of Young Dissenters Is Adventurism." Grigorenko and Kosterin can perhaps be regarded as the inspirers of this joint appeal of the twelve. Their neo-Leninist orientation led them to seek allies for the struggle against Stalinism in the world Communist movement, and others followed their lead. Their own, separate Leninist document was sent at the same time to the Budapest conference. Gabai, Yakir, and Kim had jointly authored a protest against political trials and Stalinism shortly before this (see excerpt in preface to "Memoirs of a Bolshevik-Leninist"). A year later, Gabai was arrested at the same time as Grigorenko, and investigated, for a time, under the same case. Two other signers, Krasin and Glazov, were soon to become active in the Initiative Group for the Defense of Human Rights in the USSR, together with Yakir: in 1972, Krasin and Yakir were arrested; Glazov chose to leave the USSR to avoid the same fate, and now has a teaching post in Boston, Massachusetts. Levitin-

273

Krasnov represents the "Christian socialist" point of view among
Soviet dissenters. As for the Crimean Tatar activist Zampira
Asanova, she tells her own story eloquently in another docu-
ment in this collection — one of the speeches at the funeral of
Aleksei Kosterin.

[The translation is by the editor, from the *Chronicle of Current Events*, no. 1, dated April 30, 1968. The *Chronicle*, as
we have indicated, first appeared at this time, and began to
serve as the unofficial organ of the democratic movement, especially of its Russian-speaking component. Edited anonymously,
it appeared roughly once every two months until apparently
being suppressed as the result of a special decree of the Central
Committee of the CPSU adopted in December 1971. The last
issue of the *Chronicle* known to have appeared was no. 27,
dated October 15, 1972.

[The *Chronicle* was devoted to spreading information on all
struggles for democracy and all deprivations of civil rights
by the Kremlin authorities. It provided impressive proof of
the extent and depth of the movement for socialist democracy
in the USSR in recent years. In its first issue it described itself
as "in no sense an illegal publication" but one that was forced
to remain anonymous because of "peculiar notions about law
and freedom of information which . . . have become established
in certain Soviet organizations."]

To the Presidium of the Consultative Conference of Commu-
    nist Parties in Budapest:

A number of political trials have been conducted in our
country in recent years. The essence of these trials lies in the
fact that people have been tried for their beliefs, in violation
of their basic civil rights. Precisely as a result of this, the trials
have been conducted with gross violations of legality, the major one being the absence of publicity.

People no longer wish to submit to such illegality, and this
has led to indignation and protests, which have been increasing
from trial to trial. A great many individual and collective letters have been sent to various judicial, governmental, and party
organs, all the way up to the Central Committee of the CPSU.
These letters have gone unanswered. Instead, the answer to
those who have protested most actively has been dismissal from
their job, a summons from the KGB, and threats of arrest,

or finally — the most shocking form of reprisal — forcible confinement in a mental hospital. These illegal and inhuman actions cannot produce any positive results; on the contrary, they increase tension and give rise to further indignation.

We also believe it is our duty to point out that several thousand political prisoners, about whom almost no one knows, are in camps and prisons. They are kept in inhuman conditions of forced labor, on a semi-starvation diet, exposed to the arbitrary actions of the administration. After they complete their sentences, they are still subjected to extrajudicial and frequently illegal persecution — restrictions on their choice of a place to live and administrative surveillance, which places free men in the position of exiles.

We also call your attention to the fact of discrimination against small nations and the political persecution of people who are struggling for national equality, which is particularly clear in the case of the Crimean Tatars.

We know that many Communists abroad and in our country have repeatedly expressed their disapproval of the political repressions of recent years. We ask the participants in the consultative conference to fully consider the peril caused by the trampling on human rights in our country.

Aleksei Kosterin, writer (Moscow, Malaya Gruzinskaya St., Bldg. 31, Apt. 70); *Larisa Bogoraz*, philologist (Moscow V-261, Leninsky Prospekt, Bldg. 85, Apt. 3); *Pavel Litvinov*, physicist (Moscow K-1, Aleksei Tolstoi St., Bldg. 8, Apt. 78); *Zampira Asanova*, physician (Uzbek SSR, Fergana Oblast, Yangi Kurgan settlement); *Pyotr Yakir*, historian (Moscow Zh-180, Avtozavodskaya St., Bldg. 5, Apt. 75); *Viktor Krasin*, economist (Moscow, Belomorskaya St., Bldg. 24, Apt. 25); *Ilya Gabai*, teacher (Moscow A-66, Novolesnaya St., Bldg. 18, Block 2, Apt. 83); *Boris Shragin*, philosopher (Moscow G-117, Pogodin St., Bldg. 2/3, Apt. 91); *Anatoly Levitin-Krasnov*, religious writer (Moscow Zh-337, Third Novokuznetskaya St., Bldg. 23); *Yuli Kim*, teacher (Moscow Zh-377, Ryazansky Prospekt, Bldg. 73, Apt. 90); *Yuri Glazov*, linguist (Moscow V-421, Leninsky Prospekt, Bldg. 101/164, Apt. 4); *Pyotr Grigorenko*, construction engineer, former Major-General (Moscow G-21, Komsomolsky Prospekt, Bldg. 14/1, Apt. 96).

I WILL REMAIN A BOLSHEVIK
by Aleksei Kosterin

[Following is the text of Aleksei Kosterin's letter of resignation from the Soviet Communist Party dated October 24, 1968. He had joined the Bolshevik Party in 1916, fought in the civil war, endured the tortures of seventeen years in Stalin's camps after being arrested in 1937 (and of course expelled from the party). Rehabilitated and restored to the party after 1954 he chose at the time of this letter to resign in order to protest, in his words, "the flagrant violations of party statutes and in order to free myself from that party discipline which deprives me of the right to think."

[Kosterin's action came after a series of blows had hit the movement that had flared up so boldly earlier in the year. Hundreds of protesters had been fired, threatened, arrested, and brutalized by the KGB—yet they had continued to struggle. The simultaneous development of the Czechoslovak democratization had especially spurred them on.

[Many Soviet dissidents openly solidarized themselves with the Czechoslovak reformers. Kosterin, jointly with Grigorenko, Yakhimovich, Sergei Pisarev (an old Communist—member of the party since 1920—who had been confined in a mental hospital for political reasons under Stalin), and Valery Pavlinchuk (a young physicist and party activist from Obninsk), signed a joint statement of solidarity with the "Communists, working people, and all socialist forces" of Czechoslovakia, objecting to attempts by the "Soviet party and government leadership" to interfere in the internal affairs of Czechoslovakia. That message was delivered to the embassy of the Czechoslovak Socialist Republic in Moscow by Grigorenko and Yakhimovich on July 29, less than a month before the experiment at "socialism with a human face" was brought to an end by the Kremlin-sponsored invasion (August 21).

[On August 25, eight Soviet oppositionists demonstrated on Red Square in defense of Czechoslovakia, and were immediately

276

arrested. They were Pavel Litvinov, Larisa Bogoraz, Vadim Delone, the poet Natalya Gorbanevskaya, a young worker, Vladimir Dremlyuga, a Crimean Tatar, Galina Babai, and two young intellectuals, Viktor Fainberg and Konstantine Babitsky. The trial of five of them, in October 1968, marked an intensification of repression against the protest movement. In the wake of that trial — which Grigorenko and Kosterin, among others, issued an energetic protest against — came Kosterin's illegal expulsion from the party (involving procedures that violated party regulations). Kosterin's letter of resignation was his reply.

[At the same time, he was also expelled from the Soviet Writers Union without being informed. Having been in ill health for most of the year, as this letter indicates, he died shortly after this. His reaffirmation of faith in the revolution and in Leninism, under these conditions, is an important testament, symbolizing the living link that Kosterin represented between the modern democratic movement and the generation of Old Bolsheviks who had known the party in its best years, during the revolution and civil war and the beginnings of socialist construction. The speeches at Kosterin's funeral, printed in this volume, will provide the reader with abundant biographical information about him.

[The translation is from the *Fourth International* (London), Summer 1970.[

Appeal to the Politbureau of the Central Committee of the Communist Party of the USSR. Copies to:
The editorial committee of *Pravda* for publication;
The local Frunze Committee of the party;
The party organization of the Moscow Writers' Union.

Dear Comrades,
Over the last few months I have sent several letters to my party cell and to the Central Committee criticizing a whole series of negative phenomena in the internal life of the party and the social life of our country.

I persisted so that the problems I raised would lead to public discussion.

After having debated them clearly, in the spirit of the party, I could be told how and why I was wrong; and, if sometimes I was right, I could be supported so that positive solutions to the problems I raised could be found and applied where necessary to the party and the state.

No one can deny, I believe, that I had the indisputable right guaranteed to me by the party statutes as a party member, to take this step. What followed, however, violated the party statutes as well as violating simple common sense. I was informed that the Moscow Party Committee would debate my letters on October 17 of this year. For reasons of health, I could not be at the meeting. Following a serious and painful heart attack — the second! — that recently laid me up, the doctors categorically forbade me to participate in these discussions because of the nervous tension it would have involved. And as I had set out and argued very clearly and in a convincing way the problems I was raising, I thought the discussion could go on without me.

It appears that the content of my letters was never examined. Instead of discussing them, my letters had the labels "anti-party" and "anti-Soviet" attached to them in a totally wanton way, and I was expelled from the party.

Several other CPSU statutes were flagrantly violated:

1. The question of my party membership was ruled on without consulting my local organization.

2. I was expelled for exercising the inalienable right of a party member to express himself before the party on any important question, to present his proposals and defend them until a decision is reached about the matters they concern.

3. The transcript of the proceedings of the meeting and the decision of the Party Committee were passed on to the local committee right away without informing me first.

4. Neither was I told about the local committee's deliberations; they had evidently already decided with amazing rapidity to "settle" the question of my expulsion.

This confirmed my hypothesis that only the fact that I sent the letters was considered and not the questions raised in those letters. Their content — the real problems — has not been examined.

The label "anti-party" was wantonly attached to my letters. I had already been reproached for defending the Tatars of Crimea. To be consistent, the Party Committee should have accused me at the same time for writing in defense of the Germans living in the Volga and the Turks. It should also be remembered that in 1958 I was expelled from the party for having defended the Chechen-Ingush people. I should have been reproached for having defended with arms, in the first years of the revolution, the Leninist policy of nationalities and the right of minorities to national equality.

What happened to me is not accidental. It springs from the whole line of the party leadership. The Politbureau of the Central Committee does not itself respect the party laws, does not take them into account.

In spite of the decisions of the twenty-second and twenty-third party congresses, the name and antihuman acts of Stalin are being "cautiously" but insistently rehabilitated. And, in practice, Stalinist methods are allowed more and more scope. As under Stalin, freedom of speech, freedom of the press, freedom of assembly, freedom to meet, freedom to march and demonstrate in the streets only exist in written form in the constitution. In practice, all those who try to exercise these rights are arrested; those who protest against this arbitrary injustice are expelled from the party, dismissed from their jobs and put under constant surveillance by KGB agents. Their mouths are closed by all possible methods including the most repugnant. As under Stalin, a whole series of national minorities are the victims of savage persecution, discrimination, and veritable acts of genocide.

Stalinism manifests itself with particular clarity in the domain of foreign policy. The events in Czechoslovakia are an especially striking illustration. The supreme leadership of the party and the Soviet state is not afraid to put the world on the brink of a thermonuclear catastrophe without considering the genuine interests of our country and the world Communist movement; the leadership has provided the imperialist extremists with arguments to be used for increasing international tension. The leadership has inflicted a moral defeat with very far-reaching effects on our country and on the international Communist movement. And all this with the sole end of defending the narrow interests of caste.

A climate of oppression continues to reign in the party. The carefully sorted and selected Stalinist party machinery throws itself unanimously into the assault against anyone who expresses any doubts about the machine's policies — whoever the doubter is — or tries to criticize any member of the party and state leadership.

In our party today discussion is forbidden, the right to think is refused. You are expelled for the sole reason that you have formulated proposals that appeared good to you but don't conform to the prescriptions that rain down from on high. Only those who carry out orders from on high without thinking can live in this party; only those who consider their presence in the party an assurance of safe conduct and of their own well-being can live in this party.

I foresaw what the local Party Committee's decision would be because I knew of certain other expulsions from the party, decided upon by its committees without any discussion in the lower party organizations.

But I do not want to go to the local committee to be "corrected." I don't have the strength or health for that. I could still endure these corrections in 1937 when they followed my arrest, but not today.

As a protest against the flagrant violations of party statutes and in order to free myself from that party discipline which deprives me of the right to think, I am resigning from the Communist Party of the Soviet Union and I am returning my party membership card, number 8,293,698. I am taking this step consciously and with the hope that it will compel true Communists to think seriously about what is happening inside our party as well as in all of our society.

If the Central Committee sees that it is in its interest that all party members, including the party machine, observe the statutes, it will decide on my case publicly and punish those who are guilty of violating these statutes. If this is the case I will rescind my decision to resign from the party and continue to struggle against Stalinism inside the party ranks, submitting to its discipline.

But with or without a party card, I have been, I am, and I will remain a Marxist-Leninist Communist, a Bolshevik. My whole existence, from my youth to today, bears witness to that. If I find myself outside the party I will continue to struggle for my Marxist-Leninist ideas, for their democratic application in life, as I've always struggled, making use of all the rights given to me by our constitution and the Declaration of the Rights of Man, adopted by the United Nations and signed by our government.

THE FUNERAL OF ALEKSEI KOSTERIN

[Aleksei Kosterin died November 16, 1968, only three weeks after his resignation from the CPSU. His funeral was the occasion for an open meeting of dissidents, the first to be held in the Soviet Union since the demonstrations of the Left Opposition in 1927, at the funeral of Adolph Joffe, described in the "Memoirs of a Bolshevik-Leninist." Kosterin's friends used the opportunity to attempt to evaluate and give recognition to his leading position in the democratic movement and his role in struggling for a return to a Leninist policy toward national minorities in the Soviet Union. The compiler of this collection of speeches from the funeral itself and from the reception held afterwards was Pyotr Grigorenko. One item from the collection as originally compiled by him has been omitted — a 24-line poem by his son Andrei Grigorenko, dedicated to the memory of Kosterin.

[The translation for this volume is by Marilyn Vogt.]

"Even a life lived in the most honorable way will vanish from human memory without a trace if it is not consecrated by a fitting death."

(An Oriental Proverb)

To the Memory of
Aleksei Yevgrafovich Kosterin

This collection is dedicated to Vera Ivanovna Kosterina; to Lena, the daughter of the writer; to Alyosha Kosterin, his grandson; to the daughters of the writer's brothers — to Irma, the daughter of Mikhail, and Vera, the daughter of Vasily; and to the relatives and friends of the writer.

The Compiler

From the Compiler

November 1968

The funeral of an outstanding Soviet public figure and a remarkable writer, a man with a tragic yet enviable fate— Aleksei Yevgrafovich Kosterin—has itself turned into an exceptional event. His life and death constitute a true optimistic tragedy. To keep one's faith in the ideals one chose to serve in early youth, to keep them "right up to the gravestone" and to keep them in spite of ordeals that are terrifying even to recall, let alone to survive—it is not given to many to do this. Such is the lot of the chosen few, the fate of the Dankos,[79] who remove their hearts from their own chests in order to give light to the people. At this time it is difficult for us, the direct participants in the event, to properly evaluate what took place on November 14, 1968. But it is our conviction and belief that what happened on that day will be noted by history as a landmark of no small importance in altering the destiny of our native land. For the present we shall comment simply that in the midst of our fast-moving daily lives, this event has been *the most outstanding*.

This is not only, or rather, not so much my personal opinion as it is the opinion of the many participants in the funeral ceremony. Even as we left the crematorium, even in the aftermath of such a sad rite, many friends, acquaintances, and even complete strangers began appealing to me to compile a collection that would include the eulogy and all the speeches at the funeral. This request was expressed even more persistently at the reception and dinner after the funeral. In point of fact, it had already become a demand rather than a request: on the part of Vera Ivanovna Kosterina, his closest relatives, and his numerous friends. And I understood that was my duty to my deceased friend and to his memory, which for me is immortal. Having understood this, on the following day I set about compiling the collection. But when it was almost ready, agents of that same KGB which had so zealously driven the writer to the crematorium furnace, arrived at my home and conducted a search "with the aim of finding and confiscating documents containing slanderous fabrications discrediting the Soviet political and social system."

---

79. [The figure of Danko, in Maxim Gorky's 1894 short story "Old Izergil," is supposed to be from a Moldavian folk tale.

At the time of the search (November 19), all the documents for the collection were confiscated. I had to reconstruct everything from the beginning. I am far from having been totally successful. I am not even sure that I have succeeded in remembering all the speakers. According to the information I have at present, during the entire affair — at the morgue, the crematorium, and the reception afterwards — a total of eighteen people spoke: Anatoly Yakobson (who read the eulogy), Muarrem Dzhelyaloghly Martynov, Reshat Dzhemilev, Sergei Pisarev, Ablyamit Borseitov, Refik Muzafarov, Pyotr Grigorenko, Molla Abdurakhman, Pyotr Yakir, Khalid Oshaev, Dzhafer Akhmedov, Andrei Grigorenko, Esma Ulanova, Reshat Osmanov, Leonid Petrovsky, Veli Samedlyaev, and Zampira Asanova. I have not been able to remember the name of the eighteenth person. That was the first time that he had appeared in our group and none of us knows him or how to reach him. However, the record of his speech was accidently spared. Therefore, I am including his speech in this collection under a pseudonym which I have devised for him — "the Christian."

I have not been able to reconstruct the speeches of those who do not live in Moscow and who had left before the search of my apartment; therefore, they are not included in the collection. This applies to the speeches of the following people:

The engineer Reshat Osmanov, a first-category invalid (he has lost both his arms), who read the collective greetings of the Crimean Tatars now living in Krasnodar territory.

Molla Abdurakhman, who fought in the Great Fatherland War, who was awarded orders and medals for his military service, and who was qualified to serve as a commander of a rifle battalion and is now a major in the reserves. He spoke in the name of the Crimean Tatars living in the city of Sukhumi and its environs.

A member of the CPSU, pensioner Esma Ulanova, who spoke for the small number of Crimean Tatars now living in the Crimea.

The teacher Veli Samedlyaev, who spoke for the Crimean Tatars living in the Zaporozhye and Kherson oblasts of the Ukrainian Soviet Socialist Republic.

A member of the CPSU, pensioner Dzhafer Akhmedov, who spoke for the workers of the city of Chirchik.

I earnestly request all these comrades to send me the texts of their speeches for inclusion in possible subsequent editions of this collection.

I have tried to compensate, if only partially, for the delay in the appearance of this collection — although it was not my fault — by an account of how the funeral took place. This report is entitled "Yet Another Mockery of Sacred Feelings."

I hope by this to better fulfill my duty to you and to more graphically express my gratitude and my respect to all those who attended the funeral and helped by their participation to demonstrate that the living forces of society have still not been suffocated. They demonstrated that there are people for whom the feeling of civic responsibility is many times greater than the feeling of fear with which our people have been inoculated by decades of sinister terror — that there are people who have not succumbed but have continued to fight. Vera Ivanovna, the writer's closest relatives, and his close friends express their warmest gratitude to all those who share our grief. We particularly thank those who regardless of the time and material expense involved came from many hundreds of miles away. And we express a very special thanks to the long-suffering Crimean Tatar people who sent the largest delegation to the funeral — twenty-three people, representing all those pockets of our native land where the Crimean Tatars are now residing.

There were very few Volga Germans in attendance. But their situation is even worse than that of the Crimean Tatars. Understanding this we express admiration for the bravery of those who arrived for the funeral, but we shall not mention either the names of their representatives or their speeches.

The Compiler

Yet Another Mockery of Sacred Feelings

The funeral of a Bolshevik writer and unswerving Marxist-Leninist — Aleksei Yevgrafovich Kosterin — has added yet another page to the narrative of dreadful times and of people who have lost the essence of their humanity.

Are there any among us who have not been troubled to the depths of their souls when reading how the Catholic Church persecuted the dead Paganini.[80] But something similar has hap-

---

80. [The Catholic Church would not allow Paganini's body to be buried in any Church-owned graveyard, on the basis that he had been immoral and "in league with the devil."]

pened before our very eyes. And not in some "God-forsaken hole" or on the "outskirts of civilization," but in the capital of the first socialist state in the world. And not among some kind of obscurantists but in a "cultured society," among people calling themselves "engineers of human souls." And not in the bosom of the medieval Catholic Church or some obscurantist sect but under the initiative of people calling themselves Communists who carry party cards in their breast pockets with pictures of Ilyich.

Aleksei Kosterin died November 10 at 9:20 a.m. No one, of course, thought that he would live forever. He had so much optimism — such youthful enthusiasm. His eyes had the glitter of youth and his laughter was so infectious that none of us expected the worst. His condition had deteriorated before the holiday. On the evening before (November 9) his condition was so grave that the doctor told his wife, Vera Ivanovna: "Prepare yourself for the very worst." But no one wanted to. And Aleksei did not let us have such thoughts. He joked and laughed as he always had, and discussed the perspectives of the democratization of our life with his friends. Therefore, when the terrible, the unthinkable happened, we were all dumbfounded, shaken, and in such a state of shock that the first day we were incapable of taking care of anything — either notifying friends and relatives or informing the writers' organization which he had been a member of since the day it was formed.

How surprised we were when on the following day (November 11) our representatives — the writer's niece Irma Mikhailovna and one of his friends, Pyotr Yakir — upon arriving around noon at the office of the Writers' Union — discovered that everyone knew all about it. More than that, they had already set a time for the cremation — 4 p.m., November 12 — meaning we had at best one day at our disposal. Our representatives protested, of course. Pyotr Yakir said: "That is enough time to burn the body, of course, but we also need time to say farewell to the deceased." And it was then that for the first time those words were uttered which later accompanied us all the way to the ovens of the crematorium: "You think you need a demonstration? That we won't allow!"

Our representatives appealed to Ilin [secretary of the Moscow Writers' Union]. They cited the fact that for deceased veterans of the Soviet Writers' Union the following were provided: to make an announcement of the death to the press, including the place and time of the wake and funeral; to publish an obituary and provide a place at the Writers' Club where the body could be on display and the memorial ceremony could be held; to provide for burial at the expense of the literary fund at the Novodevichy cemetery. They requested all these things be provided for Kosterin — a member of the Soviet Writers' Union from the day of its inception. But everything was denied — and again under the pretext of their pet phrase: "We will not allow you to organize a demonstration." Towards the end, everything was "smoothed over" and they provided payment from the literary fund for the hearse and the cremation. However, we had to announce that we were refusing the favor because the literary fund arranged the service of the hearse and the delivery of the coffin in such a way that we could view the deceased only during those few minutes that he would be on the crematorium pedestal. The literary fund then compromised: it agreed that the deceased would be on display in the coffin for one hour in the funeral parlor at the mortuary. It paid for two blocks of time at the crematorium, i.e., it granted us the pedestal and platform for half an hour, and chartered two buses in addition to the hearse. (Later the literary fund refused to pay the bill for the buses.) Without the aid of the literary fund we rented a dining room for the reception after the funeral. In this way everything was arranged more or less properly.

But on the day of the funeral, surprises suddenly began to happen. First, the buses bringing the people and the wreaths were not allowed to come up to the mortuary. They were stopped 800 meters away. Who stopped them? The municipal traffic-control service. By a strange coincidence the city set up a roadblock near the entrance to the Botkin Hospital exactly an hour before our arrival. It is true that the roadblock was not kept there long; it was removed immediately after we left the mortuary. During the time of its existence, it did a huge amount of work — it detained our two buses and . . . nothing more.

The second surprise, it is true, was not totally unexpected. There turned out to be increasing anxiety about our "security" on the part of the militia and agents of the KGB. A good number of people from both groups gathered around the mortuary. A couple of people with little blue passbooks went into the section where the body of the deceased was being prepared. What took place next was really remarkable. They did not bring out the deceased at 5 p.m., as was arranged; nor at 5:10, nor at 5:20. We became agitated. Several times the director of the mortuary, whom we summoned, mumbled something unintelligible and looked at us with imploring eyes. The militia officer on duty at the entrance of the mortuary was literally besieged by my friends, who were expressing their indignation in a very energetic manner. But he did not try to argue with us or to justify what was going on. He simply said: "Well, what do you want of me? I understand how you feel and I sympathize with you. But didn't you see who dropped in there? I am powerless against them."

At this time we got another surprise. The comrades who were preparing the reception and dinner for after the funeral came up and reported: "They have denied us the dining hall." Everything was all ready, but two people in civilian clothes drove up in a grey "Volga" and went in to see the director. Subsequently the superintendent and the chef were called in. After that the deposit was returned to our comrades, without any motivation being given for this repudiation of a fixed agreement.

It became clear that they wanted to wreck the funeral. The enemies of this progressive writer and outstanding social figure tried to vent on him in death the anger that had accumulated against him while he lived. We went to confer with Vera Ivanovna. She decided: "If the body of the deceased is not brought out immediately, I will have it taken, not to the crematorium, but home. Tomorrow or the day after we will organize a funeral without the participation of the literary fund. We will conduct a memorial ceremony in the courtyard."

Our conversation was overheard "in passing" by a certain person who had been dubbed by the wits among us as "the mystery man in the hat." He is the one who by our observations headed the KGB's "send-off crew" for Kosterin. He had not, apparently, made arrangements for this turn of events, and the deceased was immediately brought out. At 5:37 p.m., we finally placed the coffin on the pedestal and began the mourning ceremony. It came off without excesses. The friends of the deceased formed such a compact and monolithic mass around the coffin that no one dared to cause a disturbance and offend us in our grief. I was the last to leave the mortuary, making certain that no one was detained, that everything was taken away, and that everyone was accommodated in the buses and in the hearse.

The director of the mortuary, having heard the eulogy and the speeches of the friends of the deceased, came after me looking totally embarrassed and confused. I was already at the exit when he looked at me imploringly and said: "Please understand that I was not responsible for this." But I could express no sympathy for him. I thought then and I still think that people can make themselves into *real human beings* only by their own efforts. In no case would I allow anyone to interfere in a matter for which I was responsible. There are many among us (unfortunately, very many) who as soon as they hear the magical word "KGB" will carry out the most shameful deeds on the command of someone representing this organization. But we must someday grow out of this habit. We must, finally, recall the existence of such good words as *human dignity.*

The trip from the mortuary to the crematorium passed without incident except that the driver of one of the buses suddenly "forgot" how to get from Krasnaya Presnia to the Crimea Bridge and turned the wrong way. But our comrades were watchful enough to quickly "explain" to the driver which road he should stick with. At the crematorium our anxiety intensified. As we approached, we saw that the yard was literally overrun with members of the militia and plainclothes police who here too were being directed by "the mystery man in the hat." But now he didn't have a hat on. Apparently it got too "cold" for him and during the trip he had exchanged it for a cap. It was just like a bad detective story.

However, our anxiety turned out to be premature. Three to four hundred friends of the writer had gathered outside the crematorium hall. They entered the hall immediately behind the coffin in a dense mass. In doing this they exhibited such confidence and solidarity that the plainclothes police did not dare to wedge their way into this mass and remained by the entrance to the hall and on the edges of the crowd inside. Here too there was an attempt to delay the start of the funeral. But our people raised the coffin and carried it to the pedestal as soon as the time came (7 p.m.). The attendants, apparently not initiated in the refinements of "higher politics," turned on the lights and the second part of the mourning ceremony began. In the middle of my speech we heard "Finish it up!" over a microphone. This abrupt command was repeated several minutes later. Afterward, the "mystery man in the hat," as I learned later, shouted to the superintendent of the crematorium: "Release the coffin!" But standing firmly together our comrades declared: "Just try! We haven't even used up half our time." This was said in such a tone that the superintendent did not hasten to carry out the order and the "mystery man" did not dare repeat it.

The funeral was concluded as planned. It took exactly eighteen minutes instead of the allotted thirty. And this time, Aleksei Kosterin and not his persecutors emerged the victor. After decades of suffocating silence *the first free meeting had been held*. My friend can be proud. Even with his death he gave a new impulse to the democratic movement in our country. And the democratic public can be proud. The enemies of progress and democracy, those who stifle everything free and progressive, enlisted for their "Operation: *Funeral*" a large number of specialists — people trained in such matters and who have made them their life-long profession. They readied all these experts specially — they conducted a trial run of the impending operations, worked out contingency plans, and discussed them. But we had not prepared at all. We didn't even know who would come to the funeral. The relatives and closest friends of the deceased were busy with the organization of the funeral. Voluntary helpers were continuously coming to them. We had not even composed a list of speakers for the meeting. We simply gave the floor to anyone who asked for it. And despite that, we won. We won because justice was on our side. There was confidence that we were doing the right thing; and we had on our side the courage and initiative born of this confidence. No one delegated anyone else to carry the coffin to the pedestal. While we, the self-appointed leaders, were haggling with the superintendent of the crematorium, arguing that the time had come, the coffin was raised and placed on the pedestal. After this the light was lit and all that remained was for me to proceed to the rostrum.

No one authorized anyone to keep an eye on the activities of the "mystery man in the hat," yet all the same at the necessary moment our people turned out to be right alongside him and frustrated his sinister intentions. No one authorized anyone to carry out that measure which all in all turned out to be the most important for the unity and solidarity of the mass of people who had come to the funeral. I mean the initiative of the women among us in preparing the black bows and bands of ribbon worn in mourning. Using a way of detecting known only to them, they distributed these bands and bows only to those who had come to honor the memory of the writer. Out of all the plainclothes police only the "mystery man in the hat" ended up wearing a black band. It was precisely by this that all our friends singled him out. The presence of the mourning bands and bows made it possible to distinguish ourselves from the unwelcome arrivals and converted the mass of people, who did not know, or hardly knew, each other, into a unified monolith. This incident attests better than anything else could that the just cause triumphs no matter how the opponents of this cause may fight against it. The only thing necessary is faith.

No matter how this meeting is judged now, everyone at the time felt confident that a great victory had been won. In line with this, everyone was in a triumphant and elated mood. We did not want to disperse and we all gathered around the buses. But there was no point in tempting fate any further. Provocateurs might start something; they might try to get revenge for having suffered a defeat in the struggle against the deceased Kosterin by making trouble for us. I told those present how they denied us the dining hall in an attempt to spoil the reception and dinner after the ceremony. Then I proposed that we go to my apartment and organize the reception there.

After this, the great bulk of our "guardians" cast off from us. The "mystery man in the hat" apparently did not consider that a mere forty-five square meters of living space could accommodate the many, many people who wanted to be friends not for personal gain but out of noble convictions. At any rate, everyone who had come in the tightly packed buses crowded into my apartment. People filled every room — the kitchen, bathroom, corridor, and the stairway landing in front of the apartment. And a glass of vodka, a sandwich, and a cup of tea were served to everyone. Incidentally, all this provisioning was organized without the participation of us, whose apartment it was; and by whom, we still don't know. And there was a warm, friendly word for everyone. The memorial meeting continued there. It was very late at night before the wife of the deceased and his closest friends left my home.

I think that everyone present at the funeral left with a warm memory of a great man and a feeling of satisfaction that every one of them had fulfilled his civic duty with dignity and honor.

P. Grigorenko

To the Memory of Aleksei Yevgrafovich Kosterin (The Eulogy)

On November 10, 1968, four months before his seventy-third birthday, a man and citizen, a most honorable and untarnished Bolshevik and writer left us.

His life was a remarkable illustration of the integrity, honor, talent, energy, creative enthusiasm, and tragic fate that have characterized the Russian working class.

Alyosha was born in the Volga region to a family that had been proletarian for generations. As a sixteen-year-old youth, following after his older brothers, he joined the revolutionary movement and began to contribute to the working class press. Beginning in 1916 he was a member of the Russian Social Democratic Labor Party (Bolshevik). Three years in a czarist prison hardened him and strengthened his revolutionary views. The socialist revolution stirred even the older generation of workers. And in 1918 the mother and father of these three Communists — the Kosterin brothers — also joined the Bolshevik Party.

During the civil war Aleksei was one of the leaders of the partisan movement in the Northern Caucasus and a correspondent for the Bolshevik press. His escape under fire from a Denikin prison is but one of the many episodes which show his courage during that period. When the war was finally over he devoted himself totally to his favorite work — that of a journalist and writer. His creative abilities flourished in the twenties. Besides carrying out the exhausting day-to-day work of a journalist, he wrote and published several short novels: *While the Volga Sleeps* (1921), *Fragments of Life* (1926), *The Forest Is Green Gold* (1930); and several collections of stories: *Scarlet Oil* (1923), *At a Turn in Life*, *The Two*, *The Short Year 1918*, and *As the Day Flows On* (1924), and *Naval Heart* and *Airplane Pilot* (1928).

The distinctive feature of Kosterin's gift for writing is that he takes a fact of life as his starting point for any work and portrays it just as it is, without resorting to fiction and fantasy. And because of the author's very perceptive eye, all of his works make very engrossing reading. He knows how to pick what is most noteworthy, representative, and typical out of the normal flow of life's events and features. In writing his works he did not adhere to strict literary formulas. His main concern was to depict the relevant event as precisely as possible and to subject it to the most objective appraisal. For that reason his short novels and stories in certain cases take the form of sheer reporting, publicistic writing, philosophical judgments, and pointed political pamphlets. This gives them originality and underscores their candor.

But this special feature which had very favorable repercussions among the readers brought only trouble to the author himself. It was precisely because of this that his creative genius became unacceptable to the powers that be.

Toward the end of the twenties fewer and fewer of his works were published, and during a seven-year period in the thirties only two short books of his came out, and those were about the civil war: *Volga on Fire* (notes of a partisan) and a collection of stories, *Memorable Days*. His works did not fit in with the themes of the time. He was only able to portray what he had encountered in real life. But he was expected to "search," mainly in *Pravda* editorials, in speeches of "the leaders" or in his own head, for things that were compatible with the interests of the rulers and to write about these things as you would about real facts. Because of this, Kosterin's literary works and news reports fluttered into the editor's wastebasket.

After he had trudged all over Kalinin Province on foot in the early spring of 1934, sending in his correspondence every day to *Izvestia*, he was suspended from the special correspondents corps. And how could it have been otherwise! His daily letters, taken all together, gave a picture of the village that was quite different from the one the literary hacks of every stripe had been making a fuss about for so many years. On the contrary, Kosterin showed convincingly, with a well-argued case and a captivating literary style, that the villages remained as they were before—ignorant, illiterate, impoverished, and impotent against arbitrary rule. It is perfectly clear that such a seeker of truth is not only unsuitable as a writer for the Stalinized press; he is downright dangerous for the regime of oppressors and liars.

And in May 1938 they arrested him. Earlier—in 1937—his older brother Mikhail was arrested and shot. Mikhail was a "Red professor," from the first graduating class of the Institute of Red Professors. His older brother Vasily was expelled from the party and fired from his job.

Seventeen years were torn from Aleksei's life by prison where he was subjected to savage torture, in the Stalin-Beria death camp at Kolyma and in exile. There could be no question of any kind of literature during this time, even of the epistolary genre. It was difficult enough just to survive. But Aleksei was lucky. He did survive. His family, however, suffered heavy losses. His persecuted, terrorized brother Vasily died. His father — a highly skilled metal worker — starved to death. His older daughter, Nina Kosterina, was killed in the battles against the fascist invaders. She left a diary which is an astounding document of that era. In it an innocent and honest soul confesses that, not believing the slander about her father, she built her life after his example. She looks at many things in life with wide-eyed, naive astonishment. But what she is not able to comprehend intellectually, she perceives with her uncorrupted sense of right and wrong, which had been quite highly developed ever since her childhood. As a result, an ordinary schoolgirl, who was young and didn't have many experiences in life and was not trained in the art of writing, vividly and convincingly paints a picture of the sinister, morally corrupting influence of Stalin's regime on the life of society. For that reason, *The Diary of Nina Kosterina* after being published in *Novy Mir*, spontaneously achieved renown all over the world, side-by-side with the diary of Anne Frank. Nina's diary is not only a monument of our age, not only the solemn anthem of an impeccable and honest soul, but in addition it is an eternal and ardent tribute to the one who inspired in this soul a disposition toward lofty and impeccable ideals — Nina's father — Aleksei Yevgrafovich Kosterin. He was left with only his mother, who was expelled from the party immediately after Mikhail's arrest; his younger daughter Lena; and the daughters of Mikhail and Vasily — Irma and Vera.

His mother, as she lay dying in the arms of her youngest son — the only remaining member of what was at one time a great and closely knit family of proletarian revolutionists — left as a legacy to him a life for the people. And Aleksei religiously carried forth his mother's legacy. He again took up the pen and devoted himself totally to the struggle against illegality and arbitrariness and for democracy and humanism. He devoted himself to the struggle for the elimination of the social injustices against small nations which were the victims of unjust and brutal repression during the years of the Stalinist terror and which are still being discriminated against at the present time: Volga Germans, Crimean Tatars, Chechen-Ingush, Turks, and several others. For this he was expelled from the party and subjected to various forms of administrative repression which included being summoned for interrogation by the KGB, and being searched. But he did not stop fighting and he achieved something. His membership in the party was restored. His notes on camp life at Kolyma were published, although in a very mutilated form: the collection *Along Paths Through the Taiga* [*Taezhnymi Tropami*]. Two stories were published in *Novy Mir* and one in *Moskva*, and a piece of art criticism he had written was published in the journal *Iskusstvo* [Art].

But what was published was not even a fraction of his work during that period. The censored press would not publish his principal works. Therefore, they circulated in samizdat. These writings in essence constitute a special phase of his civic-literary work. In some of them he achieves the accusatory force and the poignancy of a great publicist. It is hard to exaggerate their impact on readers' minds and souls. For example, such works as *Reflections from a Hospital Bed* and *Meditation on a Sleepless Night* and his totally unusual appeal to someone who perished on the front lines, *To Brother Kadyr Tarpi Dzhemilev from Sister Gulkhan Tarpi Dzhemileva*—in which the true history of a typical Crimean Tatar family is revealed, in a way that attains the heights of artistry—are shocking to read, and inspire invincible indignation against the heirs of the cause and the crimes of Stalin and against the system of arbitrariness and illegality.

Naturally, in the light of all this, the Stalinists could not overlook Kosterin. Even though he was gravely ill, they began to persecute him savagely. The party organization of the Moscow writers even took part in this. And the worn-out heart of the old fighter could not endure so much. A tragic outcome ensued.

After the death of our friend, we discovered that the Stalinists, in order to finish him off more surely, had prepared one more blow. On October 30, the Presidium of the Writers' Union, unbeknownst to Kosterin and the writers' community generally, expelled him from the Soviet Writers' Union. In the past fifteen years this was the third time a writer has been expelled for political reasons (the first was Pasternak), and the second such expulsion to be pushed through by the apparatus, without the knowledge of the rank-and-file members of the local writers' organization (the first was Oksman).

An Oriental proverb says: "Even a life lived in the most honorable way will vanish from human memory without a trace if it is not consecrated by a fitting death." The death of Aleksei Kosterin was worthy of his life. He went down like a fighter, never yielding to the enemy. As a sign of protest against the violation of Leninist principles in the party and in the country, the invasion of Czechoslovakia by Soviet military forces, and the arbitrary actions of the government against him, on October 24, 1968, he declared his resignation from the party and turned in his party card to the Central Committee. Even in this case, on the very threshold of death, he acted like a genuine Bolshevik-Leninist, like a fighter — thinking not about himself but about those who would remain after him. He already lacked the physical strength for a head-on confrontation with the enemies of the cause for which he had struggled throughout his life — those who by deceit and coercion were able to seize leading positions in the party to which he had unrelentingly devoted himself. He behaved like a soldier who, although mortally wounded on the battlefield, uses his last bit of strength to throw his own dying body on the guns of the enemy in order to help his comrades who are attacking. He was a Bolshevik-Leninist and remained so until his death. He wrote these words about twenty-five days before he died:

"I am a soldier of the Leninist revolutionary army, a representative of the generation that followed Lenin; and, therefore, risking life to the last breath and even after death, I will fight for those ideas, for the teachings of Marx, Engels, and Lenin."

Yes, Aleksei Kosterin is fighting even now. And he will continue to fight through his writings and through his example of civic valor. And his name, unlike many which are now basking in the rays of fame, will not be forgotten. His friends and cothinkers will arm themselves with his cause and his name and will carry them on to our great goal — the victory of *democracy*, the genuine and complete *emancipation of humanity*, and *humanism*.

A Group of Friends and Cothinkers
(Read at the Mortuary of the Botkin Hospital
by Anatoly Yakobson.)

Speeches at the Mortuary of the Botkin Hospital

Muarrem Dzhelyaloghly Martynov
(Pensioner from the city of Bekabad, a national poet of the Crimean Tatar people; spoke in his native language, using the verse form customary to him.)

In accompanying the dear friend of our people Aleksei Yevgrafovich Kosterin on his last journey, I wish to utter my words of farewell in my native language.

To A. Ye. Kosterin [81]

O, Democrat Kosterin! You have left us forever.
Who will we look to now for support—we the exiles, the
  Crimean Tatars!
You did not die a natural death—they killed you.
Having suffered in prisons and camps, faced with repression wherever you turned,
You did not close your eyes to arbitrariness, you met
  the enemy head on.
Following Lenin's tradition, you took the offensive
  against the enemy yourself.
"Let our party be just and then there will be no
  nationalism," said our leader Lenin.
Sleep peacefully, most honorable of Russia's sons.
You will always be in the hearts of the Tatar people.
Farewell, farewell, our faithful friend!
Oh, Aleksei Yevgrafovich! You are like a son to our
  people!

---

81. [The original poem was in the Crimean Tatar language. The English translation in this collection is from the Russian translation of the Tatar original. (The translation into Russian was made from Crimean Tatar by Mustafa Abduldzhemil.)]

In mourning clothes you have dressed us, the deserted ones.
The eyes of the Tatar people you have today filled with
   tears.
We will cherish your legacy as the light of our lives.
We will keep your ashes forever.
The Crimean Tatar people are eternally grateful to you.
They are ready to become the kind of fighter that you
   were.

Sergei Petrovich Pisarev [82]
(Scientific worker, Moscow, Member of the CPSU since 1950.)

It is with severe pain and intense grief that we accompany
our dear friend Aleksei Yevgrafovich Kosterin on his last
sorrowful journey. I have worked with him since the first years
of the revolution and am proud to have been his friend. He
was always devoted to the party and to the cause of Lenin,
and he was always a principled man. When, after the death
of Vladimir Ilyich, a departure from Lenin's policies was initiated, Aleksei Yevgrafovich struggled against this tendency
and was subjected to relentless and savage persecution. He
fought against all the departures from Leninism, especially
against the departure from Lenin's policy on nationalities.
He always spoke out with great strength and courage for
the rights of minority peoples, for the return of the Crimean

82. [Sergei Petrovich Pisarev was one of the group of five who
formed a Communist circle in 1968—the others being Kosterin,
Grigorenko, Yakhimovich, and Valery Pavlinchuk (see the prefatory note to Kosterin's letter of resignation and Grigorenko's statement, "My Friend and Comrade, Ivan Yakhimovich.") After the arrest
and forcible confinement of Grigorenko and Yakhimovich in mental
hospitals in 1969, Pisarev was active in exposing that abuse of "psychiatry" for purposes of repression. Pisarev himself had been confined
in a mental hospital for political reasons in 1953, in the last days
of Stalin's rule, and was freed in 1955 as part of the post-Stalin
reforms.]

Tatars to their ancient homeland, for the restoration of national autonomy for these people and for the Volga Germans.

Aleksei Yevgrafovich placed the question of the restoration of national autonomy for these people before two party congresses. He felt that this departure from Leninism — this violation of the rights of small nations — was undermining the authority and power of the entire state and discrediting in the eyes of the whole world the great ideas advanced by Marx, Engels, and Lenin. The loss of Aleksei Yevgrafovich is agonizingly painful for his family and near ones, for all his friends; but it is also a grave loss for the minority nationalities of our country, and for all progressive people.

Aleksei Yevgrafovich immortalized his name not only as a leading Bolshevik writer, but still more as a fighter for the rights of small nations. Our children and grandchildren will not be able to name ninety-nine of one hundred present-day writers, but they will remember Kosterin and they will always take pride in him. And the cause for which he fought as a Bolshevik will be crowned with complete victory. All the progressive and honest people of the country and, most of all, we, his friends, will carry on this work — the struggle for the restoration of Leninist national autonomy to the Crimean Tatar and Volga German peoples. [83] This issue is not one of concern only to the unfortunate nationalities. Not at all!!! It is everyone's business. It involves the honor of our entire country. For precisely this reason the Leninist policy on nationalities must triumph in our country. And this will be the very best, and truly eternal, monument to our dear Aleksei Yevgrafovich. His memory, like the cause to which he devoted his whole life, will never die!

---

83. [The Volga Germans are descendants of German colonists attracted to Russia in the late eighteenth century by Catherine the Great to colonize territory along the Volga river. In 1924 the Autonomous SSR of Volga Germans was founded, one of eighteen German "national districts" established in the Soviet Union. The Republic was abolished in 1941 during the Nazi invasion and the Volga Germans were shipped wholesale to Central Asia. Their efforts to attain the right to return to their homeland along the Volga have been unsuccessful. Since 1956 the exile regimes under which they were forced to live have been lifted. Charges that they collaborated with the Nazis were dropped in a decree of 1964, but the Volga Republic has not been reestablished despite the repeated requests and actions launched for that purpose by the Volga Germans.]

Ablyamit Borseitov

(A teacher from Syr-Darya, west of Tashkent in the Uzbek SSR. He spoke in the Crimean Tatar language.)

I express my sincerest condolences to the faithful friend of our dear Aleksei Yevgrafovich, Vera Ivanovna Kosterina; to his grandson, Alyosha, to his daughter, Lena; and to all the relatives and friends of the deceased. We, the Crimean Tatars, are grieving with you. And as testimony of this, an unending stream of telegrams continues to pour in from Crimean Tatars, expressing their deepest, most heartfelt sorrow and their warm love for Kosterin.

It may be inappropriate here but I wish to express my anger and protest against those who even after Kosterin's death continue to harass him. I have in mind the barriers erected by the authorities to prevent people from expressing their sorrow and deep respect for this great and genuine *human being*.

This is inexcusable! And we here, by the remains of the one so dear to us, vow that we will struggle more persistently than ever for the cause for which he struggled. And we believe that the just cause will triumph, that our national autonomy will be restored and throughout our great country illegality will be annihilated, and that *justice, freedom,* and *democracy* will be reestablished.

May the memory of this fighter, who fell in the struggle for these ideas — our dear and unforgettable friend Aleksei Yevgrafovich Kosterin — live forever.

Reshat Dzhemilev [84]
(Engineer from Krasnodar Territory.)

Dear Comrades,

The death of Aleksei Yevgrafovich Kosterin causes sorrow for many minority peoples in our country whose rights have been and continue to be violated by great power chauvinism. It is a source of grief for the Chechen and Ingush people, the Volga Germans, and the inhabitants of the far-off tundra. It is a source of great sorrow and an irretrievable loss also for us, the Crimean Tatars. We see in Kosterin the man who organized and led the progressive Soviet intelligentsia in support of the struggle of the Crimean Tatar people for equality and for the right to return to their homeland in the Crimea.

In Kosterin, Russia lost one of its best sons, thanks to whom sincere friendship may still have been preserved between Russian and non-Russian peoples in our country. I am convinced that the greatness of a nation and its people is not determined by its ability to occupy the territory of another state with armored military units and to impose its will on smaller nations. Real greatness is now taking shape among a number of people in

84. [Reshat Dzhemilev, born in 1932, an engineer, was regularly sent as a representative of Crimean Tatars to Moscow between 1965 and 1969. He was one of twenty representatives of his people at a meeting with high state officials in June 1967, following which charges of treason against the Crimean Tatar people were dropped. In December 1967 he was tried and sentenced to one year in a labor camp on charges of organizing mass meetings of Crimean Tatars in late 1967 in defense of their rights. Active in the circles around Grigorenko, Kosterin, and the Initiative Group, he was one of five Tatars who demonstrated in June 1969 in Moscow during a world Communist conference for a return to a Leninist nationalities policy. He was expelled from Moscow and restricted to his home in Krasnodar province. After that he was charged with "anti-Soviet slander" for his speech at Kosterin's funeral and for helping Grigorenko compile the present text. He was arrested again in October 1972, as part of the drive to suppress the *Chronicle* and its supporters, a drive that culminated in the Yakir-Krasin trial of August 1973.]

our nation who are able to say decisively and resolutely *"No more!"* to any manifestation of arbitrariness and to the violation of human rights, regardless of the possible personal consequences. Kosterin was such a man.

Since the birth of the Soviet state not one Soviet writer — I emphasize — *not one Soviet writer*, even one that may have won literary prizes three times — has been so loved, respected, and renowned among the Crimean Tatars as Aleksei Yevgrafovich. We appreciated the greatness of his soul, his nobility and courage.

The name of Kosterin will occupy a lasting place in the hearts of the Crimean Tatars forever.

Farewell, our faithful friend.

Professor Refik Muzafarov [85]

(Doctor of philological science from the city of Dzhambul, Kazakh SSR.)

Comrades! Don't condemn me for not removing my ceremonial hat before addressing you. And do not condemn those among you who, like me, have not removed their hats. According to the custom of my people — the Crimean Tatars — when you accompany the deceased on their last journey you are supposed to wear a ceremonial hat.

The representatives of my people who spoke before me already told of the severe wound which the death of Aleksei Yevgrafovich Kosterin has inflicted on our small nation. In truth, the sorrow of our people knows no limits. I don't think there could be a single Crimean Tatar who has not heard of the writer Kosterin. Everyone knows of him — from the very old to the small children. There are already legends about him. Our national poets and singers praise him.

I knew little of Kosterin as a writer. His one book to be

---

85. [Professor Refik Muzafarov, a doctor of philological sciences, was a Crimean Tatar representative to Moscow for several years, attending the June 1967 meeting described above in the note about Reshat Dzhemilev. Because of his activities in defense of his nation's rights, he has been attacked in the press and dismissed from nearly a dozen teaching posts.]

published in the post-camp years — which according to Kosterin emerged from the censors as a "wretched amputee" — and
the three stories published in Moscow periodicals, don't permit us to judge his merits as a writer. But what he did for
our people serves as evidence that he was an extremely sensitive man. And for a writer to be truly great, this is essential.
I can only conclude, therefore, that he was a truly great and
talented writer who proved capable of working his way through
even those incredibly complicated conditions in which our deceased friend lived and worked. And I promise to do everything
in my power to bring his literary heritage to my people.

I was unlucky. I never had the opportunity to become personally acquainted with this writer during his lifetime. Now
I very much regret that I didn't abandon all my pursuits
and make a special trip to Moscow for this purpose. That
can't be changed now. But I was able to do one thing — to
convey here by his remains the sorrow of my people. It is
hard on me, it is hard on the entire nation to lose such a
companion in arms, such a teacher.

We, those who remain behind, will preserve his memory
and will struggle for the cause to which he devoted his whole
life.

May your memory and fame, our dear friend, live forever!

Pyotr Grigorenko

(Candidate of Military Science, Moscow.)

> *The greatest feats in time of war*
> *Which bring shame to the smitten foe*
> *In the minds of humanity*
> *And in the court of the centuries*
> *Fade when compared with civic valor.*
>   (K. Ryleev, *Ode to Civic Valor*)

And *civic valor* is a quality very few people are endowed
with. But it was an inherent and integral part of Aleksei Yevgrafovich, whose body we accompany today on its last earthly
journey.

I have seen heroic military feats performed. Many have performed them. In the name of victory over the enemy the masses
went to their death on the battlefield. But many even of those
who were genuine heros in battle are nowhere to be found

when it is time to show civic valor. To carry out feats of civic valor you have to love the people very much, to hate evil and illegality, and to believe—believe wholeheartedly—in the victory of a just cause. All of this was a matter of course for Aleksei. Therefore, today is just that much more painful.

Dear Vera Ivanovna, dear Lena and Alyosha, dear Irma and Vera, dear relatives of the deceased. We understand how difficult this is for all of you, particularly for you, Vera Ivanovna—the person who was closest to him. We understand how difficult it is for his daughter Lena and for the grandson you are raising—the heir of the name and cause of his grandfather—Alyosha Kosterin. We understand too the grief of, Irma who in Aleksei Yevgrafovich lost not only the brother of her executed father but a man she loved like a father. But believe me when I say that our grief and the sorrow of his friends and comrades in arms is also very great. Our forces have been depleted and nothing can replace this loss. We will obviously be aware of a big gap in our ranks for a long time to come and there will be a lingering pain in our hearts. That is why, while I express my very sincere condolences to you, at the same time I express my sympathy to all his friends—to the entire democratic movement and particularly to all those who are fighting for the equality of small nations. In Aleksei Kosterin they lost their ardent, unswerving, wise, and sincere defender.

I see here representatives of many small nations. More would be here if they had found out about his death in time. But, unfortunately, our press did not choose to print notifications of it. And the telegraph offices saw to it that certain telegrams did not go out very quickly. In Fergana [southeast of Tashkent, in Uzbek SSR], for example, a telegram was received only yesterday evening. Therefore, while expressing condolences to all of you, I cannot help but at the same time express my indignation and contempt for those who tried in every way to hinder us from holding the type of funeral this man deserves.

My dear comrades! My heart, too, aches with sorrow. And I am crying with you. I especially express my sympathy to you—the representatives of the Crimean Tatar people who have suffered so much. Many of your people knew Aleksei Yevgrafovich during his lifetime and were friends of his. He was always with you. He was always among you. And there he will remain.

I think that Nufret, who phoned yesterday from Fergana, expressed the general sentiment of your people when he stated: "We do not consider him dead. He will always live among us. . . ." You know that Aleksei Yevgrafovich nourished a feeling of great love for your people. It was no accident that he left his ashes to the Crimean Tatars. And we — Vera Ivanovna and all his friends — will abide by his last wishes and take the urn holding his ashes to the Crimea as soon as autonomy is restored to the Crimean Tatars in the land of your ancestors. You can be sure that Kosterin will keep fighting for this. We trust that among Soviet writers there will also be people who are prepared to take up Kosterin's banner and carry on the struggle in defense of small nations, not only in the USA, Latin America, and Africa, but right here at home in our own country.

I have known Aleksei for a very short time, less than three years. Yet we have lived a whole life together. While Kosterin was still alive, someone very close to me said, "You were made by Kosterin." And I didn't object. Yes, he made me: he turned a rebel into a fighter. I will be grateful to him for this to the end of my days. I will remember every step that I took by his side. Even when we were geographically apart, we were not really separated. I can say that I have known this man for a lifetime and I approve his every move, his every thought. And he gave me the right to call myself one of his closest friends.

As his very close friend, what can I say about him? What special force attracted me to him?

First of all, his humanity, his inexhaustible love for the people, and his faith in them; and his faith that people are meant to walk the earth with their heads held high, not to crawl before the power of money or before an "authority" or before the powers that be. Kosterin believed that people are thinking beings. Therefore, it is inherent in their nature to strive for knowledge, i.e., to critically evaluate reality, to draw their own conclusions and to freely express their convictions and views. He himself was such a person — a thinking man who looked at life with keen eyes.

Because of this, he was terribly hated by those who believe people exist in order to create a backdrop for "leaders," to applaud them and to shout *"Hurrah!"* to blindly believe them, to idolize them, to endure their mockery without a murmur, and to grunt with satisfaction if a little more slops or thicker slops are poured into their trough than into somebody else's.

Aleksei responded to such beasts in human form with equal contempt. He did not consider them people and believed that the time was not far off when humanity would rid itself forever of such abominable creatures. He hated not only them but the order they had created. He tirelessly repeated Lenin's words: "There is nothing more savage and callous than a bureaucratic machine." Therefore, he believed a Communist has no more important task than to destroy this machine.

But he was not an extremist in the current sense of the word — a wrecker or a rioter. Kosterin was convinced that the task of destroying this machine could not be accomplished by a single forceful act; but that it called for protracted work toward overcoming century-old prejudices and the mystical worship of the state; toward overcoming the belief that people can exist only under conditions of strict supervision where their thought and will are suppressed by an outside force.

In other words, the destruction of the official bureaucratic machine means first of all a revolution in the minds and consciousness of the people, which is unthinkable under totalitarianism. Therefore, the most important task of the day is the development of a genuine *Leninist democracy,* an uncompromising struggle against totalitarianism, which is hiding behind the mask of so-called "socialist democracy." He devoted all his strength to this cause.

In the life, death, and funeral of Kosterin we are today seeing with our own eyes the accuracy of Lenin's description of the ethical and moral character of the official-bureaucratic machine. Under the domination of this machine, any of those who attended the party meeting which investigated the "special case of Kosterin," anyone who listened silently to the slander of their comrade by the party, knowing that he stood at the edge of the grave; and anyone who later voted for his expulsion, realizing that this was not only a terrible spiritual and psychological blow to a man who was gravely ill but also a sanction for his further persecution; those people can say: "Well, what could I have done alone?" And with their conscience thus cleared, they can sleep peacefully. It will never occur to them — brought up not to feel responsible for what takes place in the world but rather to callously carry out "orders"— that they took part in *murder* by not only traumatizing a sick man but by striving to deprive him of what was essential to his humanity: the right to think.

And those who organized his expulsion from the party, and later, like thieves in the night, tried to deprive him of his status as a writer and even more of those advantages that flow from the bureaucratic conduits, along with the right to be a registered writer; what will they say? They received an "order" and with an air of omnipotence took up the "demotion" without even realizing that a writer does not acquire literary standing simply by being admitted to the Soviet Writers' Union. They forgot, and it's possible they never knew, that neither Pushkin nor Tolstoy was in this organization. They believe so much in the power of their bureaucratic institutions that they even tried to deprive Pasternak, one of the greatest poets of our country, of his standing as a writer. They do not understand that Solzhenitsyn even without their union remains a great writer, and his works will live for centuries, long after the time when their bureaucratic creation, without writers like Pasternak and Solzhenitsyn, will be a useless, empty shell.

It never occurred to them that every true writer would much prefer to share the fate of Pasternak and Kosterin than to sit side by side with the Voronkovs[86] and the Ilins. And there is still much more that they do not understand, those goons of the bureaucratic machine who are in charge of the "art of writing." Not one of them will show even the slightest remorse. Why should they? They were only "doing their duty." They turn the wheels of a machine they do not control. And that a man was destroyed as a result of this, what has that to do with them?!

No one is guilty. Everyone has a clear conscience. Even the director of the dining hall who on the eve of the funeral accepted our reservation for the reception and dinner after the funeral, but who, two hours before the funeral, after he was visited by two people with blue passbooks, categorically rejected and returned the deposit he had received the night before. And the crematorium official who at the prompting of a secret plainclothes policeman tried to cut short the half-hour allotted to us (two blocks of time already paid for); and the numerous characters in civilian clothes and militia uniforms who were endlessly appearing in front of us, clouding the already painful moments of our sad farewell.

All of these people have a clear conscience. They were all carrying out "orders," although none of them knows who gave the order or why.

Only in one person — an employee of the mortuary who, following the orders of some unknown individual, failed to deliver our friend's body an hour before our departure from

---

86. [K. Voronkov is the secretary of the board of the USSR Writers' Union, and of the Russian Writers' Union, and was present at the meeting of the latter in November 1969 when it approved Solzhenitsyn's expulsion from the Union. He defended that action at a meeting of the Moscow writers' organization.]

the mortuary as had been arranged, but twenty minutes before—only in this one person, after he heard the speeches of some of the Bolshevik writer's friends, did there stir any kind of human feeling. He said to us afterward with a pleading and apologetic look on his face: "Please understand that I didn't do this on my own."

This is the kind of machine we have. It is a machine which is run by our hands and heads, which is ruthlessly crushing us and annihilating the best people in our society, while making everyone feel innocent as if they bear no responsibility for the crimes which the machine commits, freeing the conscience of those who run it. It is a terrible, cruel, and heartless machine.

And it was against this very machine that Kosterin struggled throughout his life. It was this very machine that he defended people from. And people went to him, stood side by side with him, and themselves defended him. Within his circle, a person's national origin or age made no difference. Ukrainians, Germans, Czechs, Turks, Chechens, Crimean Tatars, and many other nationalities (I will not list them all), were warmly welcomed into his home. He had many close friends among all of them, particularly among the Crimean Tatars, Chechens and Ingush.

It was the same with people of different ages. Besides people of his own generation, he was friends with people of middle age and with the young—such people as the talented theoretical physicist who was sent to the grave by this same official-bureaucratic machine, 28-year-old Valery Pavlinchuk;[87] and the organizer of the demonstration in Pushkin Square in defense of Galanskov, Ginzburg, and others, who is now serving a term in the strict-regime camp—Volodya Bukovsky; and

---

87. [Valery Pavlinchuk died in 1968 at the age of thirty, just one day after he, Kosterin, Grigorenko, Yakhimovich, and Pisarev had submitted their open letter in support of the democratization in Czechoslovakia (see the prefatory note to "I Will Remain a Bolshevik"). He had been an activist in the democratic movement during the late 1960s and had lost his security pass and his position as a nuclear physicist, and had been expelled from the party in spring 1968. He signed a letter with 223 others in early 1968 to the USSR prosecutor general and the Supreme Court against the closed trial of Galanskov, Ginzburg, Dobrovolsky, and Lashkova. His funeral was attended by many activists who later suffered reprisals.]

many still younger people who for understandable reasons I will not name.

In a funeral oration it is impossible to say everything there is to say about a man like the deceased, particularly when your throat is tightened with grief and when you are choking with anger at the murderers of this remarkable man — this communist, democrat, and internationalist, this unbending fighter for *human dignity* and for *human rights*; when servants of the murderers are trying to interrupt you and not let you say everything that is crying out from the very depths of your heart.

In bidding farewell to the deceased, it is customary to say: "Rest in peace, dear comrade!" I won't do this. In the first place, because he won't listen to me. He will continue to fight anyway. In the second place, it is quite impossible for me to be without you, Alyosha. You are a part of me. And stay with me, for without you I do not live.

So, don't sleep, Alyosha! Fight, Alyosha! Let your bonfire [88] consume all that loathsome trash which wants to keep eternally running that damn machine against which you fought throughout your life. We, your friends, will not be far behind you.

There will be freedom! There will be democracy! Your ashes will be in the Crimea!

---

88. [This is a pun on Kosterin's name, which comes from the Russian word *koster*, meaning "bonfire."]

Speeches at the Reception and Feast
after the Funeral

Pyotr Yakir

(Historian, Moscow; son of Commander I. S. Yakir, brutally murdered by Stalin. Pyotr, as the son of "an enemy of the people," spent seventeen years in camps—from age 14 to age 31.)

Many good things have already been said here about the deceased. I also loved Yevgrafych very much and would like to now — and could endlessly — reminisce about him, about our meetings and conversations which, it seems to me now, were all too few. I was even too late for our last meeting. I came in response to his invitation but when I got there it was already too late for a conversation to take place. But I won't take time from those who await their turn to express their grief to their friends. Therefore, I will discuss only one feature of Yevgrafovich, that feature which I personally do not find in others of his generation. I am referring to his loyalty to ideals.

The deceased firmly retained this loyalty, uncorrupted, from his early youth until his final breath, to his last clenched fist — the gesture with which he demanded oxygen when he was no longer able to speak. I know that among those millions who were ruthlessly destroyed by the Stalinist death machine there were many, perhaps even a majority, who went to their death still retaining their loyalty to Marxism-Leninism. But many from this generation survived. And the majority of the survivors were not even subjected to repression. And *all* of them — I emphasize this — *betrayed their ideals.*

Isolated individuals, hiding in corners, maintaining their

faith deep within themselves, cannot change this appalling picture of the decline of a whole generation. Those who actually represent this generation speak, of course, about their "sacred ideals," swearing loyalty to them; but they faithfully serve the Stalinists who in general haven't the slightest regard for any ideals, no matter what they may be. Many of them serve for scraps of fat thrown to them from the feast at the rulers' table. Christian morality very aptly called such people *pharisees*. Others do it out of fear. This is a rather loathsome type—the bigots and hypocrites who speak one way at meetings—they glorify the powers and praise them—but in confidential conversations condemn the actions of the authorities. And even after unburdening their souls in this way, many of them, sensing danger, will not fail to inform on their trusting partners in conversation.

The majority of them are either fanatics or philistines. They are people who have never read any of the works of the creators of Marxist-Leninist theory but are stuffed with prejudices and on cue are ready to call any rubbish which the powers so deem Marxism-Leninism, socialism, communism, or another "ism." These people are ever prepared to support the authorities in any of their undertakings—even the Black Hundreds—and to go farther than the powers would. These are the ones who shouted to Pontius Pilate: "Crucify him!!!" They flood the streets of the cities and villages like a tidal wave howling for the execution of the "enemies of the people." They made short work of Kosterin—in the party organization and in the presidium of the Writers' Union.

How could one not be struck by the spiritual strength of this man who had preserved his convictions in the midst of a dark mass of people crammed with prejudices and biases, despite torture in the "house of Vaskov"—the terrible Magadan prison where Yevgrafych was confined in May 1938; despite the Kolyma camps and the "educational" influence of the pharisees, bigots, and hypocrites; and despite the hooting of the fanatics and philistines.

After seeing the example of this man's life, one can't help but say: "Yes, the generation which made the October Revolution was, indeed, very strong!"

I loved Yevgrafych as a man with a big heart and as a *citizen*. And a certain community of our fates no doubt played a role in the formation of this feeling. But I especially loved him for his clarity of thought and his loyalty to ideals. It is no secret that among those who survived experiences like Yevgrafych's there were many who lost faith in the ideals they fought for in their youth. They blamed not only people but also the doctrine for what had happened to them.

Aleksei Yevgrafovich perceived all this another way. In one of our conversations he said something like this to me: "As with any other doctrine, there is no such thing as a 'pure' Marxism-Leninism which is as homogeneous as a crystal and correct in all its offshoots and parts. It will bear the special features of its founders (and they are people, not gods), and of the time in which it was created (and as we know, times change). It is not surprising, therefore, that people who are devoted to it can find in the works of Marx, Engels, and Lenin any quotation needed to serve as a 'basis' for the worst crimes of any of the Stalinists, Khrushchevists, or Brezhnevites. This is particularly easy to do given the method of quoting which has been adopted in our country: in which the idea from the source being quoted is emasculated at the beginning, the end, and in the middle of the excerpt, not once but several times. And often something is added to the quotation of which there was no trace in the original source. And all this takes place with impunity, because in our country there is not one publication which would dare come out against such falsification. The practitioners distribute as much of this concocted rubbish as they want. This speculation with the ideas and names that are sacred to our people created the 'moral' basis on which Stalinism was established in the past and on which neo-Stalinism is now being developed.

"I, too, had difficulty freeing myself from delusions. For a long time I also interpreted the policies that were being consciously pursued to consolidate Stalin's personal dictatorship as isolated mistakes of local and central party and Soviet organs. And I fought against these 'isolated mistakes' and 'distortions.' More often than not these efforts brought me only bruises and bumps, but sometimes luck was with me. This inspired me. And I would again tilt with the 'windmill,' feeling fully confident that in so doing I was fulfilling my duty to the party. Only in 1934, particularly after the murder of Kirov, did my eyes begin to open. But it was not until the 'house of Vaskov' that all the scales finally fell from my eyes. Only there did I finally understand that in our country Marxism-Leninism had been buried, and the Leninist party had been annihilated."

I am leaving aside the question of whether or not his conclusions were correct. But I cannot help but admire this man's integrity, his crystal purity, his enormous courage and his incredibly strong will. Imagine a man, convinced that the people

who are governing the country hold nothing sacred even though
they rule under the auspices of a doctrine they profess to be
guided by. Imagine also that this man knows that these rulers
will stop at nothing in their efforts to silence those who are
trying to expose them. And then add the fact that he not only
knows all this, but has also experienced torture in the "house
of Vaskov" and spent many years in the Kolyma concentration camp!

If you have pictured all this, then you will bow your head
once more in respect for Kosterin.

Having failed to, as they say, come to his senses as a result
of these experiences, he took a stand in defense of the Chechens
and the Ingush. And immediately a gang of pharisees, bigots,
hypocrites, and fanatics pounced on him. All the zealous philistines and powers that be assaulted him. Then he was again
expelled from the party and expected to be arrested any minute.
Those who have not experienced the "house of Vaskov" and Kolyma or another such camp, of which we had a very large
number, very likely will not comprehend what kind of torture
this was for him. But Kosterin survived this too. There were
Communists who kept him out of prison and secured his rein-
statement into the party. To all of them, and particularly to one
woman whose name I will not give because I have not been
authorized to do so, he was grateful to the end of his days.

But even after this terrible psychological torture, Kosterin
again went to battle for his ideals. His activities in defense
of the Volga Germans, the Crimean Tatars, and other small
nations, his actions against reemerging Stalinism — how can
I enumerate everything done by this man with a big soul
and a half-broken heart. He tried to instill his faith in all of
us, his friends and comrades in arms. I remember one of our
conversations in which he countered our arguments by the
following:

"Yes, the so-called advanced capitalist countries have outstripped us in terms of social development by an entire epoch.
They satisfy the material and spiritual needs of their citizens
many times better than we do, and they provide better for the
free development of the individual. But have they really attained
the ideal? Does a person there who turns out to be living under
bad conditions either by accident of birth or because of adverse
circumstances really have a good chance of breaking out of
the vicious circle? Does each individual really have an equal
chance to fully develop? Have poverty and crime really been
completely eliminated? Have social, national, and racial inequalities been abolished?

"What do you propose as an alternative to a system which as we can see is far from perfect?"

After a short period of silence, he answered himself: "The only alternative to this regime and to Stalinist 'socialism' is Marxist-Leninist socialism, cleansed of the filth which has engulfed it and revived under conditions of freedom!"

And how elated he was when democracy began to be revived in Czechoslovakia. When he received news about the democratization of social life in that country, he would invariably exclaim: "Here, you see! What did I tell you! This is the alternative to capitalism and to Stalinism!!"

He had full confidence in the Czechoslovak Communist Party and the Czechoslovak people. He said: "Czechoslovakia is not Russia! The people there know what democracy is! They will not forever endure the barbarism which has been imposed on them. Stalin did a foolish thing," he added ironically after a pause. "He bit off a piece which his barbaric belly could not digest. Czechoslovakia is not Tuva [89] and it is not Mongolia. It is an advanced European country with very rich democratic traditions. I think that Czechoslovakia, as small as it is, will provide a spiritual force which will inspire all the greater socialist world."

He was deeply affected by Soviet intervention in Czechoslovakia. I think that this event contributed greatly to the fatal overburdening of his heart. He followed closely every development in Czechoslovakia. It was as though he wished to break out of the chains of disease which confined him to his apartment so as to fly to these people whom he trusted so much and to become a soldier in their ranks. Until the end, until his last breath, he believed in the victory of the Czechoslovak people because he believed in the strength of the ideas that lighted their way and had illuminated his entire life.

I once more bow my head before the incredible and amazing strength of this man's spirit, before his bravery and his loyalty to ideals. And I ask you to do the same.

He was the kind of person I would like to be, and the kind of person I would like my friends and relatives to be.

---

89. [Tuva Autonomous Oblast was located in southern Siberia on the Mongolian border. It was declared independent in 1921 by the Bolsheviks, and was called at that time Tannu-Tuva. It was incorporated into the USSR in 1944.]

Khalid Dudaevich Oshaev

(Writer, member of the CPSU, from the Chechen-Ingush Autonomous Soviet Socialist Republic.)

Dear Comrades! We can only admire the example of the life and death of Aleksei Yevgrafovich. I would like to end my earthly existence as he did and wish that you would see me off as warmly as you have my friend.

Of all those present, I, perhaps, am the oldest. Aleksei Yevgrafovich and I were bound together by a friendship which lasted for fifty years. In 1918, he was sent from the city of Baku to the city of Grozny[90] with a group of sixty workers, half of whom were sailors, in order to strengthen Soviet and party work. He was sent by one of the twenty-six Baku commissars, by Ivan Fioletov. I first became acquainted with Kosterin after the hundred-days battle which ended in November 1918. This acquaintance soon developed into a very warm friendship which continued until the end of his days — for fifty years.

What I will say about him briefly is what my entire fifty years of experience has confirmed. He was a brave, inflexible Leninist fighter. He was that way on the first day we met and he was that way until he died. I'll cite a few examples from our youth together.

In February 1919, the city of Grozny was occupied by Denikin's forces. At that time, Aleksei was laid up with typhus, and although he was so weak that he could have been blown over by a strong breeze, he left with the rest for the Chechen territory. More than 5,000 men moved out at that time — Bolshe-

---

90. [Grozny is the capital of the Chechen-Ingush Autonomous SSR in southern Russia. In 1943 the Chechen-Ingush population was transported en masse to Central Asia; the republic was abolished and its territories ceded to surrounding republics. Following Khrushchev's "de-Stalinization" speech, the exile regime was lifted on the Chechen-Ingush people; in 1957-58 they were fully rehabilitated and allowed to return to their homeland, and the republic was restored as an autonomous republic.]

viks, Soviet workers from Grozny, Red Army members, and rank-and-file workers. From their ranks, a strong partisan detachment was organized in the Chechen mountains. Yevgrafovich was appointed assistant commander of the detachment's operations division. While working in this post, he took part in many partisan skirmishes with the Whites. And at the time when the Whites occupied half of the Ukraine and all of South Russia and when they were approaching Tula, in the Chechen mountains there was a small speck of territory still held by the Soviets. Here, the red flag was still flying. Surrounded by the raging sea of the Denikin forces, the Chechen partisans and the Russian partisan detachment defended this flag and repelled the enemy which was pressing on them from all sides. Aleksei Yevgrafovich led the military operations of the Russian partisan detachment at this time. I well remember the great battle which took place at the Vozdvizhensky settlement on January 31, 1920. A White detachment with 1200 bayonets and sabers surrounded a partisan detachment which had about 300 bayonets and which was serving as an outpost at the entrance to the Argun River canyon.

The detachment fought from early morning until late in the evening. It seemed as though its fate was decided. But the mountaineers struck at the White forces from the south. A breach was made in the ring of White troops. And the Red fighters who were still alive passed out through it, carrying their wounded (around forty) and their thirty-three dead. The entire operation was commanded by N. F. Gikalo, Sultan Dudaev, an Ingush, who perished in this battle, and A. Ye. Kosterin. The latter was seriously wounded in the battle (the bridge of his nose was shot off), but that did not put him out of action. The detachment retreated into what was formerly the czarist fortress of Shata. Eyewitnesses told me that when the detachment entered the gate of the fortress Aleksei Yevgrafovich was in the vanguard. His head was bound with a bloody rag, and on his feet instead of boots were dirty *onoochas* [cloth wrappings] wound with twine. And the detachment was singing as it marched along. This was the young Kosterin.

Soviet power was soon consolidated in the Northern Caucasus. Aleksei Yevgrafovich was appointed Chechen military commissar. Later he worked in the city of Vladikavkaz in Kabardia. He began to write essays and stories. It was at this time that he wrote his first book — *In the Mountains of the Caucasus* (1919-20). After that Aleksei was a member of our so-called

Persian Red Army which was booting the English out of Persia. Aleksei Yevgrafovich and I maintained continuous and lively contact until 1937.

In 1937, I was sucked into the black vortex of Stalinism. I was sent to Kolyma in 1940 to serve a ten-year term. While I was there I found out that Aleksei was also near the Arctic Circle in the camps on the Nera River. It was virtually impossible for a prisoner in one of Stalin's camps to communicate with a prisoner in another. For attempting to do this one could be thrown in the camp punishment cell. But all the same I sent Aleksei two letters and received one from him.

In 1957, my people, the Chechen-Ingush, returned from exile in Central Asia to our small homeland. I found out that Aleksei was in Moscow. The bonds of our friendship were quickly renewed and were to be maintained right up to the present tragic day.

The Crimean Tatars love and respect Aleksei Yevgrafovich as a man who bravely and courageously called for a return to Leninist norms on the nationalities question in relation to the long-suffering Crimean Tatar people. So too, Aleksei proved to be a devoted friend of national minorities, a genuine fighter, and an internationalist during the first year after the Chechen-Ingush people had returned to their homeland. He wrote a letter about the Chechens and Ingush which circulated among these peoples with lightning speed. In this letter he called upon the party and the government to devote attention to the disastrous situation of the mountain peoples who had returned to their native land. But N. S. Khrushchev, who was leader at that time, not only failed to heed the cry from this Russian writer's heart, but began the persecution campaign which ultimately led to Kosterin's heart attack.

We have said farewell forever to Aleksei Yevgrafovich today. Next to his body, Pyotr Grigorevich Grigorenko — the friend and comrade in arms of our beloved deceased — made a courageous speech. It is a speech I will never forget because it vividly depicted Aleksei Yevgrafovich's personality as a Communist, a human being, an internationalist, and a fighter for human rights and justice. He said that the urn containing Aleksei Yevgrafovich's ashes will be taken to the Crimea and given to the Crimean Tatar people after a new life has been restored to them, when they have been allowed to return to the land of their ancestors and the *Crimean Autonomous Soviet Socialist Republic* has been reestablished.

When I heard this I thought: "You know, the urn should have

been given to us, the *Chechen-Ingush people.*" But later I understood that the suffering of the Crimean Tatars has been immeasurably greater than ours; and it became clear to me that our Aleksei was right about this. The urn holding his ashes should be given only to the Crimean Tatars. Their suffering and their courageous struggle has given them the right to be the keepers of the ashes of this person beloved by all national minorities.

Comrades! The Crimean ASSR was created by a decree signed by Lenin, and I believe that sooner or later the cause and the will of Lenin will triumph on this question. The Crimean Tatar people will return to their fair homeland and will build there a glorious Communist future based on close friendship with all the peoples living in the Crimea. I believe that the Leninist foundations of the nationalities policy, which were trampled underfoot by Stalin, will be restored. And if I live until that joyous time, I, as a Chechen who has tasted the bitterness of being exiled from my native land and the bitterness of inequality, will come without fail to the Crimea to rejoice with the Crimean Tatar people. Then, all of us, his friends, will recall the deceased. We will again shed tears over his ashes and again speak well of his name.

May there be eternal praise to the memory of this fighter for Leninist justice and humanity!

Zampira Asanova [91]

(A physician from the city of Fergana.)

Aleksei Yevgrafovich played a special role in my life. My
school, the institute, and life itself fostered in me an aversion
to — No! Not just an aversion — I was hostilely opposed to
Marxism-Leninism and to Lenin himself. I say that such feelings
were fostered in me, but this does not mean that anything bad
was ever said to me about Lenin. On the contrary, he was always spoken of in the most positive way, almost as if he were
a god.

But I could not love him, because all the evil things going
on in life were presented in the newspapers, in textbooks, in
the speeches of highly placed party officials, and on radio
and television, as the realization of Lenin's precepts. And I
thought: "Since he taught such bad things, he himself must
have been a very bad man." Therefore, I didn't want to read
Lenin and didn't know his teachings and didn't want to know
them.

It was from the lips of Aleksei Yevgrafovich that I first heard
a totally different interpretation of Lenin's ideas. Aleksei presented Lenin's teachings so simply and clearly that I wanted to
listen, and then listen some more. In so doing, he compared
what Lenin had said with what was going on in real life and
showed that it was only Lenin's name that was being used and
not his ideas. And his name was frequently being used dis-
honestly as a cover for sordid affairs. After this, I tried to
study Lenin's writings on my own. But I was very much ham-
pered by the prejudices which had grown up in me throughout

---

91. [Zampira Asanova, one of the representatives sent by the
Crimean Tatar people to Moscow, was living there in 1968-69 and
became active in the general democratic movement. She signed the
appeal of the twelve to the Budapest consultative conference of Communist parties in February 1968 and a similar appeal to the June
1969 world Communist conference in Moscow. At the time of the
latter conference she was one of five Crimean Tatars who demonstrated in Mayakovsky Square in Moscow, for a return to Leninist
nationalities policy and for freedom for Grigorenko. She also en-
dorsed the first appeal to the United Nations (in May 1969) by
the Initiative Group, a text reproduced below.]

my earlier years. And these prejudices still live on today.

But after hearing these speeches by Kosterin's closest friends—Pyotr Grigorevich, Sergei Petrovich Pisarev, and Comrade Oshaev—and after recalling what he himself said, I think: "No! These people are incapable of professing bad ideas. Most likely in this case, as with religion, the genuine doctrine has been distorted to satisfy the mercenary needs of those who profess to serve the doctrine."

And to you, comrades, and to this great man—Bolshevik, writer, Communist, and democrat, who was dearly loved by me and by all the Crimean Tatar people, Aleksei Yevgrafovich Kosterin—I give my solemn promise to study Lenin's ideas and to struggle to see them put into practice in their uncorrupted form.

This is very bitter and difficult for me. Tears keep me from speaking. But all the same, I will say: *Our people will never forget Aleksei Yevgrafovich!!!* We will honor him as a *prophet, as a saint. May his memory and praise live forever!!!*

Leonid Petrovsky [92]

(Historian, member of the CPSU, Moscow.)

Comrades! Many warm words were spoken today about the writer and Bolshevik Aleksei Yevgrafovich Kosterin. I want to speak about the cause for which Aleksei Yevgrafovich struggled and to which he devoted his life.

All the members of his family were Communists: his father, mother, brothers, and his daughter Nina. And they all gave their lives so that our lives might be better, in a genuine Com-

---

92. [Leonid P. Petrovsky is the grandson of Grigory I. Petrovsky, a founder of the Russian Social Democratic Labor Party, and the son of Pyotr G. Petrovsky, a prominent Bolshevik who was a victim of Stalin's purges. Leonid was a signer of the appeal to the world conference of Communist parties, and was one of ninety-five signers of a letter to supreme soviets of the USSR and the Russian republic protesting the trial and sentencing of those who demonstrated in Red Square against the invasion of Czechoslovakia. He was expelled from the party for that action.]

munist society, under conditions of real freedom and real democracy.

I, unfortunately, was not personally acquainted with Aleksei
Yevgrafovich. But I heard many things about him, particularly
from his friends, those courageous people Pyotr Grigorevich
Grigorenko and Pyotr Ionovich Yakir. And I must say at
least a few words about these people.

When I visited either of them I very often met many other
guests. Knowing that in the upper echelons both men were
condemned as anti-Soviet, I sometimes asked with astonishment: "Can it be that people *don't* go out of their way to avoid
your apartments?" Both of them only laughed and responded:
"You don't avoid us, do you?"

Today at the funeral I saw hundreds of his friends, who
are undoubtedly fighters for the cause to which Aleksei Yevgrafovich devoted his life. They came here from all parts of
Moscow and from different outlying areas of the Soviet Union
to honor the memory of this Bolshevik-Leninist, even though
they knew that he had been savagely persecuted and that as a
sign of protest against the violation of *Leninist norms* in the
life of the party and of the country he had resigned from the
party.

It is very good that people have displayed such courage
and such loyalty in their friendships. I also want to be loyal
to these noble principles. They say that a genuine and sincere
feeling of friendship can exist between people who don't know
one another. Whatever the case, I am used to thinking of
Aleksei Yevgrafovich as one of my best, most intelligent, and
sensitive old friends. His works, which I read during my visits
at the home of Pyotr Grigorevich, created a bond between
myself and the author so that I felt close to him and understood him. Therefore, the news of his death was a terrible
shock to me. Word of this found me at Pyotr Yakir's apartment. Pyotr Grigorevich telephoned Yakir first, as soon as he
had recovered from the shock. Although we weren't dressed
warmly we rushed into the street, found a taxi, and went to
be with the body of this person whom we loved and with Vera
Ivanovna, his closest friend, who was now bereft. I will not
speak about the scene we found at the Bolshevik writer's apartment. It would be too difficult for all of us. I will only say
that our presence there was not at all unnecessary.

Aleksei Yevgrafovich wrote straightforward books, which
are necessary reading for our people. But the majority of his
works are still not included in Soviet bibliographies. I am con-

vinced, however, that the time is not far off when these books will occupy the place they deserve.

I think that we should speak today not only of the deceased but of the whole Kosterin family. It is a family of Bolshevik-Leninists, Communists, who devoted their lives to the struggle for freedom, democracy, and communism. Among them was Aleksei Yevgrafovich's youngest daughter, Nina Kosterina. She based her life on her father's example, and became a brave, uncorrupted, and sincere fighter in the worldwide army of Communists. She perished in a struggle against the fascist invaders, defending a better future for those of us who survived and for her father. For the fact that we can gather here today, we are indebted to Nina and to all the young people who gave their lives defending the freedom and independence of our homeland in the struggle against the fascist invaders. But Nina did not just carry out heroic military exploits. She was distinguished by an even greater civic valor. Graphic evidence of this is *The Diary of Nina Kosterina.*

I saw this diary for the first time in a store called Politkniga [The Political Book] on Khudozhestvenny Way. I picked it up and began to turn the pages. I was captivated by it after reading the first few lines and could not put it down until I had read it through to the end. And I was sorry to part with it. I even felt like I wanted to take care of this young girl and I didn't want to believe that she was really dead. In a simple yet eloquent style, she exposed Stalin and the arbitrariness that reigned in those times, persuading everyone, without resorting to legal arguments, that her father was an honorable and honest man and a genuine Communist and Leninist. She thus carried on the tradition of the Kosterin family of proletarian revolutionaries — standing squarely for justice and never yielding an inch to the forces of injustice. All the Kosterins fought for the Leninist cause. They have passed this struggle on to us. In referring to this, I also want to reply to Zampira Asanova who spoke before me.

Dear Zampira! The crimes that have occurred in our country and the injustices that take place at times, even today, in the name of Lenin have nothing in common with Marxism-Leninism. Kosterin taught us to distinguish between the genuine and the false friends of the people. He taught us determination and perseverance in the struggle for Leninism, for the immortal Leninist cause. He devoted his entire life to this and by so doing he erected an eternal monument to himself. And those who falsify Leninism, no matter how high their position today, will inevitably be exposed and the people will condemn their names to shame in the centuries to come.

May the memory of Aleksei Yevgrafovich Kosterin — the humanist writer and fighter for the great ideals of Marxism-Leninism, for freedom, democracy and communism — live forever!!

The Christian

This is the first time that I have been among people like you. I happened to be here among you quite by accident. On the trolley-bus I overheard a conversation among some people whom I did not know about the funeral of a writer whose name meant nothing to me. But because he was a writer, and because one's fame or lack of it in our country cannot serve as a criterion for evaluating talent and social significance, I decided to go to the crematorium. What I heard there astounded me and I made a point of coming here to the reception in order to become better acquainted with the friends of such a remarkable man.

I am 28 years old. I graduated from an advanced technical institution and have worked as an engineer for over five years. I am currently in good standing on my job, although I do not like my work. I became an engineer at my parents' insistence, although my vocation most surely should be that of a writer. I began to write while I was a child, but concealed this passion of mine from others. I was ashamed to show anyone my work. I continued to write while attending the technical school. And I still write — devoting all my free time to it. These days, I occasionally give my writings to a wide variety of people to read, not as my own work, but as samizdat, distributed under a pseudonym. As a rule, after reading the work through, people will ask me to pass on to them other works by this author when I have them. From this I conclude that all my efforts have had some results. However, I have not tried to get them published because I don't think that any of my writings would be approved by the censors. I have not given my works to literary specialists. I am acquainted with several well-known writers. We got to know each other through my parents, who occupy a rather high rung on the ladder of the bureaucratic hierarchy. But I never had faith in these writers, and I did not turn to them for criticism and instruction.

After hearing what was said about Aleksei Yevgrafovich, I think that he was probably the kind of person to whom I could have given all my works for criticism. And it breaks my heart that I did not know this man during his lifetime. It is sad not only because I lost in him my probable literary mentor but also because I didn't have a chance to experience the happiness of spiritual communion with him. As I listen to the speeches I admire him all the more; and more and more I believe in the indomitability of the human intellect, in the ineradicability of the Divine Basis in Humanity. I by chance heard Pyotr Grigore-vich say to somebody who most likely knew little of Kosterin: "If a God existed, he would have sent to earth people like Aleksei Yevgrafovich in order to remind people of his own existence."

I am a deeply religious man. And I think that it was precisely for this reason that Kosterin was sent to us *by God. God* recalls his existence to us through such people and by the fact that in the midst of total skepticism and spiritual decline, people come to light who deeply believe in the *Creator* of all reality. My parents are both Communists. No — I don't think that's true. After what I've heard today I will call them party members. The word "Communist" in the sense that it was used here does not apply to them. They are people who do not believe in anything. The environment in which I grew up and was educated was saturated with skepticism. Despite this, and without any sort of outside influence I became a deep believer in Orthodox *Christianity*. I was even baptized. And the only thing that my parents accomplished by getting all up in arms about my faith was that I did not make much of it in front of them.

Until today I felt that my faith was incompatible with Marxist-Leninist ideology, just as good is incompatible with evil, light with darkness, and the divine with the depraved. Now, my confidence in this has been shattered. Now I am beginning to think that the problem lies not in the doctrine itself but in the people who are professing it. The forces of evil can even turn love into something damaging to humanity.

Therefore, I want to say to you that the memory of a man like Aleksei Yevgrafovich must unite all those who want to bar the way to evil, who want to give full scope to the *divine basis* in *human beings*—their intellect, their unhindered creativity—no matter what these people are called: Communists, socialists, Christians, or simply people.

As a sign of the complete sincerity of these words, I ask the person who spoke before me, who is standing beside me right now, the Communist Leonid Petrovsky not to refuse my friendly embraces!! (He embraces and kisses Leonid Petrovsky.)

KGB—ORGAN OF CASTE LAWLESSNESS
by Pyotr Grigorenko

[The following letter was sent by Grigorenko to USSR Attorney General Rudenko on December 4, 1968. It describes the KGB search of Grigorenko's apartment in which, among other things, the texts of the speeches at Kosterin's funeral were taken from him. It was that KGB search which forced him to reconstruct the texts of the funeral speeches, with the attendant difficulties and omissions that he describes in his statement "From the Compiler," introducing the Kosterin funeral documents.

[The Berezovsky referred to here reappears later as the prosecutor in the case against Grigorenko at the time that he was arrested in Tashkent in May 1969 and ultimately confined in a psychiatric prison hospital.

[The translation is from the June 16, 1969, *Intercontinental Press,* and is reprinted by permission.]

To the attorney general of the USSR, A. R. Rudenko:

On November 19 of this year [1968], from 7:00 in the morning until 7:00 at night, a search of my apartment was conducted.

I shall leave aside for the moment the fact that the person who—nominally—was overseeing this operation had no conception either of procedural norms or of elementary courtesy—having grown accustomed to dispensing at will with the lives of people entrusted to his hands. Those who, during the entire day, kept watch on the conduct and actions of Special Inspector for Priority Cases Berezovsky, of the attorney general's office of the Uzbek SSR, will write you about this.

I myself did not have to endure his boorishness that long. In protest against the unlawful actions of those who conducted the search, I refused to participate in it after the first half hour. Thus, I speak only of violations of principle—which were not solely the responsibility of those who actually conducted the search.

1. The search was carried out on the basis of a warrant held by Special Inspector Berezovsky of the Uzbek SSR attorney general's office. The warrant was approved by the Moscow district attorney, Malkov. In the warrant it is asserted that in the course of investigating the case of Bariev and others it was revealed that documents containing slanderous fabrications against the Soviet social and state system could be found in the apartment of P. G. Grigorenko.

I proclaim, and am ready to take full responsibility for the statement, that no proof of the likelihood of such documents in my apartment was given to Prosecutor Malkov. First, because there is no "case of Bariev and others." Second, because there never were or could be documents containing slander against the Soviet state and social system connected in any way, even indirectly, with the name of Bariev and his comrades.

What is really involved here? This is a *police provocation* pure and simple, against people who have entered into a struggle against the arbitrariness of the authorities. It is well known to you that on April 21 of this year, in the municipal park of Chirchik, an attack was made by the Uzbek police (who for some reason are still called militia) upon a peaceful outing of Crimean Tatars, which was dedicated to the birthday of the founder of the Soviet state and initiator of the Crimean Tatar National Autonomous Republic— *V. I. Lenin.*

People who were at a peaceful outing, suspecting nothing, young people dancing, groups singing national and revolutionary songs or putting on amateur performances— all were struck by high-pressure streams of heavily chlorinated, icy water from fire engines.

These streams swept people off their feet, ruined their clothes, and inflicted moral and psychological wounds that will not heal. Then the police clubs went into action. The calculation was that the outraged people would resort to measures of self-defense and that this could later be used to charge them with resisting the authorities.

But the people displayed the most incredible restraint, not giving in to the provocation. They began a peaceful demonstration against the humiliations permitted against them. In reply, arrests followed. More than 300 persons were arrested. Twelve of these, most of whom had not participated in the outing but were arrested in their homes, were subsequently placed on trial and condemned for "disturbing the peace."

Ayder Bariev — a worker, a tractor operator — who managed to avoid arrest, flew to Moscow on the same day and by the morning of April 22 the attorney general's office of the USSR had received his telegram bringing to light in detail the Chirchik events — this unprecedented violation of *human rights* and of the norms of *human morality*.

Understandably, Bariev did not mince words, but simply, in the way of a workingman, called things by their proper names. He stayed on in Moscow as the empowered representative of the people who sent him, without results, haunting the threshold of the office of which you are supervisor, and other government bodies. He and other representatives of his people sought — using every possible means they could find — to win the punishment of the Chirchik goons and a halt to the illegal persecution by the courts of the victims of the Chirchik pogrom.

You did not respond in any way to the personal telegrams and letters of Bariev or to the collective appeals of all the Crimean Tatar representatives then in Moscow. Neither you nor your deputies ever admitted any of these representatives, nor did you make any effort to look into their complaints. You did not choose any other approach either: you did not answer even one of their letters.

You also failed to respond to their complaints about the unjustified actions of the Moscow militia against the Crimean Tatar delegates. It did not concern you, the highest overseer of Soviet law, that they were rounding up people like wild animals on the streets of our motherland's capital and shipping them off by force, under conditions fit only for cattle, to uninhabited regions of administrative exile.[93]

It did not concern you, a jurist versed in the law, that these

---

93. [On May 16, 1968, some 800 representatives of the Crimean Tatars went to Moscow to lodge protests with various government bureaus over the Chirchik pogrom and to demand the right of the Tatar people to return to their homeland from their long exile in Central Asia. Moscow police and militiamen began a mass roundup of Tatars. On May 18, those Tatars still free — about 100 — went in a body to the garden near the offices of the Central Committee of the CPSU. They were accompanied by several of the most courageous representatives of the opposition intellectuals, including Grigorenko. The group was attacked by the police. The Tatars were arrested, beaten, then loaded on trains and forcibly sent to places of compulsory settlement.]

were not simply individuals but national representatives, that is, citizens concerning whom one had no right to make decisions removing them from their assigned stations without the agreement of their constituents. You overlooked this, just as you did those tragic incidents which occurred as a result of the fact that people, trying to be true to the confidence placed in them, took desperate measures, even to jumping from windows of a speeding train, in order to escape from the militia convoying them and to continue to carry out the duty entrusted to them by their people.

Bariev had no sooner been relieved in Moscow by another person and returned to Chirchik than he was placed under arrest. The grounds for this were the above-mentioned letters of individual and group representatives of the Crimean Tatars sent to various Soviet bureaus, including the USSR attorney general's office, to public organizations, and to individual representatives of Soviet public opinion, as well as the information bulletins that the Tatar representatives regularly send from Moscow as reports to their constituents. All these documents were interpreted by people of Berezovsky's type as containing slander against the Soviet state and social system.

I will not begin here to try to demonstrate how they contrived to transform a document containing a true description of an actual event into so-called slander. I will limit myself to posing several questions for you, relating directly to the fabrication of such cases. I ask you, as the highest guardian of Soviet law, whether anyone has the right to make a person answer in court for having sent you a complaint that you never took the time to examine, and when you never investigated the facts recounted in it.

I ask you—could anyone, even in his wildest imaginings, refer to the bloody encounter in Chirchik as disturbance of the peace rather than as a crude police provocation against the Crimean Tatar people, having as its aim the creation of a pretext for suppressing the just movement of this people for their national resurrection?!

I believe that if the questions raised here were answered justly, there would be no question but that everything following the Chirchik events has been a realization of the provocative aim I have indicated. And if that is so, then how could the Uzbek "guardians of order" show District Attorney Malkov proof of the existence of the documents mentioned (unless, of course, Malkov himself was participating quite consciously in the provocation)?

Such is the state of affairs concerning the legal basis for conducting a search of my apartment. With that, one might be done with the matter. But I cannot avoid speaking about something that is not clear to me, indeed, is totally obscure: your own role, both in the Chirchik affair and in the trials of Crimean Tatars—those held since the famous September 5, 1967, decree of the Supreme Soviet of the USSR, and those still being prepared.

Their unjust and often plainly provocative character is so obvious that one is amazed that this cannot be understood by a jurist of international standing, a person who diligently instructs the whole world in the methods of fighting crimes against humanity! [94]

2. Having thus clarified the fact that the Uzbek events are related to me and my apartment in the same way that "the elder tree in the garden" is to the uncle who appeared in Kiev, let us try to figure out why this search was actually carried out and whose purposes it served. An exhaustive answer has to explain the composition of the "investigative" group and tell which bureau sent the person who in fact led the search.

Attending the search, besides Berezovsky, were seven KGB personnel and three "witnesses"—also security agents. Thus for one person from the Uzbek Republic—from the attorney general's office, remember—ten Muscovites were needed, not counting those who blocked off the house at the street level. And all from the KGB.

In command of the search was also a KGB man—Aleksei Dmitrievich Vragov. That is all I was able to find out about him through Berezovsky. Vragov himself refused to tell his rank or place of work—whether it was the Moscow office or the central office—although according to law he was supposed to tell me both. This semiofficial person, only partly made known to me, then, was in charge of the search. Berezovsky got his orders from him alone.

To Vragov belonged the right to decide disputed questions, to confiscate this or that document or to leave it. Moreover, he supervised the practical activities of the other KGB personnel at the search. The only thing that the nominal head of the search, Berezovsky, did was to dictate to one of the KGB men the titles of the documents gathered up by the others.

---

94. [Rudenko was the Soviet prosecutor at the Nuremberg War Crimes Tribunal following World War II.]

Thus the search was conducted by organs of the KGB which had chosen as a "fig leaf" the "case of Bariev and others" together with the investigator in charge of that case. This search concluded another stage in the interrelations between the KGB and myself. The first stage ended, as you know, with my being freed from the Soviet Union's most dreadful kind of prison — the so-called special psychiatric hospital, where the KGB had me "settled" in order to get themselves out of the impasse they had fallen into as a result of my totally unfounded arrest and the impossibility of obtaining from me a "heartfelt confession."

The next stage began two or three months after my release, when the organs of the KGB, without any grounds being provided on my part, suddenly began to take an interest in me. Since then, for more than three years, I have been kept under constant surveillance: people assigned around the clock to follow me or members of my family or those who visit me; stationary surveillance of my apartment, both in plain sight and by special apparatus; tapping of telephone conversations; the perusal of my mail, with the occasional confiscation of a letter. Twice in these years there have been secret searches of my apartment. All these actions I protested in a letter to the head of the KGB, Yu. V. Andropov. To this letter, as is customary in our country, no reply was made. They simply began to follow me more discreetly.

The search carried out was a general inspection of my "storehouses," an attempt to look over what they hadn't seen before. But that isn't the only thing, of course. Obviously, some new provocations toward me are indicated. I do not intend to wait meekly for them.

I am a Communist and, as such, I hate with every fiber of my being the organs of caste lawlessness, violence, and coercion. In our country this means the organization created by Stalin and now called the KGB. I hide from no one my hatred for this organization; I consider it inimical to the people and I will struggle for its rapid liquidation by all legal means available to me. Therefore I do not wish to have any relations with it and I do not recognize it as having any rights to interfere in my life or public activity. A parasitic organization, that grows fat off the inexhaustible flood of the people's wealth, that takes away the best sons of the people for this purpose, and inflicts irreparable moral damage, should disappear forever from our society, and the sooner the better.

I have long known that the courts and the prosecutors' offices have a relation with the KGB that amounts to actual subordination. If examples are necessary to illustrate this, the search carried out at my apartment serves as quite an illustrative one. The prosecutor's office in this case played the role of errand boy. They can go on playing this dishonorable role, but not in relation to me. By my life, by my participation in the defense of the motherland, by the blood I have shed for it, by my Communist convictions, I have won the right to feel myself a co-owner of my country, a member with equal rights of the family of Soviet peoples. I have the right to walk around freely without being followed in my native land, to freely defend my convictions, to utilize all those rights guaranteed me as a citizen of the USSR under the Soviet constitution and the Universal Declaration of Human Rights. And no one, least of all such an organization as the KGB, has the right to interfere with my making use of such rights.

The organs of public supervision of the law are obliged to help citizens struggling for their legal rights, not to help organizations seeking to deprive citizens of those rights.

3. After all that has been said there remains only to explain why the representatives of this organization that I respect so little arrived; what I had that they needed; against whom they are fighting; and, of course, whom they plan to fight in the future. Let us try to deal with this by way of an analysis of the material confiscated.

Actually they confiscated materials having nothing to do with "slanderous fabrication." What was confiscated was not at all what was indicated in the official warrant for the search. They took all the typewritten and handwritten documents, letters and notes that I had. There was nothing slanderous, let alone anti-Soviet, in any of them. These were anti-Stalinist materials and public statements against the violation of Soviet laws by the authorities, against arbitrary justice, against the continuing discriminatory and genocidal acts toward the Crimean Tatars, the Volga Germans, and other small nationalities. The following is what was taken:

Numerous letters of the Crimean Tatars, both individual and collective, that had been sent to me — a cry from the heart of a people worn with suffering — as well as materials from the movement of the Volga German people for the restoration of their national rights.

Copies of my letters to the Politbureau of the Central Committee of the CPSU, both the ones written in connection with arbitrary treatment permitted against myself (illegal expulsion from the party, reduction from the rank of general to that of private, denial of the pension I had earned) and the ones that exposed arbitrary justice and falsification of history in the interest of reviving Stalinism.

The manuscript of *Academician Sakharov's* pamphlet and *my review* of it.

All the works of that untiring fighter against Stalinism, a writer-Bolshevik, participant in the revolutionary movement since 1912, member of the Bolshevik Party since 1916, with three years of czarist prison and seventeen in the Stalinist torture chambers and death camps at Kolyma — *Aleksei Yevgrafovich Kosterin.*

A *manuscript* in which are collected and analyzed all the facts known to me indicating that after the October (1964) plenum of the Central Committee a firm course, though one quietly carried out, was adopted *on the revival of Stalinism.*[95]

Records of public criminal trials (criminal in form, political in essence) of Crimean Tatars, who are participants in a movement for national equality, and of free-thinking people in Moscow (the trials of Sinyavsky and Daniel, Khaustov, Bukovsky, and others, Ginzburg, Galanskov, and others).

Biographical sketches of those convicted for demonstrating on Red Square against the intervention of Soviet troops in Czechoslovakia and against the shedding of blood by those who are brothers, Soviet soldiers and Czechoslovak citizens.

A *manuscript* of Academician Varga's work *The Russian Path to Socialism.*

A copy of the *letter by a group of Soviet intellectuals* (Artsymovich, Kapitsa, Kataev, Leontovich, Plisetskaya, Sakharov, Chukovsky, etc.) to the twenty-third congress of the CPSU, expressing alarm in connection with the tendencies toward the rebirth of Stalinism that have appeared.

A copy of the *letter by forty-three children of Communists* who were killed in gangster fashion by Stalin (Yakir, Petrovsky, Antonov-Ovseenko, Berzin, Yenukidze, Bukharin, Vavilov, Piatnitsky, and others), in which alarm was expressed regarding the tendencies toward the revival of Stalinism and the forgetting of the crimes committed by Stalin and his henchmen; in it, the resolution of the twenty-second congress for the

---

95. [This was the Central Committee plenary meeting that ousted N.S. Khrushchev from his posts as prime minister and first secretary of the party and placed A.N. Kosygin and L.I. Brezhnev in those positions, respectively.]

erection of a monument in Moscow to the victims of Stalinism was recalled.

Translations from Czechoslovak newspapers (the "Two Thousand Words," a speech by Smrkovsky on Czechoslovak radio, etc.).

A *list of persons* subjected to repression by the party or government because they had signed one or another of various documents protesting the violation of Soviet laws and of elementary human rights — by the courts, the prosecutor's offices, and the KGB.

A typewritten text, published in the USSR in an edition of insignificant size and meant only for jurists, of the *Universal Declaration of Human Rights*.

A typewritten text of two *UN "covenants on rights,"* not published in the USSR (the International Covenant on Economic, Social, and Cultural Rights and the International Covenant on Civil and Political Rights, both adopted by the General Assembly two years ago [1966], together with their optional protocols).

Records of all the speeches made at the funeral of the writer A. Ye. Kosterin.

Among the confiscated works of literature were: the long poem "Requiem," by Anna Akhmatova, about her only son, who, together with her, suffered in the prison cells of Stalin; several works by Marina Tsvetaeva, not published in the USSR; a powerful work on the morally degrading influence of Stalinism — the unpublished narrative poem by N. Korzhavin, "Tanka"; the manuscript of A. Marchenko's book *My Testimony* on present-day camps for political prisoners; a typewritten text of Hemingway's *For Whom the Bell Tolls*.

The material listed characterizes rather fully the principles of the confiscation. I do not think I would add anything by pointing out that *everything written by me* was confiscated, even scraps of paper bearing only a single word in my handwriting. Thus, materials of mine that have disappeared include my scientific work, personal correspondence, drafts of various documents, both those which have received wide distribution and those that have not gone beyond my desk. In general, everything typewritten or handwritten or that has not been published in the USSR. Obviously, if they had not already been given to others, my copies of *The Letters of Korolenko to A. Lunacharsky*, Gorky's *Uncontemporary Thoughts*, and the poems of Osip Mandelshtam would all have been taken as well.

I had a copy of the manuscript of a book on the opening period of the last war — *Notes of an Intelligence Officer,* the memoirs of a colonel in the reserve, V. A. Novobranets — inscribed by the author. When they put this book, too, in the pile for confiscation, I protested sharply, declaring that it could in no way be included among the materials for which confiscation had been sanctioned. Then Councilor of Justice Berezovsky, who was conducting the confiscation, having received advance permission from Vragov — "Confiscate it!" — decided to demonstrate to me the book's slanderous character, in relation to the Soviet state and social system, and he read to me from the author's preface: "Stalin died, but the poisonous seeds sown by him continue to produce shoots."

After that I refused to be present at the search any longer. But they had no need of my presence anyway. Without having listed even half of what was selected for confiscation, they dumped the remainder in a bag, marked it with a stamp saying "KGB-14," and took them away . . . and the bag . . . and the stamp. Judge for yourself to what extent the inviolability of the contents of the bag is guaranteed.

What's worse, the sealing of the bag, in which I refused to participate, considering the total senselessness of such participation, took place in the presence of those "witnesses" who themselves were personnel of the government body carrying out the search. Not one of the real witnesses whom I insisted should be called was called.

There you have the way observance of the law was assured in a concrete case. But it is not this case alone that interests me. I wanted to clarify what the attitude of a Soviet attorney general's office is toward *Soviet* law! My personal experience shows that such bodies are concerned with only one thing in political cases — choosing articles of law that will give the appearance of legality to the savage arbitrariness of the authorities. But I naively thought that, even for this, it was necessary to know the law. It turns out that that is not obligatory. The necessary articles, obviously, are chosen by legal specialists. Practical workers have no interest in the law at all. They do what is ordered without looking into the case to see if it is legal or not.

Berezovsky appeared at the search without the Code of Criminal Law or the Procedural Code for Criminal Law, and when he was taken to task for violating the law, with citations from copies that I had, he only modified his procedure, and that in only a few cases, with ever-mounting reluctance. How burdensome the law is to him may be judged from the following incident. Toward the end of the search, my wife reproved him, declaring: "That's not according to law!" At this Berezovsky could not restrain himself. He poured out all the irritation that had built up in him through the day: "Ah, you legalists! You and your husband with his shelf full of legal books!"—he yelled in anger. I think this outcry characterizes the attitude of the "guardians of the law" toward the law better than all their pompous scribblings that count on people being uninformed.

4. In conclusion I would like to try to clarify with your help one other question—*why has all this been done*? Perhaps an attempt to intimidate? I don't think so. The KGB and I are too well acquainted for either of us to consider such a thing. Perhaps, then, the wish to find some peg on which to hang a "case" and put me away somewhere where my voice will no longer be heard? This is quite possible, but stupid. To stage a trial based on a frame-up nowadays is risky, and to calculate that I will actually get involved in criminal actions . . . no, the KGB knows me too well to count on that. I don't count on the stupidity of my opponent either.

Consequently, there remains only one assumption—they wanted to find out what I am working on and at the same time to put a brake on my work by depriving me of materials and "means of production." Testifying to this, in particular, is the fact that they took both typewriters (the office one and the portable), though there was no warrant for their confiscation. Moreover, to confiscate typewriters under our conditions is such savage arbitrariness that it disturbs me even to mention it. But judge for yourself. If the typeface of the machines was needed, only a few minutes were required to take a sample. And that is supposed to be done in the presence of the owner of the machine. Then why confiscate the machines? In the best of cases, in order to deprive the owner of the use of them. And in the worst? In the worst, I'll tell you, if you don't know already—to prepare a frame-up against the owner of the machines.

When I protested the confiscation of documents not double-checked by me, Inspector Berezovsky answered: "You, what are you suspicious about?" I fear that you too may answer the same way. Thus, I reply as I did to Berezovsky: "I am not suspicious about anything. I am stating the logical possibilities flowing from the violation of procedural norms. And what in fact will be made out of these possibilities the future will show."

But I do not wish to wait impassively for what will come. I intend to demand the correction of all violations of the law made in regard to myself. Therefore, I demand: (1) the immediate return of all documents taken from me and both typewriters; (2) an end to all illegal acts toward me or my family— from the assignment of persons to follow us; to the surveillance of my apartment, either directly or by special apparatus; to the application of listening devices to the apartment and tapping of telephone conversations; to the opening and reading or confiscation of my mail. I contend that *your powers and rights* are sufficient (going by the law, of course) to force those involved to comply and to have my demands carried out. In expectation of this, I await your reply.

I hope that you will give due consideration to the fact that I held off making my complaint for *fourteen* days, giving these "searchers" that time to find out what they had confiscated. In the hope that you will take that into account, I will expect to receive your reply no later than in the time allotted by the presidium of the Supreme Soviet of the USSR— *two weeks.*

LENINISM YES! STALINISM NO!
by Ivan Yakhimovich

[In April 1968, Yakhimovich was dismissed from his post and condemned to unemployment and his family to hardship. However, his long period of enforced idleness gave him the opportunity to meet other dissidents in Moscow. It was in that period, July 1968, that he, with Grigorenko, delivered to the Czechoslovak embassy the open letter they had composed together with Kosterin, Pisarev, and Pavlinchuk. (See preface to Kosterin's "I Will Remain a Bolshevik," above.) Back in Latvia, he began to prepare a study of the post-January developments in Czechoslovakia, and when the Red Square demonstrators against the invasion were arrested, he wrote and circulated a letter supporting them. That document, along with his notes on Czechoslovakia and other "unauthorized" materials, was seized from him by police who searched his apartment in late September on suspicion of "bank robbery." In December an investigation of Yakhimovich was begun under a law forbidding "anti-Soviet slander." The investigator asked him if he still felt as he had in his letter ("If I had been in Moscow, I would have been in Red Square too.") Yakhimovich's reply was "Yes." The consequences were not long in coming, as the next document shows.

[The present translation is from the September 27, 1969, *Workers Press*.]

Since the end of the Great Patriotic War, our people has not known such an uncomfortable situation as that into which it was plunged by the events of August 21, 1968.

To occupy an allied socialist country solely because of a supposed counterrevolution, to occupy a country in which the leading role is played by the Communist Party, without its consent, with contempt for its wishes, is something which

336

runs counter to all the moral conceptions of the Soviet people. They desire peace and know how to appreciate the friendship and confidence of other peoples.

An old illness — fear, a stupor similar to paralysis — has gripped the souls of millions of people like a rebirth of the servile and degrading fear of the bloody night of Stalinism.

All that gang of Stalinists who have not and never had anything to do with Marxism-Leninism, but who, on the contrary, tended towards fascism, and who often used the methods of fascism, these Stalinists who Khrushchev relegated to the storehouses and corridors of history, considered that the time had come to take their revenge. How much they resemble those thirsty for revenge in West Germany. They also camouflage themselves behind phoney slogans. They also hope to take revenge!

Can such brutal acts of interference in the affairs of a socialist state strengthen the Communist movement? No! Can they strengthen the authority of the Soviet Union? No! Stalinism has become the principal danger which threatens the unity and solidarity of all countries, the principal danger which threatens peace and progress. It cannot be doubted that all Marxist-Leninists must unite their efforts to destroy Stalinism, to destroy this leftist deviation, this revisionism, this non-socialism, before the danger which it represents leads to catastrophe.

Whether the Stalinists are conscious of it or not, they fear their own people more than they fear the imperialists. It is this fear alone that can explain the continuous brainwashing of large sections of the population, the use of methods of intimidation and blackmail, the rude violation of the constitution, the extreme bureaucratization of the state, the immense network of spying, of informing, of prisons and concentration camps.

Is all this socialism? Where did they get this policy? Marxism-Leninism did not put forward this type of "socialism"; it does not include such principles; it knows nothing of such ideas; this is what has to be admitted when all their screen of verbiage has been swept aside and the facts brought into the light of day. No! a thousand times no!

This is why the twentieth congress of the CPSU affirmed the necessity to restore the norms and principles of Leninism. This is why the whole Communist world followed with such close attention and hope the process of democratization in Czechoslovakia. And this is why the Stalinists attacked the Czechoslovak Communist Party with such fury, because they saw in it a mortal danger for themselves personally; they make a mockery of socialism and communism and of all their principles in order to save their own skins.

Isn't it significant that those comrades who demonstrated in Red Square on August 25 with the slogans of support for Czechoslovakia, its people and government, were arrested and beaten up? This took place in the Year of the Rights of Man, and what is more, in Red Square.

They must have reached the limit of fear and panic in order to turn on their own citizens, the Soviet people. These demonstrators — Pavel Litvinov, Larisa Bogoraz-Daniel and others — were they not supporting a socialist state? Perhaps, after all, they were supporting Franco, Salazar, the Greek military junta!!!

No, the Stalinists feel the ground slipping away beneath their feet; they know that the mortal hour that history has chosen for them is approaching. Their panic is that of condemned men, it is the panic of living corpses. But it is necessary to be vigilant! They have in their hands today powerful weapons. They have in their hands the reins of power. But their hands are frail; they are the hands of criminals. Communists of the world, stop them before it is too late. . . .

We know the fate that awaits Pavel Litvinov and [his] comrades. We know what the accusations will be like — they will be false accusations, dirty accusations. I do not base this upon a simple hypothesis, but upon my personal experience. On September 27, five individuals carried out a search of my home because I was "suspected of having stolen 19,000 roubles from the State Bank of the town of Yurmala."

They went through my flat and found some political literature concerning events in Czechoslovakia, and they took it away, including *Pravda* and *Izvestia*, because comments had been written in the margin on some of the statements. There is no need for the least doubt that "they" will now have material for a direct intervention of the KGB and for my arrest.

The examining magistrate asked me why I had been so long without working (since April 1 this year). I was sacked while on holiday for a letter written to Politbureau member Suslov and addressed to the Central Committee [see p. 263]. Besides, I have not been given a registration permit to allow me to join my family. Everybody knows that without this in the USSR one cannot obtain work even as a porter or be admitted to a hospital. What sort of hypocrisy is it to ask someone unemployed under these conditions: "Why are you not working?" when it is obvious on whose orders the things just mentioned have been decided!

When a torrent of slander floods all our papers, when the fraternal Communist Party of the socialist republic of Czechoslovakia is also slandered, what does a further slander against the former chairman of a collective farm matter?

Those Communist parties which support the CPSU in its crude mistakes render it, whether they want to or not, the worst of services: they contribute to deceiving the Soviet people, they weaken our country in practice, because they strengthen the adventurist elements within the leadership of the party and weaken the healthy and progressive elements.

We repeat: Come to your senses! We repeat: Hands off Czechoslovakia! We repeat: Free the political prisoners!

We repeat: LENINISM YES! STALINISM NO!

APPEAL ON CZECHOSLOVAKIA
by Pyotr Grigorenko and Ivan Yakhimovich

[Printed below is the full text of the February 1969 call for withdrawal of Soviet troops from Czechoslovakia that was circulated in the Soviet Union by Grigorenko and Yakhimovich.

[The translation is from the March 31, 1969, *Intercontinental Press,* and is reprinted by permission.]

The campaign of self-immolation initiated on January 16, 1969, by the Prague student Jan Palach as a protest against the intervention in the internal affairs of the Czechoslovakian Socialist Republic has not ended. Another human torch [the student Jan Zajic], the latest, flared up in Prague's Wenceslas Square on February 21.

This protest, which took such a frightful form, was intended above all for us, Soviet citizens. It is the unsolicited and unjustified presence of our troops that arouses such anger and despair among the Czechoslovak people. For good reason the death of Jan V. Palach stirred the whole of working Czechoslovakia into action.

We all share a part of the guilt for his death, as well as for the death of other Czechoslovak brothers who have committed suicide. By our approving the venture of our troops, justifying it, or simply keeping silent, we contribute to the continued burning of human torches in the squares of Prague and other cities. The Czechs and Slovaks always considered us their brothers. Will we let the word "Soviet" become synonymous in their eyes with the word "foe"?

Citizens of our great country! The greatness of a country is not shown by the power of its armies being brought down upon a small, freedom-loving people, but by its moral power. Shall we really continue to look on in silence while our brothers perish? By now it is clear to everyone that the presence of our troops on the territory of the Czechoslovakian Socialist Republic is not called for by the defense needs of our country nor the needs of the socialist community. Do we not have enough courage to admit that a tragic mistake has been made and to do everything in our power to correct it? That is our right and our duty!

We call upon all Soviet people, without doing anything rash or hasty and by all legal methods, to bring about the withdrawal of Soviet troops from Czechoslovakia and the renunciation of interference in its internal affairs. Only by this means can the friendship between our peoples be restored.

Long live the heroic Czechoslovak people!

Long live Soviet-Czechoslovak friendship!

APPEAL TO THE SOVIET PEOPLE
ON THE EVE OF ARREST
by Ivan Yakhimovich

[Yakhimovich was arrested on March 25, 1969, for "spreading anti-Soviet fabrications." Anticipating arrest, he wrote this defense of his position just days before the police took him into custody.

[The following excerpts from his statement, translated in the May 12, 1969, *Intercontinental Press,* are reprinted by permission.]

My days of freedom are numbered. On the threshold of captivity, I address myself to those whose names I cannot forget. Hear me!

I am thirty-eight years old. I was born in Daugavpils as the tenth child of a washerwoman and a day laborer. After I graduated from high school, I studied at the Latvian Pyotr-Stuchka state university. Then I worked in the countryside as a high-school teacher, school inspector, and as the chairman of the Yauna Gvarde [Young Guard] collective farm in the Kraslava district. At present I am working as a stoker in the Belorussiia sanatorium in Yurmala, Latvian SSR. I was a member of the Young Communist League for ten years and a member of the party for eight years. I grew up among people to whom Lenin's name was more respected than any other, to whom his name was the authority for determining the truth. At the beginning of 1942, my brother Kasimir Yakhimovich, a bearer of the Order of the Red Star, fell before Moscow. My brother-in-law Nikolai Kirkhenstein, a nephew of the present chairman of the Supreme Soviet of the Latvian SSR, lost his life in the defense of Leningrad. My uncle Ignat Yakhimovich, an old revolutionist, spent eight years in prison under the Latvian bourgeois regime. . . .

In 1956, I went to the virgin lands as a Young Communist volunteer. I met my future wife there, although we had studied at the same school, the school of history and philosophy, at home. She was in her first year of study, I in my fifth. We married in 1960.

I must tell my history because a flood of lies and slanders against me will come out of the court chambers. I must tell about myself because my fate is the fate of my people and my honor is their honor.

I am accused under Paragraph 183, Section I, of the Criminal Code of the Latvian SSR, of spreading fabrications slandering the Soviet state and social system. The maximum penalties for this offense are three years deprivation of freedom, a year at hard labor in a prison camp, or a 100 ruble [1 ruble = US $.90] fine. My letter to Suslov, which I sent to the office of the CPSU and which also became known in the West, is supposed to have been anti-Soviet. The appeal to world public opinion by P. Litvinov and L. Bogoraz, which I helped disseminate, is alleged to have been slanderous.

On September 27, during a search of my apartment, newspapers, periodicals, excerpts from Lenin's works, two notebooks with my notes on the events in the Czechoslovak Soviet Republic, my wife's diary, an unsent letter in defense of P. Litvinov, and a report by P. G. Grigorenko on the beginning of the 1941-45 war were confiscated. This search was carried out under the pretext that I had stolen over 19,000 rubles from my bank, although at that time the real bank robber had already been captured and all police stations had received the order to discontinue the search.

On February 5 and March 19 and 24, I was summoned to appear before E. Kakitis, the investigating judge of the Lenin district in Riga, despite the fact that I live in Yurmala. From the negative report made by the first secretary of the Kraslava district, G. M. Kirilov, and by the chief of production direction, A. I. Oralov; from the evidence presented by the dean of the Jelgava agronomy school, Comrade Pakalnietis (who maintained that I had admitted visiting P. Litvinov in Moscow and that I recorded my letter to Suslov on tape to send abroad); and from a whole series of similar indications, one thing became clear to me. Previously the alternative was whether or not I should be brought before a court, and if I were, whether or not I should be sent to prison, but now all that remained was to bring me to trial and lock me up. . . .

Bertrand Russell, you are a philosopher, can you perhaps understand better what their accusations are based on? From what position do they approach this? From the class standpoint? By my social origin I am a worker and I am a worker now by the criterion of the job I am actually doing.

What law have I broken? The constitution of the Latvian

SSR and the Universal Declaration of Human Rights guarantee the freedom to write, to propagate ideas, to demonstrate, and so forth. Do they fear perhaps that I am about to become a capitalist? But as a collective farm chairman, I did not possess a private plot or a cow or a sheep or even a hen, but I lived on my wages. I have no house of my own, no car, no savings book. My only capital is my books and my three children. Do they think that I did not work and am not working for socialism? If not, what system am I working for, then? Whom does my freedom threaten and why must it be taken from me?

Comrade Alexander Dubcek: When seven people went out on Red Square on August 25 with the slogan "Hands Off Czechoslovakia," and "For Your Freedom and Ours," they were beaten bloody, they were called "anti-Soviet slanderers," "dirty Jews," and the like. I could not be with them, but I was on your side and I shall always be on your side as long as you serve your people honestly. "Remain firm, the sun will rise again. . . ."

Aleksandr Isaievich [Solzhenitsyn]: I am happy that I had the opportunity to read your works. May "the gift of the heart and the wine" be yours.

Pavel [Litvinov] and Larisa [Bogoraz-Daniel]: We saluted your courage like the gladiators of old: "Hail Caesar, we who are about to die salute you!" We are proud of you. "Deep within the Siberian mine, keep your patience bright . . . not in vain are your sufferings nor the lofty flight of your thought" [from Pushkin's poem dedicated to the survivors of the 1825 Decembrist uprising against czarism].

Yevgenii Mikhailovich, old friend and fellow fighter from World War II days: My arrest should not come as a surprise to you. Do not believe them, do not believe them! I cannot be an enemy of Soviet power.

Peasants of the Yauna Gvarde collective farm: I worked with you for eight years. That is long enough to get to know a person. Judge for yourselves and may your judgement serve the truth. Don't let them deceive you.

Workers of Leningrad, Moscow, and Riga, dockers of Odessa, Liepai, and Tallinn: By going out onto Red Square to say "No" to the occupiers of Czechoslovakia, the worker Vladimir Dremliuga saved the honor of his class. He was thrown into jail. On the pretext that he violated the police passport regulations, the transport worker Anatoly Marchenko was thrown into jail. His letter exposed the duplicity of the leading circles— their interference in the internal affairs of the Czechoslovak Socialist Republic. Previously he languished six years in the camps in Mordovia because of the evidence given by an informer, losing his hearing and his health there.

Who should help a worker if not another worker? One for all and all for one! Comrade Grigorenko, Comrade Yakir, seasoned fighters for the truth! May life preserve you for the just cause!

Crimean Tatars! He who has robbed an entire people of their homeland, he who has defamed an entire people, from infants in arms to old men, is the mortal foe of all peoples. For your homeland, the Crimean Tatar Autonomous Soviet Socialist Republic! For your sons and daughters who are being thrown into prison! For your rights that are being trampled underfoot!

I address myself to people of my own nationality — to the Poles wherever they are living and wherever they work. Do not keep silent when injustice is being done. Poland is not lost yet while still we live.

I address myself to Latvians, whose land has become my homeland, whose language I know as I know Polish and Russian. . . . Do not forget that in the labor camps of Mordovia and Siberia thousands of your fellow countrymen languish! Demand their return to Latvia. Watch carefully the fate of everyone deprived of freedom for political reasons.

Academician Sakharov: I heard about your "Reflections." I regret that I did not manage to write to you. The debt is mine. "There is so much evil in the world and so few are outraged at it" [from Yussuf Has-Habzhib Balassagunskii].

Communists of all countries, Communists of the Soviet Union: You have *one* lord, *one* sovereign — the people. But the people is made up of living persons, of real lives. When human rights are violated, especially in the name of socialism and Marxism, there can be no two positions. Then your conscience and your honor must command.

Forward Communists! Forward Communists! Most of all, it is dangerous for Soviet power when people are deprived of their freedom because of their convictions, for it will not be long before it too loses its freedom.

The great of this world are only great because we are on our knees. Let us rise!

MY FRIEND AND COMRADE,
IVAN YAKHIMOVICH
by Pyotr Grigorenko

[When Yakhimovich was arrested in March 1969, Grigorenko wrote this stirring tribute to him; other protests were registered by Soviet dissenters as well. But to no avail. Rather than try their victim publicly, and face the possibility of a political challenge from the dock by the accused, the Brezhnev regime pressured psychiatrists into ruling Yakhimovich "psychologically irresponsible." (For the text of the second in a string of three "expert diagnoses," the bases for Yakhimovich's confinement, see *International Socialist Review,* June 1972.) After two years of hell in a prison-madhouse, Yakhimovich was released — in April 1971, according to the *Chronicle of Current Events.* Release probably entailed a promise on his part to renounce political activity, for he has not raised his voice since then so far as we know. He is still classified as an "invalid of the second category," meaning he is required to report regularly for a checkup on the "healthiness" of his ideas. The authorities thus have a ready pretext for reconfining him any time they see fit.

[This translation is from the October 20, 1969, *Intercontinental Press,* and is reprinted by permission.]

And so the first circle in the process whereby a man gains enlightenment in this country has now been completed for Ivan Yakhimovich, too. On March 24 he was arrested, and a fabricated case is being built up against him.

This is the end of all illusions, of the secret hopes that frightful deeds were simply mistakes and that the views of the party and government leaders actually correspond to the ideals they speak about from official rostrums. With arrest, these illusions disappear. Anyone who is a real Communist can never again be deceived by flowery declarations. For especially sensitive people this is the most difficult and frightful turning point in their lives. I experienced all this myself at one time. Now this experience has fallen to the lot of my dear friend as well. How it was for him you may judge from the letter he wrote just before his arrest.

The history of how this letter came into being is also instructive. A legal case was underway involving him. At the last interrogation before he was arrested he was confronted with slanderous testimony by one of the instructors at the agricultural college and a characterization of him, of similar quality, by the first secretary of the Kraslava region party committee. Ivan drew the correct conclusions: if the investigation had reached the point where such documents were fabricated, the question of his arrest and conviction had already been decided beforehand. Making use of the fact that at that time they let him return home, he drew up the letter. Whoever reads it will see what unbearable anguish echoes in its every line. Anguish not for himself, not for his life that was being mutilated, but for the ideals dear to his heart that have been trampled so mercilessly.

Yes, Ivan is a person of acute sensitivity, wholeheartedly devoted to the ideals he absorbed in childhood, a person of great honesty, trustfulness, and love for people. In his every step, in every action, there is moral purity, integrity of character, a faith in people and in the rightness of the cause to which he has devoted himself completely.

One would have had to see how he talked with people, how they behaved toward him, what a moving friendship there was between him and his wife, how his three daughters — the oldest being only eight — loved their father, in order to understand what a pure, honest, radiant person this is.

I came to know Yakhimovich in March 1968. He had traveled to Moscow in order to find Pavel Litvinov and Larisa Bogoraz. Their appeal "To World Public Opinion" he had heard on the foreign radio. Under the immediate impact of it, he wrote a comradely letter — as one Communist to another — to one of the secretaries of the Central Committee, Suslov. The latter, as is customary in the relations between highly placed party officials and rank-and-file Communists, never answered the letter. On the other hand, it was received with great interest by the samizdat. It quickly began to circulate and soon showed up abroad. After it was broadcast by the foreign radio, Yakhimovich was called in to the KGB. During a long interview it was made known to him, in particular, that Litvinov and Bogoraz had not signed any appeal, that this was a fabrication made up by the BBC. In order to clear up who was right — the KGB or the BBC — he came to Moscow.

From our first conversation I knew that I was talking to

a convinced Communist, a highly developed Marxist-Leninist. This brought him close not only to me but to my fellow Communists as well — the seventy-two-year-old writer, Aleksei *Kosterin*, a member of the Bolshevik Party since 1916, who had spent three years in czarist prisons and seventeen in Stalin's death camps; the sixty-four-year-old scientific worker, Sergei *Pisarev*, a member of the party since 1920, who had suffered the most frightful abuses in the secret police prisons, leaving their permanent mark on his life (a ruptured spinal cord); and the theoretical physicist Valery *Pavlinchuk*, a talented young scientist and one of the authors of the books *When Physicists Joke* and *More Physicists' Joking,* who was secretary of the party organization at one of the scientific research institutes in Obninsk. Many questions were discussed by this group of five people devoted to the ideas of communism. And when, in the summer of 1968, clouds gathered over Czechoslovakia, we decided to express openly what we thought about the events in that country. The delivery of our collective letter to the embassy of the Czechoslovak Socialist Republic was entrusted by our friends to Yakhimovich and me. On July 28, 1968, we fulfilled this mission.

The last time Ivan Antonovich and I saw one another was at the end of February this year. During his very short trip here (two days in all) the two of us probably discussed more than we had in all the time that had gone before. It was very hard to part. Perhaps because at that time the investigation involving Yakhimovich was already under way and his arrest was to be expected; and perhaps because by that time, of our group of five, only we two remained. Aleksei Kosterin and Valery Pavlinchuk, hounded by the savage bureaucratic machine, had passed away; subjected to harsh persecution, Sergei Pisarev had fallen seriously ill.

The deepgoing analysis of the internal and international political situation of the USSR and of the contradictions within the international Communist movement which I heard from my companion at that time showed that during the time we had been apart he had studied these questions intently, had done a great deal of thinking, and experienced a lot. The anguish and alarm with which he spoke about the ill-considered actions that had gotten our party and country into an exceptionally unfavorable position, weakening and undermining their international authority, are something that would have to be heard. The culmination of these discussions was our joint "Appeal on Czechoslovakia" to the citizens of the USSR concerning the self-immolations in Czechoslovakia.

Yakhimovich has spoken about himself quite movingly in his prearrest letter. I will therefore cite only some details of his biography. At the age of twenty-three he completed his university courses. The honorable labor of teaching, to which he devoted himself thereafter, enchanted him; he fell in love with it. However, he only worked in the schools for four years. The CPSU leadership summoned the party's cultural forces to the village — to save agriculture, which had been crushed by the whole preceding criminal policy. And for that reason, the young Communist Yakhimovich decided to abandon the work he loved. It was not for the sake of a career or for glory, but simply out of his Communist sense of conviction.

Joining the party in 1960, he spent a lot of time studying the classics of Marxism-Leninism and the current party documents. Everything he studied, assimilated in his mind, became part of his personal world outlook, the constant basis for all his actions. The proper development of his Communist consciousness was made possible by the fact that his life in the party began after the twentieth congress of the CPSU; therefore he did not experience in its entirety the deadly workings on the mind, the dogmatism, of the personality cult period. But without having experienced it, he nevertheless acquired an accurate enough picture of that period, and this made itself felt in the formation of his views. By himself he came to the firm conclusion that never again should the party oligarchy be permitted to get into position to run the show as it pleased, free of any control whatsoever, in both the party and state. Every Communist, no matter what post he holds, has an equal right to participate in the decisions affecting all internal party matters and in government affairs. Yakhimovich was certain that this was not only his conclusion but the general line of the party as well. He did not yet know then that the words of party and government leaders are one thing and their actual practice another. It would never have occurred to him that precisely the defense of the views he had worked out would bring him to the prisoner's dock.

So long as he proclaimed his right only to the first part of the formula by which he had chosen to live, everything was fine. No one objected when he renounced the privileges provided by the teaching work he loved, and expressed the desire to go to work on a backward collective farm, paying no heed to the difficulties this new way of life would bring. On the contrary, this action met with the approval of the party apparatus.

In 1960 he was elected chairman of the Yauna Gvarde collective farm. He worked selflessly to master his new, unfamiliar, and complicated job. He approached everything through first-hand experience, learned from the rank-and-file farm workers. Because of his work, no time remained even for his family, whom he dearly loved. Nevertheless he resolved to find time even to do some studying in his new profession. In 1964 he began to attend the Latvian Academy of Agriculture. This exacting labor did not go unrewarded. Things began to go better for the collective farm. Even the central press began to talk about it. The collective farmers evaluated their chairman rightly, feeling a sense of respect and confidence toward him: four times they reelected him to that post.

But then came the time for the second half of Yakhimovich's chosen formula. He expressed his views on a very small question, and suddenly it became clear that his opinion was not only not needed by the party leaders but even irritated them with its reference to the usurped rights of party members. It turned out that the leaders were only for equal rights within the party in words, while in reality they were content with the inner-party situation established under the personality cult — a situation of total freedom from control for the leaders, their full independence from the party mass. It is no secret that in those accursed times a goodly number of scoundrels and careerists, of morally degenerate types, penetrated into the party. The remaining mass of party members, as a result of the innumerable brutal purges directed against thinking members of the party, were turned into politically indifferent people who lived by the principle: "the Central Committee knows best what should be done; our job is to submit unquestioningly to the party 'bosses.'" The ideology of precisely that element of the party mass was supported and encouraged by the party leadership.

The highest party leaders themselves, trained in the stuffy, family-circle atmosphere among the "Boss's" retainers, responded to "guerrilla sorties" such as Yakhimovich's letter the way a bull responds to the color red. And whatever he wrote and however he wrote it, as long as it was done on his own initiative and not by order from above, he could expect only that fate which in fact has overtaken him. Bypassing the base-level party organization, they expelled him from the party; in essence he was thrown out by decision of the regional committee apparatus of party bureaucrats; then, when he had gone to take his exams for his fourth course at the agricultural academy, they removed him from his post as collective-farm chairman, in violation of the collective-farm charter. At the same time they dismissed his wife from the school where she was teaching Russian.

Yakhimovich, with three young daughters to care for, had to look for work and a place to live. They went to the city of Yurmala, to his wife's mother with whom they shared a room of *eight* square meters. They had been given permission to move, but after several days Ivan Antonovich was denied permission to stay where he was. It was necessary to go through all sorts of harassment to finally receive permission for temporary registration and, therewith, a chance to find work. Ivan was hired as a stoker at the sanatorium, and Irina as a kindergarten teacher, apparently with the not unfounded hope that the children, at that age, would not yet be prone to the influence of her "alien" ideology.

While Yakhimovich was trying to get permission to register and therefore was not working, he suddenly came under "suspicion" of robbing a bank, and a search was made of his home. But strange to say, the search was conducted not by the proper authorities but by the KGB, and for some reason they did not hunt for the weapon used in the crime or for stolen money but leafed attentively through his books, confiscating all samizdat material, as well as the notes, diaries, and letters of the "suspect." Soon an investigation began, not into the crime for which the search had been conducted, but into suspected "spreading of slanderous rumors discrediting the Soviet state and social system." Incidently, during this investigation it came out by chance that the real criminal, the one who had actually robbed the bank, had been detained long before the search of Yakhimovich's home.

What is the meaning of all this?! For the KGB, laws do not exist. If a person is arrested by this body, the case will be drawn up, the prosecutor will support the indictment, and the Soviet court, "fairest in the world," will condemn ·him. Past experience offers no examples to the contrary. Tens of millions of those rehabilitated posthumously or after long years of sitting in Stalin's camps are the best proof of the "fairness" of past sentences. And the present system differs from the former one only quantitatively (fewer are jailed), not in essence. At bottom it remains as before—"The KGB makes no mistakes." Therefore, Yakhimovich too will necessarily be condemned unless forces capable of stopping the criminal hand of the latter-day Stalinists can be found.

A single individual is nothing to the Stalinists. They will never take something on that small a scale into account.

DIARY FROM PRISON
by Pyotr Grigorenko

[Pyotr Grigorenko was arrested on May 7, 1969, in Tashkent, where he had been invited to appear in behalf of the defendants in a trial of Crimean Tatars. What happened there is related in the excerpts from his diary presented here. In August, a Tashkent psychiatric commission declared him sane and commented on the clarity of his thinking; however, he was sent to the notorious Serbsky Institute of Forensic Psychiatry, where the ruling was reversed and Grigorenko was declared non-accountable. When his trial was finally held, in February 1970, he was not permitted to attend it (he was "too ill") and was denied interviews with his wife and his defense attorney. On My 26, 1970, he was transported to the special psychiatric prison hospital at Chernyakhovsk.

[In Soviet practice, "psychiatric" cases are reviewed by a board of experts every six months, to determine whether the "patient's" status should be altered. In Grigorenko's case, according to Zinaida, who manages to see him rarely (special permission and a long trip from Moscow to Chernyakhovsk are required), the doctors are mainly interested in whether his ideas have changed. "One does not change one's convictions like taking off a pair of gloves," is his reply.

[In late August 1973, Solzhenitsyn spoke strongly in defense of Grigorenko: "The unyielding General Grigorenko has had to show incomparably more courage than was ever required on the battlefield in order to survive for four years in the hell of a psychiatric prison hospital. He refuses the temptation to buy freedom from torment at the price of his convictions, at the price of accepting injustice as just."

[Unless sufficient protest is heard, around the world as well as in the Soviet Union, the Kremlin will keep Grigorenko confined until he either renounces his ideas or is physically destroyed. He is in poor health, and his condition has deteriorated because of the harsh circumstances of his confinement. He has suffered two heart attacks. Cataracts have caused loss of vision in one eye and there is a danger that he may soon be totally blind. The authorities refuse to provide the necessary medical treatment.

[A recent unconfirmed report from the Soviet Union that

352

Grigorenko has been transferred from the Chernyakhovsk "special" psychiatric prison to a "normal" mental hospital may mean the Brezhnev regime is beginning to feel pressure from the protests around his case. These protests ought to be redoubled to free this model of courage and loyalty to revolutionary convictions.

[The first and last of the excerpts are reprinted by permission of the Working Group on the Internment of Dissenters in Mental Hospitals; they were translated from a condensed version of the diary that appeared in the *Chronicle of Current Events.* The translation of the middle excerpt, from the full Russian text of the diary, is by the editor.]

3 May [*1969*]— Arrive in Tashkent by air, go to Ilyasov's flat. The call to appear in court at Tashkent turns out to be a provocation. Decide to return to Moscow, but fall ill.

4 May — Notice that the flat is being watched.

7 May — Arrested just before the departure of flight for Moscow, after a search which furnishes the investigators with no evidence.

15 May — Charged under article 190-1 of the Russian Criminal Code.

8 May-11 June — Statements to procurator-general of the Uzbek Republic, Ruzmetov, and to the procurator-general of the USSR, Rudenko. Demands: to release me or to transfer the investigation to Moscow, my place of residence, and (in accordance with the Criminal Procedure Code) the "scene of the crime" (the incriminating documents were found in Moscow); or to permit me a meeting with my wife. If none of these demands are met, I announce a hunger strike.

13 June — Hunger strike begins.

15 June — Forced feeding begins. They beat me, half-choke me.

16-19 June — Forced feeding. They're beating me, making me choke. They twist my arms. They beat me on my wounded leg, on purpose. The most zealous are the "Lefortovo [Prison] boys" sent specially from Moscow.

17 June — Statement that my continued hunger strike will be in protest at this bestial treatment.

18 June — Write a statement about whom to blame for my death. After these two statements the acts of cruelty are cut short. They begin simply using force to bundle me into a straitjacket. I resist. The number of my attackers rises from

five to twelve. The struggle goes on and on. Most often I collapse with terrible pains in the heart. I hope that my heart
will give out. I long to die, calculating that my death will
serve to expose this tyranny.

20 June—Naumova, the procurator responsible for ensur-
ing the observation of legality, comes to my cell and gives
me to understand that my death is desirable. She confirms
what Major Lysenko, the head of the detention prison, had
told me earlier: "Don't you think you'll earn yourself a funeral
with lots of speeches. No, you won't get the sort Kosterin
got. And we won't hand your body over to your relatives.
They won't even learn the exact date of your death. They'll
be informed perhaps three days later, or perhaps three months,
or perhaps six months. And the exact place of your burial
won't be revealed."

Why am I helping them to achieve their aims? I begin to
waver in my decision to aim for death. . . .

Obushayev and I started a discussion on our own. Suddenly Berezovsky interrupted Obushayev, shouting at the top of
his voice: "What are you arguing with him for? You know
he'd happily hang us from the nearest tree!" He went on shouting variations on this theme, obviously expecting me to ex-
plode. But I just waited until he'd finished, and said calmly:
"Let me answer with a paraphrase of Lydia Chukovskaya's
words: 'Perhaps you deserve to be hanged, but our people
doesn't deserve to be fed on hangings any more. I refuse to
hang you—out of respect for our people.'"

It is clear to me that the whole situation has been designed
to inspire a feeling of "no way out"—of hopelessness and despair. What the head of the detention prison had said about
the consequences of my death was aimed to produce the same
result, for it emphasized that "you're utterly at our mercy,
even after death." Nor is it surprising that people seek death
in such a situation. It was chance that saved me from death.

Only now have I realized the special horror of the fate that
overtook those unfortunate people who perished by the million in the torture chambers of Stalin's regime. It wasn't the
physical suffering—that's bearable. But they deprived people
of any hope whatsoever; they reiterated to them the omnipotence of their tyranny, the absence of any way out. And that
is unbearable.

Throughout my period in solitary there is no psychiatric
investigation of any sort. True, Maiya Mikhailovna does in-
vite me once for a chat. But the chat doesn't come off. I put

a stop to everything by announcing that I don't want the doctor to note my answers down just as he wants. "I'll talk about anything you like, on one condition: that *I* note down the content of my answers." Past experience had taught me that this was vital.

The doctor responsible for me in 1964, Margarita Feliksovna, wrote down my answers in an unbelievably distorted form. And she did so not just because of her fervent desire to present me as "of unsound mind," but from sheer political illiteracy and ignorant narrow-mindedness. It was perhaps the last that prevented her from understanding me. For example, she asked me: "Pyotr Grigorevich, at the Academy you used to get 800 rubles a month. So what turned you to your anti-state activities? What did you lack?" Glancing at her, I realized that any answer would be fruitless; for her, a man who made material sacrifices was "of unsound mind," however lofty the causes that prompted him. So I answered briefly: "You won't understand. I couldn't breathe." And you should have seen the joy that flashed in her eyes, how quickly she jotted down my answer in her notebook, because in her opinion it testified to the fact that before her sat a crazy lunatic. . . .

19 November—the diagnostic commission: Morozov, director of the Institute of Forensic Psychiatry and corresponding member of the USSR Academy of Sciences; Lunts; Maiya Mikhailovna; and a man in a brown suit (the only one not in a white coat). The questions are asked by Morozov, the chairman of the commission. They all involve an attempt to reveal some inconsistency in Grigorenko's view of himself and his attitude to his actions. The line is: "Grigorenko has no doubts about the normality of his actions, which have led to this diagnostic session; yet Grigorenko himself recognized, after treatment in the Leningrad special psychiatric hospital, that similar actions of his which led to the diagnosis of 1964 were mistaken. As a result of the intervention of the psychiatrists Grigorenko had been behaving 'normally, in the accepted way'—before he 'went back to his old ways.'"

Grigorenko answers that he considers his previous activities (before 1964) to have been mistaken in the ideological and political senses, and in no way because of any damage to his psyche:

* * *

"Not every mistake a person makes is the result of damage

to the psyche. My mistakes were the result of my incorrect
political development — an overly one-sided Bolshevik-Leninist training. I had been accustomed to thinking that the way
Lenin had taught was the only correct way. Therefore, when I
encountered disparities between what Lenin had written and
what was being done in real life, I saw only one way out:
to go back to Lenin.

"But this was a mistake. Irreversible changes have taken
place in our life, and no one has the power to return life to
what it was, not to 1921, and not even to 1953. One can
move ahead to the next step only by starting out from the
present, making creative use of Lenin's theoretical heritage
and taking into account all the accumulated experience since
then. This I did not understand at that time [1964], and that
was my main error. I was thinking of this first of all, when
I acknowledged the error of my ways. I did not go into the
essence of my errors in that situation. Nor was that required
of me. Therefore it remained unclarified at that time that my
mistakes were not of the kind that can be corrected by the
intervention of psychiatrists.

[Grigorenko was then asked how he explained the fact that
for a year or a year and a half after the "intervention of psychiatrists" he had behaved "normally" and only later on, returned to "his old ways."]

"The psychiatrists had nothing to do with my so-called
'normal' behavior. I think what you have in mind by that is
that I did not write anything for distribution. (The presiding
doctor nods his head affirmatively.) But I did not write anything in 1965 and [early] 1966 for two reasons, which were
dependent neither on myself nor any psychiatrists.

"First: There was no time. In order to earn a crust of bread
for myself and my family I worked as a loader at two different warehouses. I earned a total of 132 rubles for this work,
i.e., almost as much as I used to pay in income tax on the
salary I got at the Military Academy. It was very hard work:
twelve hours a day with no days off. As a result I would
come home completely exhausted, with barely enough strength
to crawl into bed. I lost so much weight that my clothes hung
on me as though from a coat hanger.

"Second: During that first year and a half I still hoped that
I would succeed in winning back the pension I had earned
which had been illegally denied me. If I had succeeded we
would not be talking here now, for while still in the Leningrad
Special Psychiatric Hospital I had decided that when I was
free I would concentrate on writing a history of the Great

Patriotic War. I had my "heart set," as they say, on doing that work. But experience showed not only that cases of illegal repression were not diminishing but that they were increasing all the time. The refusal to let me get a job, leaving me purposely in a state of semistarvation, and the constant, humiliating, and illegal surveillance over me demonstrated conclusively that the time had not yet come when one could climb into an ivory tower and engage in 'pure scholarship.' Until a real stop was put to the abuse of power in our country, every honest person had to take part in the fight against it, no matter what the danger. And I joined the ranks of fighters against such abuse.

"But you are mistaken when you say I went back to my old ways. What I have been doing during roughly the last two years has not borne even a superficial resemblance to what I did before."

*   *   *

This last statement of Grigorenko's makes the man without a white coat ask him: "What's the difference? Your tactics may have changed, but in essence there's no difference. . . ."

"No! The essence is different," says Grigorenko. "The old approach was typically Bolshevik: the creation of a strictly conspiratorial illegal organization and the circulation of illegal leaflets. But now there's no organization, no leaflets, just open, bold attacks on obvious tyranny, falsehood, and hypocrisy, attacks on the perversion of truth. Before, the call was for the overthrow of the regime of that period and for a return to the point at which Lenin left off. Now the call is to remove the visible evils of society, to fight for strict observance of the existing laws, and for the realization of constitutional rights. Then the call was for revolution. Now the struggle is an open one, within the framework of the law, for the democratization of the life of our society. What, then, is there in common, either in tactics or in essence? Of course, if it is only a person who bows submissively before any arbitrary act of the bureaucrats that is considered a normal Soviet person, then I am 'abnormal.' I am not capable of such submissiveness, no matter how, or how much I may be beaten up.

"I have said, and I repeat once again that in 1963-64 I made mistakes. But I did not need psychiatry to correct them. I had already begun to understand these mistakes before my arrest. . . ."

OFFICIAL "PSYCHIATRIC DIAGNOSIS" OF GRIGORENKO

[The following are excerpts from the official diagnostic report, No. 59/S, drawn up in November 1969 at the Serbsky Institute by a team of forensic psychiatric experts, including D.R. Lunts, identified by dissenters as a KGB agent. On the basis of this report the court ruled Grigorenko "of unsound mind" and ruled that he be forcibly confined in the Chernyakhovsk "special" psychiatric prison hospital.

[It is important to stress that the Stalinist regime uses the technique of forced psychiatric confinement to avoid political trials that would be too embarrassing. The KGB requires Soviet psychiatrists to examine the "patient" who is too dangerous to put on trial. An expert commission of such psychiatrists has long sessions with the victim, goes over his records, reviews his whole life, and writes a report summing up all this information. The actual texts of two such reports on Grigorenko, the basis on which he is currently confined, were never published in the Soviet Union. The regime wants to avoid such publicity. But these texts did reach dissident circles.

[Democratic oppositionists managed to obtain exact copies of these and other official records on dissident victims of this kind of treatment. These have circulated and been commented on widely in samizdat. The courageous young rebel Vladimir Bukovsky sent 150 pages of such documents, including the official diagnoses of Grigorenko and Yakhimovich, out of the USSR in March 1971. He appealed to Western psychiatrists to comment on the question: "Do the above-mentioned diagnoses contain enough scientifically-based evidence not only to indicate the mental illness described . . . but also to indicate the necessity of isolating these people completely from society?"

[In response to this act exposing them, the Kremlin bureaucrats put Bukovsky on trial in January 1972 and sentenced him to seven years in a labor camp and five in a penal exile.

[Readers will not need psychiatric training to form an opinion on how well or poorly based the "diagnosis" is.

[Grigorenko wrote his own refutation to the "conclusions of the experts" in his prison diary: "If it is only a person who bows submissively before any arbitrary act of the bureaucrats that is considered a normal Soviet person, then I am 'abnormal.'"

358

[The excerpts from Report No. 59/S are reprinted by permission of the Working Group on the Internment of Dissenters in Mental Hospitals.]

. . . . He was a weak, sickly child who began school at eight. In character he was lively and sociable; had an inquiring mind, was easily carried away, stubborn, always defended his own point of view, and defended the weak. He was a good pupil. After four years of school he worked as a metal worker's apprentice. From this time onwards he took an active part in community life. He joined the Communist Youth. He studied in the Workers' Faculty of the Kharkov Technical Institute. In 1931 he was mobilized into the army and sent to the Military Engineering Academy. During his training at the Academy and in the following years he remained active and purposeful, was interested in all the events that took place in the country, and as he himself observes, was energetic, "brought order," and enjoyed prestige among his comrades; but at the same time he did not like contradiction, was easily irritated, and in argument could say rude sharp things to someone's face. In 1934 he finished his course at the Academy and, although he could have remained a post-graduate there, he managed to get directed to a building project.

He then graduated from the General Staff Academy and was stationed in Khabarovsk till 1943. In his own words he worked with enthusiasm, trying to reach the heart of any matter and always tried to understand what, to his way of thinking, had significance for the solution of this or that question.

In the early years of the war he was reprimanded within the party for critical comments on the state of the armed forces of the USSR.

From 1943 he took part in the Patriotic War. In 1944 he received a wound (in the leg) and was concussed, with a brief loss of consciousness. He was not hospitalized.

After the war he worked in the Frunze Military Academy as senior lecturer; in 1949 he defended his master's thesis. According to him, the defense was postponed because in discussion he expressed critical views on several points. In 1959 Grigorenko was appointed head of the Department of Military Administration.

At this time he made no complaints about the state of his health, was active, conducted scientific work, published articles, followed social and political events in the country, thought a great deal about what took place at the twentieth party congress, and came to the conclusion that all the consequences of the "personality cult" had not been liquidated, that there remained in the party "Bonapartist methods of work."

In 1961 he made a speech at a district party conference which contained "critical remarks," after which he was dismissed from his post. He took this very hard, was convinced of his rightness and struggled for a restoration of his rights. At this time he had headaches, noises in the head, and pains in the heart. He became more hasty-tempered and irritable, and could not bear contradiction. In 1962 Grigorenko was appointed chief to the operations section of the army of the [Pacific] Maritime Province.

As is evident from report No. 25/S of the forensic psychiatric diagnosis of 1964, in which there are data relating to his period of service in the Maritime Province, Grigorenko, along with his energy and an exceptional industriousness, suffered from "extreme conceit" and overestimated his own knowledge and capabilities; was hasty-tempered, lacking in restraint, and did not have authority. He observes that he was insulted by his transfer from Moscow, and considered that he had been "sent away" on purpose. Then he came to the conclusion that the government was "becoming rotten" and had departed from Leninist norms and principles, and that it was essential to conduct explanatory work among the people, aimed at "breaking down" the existing order. He studied Marx and Lenin and pondered over the mistakes of the political leadership, tried to map out the right course. He was engrossed in these thoughts, and considered this "a matter for his conscience and his honor."

In 1964 when on leave in Moscow he distributed leaflets with contents of this kind. . . .

His psychological condition was characterized by the presence of reformist ideas, in particular for the reorganization of the state apparatus; and this was linked with the ideas of overestimation of his own personality that reached messianic proportions. He felt his experiences with affective intensity and was unshakeably convinced of the rightness of his actions. At the same time elements of a pathological interpretation of his surroundings were observed, together with morbid suspicion and sharply expressed affective excitability. . . .

In about 1967 he once again started to be involved in questions of "general politics" and all his energy, he says, he devoted to the struggle for truth. He soon became acquainted with people whose views he found acceptable, readily consorted with them, and worked on articles in which he set forth his ideas on various events taking place in the country. At the same time he wrote letters to government leaders in which he "openly" criticized their actions and expressed his point of view. He was enthusiastic about his work, considering it useful and necessary, and saw in it an "outlet" for the inactivity which in his opinion the KGB was trying to thrust upon him. In character he remained alert and lively but he became even more hot-tempered, irritable, and emotional. At the same time he considered it necessary to react to any events which he considered unjust, although they had no relation to him. It is precisely by his endeavor to do this that he explains his activity at the time of the trials of certain people charged under Articles 70 and 190-1 of the Russian Criminal Code and the active help he gave to Crimean Tatars trying to return to the Crimea. . . .

Among the documents of the criminal case are the testimonies of witnesses, including his relatives, in which Grigorenko is described as a man of honor and integrity, well-balanced and friendly; and no eccentricity in his behavior had been observed. At the same time in other witnesses' testimonies it is pointed out that Grigorenko had "dictatorial ways," that he talked a great deal and with heat when he was proving his point of view, thrusting it on his interlocutor. Witnesses who saw Grigorenko near the court building on 9-11 October 1968 at the time of the trial of persons charged under Articles 190-1 of the Russian Criminal Code observe that he "stood out" by his behavior, that he was active, gave loud voice to his opinions, was abusive, insulted the *druzhinniki* [voluntary police], calling them fascists and Black Hundreders, that he drew a crowd around him, to which he spoke about himself, shouting that he would fight for democracy and truth. In the period of investigation, as is evident from the documents in the case, when exercising and in his cell, Grigorenko would shout in answer to rebukes, insulted the prison staff, was irritable during interrogation, and for a time went on hunger strike. . . .

At the same time he affirms that all that he wrote during that period was perfectly correct: he does not, even now, renounce the views he expressed then. After discharge from the hospital and subsequently he also felt quite well, and if it had not been for the unpleasant situation which developed for him, he would, in his opinion, have obtained a post suiting his qualifications and written scientific works. However, the things that happened to him "pushed" him, in his words, along the path of struggle against injustice and lawlessness. From that time on, all his energy and activity were "devoted" to the fight for "truth" and the creation of conditions which would exclude injustice in the life of the community.

He considers his struggle absolutely legitimate, and the path he has entered on to be the only correct one. When attempts are made to dissuade him he becomes angry and ill-tempered and declares to the doctor that the whole of life consists of struggle, that he had foreseen the possibility of arrest, but that that never stopped him, as he could not renounce his ideas. At the present time he considers himself to be mentally fit.

He formally declares in conversation with the doctor that he does not rank himself among outstanding people and alleges that he does not consider his activity to have historical significance; he says that he acted at the behest of conscience and he hopes that his struggle will not be without effect.

But in his letters, which are among the documents of the case, one finds a clear overestimation of his own activity and of the significance of his personality and reformist ideas, of the rightness of which he is unshakeably convinced.

In addition he distinctly reveals a tendency to write much and at length, and in his writings it can be observed that side by side with disturbances of the critical faculty he has preserved his former knowledge and ability to present, formally, a consistent account of facts. In his wing of the Institute the patient tries to behave calmly, is polite, sociable, with those around him, and reads literary works. . . .

Part III:

Documents
of the Protest Movement
(1969 and After)

(Top left) Aleksandr Ginzburg, samizdat editor, defendant in 1968 Trial of the Four, imprisoned since then. (Top right) Yuri Galanskov, poet and editor, codefendant with Ginzburg in 1968; died in Mordovian prison camp in late 1972. (Bottom left) Valery Ronkin, of *Kolokol* and Union of Communards in Leningrad, cosigner with Ginzburg, Galanskov, and others of 1969 appeal by political prisoners to Supreme Soviet. (Bottom right) Valentyn Moroz, Ukrainian historian and oppositionist, imprisoned since 1970, gravely ill.

INITIATIVE GROUP
APPEAL TO THE UNITED NATIONS

[This appeal, circulated by the Initiative Group for the Defense of Human Rights, was dated May 20, 1969. Most of its initiators and signers have figured prominently in the struggles for political rights in the Soviet Union, struggles impressively summarized in this document.

[Noteworthy is the insistence on the right to hold and impart political ideas — a direct challenge to the monopoly of political power exercised by the Stalinist bureaucracy. Similarly noteworthy is the deliberateness with which the signers decided to make an international appeal. That the document is directed to the United Nations reveals that the signers have illusions about the role of the UN as an instrument of imperialist policy. The appeal would have been better directed to workers' and radical organizations abroad. However, the Soviet government played a decisive role in creating the UN and was a signatory to its key documents, including the Universal Declaration of Human Rights. Perhaps the signers of the appeal had this fact in mind.

[Among the signers were N. Gorbanevskaya, who had participated in the demonstration at Red Square protesting the invasion of Czechoslovakia and had been imprisoned for that act; Zinaida and Andrei Grigorenko, the wife and son of Pyotr, who had been imprisoned May 7 for attempting to act as defense counsel for ten Crimean Tatars.

[The translation is from the June 16, 1969, *Intercontinental Press,* and is reprinted by permission.]

1. We, the undersigned, deeply disturbed by the unceasing political repressions in the Soviet Union, and seeing in this a return to Stalinist times when our entire country found itself in the grip of terror, appeal to the Human Rights Commission of the United Nations to defend the human rights being trampled on in our country.

2. We appeal to the UN because we have had no response to the protests and complaints that we have sent for quite a number of years to the highest government and judicial offices of the Soviet Union. The hope that our voice might be heard, that the authorities would cease their illegal actions, which we have repeatedly called attention to — this hope has died.

3. Therefore we are appealing to the UN, assuming that the defense of human rights is a sacred obligation of that organization.

4. In this document we shall speak of the violation of one of the most basic human rights — the right to hold one's own opinions and to impart them by any legal means.

5. At political trials in the Soviet Union one often hears the statement, "You are not being tried for your opinions."

6. This is totally untrue. We are tried precisely for our opinions. When they tell us they are not trying us for our opinions, they are in fact saying: "You can have any opinions you want, but if they contradict the official political doctrine, then don't you dare impart them." And in truth, arrests and trials, of which we shall speak, have occurred whenever people with opposition views have begun to impart those views.

7. But the imparting of opinions is the natural consequence of holding opinions. Therefore in Article 19 of the Universal Declaration of Human Rights it says: "Everyone has the right to freedom of opinion and expression; this right includes freedom to hold opinions without interference and to seek, receive, and impart information and ideas through any media and regardless of frontiers."

8. Thus while the formal basis for the repression is the imparting of opinions, in fact people are being tried for the opinions themselves.

9. They are tried on charges of slandering the Soviet state and social system, whether with the intention of subverting the Soviet order (Article 70 of the Criminal Code of the Russian Republic) or without such intent (Articles 190 and 191 of the Criminal Code of the Russian Republic). None of the people convicted at the political trials known to us set as their goal the slandering of the Soviet system, let alone acting to subvert it. Thus at all these trials people were convicted on fictitious charges.

10. We shall cite several examples, which have been the object of broad publicity both in the Soviet Union and beyond its borders.

11. The trial of Sinyavsky and Daniel, who were convicted

for publishing outside the country literary works critical of Soviet reality.

12. The trial of Ginzburg, Galanskov, and others, who were tried for publishing the literary journal *Phoenix-66* and a white book on the Sinyavsky-Daniel trial.

13. The trial of Khaustov and Bukovsky, who organized a demonstration against the arrest of Ginzburg and Galanskov.

14. The trial of Litvinov, Laris Daniel, and others for demonstrating against the introduction of Soviet troops into Czechoslovakia. An important feature of the two last-mentioned trials was the fact that the participants were charged in relation to the content of their slogans.

15. The trial of Marchenko, formally convicted of violating passport regulations, a charge, incidentally, that was not proved at the trial; actually he was condemned for his book *My Testimony,* which is about the conditions of prisoners in the post-Stalin years.

16. The trial of I. Belogorodskaya for trying to distribute her letter in defense of Marchenko.

17. The trial of Gendler, Kvachevsky, and others in Leningrad, who were sentenced for distributing the books of foreign publishers.

18. The trials of people who advocated national equality and preservation of national culture.

19. In the Ukraine—the trial in Kiev in 1966 at which over ten persons were convicted; the trial of Chornovil in Lviv, convicted for his book on the political trials; and many other trials.

20. The trials of the Crimean Tatars who are struggling to be returned to their native land of Crimea; in recent years some twenty political trials took place, at which more than a hundred persons were convicted; in the near future in Tashkent the most recent and biggest trial is to take place, at which ten representatives of the Crimean Tatars will be placed on the stand.

21. The trials in the Baltic republics, in particular the trial of Kalninsh and others.

22. The trials of Soviet Jews desiring the right to emigrate to Israel; at the recent trial in Kiev, the engineer B. Koshubiyevsky was sentenced to three years.

23. The trials of religious believers demanding the right to freedom of religion.

24. All these political trials, as a result of their illegality, were accompanied by the crudest violations of procedural

norms, above all, not being open to the public, but likewise not providing an impartial hearing.

25. We wish also to call your attention to that particularly inhuman form of repression — the confinement of normal persons in mental hospitals because of their political beliefs.

26. Recently a series of new arrests has occurred. At the end of April, the artist V. Kuznetsov of the city of Pushkin in the Moscow region was arrested on charges of distributing samizdat — that is, literature not published by state publishing houses.

27. In the recent past, in Riga, I. Yakhimovich, former chairman of a collective farm in Latvia, was arrested and charged for having written letters protesting political repression in the Soviet Union.

28. At the beginning of May former Major General P. G. Grigorenko was arrested; one of the best-known participants in the movement for civil rights in the Soviet Union, he had gone to Tashkent on the request of some two thousand Crimean Tatars as a public defender at the coming trial of the ten Tatars.

29. And lastly, on May 19, in Moscow, Ilya Gabai, a teacher of Russian literature, was arrested several days after his home had been searched and documents confiscated that contain protests by Soviet citizens against the political repression in the Soviet Union. (In the spring of 1967, Gabai spent four months under surveillance for having participated in the demonstration of Khaustov and Bukovsky.)

30. These recent arrests have compelled us to conclude that the Soviet punitive organs have decided to suppress once and for all the activity of persons protesting arbitrariness in our country.

31. We judge that the freedom to hold and spread opinions is being critically imperiled.

32. We hope that what we have said in our letter will give the Human Rights Commission a basis for reviewing the question of the violation of basic civil rights in the Soviet Union.

33. The Initiative Group for Defense of Human Rights in the USSR: *G. Altunyan*, engineer (Kharkov); *V. Borisov*, worker (Leningrad); *T. Velikanova*, mathematician; *N. Gorbanevskaya*, poet; *M. D. Dzhemilev,* worker (Tashkent); *S. Kovalyov*, biologist; *V. Krasin*, economist; *A. Lavut*, biologist; *A. Levitin-Krasnov*, religious writer; *Yu. Maltsev*, translator; *L. Plyushch*, mathematician (Kiev); *G. Podyapolsky*, scientific worker; *T. Khodorovich*, linguist; *P. Yakir*, historian; *A. Yakobson*, translator.

34. The appeal is supported by *Z. Asanova,* doctor (Begovat, Uzbek Republic); *T. Bayeva,* office worker; *S. Bernshtein,* writer; *L. Vasilyev,* lawyer; *Yu. Vishnevskaya,* poet; *A. Volpin,* mathematician; *O. Vorobyev,* worker (Perm); *G. Z. M. Gabai,* teacher; *E. Yegaidukov,* mathematician; *V. Gershuni,* bricklayer; *Z. M. Grigorenko,* pensioner; *A. Grigorenko,* student-technician; *N. Yemelkina,* office worker; *L. Zigikov,* worker; *A. Kalinovsky,* engineer (Kharkov); *A. Kaplan,* physicist; *S. Karasik,* engineer (Kharkov); *L. Kats,* office worker; *Yu. Kim,* teacher; *Yu. Kiselev,* artist; *A. Levin,* engineer (Kharkov); *V. Kozharinov,* worker; *L. Kornilov,* engineer; *V. Lapin,* writer; *T. Levin,* engineer (Kharkov); *D. Lifshits,* engineer (Kharkov); *S. Mauge,* biologist; *V. Nedobora,* engineer (Kharkov); *L. Petrovsky,* historian; *S. Podolsky,* engineer (Kharkov); *V. Ponomarev,* engineer (Kharkov); *V. Rokitiansky,* physicist; *I. Rudakov*; *L. Terpovsky,* doctor; *Yu. Shtein,* movie director; *V. Chornovil,* journalist (Lviv); *M. Yakir,* office worker; *R. Dzhemilev,* worker (Krasnodar region); and *S. Vintovsky,* student.

APPEAL TO WORLD
COMMUNIST CONFERENCE IN MOSCOW

[Intensifying their activities in response to stepped-up repressions by the Kremlin bureaucracy, Soviet oppositionists appealed in a statement dated June 1, 1969, to a conference of pro-Moscow Communist parties that opened in the Kremlin on June 5. The appeal is signed by ten activists in the Soviet civil rights movement, several of whom are members of the CPSU. Among them was Irma Kosterina, niece of the late Aleksei Kosterin.

[The translation is from the June 23, 1969, *Intercontinental Press,* and is reprinted by permission.]

We are appealing to the international conference of Communist and workers' parties in regard to the revival of Stalinist methods in our country.

The twentieth and twenty-second congresses exposed and condemned Stalin and his serious crimes against the party and the people. Stalin's one-man dictatorship; the arbitrary practices of the security forces, which kept society in an atmosphere of fear and terror for decades; the concentration camps, in which millions of innocent people perished; the criminal nationalities policy, under which entire nations were repressed; the impasse into which the national economy fell; the stagnation of culture and science; the low level at which wages and the production of consumer goods were kept; the catastrophic housing crisis; and the many other deformations of Stalin's dictatorship — all these were condemned.

The party solemnly promised the Soviet people that the personality cult and its consequences would never be repeated in the life of our country. It was said that the Leninist norms of democracy would be restored.

Soviet society believed these announcements, and in fact a

good deal was done toward revitalizing the life of our people.

A certain amount of anxiety was aroused by the slow and partial character of de-Stalinization. Togliatti wrote of this in his political testament.

Still greater anxiety was felt when, after the removal of Khrushchev, the democratization process began gradually and bit by bit to give way to the restoration of Stalinist methods.

At that time a movement for civil rights arose in the Soviet Union. The milestones of this movement are well known to the entire world. They are dated by the trials of Sinyavsky and Daniel; Ginzburg and Galanskov; Khaustov and Bukovsky; Litvinov and Larisa Daniel; the trials of the Crimean Tatar participants in a national movement for returning to the Crimea; the trials in the Ukraine; the trials of Marchenko and Belogorodskaya; and the recent arrests of Yakhimovich, General Grigorenko, and Gabai. This list could be expanded many times over.

In this connection it is necessary to speak of illegal arrests and unjust sentences, the lack of publicity and the bias of the courts, numerous violations of procedural norms, searches of homes, and shadowing of people, eavesdropping on phone conversations, and opening of mail. Thus, free citizens of the USSR, who have been convicted of nothing, can be placed in the position of outcasts if they don't please the KGB: mail is not delivered to them; they cannot use the telephones freely; all who have dealings with them immediately come under KGB surveillance.

Citizens who dare to express criticism of any government position whatsoever (whether they are Communists or non-party people) are subjected to humiliations and persecution and unlawful dismissal from work. For the slightest attempt to criticize, Communists are subjected to immediate expulsion from the party (in violation of the party constitution). Recently, the commitment of completely normal people to mental hospitals has become more and more frequent.

We ask the representatives of the international Communist movement to help in the liquidation of such phenomena, which, like the distortions of Stalinism, constitute a shameful blemish on the entire international Communist movement. All of these judicial and extrajudicial repressions are aimed at suppressing independent beliefs. Again, as under Stalin, the alternative is silence. Again, as during that fearful time, we are being deprived of the opportunity to express our beliefs.

But despite persecution, people will not remain silent; they are protesting. After the fifty-year history of socialism in our country, Soviet people are not willing to equate socialism with Stalinism.

At the same time, recent years have seen the undertaking of more and more frequent attempts in literature and historical writing to restore to Stalin his former greatness and thereby to place in doubt the decision of the twenty-second congress to remove Stalin from the mausoleum. The growing influence of people who are striving to revive the Stalinist past has become more and more noticeable. Once again in the state and party apparatus old Stalinist cadres are setting the tone. How else can the introduction of Soviet troops into friendly Czechoslovakia be interpreted?

We ask the representatives of the Communist parties, whose ideal is the building of a totally just society: Does it not alarm you that such an obvious restoration of Stalinism is occurring in our country, which is in the position of being the foremost Communist society? Is it really not possible to forestall the catastrophic consequences of this?

We appeal to you to examine the full seriousness of the situation and to do everything that your conscience and reason demand, everything in your power, to prevent the sinister shade of Stalin from darkening our future.

G. *Altunian,* engineer, Communist (Kharkov); Z. *Grigorenko,* pensioner, Communist; *Ilya Gabai,* teacher — from the KGB investigation prison in Tashkent, signed for him by Galina Gabai; R. *Dzhemilev,* worker (Krasnodar region); I. *Kosterina,* office worker; *Krasnov-Levitin,* writer on religious subjects; L. *Petrovsky,* historian, Communist; S. *Pisarev,* pensioner, Communist; L. *Plyushch,* mathematician (Kiev); P. *Yakir,* historian.

INITIATIVE GROUP
STATEMENT OF PURPOSES

[In May 1970, the Initiative Group for the Defense of Human Rights in the USSR issued an open letter which, among other things, described the group's principles and method of functioning. We are printing here a summary of the letter, rather than the full text. The summary appeared in the *Chronicle of Current Events,* no. 14, dated June 30, 1970, in its section "News About Samizdat."

[The full text describes the group as including believers and non-believers, optimists and skeptics, Communists and non-Communists, who are united on the basis of an effort to defend human rights, agreement that extension of liberties is progressive, and the intention to act openly, in the spirit of legality, regardless of personal convictions about particular laws. It also comments that "to describe our activities as anti-Soviet is to assume that the violation of human rights is one of the basic precepts of the Soviet state order."

[The Initiative Group takes issue with people who condemn acting openly against the violation of Soviet law because they believe that protests will drive the rulers to even greater severity and to increased reprisals. "We remember that the rulers in our land employed the most unmerciful suppression exactly in those times when no one 'provoked' them. Actually, a favorable atmosphere for repression is created simply by the lack of opposition, by that undignified submissiveness with which we inwardly sanction the violation of our rights. . . . Society needs publicity, needs public opinion. This hinders extremism and acts of force, not only those stemming from above but also those from below."

[The letter, as summarized by the *Chronicle of Current Events,* was translated for this volume by Marilyn Vogt.]

Addressed to: (1) Novosti Press Agency, Moscow; and (2) Reuters, London.

Beginning in May 1969, the Initiative Group addressed itself five times to the Human Rights Commission of the United Nations with statements enumerating concrete instances of civil rights violations in the USSR and discussing acts of repression against dissidents.

In this letter the Initiative Group explains what it stands for, what its aims are, and what its conception is of the significance of its activities.

The Initiative Group has no program or constitution. Its members are bound to one another, not organizationally, but morally; they are united by respect for human beings and for their civil rights, devotion to freedom, and a feeling of responsibility for everything that takes place in this country.

The Initiative Group is not engaged in politics and does not propose any sort of constructive solutions in this area. But it is unwilling to accept the policy of penalizing and persecuting dissenters. The Initiative Group's cause is opposition to illegality.

The Initiative Group believes that there is only one antidote for despotism — an open, public airing of views. Hence the appeals to the United Nations, the most representative international organization (to which, by the way, the USSR belongs), and through the UN, to the entire world democratic public.

"We are not at all sure," the letter states, "that our appeal to the UN is the most correct form of action; and even less, that it is the only one possible. We are trying to do something under conditions in which, from our point of view, it is impossible to go without doing anything. The Initiative Group is convinced of the urgency and advisability of a variety of actions on the part of many people and of the fruitlessness of inaction."

Six of the founding members of the Initiative Group have been subjected to repression. This letter is signed by the seven members who are still free.

Signers: *T. Velikanova, S. Kovalyov, A. Lavut, L. Plyushch, G. Podyapolsky, T. Khodorovich, P. Yakir, A. Yakobson.*

POLITICAL PRISONERS
IN MENTAL HOSPITALS

[The following article is from the May 1971 issue of *Wiener Tagebuch* (Vienna Diary), the journal of the Ernst Fischer-Franz Marek grouping, which was expelled from the Austrian Communist Party in May 1970 because of its opposition to the Soviet invasion of Czechoslovakia. It consists mostly of excerpts from several issues of the samizdat journal *Chronicle of Current Events* documenting cases of "psychiatric repression." *Wiener Tagebuch*'s action in publicizing this information represents the kind of solidarity Soviet dissenters have hoped for, more often in vain, from pro-Moscow Communist parties in the West.

[The translation is from the July 19, 1971, *Intercontinental Press*, and is reprinted by permission. The subheads have been added.]

This is documentation. As that excellent phrase puts it, any commentary would be superfluous. Where other sources are not indicated, the information comes from the samizdat *Chronicle of Current Events*, an information bulletin in the Soviet Union exclusively devoted to publicizing factual material on cases of violations of human rights by state and judicial bodies.

J. S. Gorbanevskaya, the mother of Natalia Gorbanevskaya, testifying before the court:

"If my daughter has committed a crime, then sentence her to any punishment, no matter how strict. But don't send a completely healthy person into a psychiatric institution."

Natalia Gorbanevskaya wrote a letter to *Rude Pravo* on August 29, 1968, that is, four days after the demonstration in Red Square [protesting the invasion of Czechoslovakia]. (The following excerpt from the letter was read to the court by the prosecutor because it was considered especially incriminating.)

"My comrades and I are happy that we were able to take

part in this demonstration, that it was possible, at least for a moment, to break through the flood of unrestrained lies and the cowardly silence and to show that not all the citizens of our country approve of the force that was used in the name of the Soviet people. We hope that the Czechoslovak people will hear of the demonstration, and we gain strength and perseverance from the belief that when the Czechs and the Slovaks think of Soviet citizens, they will think not only of the occupiers, but of us also."

The Sentencing of Natalia Gorbanevskaya

After summing up all the crimes charged against Gorbanev-skaya — such as participation in the Red Square demonstration against the occupation of Czechoslovakia, writing the letter just quoted, helping to edit the *Chronicle of Current Events*, and writing a report entitled "Free Medical Care" (about her first forced psychiatric treatment) — after citing Section 190-1 of the Criminal Code of the Russian Republic and the defendant's opposition to the state authority (see below), after citing Section 191 of the Criminal Code, the prosecutor came to the following conclusion:

Of course, the opinion of a juridical medical commission of experts is attached to the court record. The expert, Professor Lunts, a recognized psychiatrist, explained to the court in great detail that Gorbanevskaya suffered from a mental illness and needed treatment in a psychiatric special clinic. We must heed such a weighty medical diagnosis and release Gorbanevskaya from any legal punishment, in accordance with Article II of the Criminal Code. However, mandatory medical treatment must be ordered as prescribed by Section 53 of the Russian republic's penal code, and Gorbanevskaya committed to a psychiatric institution "of a special type," in accordance with the recommendation of the commission of experts.

Number 8 of the *Chronicle of Current Events* in June 1969 reported exhaustively on the nature and practical workings of these "psychiatric special clinics." Amnesty International also circulated this report. The special psychiatric hospitals take persons who have committed serious crimes (murder, rape, robbery) but cannot be held legally responsible for their actions. In addition, it often happens that when they want to exclude persons from society they declare them mentally ill if the authorities are convinced of their guilt and the investigation has not been able to prove anything. The length of internment in a hospital is not set by the court and can be drawn out indefinitely. Together with those who are really sick, completely healthy persons are taken to these hospitals because of their opinions. In this manner, they lose the right to defend themselves before a court, and they live in considerably worse conditions than in the prisons or camps.

The first so-called hospital of this kind existed even before the war, in Kazan. It still has a special section for political inmates, which originated in that period. After the war a special colony was established at Sytskhovka in the Smolensk region. Even now chronic cases are sent there, including politicals who are considered the most dangerous by the state security service and the directors of the special hospitals. The persons in this colony are driven into a state of complete mental collapse.

A special hospital was opened in Leningrad in 1952; another in 1965 in Chernyakhovsk in Kaliningrad region, in a former prison for Germans; still another in Minsk in 1966; and another in Dnepropetrovsk in 1968. All these institutions have the following characteristics in common: Although mentally normal, political prisoners are held in the same cells as patients with severe mental illnesses. If they refuse to renounce their opinions, they are tortured under the pretext of treatment, receiving large doses of aminazin and sulfazin, which cause depressive shock reactions and severe physical harm. The rules are the same as in a prison. One hour of exercise a day is permitted.

Often patients are injected with natriumaminat, a strong narcotic, in order to weaken them. After the injection they are questioned.

The personnel consist of employees of the state security service, whose uniforms are hidden under white coats; male attendants (thieves and incorrigible murderers) selected from the penal camps, also in white coats; and finally, higher and lower medical personnel, many with officers' stripes under their coats.

The brick walls that surround these prison hospitals are even more imposing than those around other prisons.

The most horrible despotism exists in the hospitals, from Sytskhovka to Chernyakhovsk, where the really sick and the politicals are equally victims of daily beatings and sadistic humiliation by the supervisory personnel and the attendants, who possess unrestricted power. The patient Popov, for example, was beaten to death in the spring of 1969 in the hospital of Chernyakhovsk. In his medical record, the cause of death was given as cerebral hemorrhage.

Prisoners in the strict regime camps who feel that they can no longer bear the terrible conditions often try to feign madness, and many are successful. But when they are transferred to a psychiatric prison hospital, they recognize immediately that they are worse off now than in the most dreadful camps. Many even beg the doctors—on their knees—to send them "back to the camp."

Like ex-convicts, persons who manage to be released from these hospitals receive a special passport. Those who refuse to confess their illness generally have no hope of ever winning freedom.

Testimony of the Government "Experts"

From the court proceedings against Natalia Gorbanevskaya, Moscow, July 7, 1970:

The proceedings concern the deposition of the legal psychiatric expert commission. The chairman of the court asks the lawyers to put questions to the experts. The defense attorney proposes eleven questions, six of which are permitted by the court. The last question by the defense concerns the methods of treatment proposed by the commission of experts when it recommended commitment to a special hospital. The defense wanted to know if this treatment could not be carried out in a hospital of the usual sort.

The witness, Professor Lunts, explained that in Gorbanevskaya a stealthily progressing form of schizophrenia had been diagnosed in which "definite symptoms are absent." In this illness, the only changes that can be established are in the emotional sphere, in the thinking and critical faculties, while there is no loss of memory, earlier acquired knowledge, or acquired abilities. The commission of experts is of the opinion that slowly increasing changes are occurring in Gorbanevskaya's psyche, which "from the theoretical standpoint cannot be classified as a remission (that is, a weakening of the symptoms), although they have superficial similarities with it."

To the defense's question about the need for a special institution, Professor Lunts answered that in these hospitals, in addition to the direct treatment, a regimen was maintained suited to achieving adaptation by the patients to the conditions that they would find on leaving the hospital. The combination of pathological changes in the psyche with certain unimpaired faculties, Professor Lunts continued, increased the dangerousness to society of patients, as long as they lacked a critical insight into their own behavior and were not conscious of their illness. Thus the defense was unable to obtain concrete answers to its questions.

From the court proceedings against N. Gorbanevskaya, Moscow, July 7, 1970:

The attorney for the accused, Mrs. S. V. Kalistratova, proposed a second medical examination, because on November 19, 1969, the accused Gorbanevskaya had been presented to a medical expert commission chaired by the psychiatrist I. K. Yanushevski. After studying the course of the illness and the ten-year-long psychiatric history, and on the basis of its investigation, this commission came to the conclusion that Gorbanevskaya did not suffer from a mental illness and that confinement in a psychiatric institute was not indicated. On the other hand, the commission of experts from the Serbsky Institute came to the opposite conclusion, in that it confirmed that Gorbanevskaya had a chronic mental illness, namely schizophrenia, declared her incompetent, and prescribed compulsory treatment in a psychiatric institute of a special type.

In the opinion of the defense, the presence of two mutually contradictory medical diagnoses of Gorbanevskaya's psychic state demanded an especially thorough study of the question of whether the defendant was mentally competent. This was all the more true since the record of the institute's examination aroused legitimate doubts as to the accuracy of the experts' conclusions. It did not name the form of schizophrenia nor present a single symptom of psychic disturbance. All this was basis for asserting that the experts' deposition was a criminal falsification. From this followed the demand for a detailed examination of the deposition of the institute's experts.

The indictment indicates the view of the experts concerning testimony by Gorbanevskaya and her presence at the trial. The witness, Professor Lunts, explains that the commission of experts as a rule pleads against bringing the mentally ill into court, because the latter must be regarded not only as the object of an investigation but also as patients whom the doctors are obligated to care for. The indictment declares pointless the request of the defense for an additional psychiatric examination. The commission of experts had at its disposal all the judicial records and knew which actions could be held against Gorbanevskaya. The commission of experts was aware that she had spread slanderous material and provided it to "our opponents" (in the West).

The Expert Qualifications of Doctor Lunts

In Stalin's time, Professor D. R. Lunts directed the division for political prisoners in the Serbsky Institute. Today this division is distinguished as a ward for special examinations.

Professor Lunts is simultaneously a collaborator of the KGB. As a witness, Professor Lunts in 1963 confirmed the mental incompetence of Bukovsky and in 1967 his competence; the incompetence of Dobrovolsky in 1964 and his competence in 1967. On the bases of Lunts's testimony, General Grigorenko was declared incompetent in 1964 and spent fifteen months in the psychiatric prison-clinic in Leningrad. The forced hospitalization of the participants in the August 25, 1968, demonstration, Gorbanevskaya and Fainberg, as well as Victor Kuznetsov, who was arrested in March 1969, also rests on Lunts's testimony.

From the interrogation of the witness Shilov, examining magistrate of the Moscow bar, at the trial of N. Gorbanevskaya:

The witness states that on December 24, 1969, he had to carry out a search of Gorbanevskaya's home. The action was almost at its end, he was about to complete a list of confiscated documents, while Gorbanevskaya sat nearby and sharpened a pencil for her small son with a razor blade. In order to hasten the completion of the list, he suggested to her that she number the pages of a manuscript he was going to confiscate — it was the "Requiem" of Akhmatova.

Suddenly Gorbanevskaya leaped up and tried to tear the manuscript away from him. In the course of the "struggle lasting several seconds" he suffered a number of cuts on his fingers. . . . Under questioning, the witness states that after the incident, Gorbanevskaya had apologized and assured him that the cuts had been unintentional.

The defense wanted to know on what basis the poems of the well-known and recognized Soviet poet Anna Akhmatova were supposed to be confiscated. The witness answers that the examining authorities need all the information about the philosophy, tastes, and habits of accused persons in order to make a complete study of their personalities. To the question of the defense whether he, the witness, was aware why Gorbanevskaya had been so excited about the confiscation of this manuscript, he answered that the title page bore a personal dedication by Akhmatova and therefore the manuscript possibly had a special value for Gorbanevskaya.

A Letter from Sakharov

In connection with the preventive arrest and confinement in mental hospitals of oppositionists because of the twenty-fourth congress of the Communist Party, Andrei Sakharov, a member of the Academy [of Sciences], sent a protest letter to the interior minister. Among other things, it said: "The heroic hunger strike of Fainberg and Borisov, political prisoners in the psychiatric prison of Leningrad, has already lasted seventeen days. They oppose the forcible application of treatment endangering mental capacity . . . and demand the opening of their trial. They are defending the intellectual freedom of humanity and its future. I support their demand and offer to serve as a mediator for them.

"I am disquieted by the illegal arrests of representatives of public opinion during their visit to the state attorney of the USSR. I am especially upset by the arrest of the great scholar Michael Zand, who is seriously ill, and by the forcible hospitalization of Stoliyeva and Titov in a psychiatric clinic. They violated no official rules as they waited in the state attorney's building for their legal petition to be examined, as had been promised to them. I demand the release of all those arrested. . . ." (*Le Monde,* April 4-5, 1971)

An Incident in a Prison Psychiatric Hospital

From the *Chronicle of Current Events,* Number 15, August 1970:

On May 3, 1970, around 1:00 p.m., the patient Baranov attempted to escape from the twelfth (psychiatric) hospital ward of Dubrovlag labor camp. He succeeded in getting out of the hospital and ran into the prohibited area around the camp. He was fired on from a watchtower. Eleven shots from a machine pistol were fired, of which at least five struck home. The last two shots were fired as he already lay wounded.

This incident was observed from the hospital and the camp. The next day fifteen prisoners announced a three-day strike to protest this arbitrary act against a mentally sick person. They refused to go to work. Three of the strikers were then transferred to the dreaded prison of Vladimir. Two others were locked up for seven days each. The strike was broken.

After the incident, two Armenian soldiers, Ruben Davidian and Gensel Derbinian, refused to serve their watch on the guard towers.

A Visit to P.G. Grigorenko

Pyotr Grigorevich Grigorenko is still in the prison mental hospital of Chernyakhovsk (formerly Tilsit). On July 3, Grigorenko's wife, Zinaida, his son Andrei, and the latter's bride came from Moscow to visit him. Without any explanation, the director of the institution, Major Belokopytov, refused visiting permission, although Doctor Bobylev had no reason to object on the basis of Grigorenko's condition. Grigorenko's wife then asked for at least a five-minute visit, so that Grigorenko could give the young couple his blessing. Major Belokopytov answered, "Don't ask me. On duty I have no feelings, only instructions." Only on August 3 were the son and his young wife granted a visit. Grigorenko is in a solitary cell, and is denied the right to pencil and paper.

In July 1970, Revolt Pimenov, a collaborator of the mathematical institute, was arrested in Leningrad. He was later sentenced for allegedly distributing samizdat publications. From his biography:

R. I. Pimenov, born 1931. Graduate of the Leningrad University school of mathematics. 1949 — Forcible confinement in a psychiatric clinic after filing a request to leave the Communist Youth. Diagnosis: schizophrenia. After a second hearing under the chairmanship of Professor Holand, he was declared healthy; the only thing on which the professor insisted was the retraction of his resignation.

In 1950, after threats of additional forced psychiatric treatment, Pimenov declared himself ready to remain in the Communist Youth. In 1951 he was expelled but readmitted on the decision of the district committee, was expelled from the university and readmitted, and in 1954 completed his studies.

In 1957 he was sentenced to six years' forced labor for writing an article on, among other things, the Hungarian revolution. On appeal the sentence was increased to ten years. Released on probation in 1963.

1969 — Doctoral dissertation. Member of the gravitation department of the Academy of Sciences. Author of *Kinematic Spaces* (on mathematical space-time theory), which has been published in the Soviet Union and England.

APPEAL TO THE SUPREME SOVIET

[The open letter to the Supreme Soviet published below was written apparently in March 1969. Its signers were all dissidents who became political prisoners at the Dubrovlag complex of strict-regime labor camps in Mordovia. Yuli Daniel was the co-defendant with Andrei Sinyavsky at the notorious 1966 trial. Yuri Galanskov and Aleksandr Ginzburg were codefendants in the 1968 trial that sparked the unprecedented protest movement that year. Further information on Galanskov is in the introductory comments to the document by him succeeding this. Like Galanskov, Ginzburg was a literary rebel of the fifties who developed into a major figure of the "democratic movement." He edited the uncensored magazine *Syntax* (three issues in 1958-60). Railroaded for a two-year stint in a labor colony (for having taken a university exam for a friend), he continued his dissident activities after being released, compiling the "white book" on the Sinyavsky-Daniel case. For this he was arrested in January 1967, and held for a year before the notorious Trial of the Four.

[Valery Ronkin and Sergei Moshkov were active in the Union of Communards, which produced the underground magazine *Kolokol.* More on Ronkin is in the preface to "On a Multiparty System." Victor Kalninsh, a Latvian journalist, was convicted in 1962 in a case involving an alleged "anti-Soviet underground nationalist organization." Despite the fact that the public prosecutor of the Latvian SSR appealed his ten-year sentence, it remained in force.

[The present translation is from the December 1, 1969, *Intercontinental Press,* and is reprinted by permission.]

To the Presidium of the Supreme Soviet of the USSR:

This is not a complaint intended for consideration by those bodies under whose administration the prisons and labor camps fall. We do not exclude use of our letter for establishing and verifying the facts stated in it and the adoption of the measures justified in the light of these facts. But we beg that *this letter be brought to the attention of all the deputies of the Supreme Soviet.*

Citizen Deputies,

A session of the Supreme Soviet of the Soviet Union is soon to discuss and adopt the Principles of a Corrective Labor Code for the USSR. This was announced in the press, and so far as we know the draft principles are already being discussed in certain official bodies.

Inasmuch as the passage of this law depends to some extent on you, and, as it were, concerns us, we consider it essential to explain to you the facts about the present situation in this area of Soviet jurisprudence, the facts about the interpretation and application of the laws today in the existing camps.

Our personal experience enables us to write to you only about the situation in the strict regime camps where the main body of political prisoners (according to the official terminology, "especially dangerous anti-state criminals") are being held. Of the practices in the special regime prisons and camps, where as a rule persons convicted more than once of violating the political statutes are sent, we have only secondhand knowledge, and therefore we cannot write about them.

We are not now concerned with the right which you, the legislators, grant the state to imprison (call it what you like — persuade, reeducate, isolate, punish) dissenters who propagate their own views or opinions. What is in question is only the methods of punishment (isolation, persuasion, etc.). And so to the point. Our situation is regulated now (formally) by one legislative act — the penal code (Article 20, "The Aims of Punishment"), one supplementary statute ("The Rights and Duties of Prisoners"), and many secret (so they tell us) directives. Incidentally, the directives do not agree with the rules and both contradict the direct provisions of the law: "Punishment is not intended to cause physical suffering or degradation of human dignity." Although the corrective labor code of 1926 has not yet been repealed, it not only does not reflect life in confinement today but some of its provisions even seem pure fantasy — work at your own trade, no restrictions on correspondence and receiving aid from relatives, etc. We note, incidentally, that the 1926 code actually became a dead letter and was replaced by secret directives in the unhappily remembered

1930s. And this system of keeping the documents that govern our existence secret has been maintained to this day.

Therefore, we cannot tell anything either about these directives themselves. We cannot tell whether they are really what they are claimed to be, or whether they are an invention to justify the arbitrariness of the camp administration. This means that what we can discuss is the "rules" ("The Basic Rights . . .") that we know about, and, in the first place, the actual practice.

What we have in mind is *restricted rations, cold, and humiliations*. Perhaps jurists will find words to square this with Article 20 of the Criminal Code, but we are not jurists. Here are the facts.

1. The nutritional norm in the camp is 2,413 calories. Such a diet (according to the information in the journal *Zdorove* [Health]) is the minimum for a healthy nonworking person under normal conditions. But we get far less than this norm. Our food is tasteless, monotonous, and almost entirely lacking in vitamins. If we do not have sufficient basis for saying that there is real hunger, constant vitamin starvation is an unquestionable fact. It is no coincidence that so many in the camp suffer from stomach disorders.

There is a canteen where you can buy necessities, smoking accessories, and tobacco products with the extremely limited sum of five rubles [1 ruble equals US$.90] a month. The possibility is deliberately excluded of obtaining green vegetables or other vitamin-rich products at the canteen or by any other means. It is forbidden to obtain food products by mail (*only* books, journals, papers, and written materials may be obtained this way).

According to the official rules, we can receive packages three times a year (after serving half our sentences), but (in accordance with the directives, they tell us) the only ones who get packages are those in favor with the administration. Altogether, the signers of this letter have been in confinement for more than twenty-two years but in that time not one of us has received even one food parcel in the camp.

So far we have been talking about the "upper limit" of our diet. At any time, any of us can be deprived of the right to use the canteen (this is a favorite punishment here) or be locked up in solitary confinement where the dietary norms can be reduced to 1,300 calories (and, in fact, as in the first case, still lower). That is already outright starvation.

2. A normal temperature is maintained in the dormitories and workshops only in summer weather. In the fall, winter,

and spring, the temperature hovers around the low fifties. The temperature could be raised only by a consumption of firewood beyond the capacities of the administration, because the buildings are old and the climate is not exactly like the Mediterranean. Protection against the cold is provided for in a peculiar way in the camp. They have taken away all our warm clothing — sweaters, jackets, etc.

3. We have already mentioned certain punitive measures. We should add that the isolation cell means not only hunger but miserable cold because they give you a jacket only at night. All the rest of the time you have nothing but a bare plank-bed and the cement floor.

What are the pretexts for such punishments? We did not use the term pretexts instead of reasons accidentally, because in fact there are no actual violations of the rules in the political prison camps. But "punishment is essential," and they do inflict punishment: for not waking up after a blow in the ribs; for not standing in the presence of an officer; for brewing coffee or toasting bread; for not going to the political lecture; for growing a few wild carrots in the area (for vitamins, by the way) or for refusing to stamp them out; for not fulfilling production quotas, etc.

"In combination" such transgressions can get you a half year's detention in the isolation cell ("the indoor diet") and transfer to a prison for a period of up to three years. The latter is decided by a judge, but in such cases we are deprived of counsel.

4. Denying prisoners their regular visits by relatives is also one of the penalties the rules provide for. Altogether we have the right to one "private" visit a year (up to three days) and three "public" visits (in the presence of a guard) for up to four hours. But three-day or four-hour visits are as much of an exception as packages. Without any formal grounds, the administration can shorten personal visits to one day (and, subtracting work time, this comes to twelve to fourteen hours), and public visits to one hour.

Add to this the restrictions on correspondence (we are allowed to send no more than two letters a month and any one of them, as well as any letter to us, can be confiscated both officially, for example, "in connection with the suspicion of conspiracy between the sender and the addressee," and unofficially — a considerable number of our letters and the letters sent to us disappear without a trace.

Add also the censorship of our letters (we cannot write about our conditions; such letters always "disappear") and you will understand how difficult it is made for us to defend the last pitiful scraps of our rights against any arbitrary action.

5. We should pause separately on each of the special methods used to persuade dissenters.

The first and most important of these is the regular so-called political lectures. Year in and year out the same elementary political course is repeated. Half-literate officers spelling out the handbooks, word for word, or rehashing them in their own words, scandalously butcher even this. On the same level, from time to time, editorials a week or more old are read from the newspapers. Questions which the officers cannot answer (and that means most of them) can be considered "provocations" and the questioner will be punished in one way or another. The expression of your own views means risking a new trial and sentence. We are required to attend these "political lectures"—also under threat of punishment.

Occasional "lectures" given by the same officers, or lecturers brought in, are as a rule offensive to the religious and national sentiments of the political prisoners.

Among these "educational" measures must apparently be listed the refusal to allow believers (imprisoned for religious activity) to receive religious literature (even a bible is forbidden); the prohibition against receiving or ordering literature and periodicals published outside the borders of the Soviet Union, including the Communist press and the press of the socialist countries, as well as the publications of international organizations (UNESCO, the UN, etc.).

The constant degradation of human dignity and physical violence must, presumably, also be termed "education." The chief of Section 17A of this camp, Major Annenkov, orders paper taken away from the political prisoners in the isolation cells and recommends that they use their fingers instead of toilet paper.

Officer of the day Lieutenant Taktashev ordered handcuffs put on political prisoners and then the guards beat them savagely "in performance of their duty." None of the victims in any case is ever "punished"—their "education" is being carried on.

We cannot list all such cases here; that would require a whole book. For those of you who are interested in the details, we refer you to the complaints sent by us and others to various official bodies, including the Presidium of the Supreme Soviet of the USSR, over the last two years. In particular, we refer you to the declarations giving the grounds for the hunger strike in February of last year, in which some of us took part.

Naturally, all these physical and psychological pressures on the political prisoners do not and cannot produce the intended result, unless the intent is to try our steadfastness and firmness. Privations and humiliations can only break the weakest, but weaklings are not worth the effort.

We use the words "arbitrariness" and "humiliations," etc., in the meaning in which they are used in the Soviet press with respect to similar phenomena in other countries, including countries of the socialist camp. For example, the newspaper *Izvestia*, reprinting anonymous articles from a Czechoslovak "historian" (see No. 171 for 1968 and No. 6 for 1969) described the censorship of letters, the procedure of sorting out prisoners' complaints, and other "firm and uncompromising consistent educational measures" used in forced labor čamps as "inhuman and illegal activities."

Of course, the conditions under which political prisoners are held now cannot in any way be compared with those of Kolyma, Vorkuta, or Taishet in the forties. But those conditions cannot be used as a standard or as an excuse either, although there are still those among us who want to emulate them.

It is no coincidence that the Dubrovlag camp where we are is run by Colonel Gromov, who in 1949 was the warden of one of the most dreadful political camps in Taishet It is no coincidence that today Lieutenant-Colonel Suchkov, the deputy chief of the political department at Dubrovlag, told a sick prisoner with a temperature of over a hundred, "In my day in *our* camp people with such temperatures worked."

Citizen Deputies!

In appealing to you, we realize that you cannot answer for the present situation. But tomorrow in adopting the Principles of Corrective Labor Legislation, the responsibility for the fate of the persons falling under this law will be shifted onto your shoulders. Therefore, we considered it our duty to appeal to you with this letter. It is in your power today either to confirm and endorse the existing situation or to change it in one or the other direction — to legitimize arbitrariness or restrict it by real guarantees that our rights, our human and civil rights, will be respected.

Signed: *Yu. Galanskov*; *Moshkov*; *V. Kalninsh*; *Yu. Daniel*; *A. Ginzburg*; *Ronkin*.

FOR A REVERSAL OF
THE POLICY OF REPRISALS
by Yuri Galanskov

[Yuri Galanskov, a dissident poet who emerged from the student literary circles of the late fifties, compiled the early samizdat anthology *Phoenix* in 1961, for which he was arrested and confined to a psychiatric hospital for several months. After the Sinyavsky-Daniel trial, he compiled another, more political, anthology — *Phoenix-66*. In retaliation he was made, with Ginzburg, one of the defendants in the "Trial of the Four."

[Like Ginzburg, Daniel, Ronkin, and others, Galanskov was very active in the protests and struggles of political prisoners during the years of his seven-year term at forced labor, even despite his serious ill health. He died November 4, 1972, in the Mordovian complex, at Potma, at the age of 33, after undergoing an operation for a severe ulcer condition at the prison-camp hospital. He had been warned by a hospital surgeon that hospital conditions were too poor to guarantee a successful operation, and because of this he had asked not to be subjected to the operation. Nevertheless, an operation was performed, on October 18, by a doctor who had had no surgical training.

[The essay by Galanskov from which the excerpts below were taken was probably written toward the end of 1969. The appeal to Western Communists, with the hope that they would champion the cause of Soviet democratization, is a frequent theme among Soviet and East European dissenters. Too often such appeals have fallen on deaf ears, as was the case with Soviet and Czechoslovak prisoners' appeals to Angela Davis in 1972.

[The translation for this volume is by Marilyn Vogt.]

Fortunately, such events as the hunger strike in February 1968, the "Letter of the Six," and the collective hunger strike in support of Aleksandr Ginzburg have eventually fallen within the realm of public discussion both in this country and abroad. The latter is especially important and valuable from the point of view of our national interests. The Western press, and particularly Russian-language radio broadcasts originating in the West, make specific instances of official despotism and administrative excesses widely known; they explain the nature of the social origin of these distortions, and confront the governmental organs and functionaries with the necessity of adopting urgently needed measures. This helps overcome the natural inertia and conservatism of the bureaucracy, which by nature gravitates toward official formalism, red tape, and procrastination. Functioning in this capacity, the Western press and radio are fulfilling the tasks of an organized opposition, which is lacking at the present time in Russia; in this way they are a stimulant to our national development. Unfortunately, the West often limits itself by its sensationalism and out of consideration for immediate ideological needs, and does not demonstrate the necessary persistence in posing problems that for us are of vital importance.

In the years of Stalin's dictatorship, the Western intelligentsia was more shocked by what was going on than opposed to it. It was astounded by the savageness of the evil and by the extent of our tragedy. But the Western intelligentsia lacked the spiritual determination and the moral strength to effectively oppose the outburst of these diabolical forces. It proved to be unprincipled: it made political compromises and deals with its conscience. The Western intelligentsia could no longer hear behind the sensational news about Russian concentration camps the groans from the other side of the barbed wire. And no amount of sensationalism could help us safeguard our intelligentsia from physical annihilation. No amount of sensationalism helped us to stop the process by which the human resources of our nation were being exhausted. . . .

In 1964, General Secretary of the Italian Communist Party Palmiro Togliatti posed the question decisively in his "Memorandum," which was published in *Pravda*: It was impossible for the Italian Communist Party to understand why the regime of suppression and restriction of democratic and personal freedoms that was introduced by Stalin had been retained up to the present time in Russia. The question is still unanswered. . . .

But if this question provokes perplexity and, at worst, annoyance, among the Communists of the West, for us it is a question of life and death. For us the regime of suppression and restriction of democratic and personal freedoms means the suppression of political and economic activity by the national forces. It crushes and smothers all creative initiative; it kills one's faith in others; it deprives one of hope. . . .

We need freedom in order to develop our national forces. We need freedom in order to put into motion all the mechanisms necessary for the fulfillment of this task. We need freedom in order to fulfill our obligations to Russia and to life itself. . . .

The position of P. Togliatti and the criticism of the domestic and foreign policy of the CPSU by representatives of the Western Communist parties are no accident. The very existence of the Western Communist parties is directly dependent on the character of the domestic and foreign policy of the CPSU. It works like this:

The people of Italy, France, England, America, Austria, Japan, etc. are asking the Communists of Italy, France, England, America, Austria, and Japan: You are proposing to us a social system in which all political freedoms will be eliminated? In which opposing ideas will be forced into a course of unofficial and illegal actions, and afterwards suppressed and their supporters herded behind barbed wire, machine guns at their backs? You are proposing we adopt a social system in which not only are opposition parties forbidden but even members of a "Union of Communards" will have to be in prison camps? You offer us a social order that tears a mother away from her child (the case of L. Bogoraz-Brukhman), a father from his children (K. Babitsky), and a husband from his wife (P. Litvinov) and condemns people to exile for an ordinary protest demonstration?

"By no means!" the Western Communists will be compelled to say. "We condemn such policy and dissociate ourselves from it. Our communism will insure all political and creative freedom; we will be tolerant toward dissidents."

Then the Western Communists will be asked: "But why should we believe you? You yourselves say that practice is the criterion for judging the truth of a theory. And practice has shown that the two greatest Communist powers (the USSR and China) have carried out and continue to carry out policies that you yourselves have condemned and are condemning. Furthermore, practice has shown that the two greatest Communist powers are on the brink of a war that could annihilate the Russian and Chinese people. You speak of difficulties and mistakes, but how can you prove to us that Stalinism and Maoism do not represent the essence of communism? How can you prove that your Italian, French, and English communism will not become a national tragedy for the Italian, French, and English people?

You want to convince us that communism can safeguard democratic and personal freedoms more fully than they are safeguarded in the Western world. Here, the Western system, which your work is directed toward destroying, gives you every organizational and technical opportunity for the implementation of your work. You have your party, your newspapers, your publishing houses, your bookstores, and you enjoy all the political freedoms. But in Russia, a group of young Marxists, the "Union of Communards," is imprisoned. . . .

You condemn such policies; you wash your hands of them. You assure us that a regime of repression and limitation of democratic and personal freedoms is not fundamental to the very nature of Marxism. You assure us that this regime is after all only the result of difficulties and mistakes. You assure us the CPSU can overcome its mistakes and get rid of the oppressive regime and the restrictions on democratic and personal freedoms. You try to persuade us of this. If that is the case, bring before the CPSU the demand for:

1. full and general amnesty for persons convicted for political and religious reasons; and

2. a revision of the policies of punishment for political and religious reasons.

You, as partisans of the CPSU, carry moral and political responsibility for all of this. But if you keep dodging this responsibility, if you shield the punitive policies of the CPSU by saying that you cannot interfere in the internal affairs of a fraternal Communist Party, we will bring against you charges of immorality and political unscrupulousness. And we will say frankly to the voters that suppression of democratic and personal freedoms is indeed inherent in Marxism and is a necessary result of the political practice of Communists. We will declare you illegal, drive you underground, confine you behind barbed wire, and guard you with machine guns as long as the CPSU confines all dissidents behind barbed wire.

Thus, not only the political popularity but the very existence of the Western Communist parties is directly dependent on the character of the domestic and foreign policy of the USSR. All the distortions of the CPSU's domestic policy leads of necessity to an intensification of the contradictions, to theoretical differences, and to a political splintering within the international Communist movement.

Internal ideological dialogue between the CPSU and the Western Communist parties is becoming inevitable. Abstracting ourselves from the various sides of this complex process, we will single out only what is immediately necessary for us.

With ever more frequency and persistence the representatives and organs of the different Western Communist parties are emerging as a free opposition within the Communist movement with respect to the policies of the CPSU. This state of affairs takes on extraordinary value in view of the fact that it makes possible a dialogue within the Communist movement, safeguarding progress.

No matter how much one may speak of the independent nature of the laws of national development, it is impossible to deny that the fate of Russia depends in many ways on the nature of the evolution of the CPSU as the ruling party. The nature of this evolution is directly dependent not only on dialogue with the West, but most of all on the internal dialogue within the system of international Communist relations. The leadership of the Western Communist parties must clearly understand that the CPSU maintains an oppressive rule and restrictions on democratic and personal freedoms not because the CPSU *does not want to*, but because it *cannot* abandon such policies and *does not know* what to do. . . .

Hence, the extraordinary responsibility that falls to the Communist parties of the West — as the free opposition in the international Communist movement — also becomes obvious. On their initiative, on their commitment to principle, on their unwillingness to compromise themselves depends the evolution of the policies of the CPSU and correspondingly, the fate of Russia. And the political future of the world, in a decisive fashion, will depend on the fate of Russia.

Therefore, lack of initiative, unscrupulousness, and compromises with one's conscience in the present situation are tantamount to a betrayal of the cause of peace.

THE NEW PROCESSES
ARE ONLY BEGINNING
by Valentyn Moroz

[Valentyn Moroz was arrested in August 1965 in a wave of repression that caught up dozens of other Ukrainian intellectuals as well. They were charged with encouraging "bourgeois nationalist" views. After serving four years' hard labor in a Mordovian prison camp, Moroz was released, but was soon arrested again and sentenced in a closed trial in November 1970. This time it was six years imprisonment, three years of hard labor in a special strict-regime camp, and five years of exile. His statement at his trial, printed below, is especially significant as an outstanding expression of confidence in the developing power of a mass movement in the Soviet Union that no amount of repression will be able to stop.

[The translation is by the New York-based Committee for the Defense of Soviet Political Prisoners, and is reprinted by permission.]

I will not cite the Criminal Code to offer proof of my innocence. You know very well that we are not being tried for crimes. In putting us on trial, you take into consideration the role we play in processes which you consider undesirable. There are persons for whose arrests you have more formal legal grounds than for my arrest. But it suits your purposes better to keep these people at liberty because, although they are unaware of this, they lower the tone of the Ukrainian renaissance and slow down its progress. You will never touch these people, and if they should accidentally find themselves in your hands, you would see to it that they were immediately released. You have come to the conclusion that V. Moroz raises the temperature of unwanted processes in the Ukraine. Therefore, it is better to put bars between him and his surroundings.

This would be quite logical if it were not for one "but.". . .

Since 1965 you have put several dozen people behind bars. What have you achieved by this? I will not speak of the tendency as such — so far no one has been able to stop it. But have you managed to liquidate at least its concrete, material manifestations? Have you, for instance, halted the stream of unofficial, uncensored literature which is called "samvydav" [the Ukrainian equivalent of samizdat]? No. This has proved to be beyond your powers. Samvydav is growing, is being enriched by new forms and directions, is gaining new authors and readers; and what is most important, it has sent its roots so deep and so wide that no increases in your staff of informers and no Japanese tape recorders can help. Your endeavors have had no results. In Russian, what you do can best be described as "the labors of Martyshka" [continuous but ineffective work]. But the point is that "the labors of Martyshka" entail work which brings no results. Whereas one cannot say the same of your work, which has already had a tangible effect, even though this effect has been quite different from the one you anticipated. It has become evident that instead of intimidating people, you have aroused their interest. You wanted to extinguish the fire, but instead you added fuel to the flames. Nothing has contributed so much to stimulating political life in the Ukraine as your repressions. Nothing has drawn so much attention to the processes of the Ukrainian renaissance so much as your trials. To tell the truth, it was these trials that demonstrated to the public at large that political life has been revived in the Ukraine. You wanted to hide people in the Mordovian forests; instead, you placed them in a large arena for the whole world to see. It was this atmosphere of awakening produced by your repressions that created the majority of the activists in the Ukrainian renaissance. In a word, enough time has passed for you to have finally understood that you are the ones who are most hurt by the repressions. Still, you continue to hold trials. . . . What for? In order to fulfill your plan? To appease the official conscience? To find an outlet for your anger? More than likely, you do this from inertia.

You introduced into the present-day post-Stalinist era something without which it was still immature and unripe: you introduced *the element of sacrifice*. Faith is born when there are martyrs; these you have given us.

Each time that something alive appears on the Ukrainian horizon, you throw a rock at it. And each time it has become apparent that what you threw was not a rock but a boomerang. It always turned back and hit . . . you! What has happened? Why do repressions not produce the usual results? Why has a tried and tested weapon become a boomerang? The times have changed — there is your whole answer. Stalin had enough water to extinguish the fire. But you find yourselves in a completely different situation. You are fated to live in an age in which your possibilities have been exhausted. And if you have only a little water it is better not to tease the fire with what you have. For then it burns even better — every child knows this. You took a poker in your hands in order to scatter the coals, but you only stoked the fire instead. You lack the strength to do more. This means that the social organism in which we live has entered a phase of development in which repressions are counterproductive. And thus each new repression will become a new boomerang.

In placing me behind bars on June 1, you again threw a boomerang. You have already seen the result. Five years ago I was placed in the prisoner's dock and an arrow flew out. Then I was put behind barbed wire in Mordovia and a bomb flew out. Now, having understood and learned nothing, you begin all over again. Only this time the action of the boomerang will be much more powerful. In 1965 Moroz was an unknown history instructor. Today he is known. . . .

And so Moroz will eat prison cabbage. But as the Jewish saying goes: "So what do you get out of it?" The only Moroz that would be of real value to you would be a submissive Moroz who has written a penitent statement. This would deal a truly stunning blow to all thinking Ukrainians. But you will never live to see this Moroz. If, on the other hand, you hope to create some sort of vacuum in the Ukrainian renaissance by putting me behind bars, you cannot be thinking seriously. Try to understand once and for all: there will never be another vacuum. The density of the Ukraine's spiritual potential is now sufficient to fill any vacuum and produce new political leaders to replace both those in jail and those who have retired from public activity. The sixties brought a marked revitalization of Ukrainian life. The seventies, too, will not go down as a vacuum in Ukrainian history. That golden age when all of life was forced to conform to official patterns has disappeared never to return. Today there is culture outside the ministry of culture and philosophy outside the journal *Voprosy filosofiyi* [Questions of Philosophy]. Now there will always be phenomena that appear in the world without official sanction, and with each year this stream will grow.

The court will now try me behind closed doors. Nevertheless, this trial too will become a boomerang, even if no one hears me, even if I am kept silent in a cell isolated from the world in Vladimir prison. There is a silence which is louder than shouting. And even by destroying me you will not be able to muffle it. It is easy to destroy, but have you considered the old truth that a victim sometimes weighs more than the living? The victims become an inspiration. The victims are the flint from which crystal fortresses are built in pure souls.

I am fully aware of what you will say to this. Moroz thinks too highly of himself. But it is not a question of Moroz. It is a question of every honest person in my position. And anyway, in cases where people are prepared to die in Vladimir prison from some secret drug, there is no room for petty ambition.

The national renaissance is the most profound of all spiritual processes. This is a rich and diversified phenomenon, which can manifest itself in a thousand forms. No one can foresee all of them and fashion a dragnet wide enough to trap and contain the whole process. Your dams are strong and reliable, but they stand on solid ground. The spring floods have simply circumvented them and found new channels. Your toll gates are closed. But they will not stop anyone, because the roads have bypassed them long ago. The national renaissance is a process with virtually unlimited resources, because national feeling is alive in the soul of all human beings, even of those who, it would seem, have long since died spiritually. For example, this was revealed in the Writers' Union debate, when I. Dzyuba's expulsion was opposed by people whom no one expected to do so.

You stubbornly reiterate that the people who sit behind bars are ordinary criminals. You close your eyes and pretend that there is no problem. So, all right, you can maintain this stupid position for another ten years. And then what? After all, the new processes in the Ukraine (and in the Soviet Union as a whole) are only beginning. The Ukrainian renaissance has not yet become a mass movement. But do not console yourselves that this will always be the case. In an age of total literacy, when there are 800,000 students in the Ukraine, and all have radios, in such an age, every socially significant phenomenon becomes a mass phenomenon. Is it possible that you do not understand that soon you will have to deal with mass social tendencies? New processes are only beginning, but your repressive measures have already ceased to be effective. What will happen in the future?

There is only one alternative: to reject the obsolete policy of repression and find new forms of coexistence with the new phenomena which have permanently established themselves in our life. That is reality. It appeared asking no one's permission and brought with it new things that require a new approach. People called upon to deal with affairs of state have plenty to think about. But you still amuse yourselves throwing boomerangs. . . .

There will be a trial. Well then, we will fight. Especially now when one of the accused has written a repentant statement and another has changed his profession to translator; especially now when we need someone to give an example of strength and in one sweep erase the depressing effect produced by the retirement of certain people from active political life. It has fallen to me. . . . This is a difficult mission. No one finds it easy to sit behind bars. But it is even harder to have no respect for oneself. And therefore we will fight!

There will be a trial and everything will begin from the beginning once more: new protests and signatures, new materials for the press and radio of the whole world. The interest in what Moroz wrote will grow tenfold. In a word, a fresh measure of fuel will be added to the fire that you wish to extinguish.

This then is subversive work. But I am not the guilty one. I was not the one who placed Moroz behind bars. I was not the one who threw the boomerang.

APPEAL FOR
A GRADUAL DEMOCRATIZATION
by Andrei Sakharov, Roy Medvedev,
and Valery Turchin

[This letter, dated March 19, 1970, presents a draft program for the gradual democratization of the Soviet Union. Its perspective is similar to that held by those who began democratization in Czechoslovakia in 1968. Soviet physicist Andrei Sakharov, a member of the USSR Academy of Sciences, played a key role in developing Soviet nuclear weapons. He earned prominence as a critic of the regime with his 1968 memorandum on "Progress, Coexistence, and Intellectual Freedom," followed by similar works circulated privately in the following years. He has recently moved rightward, announcing that he no longer holds socialist views. At the same time, his persistence in defending persecuted dissidents and his criticism of the 1972-73 detente for not including democratization led to serious reprisals against him in autumn 1973. Valery Turchin, a physicist of some stature, has contributed a number of essays to samizdat, including "The Inertia of Fear," about the Stalin heritage. Historian Roy Medvedev is the author of *Let History Judge* (1968) and *On Socialist Democracy* (1971). In the fall of 1973 he circulated a statement defending Sakharov against the campaign of vilification in the Soviet press, while differing with him on his assessment of the detente.

The translation for this volume is by Marilyn Vogt.]

To L. I. Brezhnev, Central Committee of the CPSU; A. N. Kosygin, USSR Council of Ministers; N. V. Podgorny, Presidium of the Supreme Soviet of the USSR:

Dear Comrades,
    We are appealing to you on a question of great importance. Our country has made great strides in the development of

production, in the fields of education and culture, in the basic improvement of the living conditions of the working class, and in the development of new socialist human relationships. Our achievements have universal historical significance. They have deeply affected events throughout the world and have laid a firm foundation for the further development of the cause of communism. However, serious difficulties and shortcomings are also evident.

This letter will discuss and develop a point of view which can be formulated briefly by the following theses:

1. At the present time there is an urgent need to carry out a series of measures directed toward the further democratization of our country's public life. This need stems, in particular, from the very close connection between the problem of technological and economic progress and scientific methods of management, on the one hand, and the problems of freedom of information, the open airing of views, and the free clash of ideas, on the other. This need also stems from other domestic and foreign political problems.

2. Democratization must promote the maintenance and consolidation of the Soviet socialist system, the socialist economic structure, our social and cultural achievements, and socialist ideology.

3. Democratization, carried out under the leadership of the CPSU in collaboration with all strata of society, should maintain and strengthen the leading role of the party in the economic, political, and cultural life of society.

4. Democratization should be gradual in order to avoid possible complications and disruptions. At the same time it should be thoroughgoing, carried out consistently in accordance with a carefully worked-out program. Without fundamental democratization, our society will not be able to solve the problems now facing it, and will not be able to develop in a normal manner.

There are reasons to assume that the point of view expressed in the above theses is shared to one degree or another by a significant part of the Soviet intelligentsia and the advanced section of the working class. This attitude is also reflected in the opinions of student and working youth, as well as in numerous private discussions within small groups of friends. However, we believe it is urgent and advisable to set forth this point of view in coherent written form in order to facilitate a broad and open discussion of these most important problems. We are in search of a positive and constructive approach that will be acceptable to the party and government leadership of the country; we seek to reduce certain misunderstandings and unfounded apprehensions. [96]

Over the past decade menacing signs of disorder and stagnation have begun to show themselves in the economy of our country, the roots of which go back to an earlier period and are very deeply embedded. There is an uninterrupted decline in the rate of growth of the national income. The gap between what is necessary for normal development and the new productive forces being introduced is growing wider. A large amount of data is available showing mistakes in the determination of technical and economic policy in industry and agriculture and an intolerable procrastination about finding solutions to urgent problems. Defects in the system of planning, accounting, and incentives often cause contradictions between the local and departmental interests and those of the state and nation. As a result, new means of developing production potential are not being discovered or properly put to use and technical progress has slowed down abruptly. For these very reasons, the natural wealth of the country is often destroyed with impunity and without any supervision or controls: forests are leveled, reservoirs polluted, valuable agricultural land inundated, soil eroded or salinized, etc. The chronically difficult situation in agriculture, particularly in regard to livestock, is well known. The population's real income in recent years has hardly grown at all; food supply and medical and consumer services are improving very slowly, and with unevenness between regions. The number of goods in short supply continues to grow. There are clear signs of inflation.

Of particular concern regarding our country's future is the

---

96. Since January 1970 a "Letter to Brezhnev" signed with the name "Sakharov" or "Academician Sakharov" has circulated widely in Moscow. Various versions of this letter were later published in the Western press. In issue no. 1 of the anti-Soviet emigre journal *Posev* in 1970 an article with the pretentious title "The Truth About the Present Time" was published signed with the name "R. Medvedev." This article, full of absurd fabrications, was later broadcast in the Russian language by Radio Liberty (West Germany). We hereby declare that none of us were the authors of the letter or the article. These "documents" are clearly forgeries and are apparently being circulated for purposes of provocation.

lag in the development of education: our total expenditures for education in all forms are. three times below what they are in the United States, and are rising at a slower rate. Alcoholism is growing in a tragic way and drug addiction is beginning to surface. In many regions of the country the crime rate is climbing systematically. Signs of corruption are becoming more and more noticeable in a number of places. In the work of scientific and scientific-technical organizations, bureaucratism, departmentalism, a formal attitude toward one's tasks, and lack of initiative are becoming more and more pronounced.

As is well known, the productivity of labor is the decisive factor in the comparison of economic systems. It is here that the situation is worst of all. Productivity of labor in our country remains, as before, many times lower than that of the capitalist countries, and the growth of productivity has fallen off abruptly. This situation causes particular anxiety if one compares it with the situation in the leading capitalist countries, in particular with the United States. By introducing elements of state regulation and planning into the economy, these countries have saved themselves from the destructive crises which plagued the capitalist economy in an earlier era. The broad introduction of computer technology and automation assures a rapid rise in the productivity of labor, which in turn facilitates a partial overcoming of certain social problems and contradictions (e. g., by means of unemployment benefits, shortening of the work day, etc.). In comparing our economy with that of the United States, we see that ours lags behind not only in quantitative but also — most regrettable of all — in qualitative terms. The newer and more revolutionary a particular aspect of the economy may be, the wider the gap between the USSR and the USA. We outstrip America in coal production, but we lag behind in the output of oil, gas, and electric power; we lag behind by ten times in the field of chemistry, and we are infinitely outstripped in computer technology. The latter is especially crucial, because the introduction of electronic computers into the economy is a phenomenon of decisive importance that radically changes the outlines of the production system and of the entire culture. This phenomenon has justly been called the second industrial revolution. Nevertheless, our stock of computers is *1 percent* of that of the United States. And with respect to the application of the electronic computer, the gap is so great that it is impossible to even measure it. We simply live in another age.

Things are no better in the sphere of scientific and technological breakthroughs. Our role in this area has not advanced either. Rather, the contrary has been true. At the end of the 1950s our country was the first in the world to launch a satellite and send someone into space. By the end of the 1960s we had lost our lead in this area (as in many others). The first people to land on the moon were Americans. This fact is one of the outward manifestations of the gulf that exists and is continually growing between us and the Western countries all along the line in scientific and technological work.

In the 1920s and 1930s the capitalist world went through a period of crises and depressions. During this period, we utilized the upsurge of national energy engendered by the revolution to build up our industry at an unprecedented rate. The slogan raised at that time was "Catch up with and surpass America." And we actually caught up with America in the course of several decades. Then the situation changed. The second industrial revolution began, and now at the beginning of the 1970s we see that not only have we not succeeded in catching up with America, we are falling more and more behind it.

What is wrong? Why have we not only failed to be the pioneers of the second industrial revolution, but have in fact found ourselves incapable of keeping pace with the developed capitalist countries? Is it possible that socialism provides fewer opportunities for the development of productive forces than capitalism? Or that in the economic competition between capitalism and socialism, capitalism is winning?

Of course not! The source of our difficulties does not lie in the socialist system, but on the contrary, it lies in those peculiarities and conditions of our life which run contrary to socialism and are hostile to it. The source lies in the antidemocratic traditions and norms of public life established in the Stalin era, which have not been decisively eliminated to this day.

Noneconomic coercion, limitations on the exchange of information, restrictions on intellectual freedom, and other examples of the antidemocratic distortion of socialism which took place under Stalin were accepted in our country as an overhead expense of the industrialization process. It was believed that they did not seriously influence the economy of the country, although they had very serious consequences in the political and military arenas, in the destinies of vast layers of the population, and for whole nationalities. We will leave aside the question of the extent to which this point of view is justified for the early stages of the development of a socialist national economy; the decline in the rate of industrial development in the prewar years rather suggests the opposite. But there is no doubt that since the beginning of the second industrial revolution these phenomena have become a decisive economic factor; they have become the main brake on the development of the productive forces in this country. As a consequence of the increased size and complexity of economic systems, the problems of management and organization have moved to the forefront. These problems cannot be resolved by one or several persons holding power and "knowing everything." These problems demand the creative participation of millions of people on all levels of the economic system. They demand the broad interchange of information and ideas. In this lies the difference between modern economics and economics, let us say, in the ancient Orient.

However, we encounter certain insurmountable obstacles on the road toward the free exchange of ideas and information. Truthful information about our shortcomings and negative manifestations is hushed up on the grounds that it "may be used by enemy propaganda." Exchange of information with foreign countries is restricted for fear of "penetration by an enemy ideology." Theoretical generalizations and practical proposals, if they seem too bold to some individuals, are nipped in the bud without any discussion because of the fear that they might "undermine our foundations." An obvious lack of confidence in creatively thinking, critical, and energetic individuals is to be seen here. Under such circumstances the conditions are created for the advancement up the rungs of the official ladder not of those who distinguish themselves by their professional qualities and commitment to principles but of those who proclaim their devotion to the party but in practice are only worried about their own narrow personal interests or are passive time-servers.

Limitations on freedom of information mean that not only is it more difficult to control the leaders, not only is the initiative of the people undermined, but that even the intermediate level of leadership is deprived of rights and information, and these people are transformed into passive time-servers and bureaucrats. The leaders in the highest government bodies receive information that is incomplete, with the rough spots glossed over; hence they are also deprived of the opportunity to effectively utilize the authority they have.

The economic reform of 1965 was an extremely beneficial

and important start toward resolving key problems of our economic life. However, we are convinced that purely economic measures alone are not enough to fulfill all its tasks. Furthermore, these economic measures cannot be fully implemented without reforms in the sphere of management, information, and open public discussion.

The same can be said regarding such promising undertakings as the organization of complex industrial associations with a high degree of autonomy in economic, financial, and personnel matters.

Whatever concrete problem of the economy we may take up, we very soon will come to the conclusion that its satisfactory solution requires a scientific resolution of such general problems of socialist economics as the forms of feedback in the managerial system, price formation in the absence of a free market, general principles of planning, etc.

There is much talk these days about the need for a scientific approach to the problems of organization and management. This is true, of course. Only a scientific approach to these problems will allow us to overcome the difficulties that have developed and realize those opportunities for controlling the direction of the economy and of technical-economic progress which in principle the absence of capitalist property relations allows. But a scientific approach demands full information, impartial thinking, and creative freedom. Until these conditions are established (not for certain individuals but for the masses), talk about scientific management will remain hollow.

Our economy can be compared with traffic moving through an intersection. When there were only a few cars, the traffic police could easily cope with their tasks and traffic flowed smoothly. But the stream of traffic continually increases, and a traffic jam develops. What should be done in this situation? It is possible to fine the drivers and replace the traffic police, but this will not save the situation. The only solution is to widen the intersection. The obstacles hindering the development of our economy lie outside of it, in the social and political sphere, and all measures that do not remove these obstacles are doomed to ineffectiveness.

The vestiges of the Stalin era are having a negative effect on the economy not only directly, because they preclude a scientific approach to the problems of organization and administration, but no less so indirectly, because they reduce the creative potential of people in all fields. But under the conditions of the second industrial revolution, it is precisely creative labor that becomes increasingly important for the national economy.

In this connection the problem of relations between the state and the intelligentsia cannot be left unmentioned either. Freedom of information and creative work are necessary for the intelligentsia due to the nature of its activity and its social function. The intelligentsia's attempts to increase these freedoms are legitimate and natural. The state, however, suppresses these attempts by employing all kinds of restrictions — administrative pressures, dismissals from employment, and even courtroom trials. This all gives rise to a social gulf, an atmosphere of mutual distrust, and a profound lack of mutual understanding, making fruitful collaboration difficult between the party and state apparatus, on the one hand, and the most active layers of the intelligentsia, i.e., the layers that are most valuable for society, on the other. Under the conditions of modern industrial society, in which the role of the intelligentsia is constantly increasing, such a gulf can only be described as suicidal.

An overwhelming part of the intelligentsia and the youth recognize the need for democratization, and the need for it to be cautious and gradual, but they cannot understand and justify measures of a patently antidemocratic nature. And, indeed, how can one justify the confinement in prisons, camps, and insane asylums of people who hold oppositionist views but whose opposition stands on legal ground, in the area of ideas and convictions? In many instances, there was no opposition involved, but only a striving for information, or simply a courageous and unprejudiced discussion of important social questions. The imprisonment of writers for what they have written is inadmissible. It is also impossible to understand or justify such an absurd and extremely harmful measure as the expulsion from the Soviet Writers' Union of the most significant popular writer [Solzhenitsyn], who has shown himself to be deeply patriotic and humane in all that he does. Equally incomprehensible is the purging of the editorial board of *Novy Mir,* around which the most progressive forces in the Marxist-Leninist socialist tendency had rallied.

It is indispensable to speak once again about ideological problems. Democratization, with its fullness of information and clash of ideas, must restore to our ideological life its dynamism and creativity — in the social sciences, art, and propaganda — and liquidate the bureaucratic, ritualistic, dogmatic, openly hypocritical, and mediocre style that reigns in these areas today.

A course toward democratization would bridge the gulf between the party and state apparatus and the intelligentsia. The mutual lack of understanding will give way to close cooperation. A course toward democratization would inspire a wave of enthusiasm comparable to that which prevailed in the 1920s. The best intellectual forces in the country would be mobilized for the solution of economic and social problems.

Carrying out democratization is not an easy process. Its normal development would be threatened from one direction by individualist and antisocialist forces, and from the other by the supporters of a "strong state" and demagogues on the fascist model, who might try to exploit for their own ends the economic problems of our country, the lack of mutual understanding and lack of confidence between the intelligentsia and the party and government apparatus, and the existence of petty-bourgeois and nationalist sentiments in certain sectors of our society. But we must realize that there is no other solution for our country and that this difficult task must be worked out. Democratization, conducted on the initiative and under the control of the highest official bodies, will allow this process to be realized in a systematic fashion, taking care that all levels of the party and government apparatus succeed in adopting a new style of work, differing from past work by its greater openness and fuller public airing of views, and its broader discussion of all problems. There is no doubt that the majority of apparatus workers — people educated and trained in a modern, highly-developed country — are capable of making the transition to a new style of work and will very soon realize its advantages. The sifting out of an insignificant number of incompetents will only be to the good of the cause.

We propose the following draft program of measures which could be realized over a four-to-five-year period:

1. A statement from the highest party and government bodies on the necessity for further democratization and on the rate and means of achieving it. The publication in the press of a number of articles containing a discussion of the problems of democratization.

2. Limited distribution (through party organs, enterprises, and institutions) of information on the situation in the country and theoretical works on social problems which at the present time would not be made the object of broad discussion. Gradual increase of access to these materials until all limitations on their distribution have been lifted.

3. Extensive, planned organization of complex industrial associations with a high degree of autonomy in matters of indus-

trial planning, technological processes, raw material supply, sale of products, finances, and personnel. The expansion of these rights for smaller productive units as well. Scientific determination after careful research of the form and degree of state regulation.

4. Cessation of interference with foreign radio broadcasts. Free sale of foreign books and periodicals. Adherence by our country to the international copyright convention. Gradual expansion and encouragement of international tourism in both directions (over a three-to-four-year period), expansion of international postal communications, and other measures for broadening international communications, with special emphasis in this regard on member nations of Comecon.

5. Establishment of an institute for public opinion research. The publication (limited at first but later complete) of materials indicating public attitudes on the most important domestic and foreign policy questions, as well as of other sociological materials.

6. Amnesty for political prisoners. An order requiring pubcation of the complete record of all trials of a political character. Public supervision of all prisons, camps, and psychiatric institutions.

7. Introduction of measures to improve the functioning of the courts and the procuracy and to enhance their independence from executive powers, local influences, prejudices, and personal ties.

8. Abolition of the indication of nationality on passports and questionnaires. Uniform passport system for the inhabitants of cities and villages. Gradual elimination of the system of passport registration, to be accomplished simultaneously with the evening up of economic and cultural inequalities between different regions of our country.

9. Reforms in education: increased appropriations for elementary and secondary schools; improving the living standard of teachers and increasing their autonomy and leeway to experiment.

10. Passage of a law on information and the press. Guaranteeing the right of social organizations and citizens' groups to establish new publications. Complete elimination of prior censorship in every form.

11. Improvement in the training of leadership cadres in the art of management. Introduction of special managerial training programs on the job. Improvement in the information available to leading cadres at all levels, increasing their au-

tonomy, their rights to experiment, to defend their opinions, and to test them in practice.

12. Gradual introduction of the practice of having several candidates in elections to party and Soviet bodies on every level, even for indirect elections.

13. Expansion of the rights of Soviets; expansion of the rights and the responsibilities of the Supreme Soviet of the USSR.

14. Restoration of the rights of those nationalities deported under Stalin. The reestablishment of the national autonomy of deported peoples with the opportunity for them to resettle in their homeland (in those cases where until now this has not been realized).

15. Measures directed toward increasing public discussion in the work of governing bodies, commensurate with the interests of the state. Establishment of consultative scientific committees to work with the government bodies at every level, such committees to include highly qualified specialists in the different disciplines.

This plan must, naturally, be viewed as a draft plan. It is clear also that it must be supplemented by a plan for economic and social measures worked out by specialists. We emphasize that democratization alone in no way solves the economic problems, but will only create the prerequisites for their solution. Without these prerequisites the economic and technical problems cannot be solved. We have occasionally heard our friends abroad compare the USSR with a truck whose driver is pressing the accelerator all the way to the floor with one foot, while with the other foot he is simultaneously pressing down on the brake. The time has come to use the brake more wisely.

The proposed plan proves, in our opinion, that it is fully possible to mark out a program for democratization which is *acceptable* to the party and government and which, even at the first stage of approximation, *satisfies* the vital needs of the country's development. Naturally, a wide discussion and deep scientific, sociological, economic, and socio-political investigations in actual practice will introduce vital corrections and additions. But it is important, as the mathematicians say, to demonstrate "the existence theorem of a solution."

It is also necessary to dwell for a moment on the international consequences of our taking a course toward democratization. Nothing could be more favorable to enhancing our international authority and strengthening the progressive Communist forces in the world than further democratization, accompanied by a reinforcement of technical and economic progress in the first land of socialism in the world. Undoubtedly the possibilities for peaceful coexistence and international cooperation would grow, the forces of peace and social progress would be strengthened, the attractiveness of Communist ideology would increase, and our international position would become more secure. It is particularly important that the moral and material position of the USSR in relation to China would be strengthened and we would have increased possibilities for influencing the situation in that country indirectly (by example and by economic and technical aid) in the interests of the peoples of both countries.

A number of correct and necessary foreign policy steps by our government have not been properly understood because the information provided to citizens on these questions is very incomplete and, in the past, obvious inaccuracies and tendentiousness was evident in the information provided. This, naturally, is not conducive to building confidence. One such instance involves the question of economic aid to underdeveloped countries.

Fifty years ago workers of war-ravaged Europe extended aid to those who were starving to death in the Volga region. The Soviet people are no more callous and self-centered. But they must feel confident that our resources are being expended for genuine assistance and for resolving serious problems, not for the construction of pompous stadiums or the purchase of American automobiles for local officials. The situation in today's world and the opportunities and tasks facing our country demand broad participation in economic assistance to underdeveloped countries in collaboration with other countries. But for the public to correctly understand these problems, verbal assurances are not enough; what is called for is fuller information and democratization.

Soviet foreign policy is fundamentally a policy of peace and cooperation. But the failure to inform the public fully arouses discontent. In the past there were certain negative features in Soviet foreign policy that bore a messianic and overly ambitious character and prompted the conclusion that imperialism does not bear the only responsibility for international tensions.

All these negative aspects of Soviet foreign policy are closely linked with the problem of democratization, and this link has a dual character. There was a great deal of unrest over the absence of democratic discussion concerning such questions as arms aid to other countries, for example, Nigeria, where a bloody war was going on, whose causes and development the Soviet public knows very little about. We are convinced that the UN Security Council resolution on the Israeli-Arab conflict is a just and reasonable one, though perhaps it is not concrete enough on several points. But there is uneasiness over whether our position does not in fact go substantially beyond this document and whether our position may not be too one-sided. Is our position on the status of West Berlin realistic? Is our effort to extend our influence to areas far beyond our borders always realistic, considering the difficulties in Sino-Soviet relations and the serious problems in our country's economic and technical development? Such a "dynamic" policy may be necessary, of course, but it must accord not only with the basic principles of our country but also with its real possibilities.

We are convinced that the only realistic policy in the age of nuclear weapons is a course toward more far-reaching international cooperation; persistent search for lines of rapprochement in scientific-technical, economic, cultural, and ideological areas; and the rejection in principle of weapons of mass destruction. We take this opportunity to express our opinion that it is urgent and advisable for the nuclear powers to make unilateral and joint declarations of principle that they will not be the first to use weapons of mass destruction.

Democratization will be conducive to a better public understanding of foreign policy and the removal of all the negative features in this policy. This, in turn, will wrest the "trump card" from the hands of those opposed to the democratic movement.

What is in store for our nation if it does not take the course toward democratization? The fate of lagging behind the capitalist countries and gradually becoming a second-rate provincial power (history has seen cases of this); the growth of economic difficulties; increasingly tense relations between the party and government apparatus, on the one hand, and the intelligentsia, on the other; the danger of ruptures to the "left" and to the "right"; exacerbation of national problems, because the movement for democratization emanating from below in the national republics inevitably assumes a nationalistic character. This perspective becomes particularly ominous if one also takes into account the danger of Chinese totalitarian nationalism (something we regard as a temporary phenomenon from a historical point of view but as an extremely serious one for the next few years). We can only withstand this danger if we widen or at least maintain the existing economic and technical distance between ourselves and China, increase the number of our friends in the world, and offer the alternative of cooperation and aid to the Chinese people. This becomes an obvious necessity if we consider the numerical superiority of this potential enemy's population, its militant nationalism, the length of our eastern borders, and the sparse population of our eastern regions. Therefore, the economic stagnation and the lag in our rate of growth, coupled with an unrealistic (often overambitious) foreign policy on all continents, can lead to catastrophic consequences for our country.

Dear comrades!

There is no other way out of the difficulties now facing our country except a course toward democratization, carried out by the CPSU in accordance with a carefully worked-out plan. A turn to the right — that is, a victory for the forces that advocate a stronger administration, a "tightening of the screws," would not only fail to solve any of the problems, but on the contrary, would aggravate them to an extreme point and lead our country into a tragic impasse. The tactic of waiting passively would ultimately have the same result. Today we still have the chance to set out on the right path and to carry out the necessary reforms. In a few years it may be too late. The recognition of this is a necessity on a nationwide scale. The duty of all who see the causes of these problems and the road to their solution is to point out this road to their fellow citizens. Understanding the need for, and possibility of, gradual democratization is the first step along the road to its achievement.

HUMAN RIGHTS COMMITTEE
STATEMENT OF PURPOSES

[In a continuing attempt to wage an open, public campaign in the Soviet Union against arbitrary abuses and violations of the guarantees written into the Soviet constitution and legal system, three leading nuclear physicists—Andrei Sakharov, Andrei Tverdokhlebov, and Valery Chalidze—formed the Committee for Human Rights on November 4, 1970. Chalidze was pressured by the regime into leaving the USSR in late 1972. He now has a teaching post in New York. Tverdokhlebov has apparently drawn back from active participation in the Committee. But Sakharov has continued to defend human rights, coming under increasing government pressure in 1973. In the wake of the Yakir-Krasin trial of August 1973, a full-fledged press campaign was waged against Sakharov, and his life was threatened. The famous novelist Solzhenitsyn—an advisory member of the Committee—spoke out in defense of Sakharov, and by publishing his explosive documentary *Gulag Archipelago* in effect challenged the regime to try him, Solzhenitsyn, instead. The fate of these two and the committee they represent remained unresolved at time of writing.

[The translation is from the February 8, 1971, *Intercontinental Press*, and is reprinted by permission.]

Proceeding from the conviction that safeguarding human rights is an important part of creating salutary conditions in which people can live, and that strengthening peace and promoting mutual understanding is an integral component of present-day culture;

Striving to assist international efforts to propagate the concept of human rights and to cooperate in the search for constructive ways of safeguarding these rights;

Noting the increased interest in this area of culture among the citizens of the USSR in the past few years;

Expressing satisfaction with the achievements in the field

of human rights in the USSR since 1953 and striving in a consultative manner to promote further efforts by the state in creating guarantees for the defense of these rights, in accordance with the specific character of the socialist system and the specific features of Soviet tradition in this field;

A.D. Sakharov, A.N. Tverdokhlebov, and V.N. Chalidze have decided to work together to continue their activity to promote constructive study of this problem by forming the Committee for Human Rights, which is based on the following principles:

1. The Committee for Human Rights is a creative association, acting in accordance with the laws of the state and the principles and regulations of the committee here set forth.

2. Conditions for membership are as follows: Members, when acting in the name of the organization, must abide by the principles and regulations of the committee. They must be recognized as members by the committee in accordance with the procedure stipulated by the regulations.

3. The aims of the committee are the following:

To cooperate in a consultative way with the organs of state power in developing and applying guarantees of human rights, acting either on its own initiative or following the lead of the interested governmental bodies.

To offer creative assistance to individuals interested in constructive investigation of the theoretical aspects of the human rights question and in studying the specific character of this question in socialist society.

To conduct civic education on legal questions, in particular to make known to the public, international and Soviet legal documents dealing with the question of human rights.

4. In theoretically investigating and constructively criticizing the present status of the body of individual rights guaranteed by Soviet law, the committee will be guided by the humanist principles of the Universal Declaration of Human Rights, proceed from the specific features of Soviet law, and take into account the established traditions and real difficulties of the state in this field.

5. The committee is prepared for creative contacts with social and scholarly organizations and with international nongovernmental organizations, if they follow the principles of the United Nations in their activities and do not have the aim of attacking the Soviet Union.

OPPOSITION ORGANIZATIONS
IN THREE CITIES

[Oppositionist youth groups considering themselves Marxists have appeared in three separate Soviet cities in the late 1960s. Some information about them is contained in the following reports from the February 1970 issue of the *Chronicle of Current Events*.

[The difficulties of the movement as well as its significant trends are highlighted by the *Chronicle* reports. The high level of police pressure and the still low level of oppositionist development that resulted in the Saratov youths' "repentance" are indicative. The same elements probably lie behind the two Ryazan students' "confessions" and turning-in of their comrades.

[Limited information exists about the programmatic basis of these youth groups. One can only surmise the nature of the program of the Ryazan group—a document entitled "The Downfall of Capital." According to one report, the Saratov group had over two hundred members and based itself on Lenin's *State and Revolution* and on the 1940 letter by the Old Bolshevik F. Raskolnikov denouncing Stalin. The *Chronicle* describes the Saratov program vaguely, as "liberal-democratic." Since the group defines itself as "True Communists," the term liberal-democratic obviously does not mean procapitalist, as it would in the West. Presumably it means favoring *socialist* democracy, that is, freedom for differing views within the framework of support to the workers' state.

[An earlier *Chronicle* report on the Gorky group stated that its members were apparently the authors of a document entitled *The State and Socialism*. If this document is an attempt to analyze the Soviet state in Leninist terms, as the parallel with the title of Lenin's *State and Revolution* suggests, the group's position may be close to revolutionary socialism. Plainly, the group is interested in getting back to the buried traditions of Bolshevism. Leaflets circulated by its members demanding that the truth be told about the trials of the thirties are a sign of that.

[The translation is from the July 25, 1970, *Intercontinental Press,* and is reprinted by permission.]

In Saratov on January 5-13, six young people were put on trial on charges of creating an anti-Soviet organization and conducting anti-Soviet propaganda and agitation — Articles 70 and 72 of the Criminal Code of the Russian Soviet Federated Socialist Republic [Article 70 forbids "anti-Soviet" propaganda and agitation]. The head of the organization was named Senin (a student at the juridical institute). The others were as follows: Romanov (fourth year student in the history division at Saratov State University); Kulikov (a graduate of the physical education division of Saratov State University and, at the time of his arrest, a gymnastics coach there); Kirikin (a student at the juridical institute); Bobrov (the same); and Fokeev (a night student at Saratov State University).

Kulikov — the oldest of those being tried — was twenty-eight. All the accused acknowledged themselves guilty and expressed repentance. During the trial some fifty witnesses appeared, most of them students. According to unverified information, the organization called itself "The Party of True Communists," had a program of liberal-democratic persuasion, and set itself the goal of creatively studying Marxist literature in the original sources as well as other works by Soviet and foreign authors, both forbidden and published ones.

At the trial the accused stressed in particular that they were carrying on propaganda ("many ideas for a few") rather than agitation ("a few ideas for many") and that new members were taken into the organization only after their familiarization with this propagandistic literature and only in the event of agreement of views.

The trial was organized on the model of analogous trials in Moscow (a specially invited audience, a few relatives). Outside the courthouse there was a crowd of 100-150 people, mostly young.

In the second half of 1968, in the city of Ryazan, six students of the city's radiotechnological institute formed an illegal group, "The Marxist Party of a New Type." They were Yuri Vudka, Valeri Vudka, Shimonas Grilius, Frolov, Martimonov, and

Zaslavsky [the *Chronicle* gives no first names for three of the students]. Yuri Vudka (a correspondence-course student and a lathe operator at the Ryazan Agricultural Machinery Plant) wrote a pamphlet under the pseudonym L. Borin, entitled "The Downfall of Capital," the programmatic document of the group.

In August 1969 the group was arrested by the KGB. The arrests were precipitated when two members of the organization, Martimonov and Zaslavsky, turned themselves in to the authorities with confessions and denunciations of their fellows. The charges were under Articles 70 and 72. The case was tried in February 1970 in the Ryazan Region People's Court Building. There were witnesses from the Moscow area, Leningrad, Kiev, Saratov, and other cities. (Apparently, the Ryazan group had connections with various cities. The group headed by Senin, tried a month earlier, had the same "Downfall of Capital" as a programmatic document.)

Yu. Vudka was sentenced to seven years; Sh. Grilius and Frolov to five each; and V. Vudka to three (all under a strict regime). Zaslavsky and Martimonov (who had been freed under surveillance) were given suspended sentences.

In Gorky the case of Mikhail Kapranov, Sergei Ponomarev, and Vladimir Zhiltsov and the related case of Vladlen Pavlenkov have continued. M. Kapranov was formerly a student at the Gorky State University. (He was twice expelled from the university for statements he made about the politics and economy of the USSR—once at a Young Communist meeting and once in a personal letter.) He is the father of two boys. S. Ponomarev is a philosophy student, a staff member on the newsletter of a local plant, and father of a four-year-old girl. V. Zhiltsov is a fifth-year student in the history division at Gorky State University, an exceptional student during his entire time there. At the time of his arrest his leg was broken. He was arrested just before he was to defend his dissertation.

All three were arrested in the summer of 1969, and the charges against all three were changed in January 1970 from Article 190-1 of the Russian Federation Criminal Code to Articles 70 and 72 [Article 190-1 forbids "slander against the Soviet state and social system"]. The investigators are Khokhlov, Belovzorov, and Savelyev.

They are charged with having composed and distributed leaflets.

(In spring 1968 at the time of Gorky University's hundredth anniversary celebration leaflets were distributed and pasted up on the city streets, especially opposite the KGB building and at the university building. They contained an appeal with the following points: A demand for the full rehabilitation of those convicted in the political trials of the thirties and full public disclosure of the true character of those trials. A demand that the conditions under which political prisoners are currently being held be improved. A demand for democratic liberties.)

They are also charged with an attempt to form an anti-Soviet organization. (Possibly there was the intent to found a group for combating violations of legality — nothing more.)

In October 1969 Vladlen Pavlenkov was arrested. He was a history instructor at the university, born in 1929. It is not known to the *Chronicle* what Pavlenkov is charged with or whether his case is tied with the case of the other three, or whether it is simply one and the same case.

The investigators turned V. Pavlenkov over for psychiatric examination. His wife Svetlana [an earlier issue of the *Chronicle* had reported her also arrested, but issue no. 11 corrected the earlier report] wrote to the KGB senior investigator A.M. Khokhlov that she would answer any finding that her husband was mentally incompetent with her own self-immolation. She sent the same declaration to the USSR Prosecutor General Rudenko and to KGB Chairman Andropov. V. Pavlenkov was declared sane.

WORKERS' DEMONSTRATION IN KIEV

[The following item appeared in *Chronicle of Current Events,* no. 8, dated June 30, 1969. It points eloquently toward independent organizational efforts among workers, with the appearance of obviously capable and exceptional workers' leaders (the figure of Hryshchuk). Although this development occurred among Ukrainian workers, probably more radicalized because of their dual oppression by the Russifying bureaucrats, it is not an isolated incident in Soviet society at the present time.

[The translation is from the February 9, 1970, *Intercontinental Press,* and is reprinted by permission.]

In the middle of May 1969, in the Berezka settlement at the Kiev hydroelectric power plant, the workers held a meeting to discuss the housing problem.

Many of them were still living in barracks and railway cars despite promises by the authorities that housing would be provided. The workers declared that they no longer trusted the local authorities and resolved to write to the Central Committee of the Communist Party of the Soviet Union. After the meeting, the workers went out with slogans, one of which was "All Power to the Soviets."

KGB agents arrived in vehicles such as are used by veterinarians. They were met by shouts of "What are we, dogs?" Lecturing the crowd, the KGB men tried to arouse feelings of "class hatred" toward one of the active participants in the events, a retired major, Ivan Aleksandrovich Hrishchuk. They explained that he was getting a very big pension, yet here he was stirring up trouble. Hrishchuk declared that he definitely considered his pension bigger than was justifiable and that for two years he had been donating it to a children's home

419

and earning his livelihood, unlike the KGB men, by working.

On the next day at an official meeting several speakers tried to discredit and smear Hrishchuk, but had to leave the platform, for they were literally spat upon by the workers.

The workers sent a delegation to Moscow with a letter about their housing problem, with about five hundred signatures. At the end of June, Hrishchuk was arrested in Moscow. The workers sent a second letter, this time with the demand that he be freed.

Before the arrest, on June 24, in the newspaper *Vechernii Kiev* [Evening Kiev], a satirical article entitled "Khlestakov's Double,"[97] by one I. Pereyaslavsky, was published. It contained the standard assortment of slanders, aimed at Hrishchuk. He was alleged to be a drunkard and a foul defaulter on alimony payments. Suspicion was cast, by hints and indirection, on his role in the Great Patriotic War and on his conduct in the fascist concentration camps.

The author of the article also wrote that the delegation — consisting of certain "neighbors," not a word about the workers of the power plant — having collected nine hundred rubles from gullible people, was spending its time drinking in Moscow restaurants.

---

97. [Khlestakov, the chief character of Gogol's play "The Inspector General," is the personification of the swindler.]

UKRAINSKY VISNYK
STATEMENT OF PRINCIPLES

[*Ukrainsky Visnyk* (Ukrainian Herald) began publishing in early 1970 to provide a vehicle for news about the movement for democratic rights in the Ukraine. Like the *Chronicle of Current Events, Ukrainsky Visnyk* considered itself "entirely legal and constitutional in its content and task," and attributed the circumstances under which it was published to the "frequent infringements of constitutional rights and illegal persecutions of individuals who are active in public affairs." Unlike the *Chronicle,* however, the *Visnyk* was explicitly pro-Soviet and pro-Communist, not limiting itself to an agnostic statement in favor of civil rights.

[The statement of principles printed below was published in the first number of *Ukrainsky Visnyk* and included in each subsequent one. The sixth number, which circulated in the first half of 1972, was the last known to appear. A wave of arrests and searches affecting hundreds of dissident Ukrainians was carried out by the secret police early in 1972, aimed primarily at stopping the *Visnyk*—just as a similar campaign in Soviet Russia was aimed against the *Chronicle*. The tactic of holding individual dissenters as hostages liable to punishment "if another issue appears," applied against the *Chronicle,* was probably used in the Ukraine too.

[The translation, by the Committee for the Defense of Soviet Political Prisoners, is printed by permission.]

The need for such an uncensored publication has been ripe for a long time in the Ukraine. There are many problems of general interest which cause concern among wide sectors of Ukrainian society and which are never dealt with in the official press. But if on rare occasions, due to the force of circumstances, the press does mention these problems, it resorts to deliberate falsification.

The *Visnyk* will present information, without generalizations, on the violations of the freedom of speech and other democratic freedoms which are guaranteed by the constitution, on judicial and extrajudicial repression in the Ukraine, on the violations of national sovereignty (instances of chauvinism and Ukrainophobia), on attempts to misinform the public, on the condition of Ukrainian political prisoners in prisons and labor camps, on various acts of protest, etc. The *Visnyk* will review, or present in full, articles, documents, literary works and other materials which have become public and have already been circulated in samvydav.

The *Ukrainsky Visnyk* is in any case not an anti-Soviet or anticommunist publication. It is entirely legal and constitutional in its content and task. Criticism of individuals, agencies, and establishments, including the highest ones, for mistakes committed in decision-making on internal political problems, particularly the violations of the democratic rights of the individual and a nation, is not regarded by the *Visnyk* as being anti-Soviet activity, but is considered the guaranteed right and the moral duty of every citizen provided for by the [fundamental] principles of socialist democracy and the constitution. The abnormal circumstances under which the *Visnyk* is published is explained solely by the fact that there exist in our country frequent infringements of constitutional rights and illegal persecutions of individuals who are active in public affairs.

The *Visnyk* is not an organ of any organization or group unified by a program or organizational unity and, therefore, it will print samvydav materials which have been written from various points of view. The *Visnyk* undertakes to provide objective information on events and phenomena in Ukrainian political life that have been kept from the public's knowledge. Therefore, the *Visnyk* will not carry any material that has been written especially for it and has not been circulated. The *Visnyk* will not reproduce documents (usually anonymous) which are anti-Soviet, that is, which repudiate the democratically elected Soviets as a form of citizen participation in governing the state, or anticommunist, that is, which reject the entire Communist ideology as such.

The *Ukrainsky Visnyk* will only be able to function with the active support of the community, which will not only circulate the publication, but which will also not allow any anti-democratic or Ukrainophobic act or any instance of illegal persecution of individuals for their convictions to go without being publicized or suitably acted against.

The *Visnyk* guarantees an impartial approach to information material. Any errors and inaccuracies that may be detected and which are unavoidable under the circumstances of publication will be noted in subsequent issues.

UKRAINIAN JOURNAL EVALUATES
RUSSIAN DISSIDENTS

[In late 1971, *Ukrainsky Visnyk* published an editorial evaluation of Soviet Russian civil-rights groups and samizdat publications. The editorial was reprinted in abridged form in the Russian-language *Chronicle of Current Events,* no. 22, dated November 10, 1971.

[This translation of the *Chronicle's* abridgment is from the April 10, 1972, *Intercontinental Press,* and is reprinted by permission.]

That section of Ukrainian public opinion that is familiar with Russian samizdat has taken an interest in the attitude held by the Russian oppositional forces, which have been visibly active since the second half of the 1960s, toward the national question in general and the Ukrainian question in particular.

In late 1970, Academician Sakharov and the physicists Tverdokhlebov and Chalidze founded the Human Rights Committee in Moscow — a moderate opposition group whose aim is to defend the constitutional rights of Soviet citizens. The committee has not defined its attitude in any way toward the national question in the USSR, nor toward the question of the rights of the non-Russian nations, nor toward the guarantees of those rights. There are only some broad generalities.

In the first appeal to the CPSU Central Committee by Academician Sakharov and scientists [V.] Turchin and R. Medvedev, there is a statement to the effect that a gradual democratization of life in the USSR is necessary because that would diminish the threat of nationalism. In the same appeal there is a proposal that, instead of one's nationality, the words "citizen of the USSR" be stamped on everyone's passport. (Similar proposals were made even under Khrushchev and were viewed in the Union Republics as attempts at further encroachment upon their sovereignty.)

In May 1969 the Initiative Group for the Defense of Human Rights in the USSR was founded in Moscow; it sent a petition to the United Nations at that time, protesting the persecution of people in the USSR for their opinions and for communicating their opinions. Among other things, the appeal mentioned repression against people who supported national equality. No further statement of position on this question has been made by the Initiative Group. The majority of its members were soon arrested.

The periodical *Chronicle of Current Events* is guided by the same principles of struggle for freedom of speech and opinion as held by the Initiative Group. . . . Without listing any articles of program other than freedom of speech and information, the periodical tries to shed an impartial light on acts of political persecution throughout the Soviet Union and to briefly characterize new works of Russian samizdat (and sometimes, those of one or another nationality). From time to time the *Chronicle* also provides material on the Ukraine, with no loss in objectivity. The brevity of the accounts and the isolated inaccuracies are, apparently, caused simply by the lack of more detailed information.

For example, in issue No. 17 the *Chronicle* reports on the trial of V. Moroz, gives the most detailed account known so far on the case of the Ukrainian National Front (we are reprinting this information), and in its supplement on victims of the repression of 1969-70, it lists those victimized in the Ukraine.

The Ukrainian reader has welcomed the appearance of the *Chronicle.* It is notable for its objectivity, extensive coverage, and relative accuracy of information, providing a rounded picture of the political trials unknown to the majority of people in the USSR.

However, some have raised their voices to point out, without denying the importance of the *Chronicle,* that it has rather unilaterally and pretentiously assumed the stance of a supranational or all-union journal, when in fact it is the product of Russian (and possibly, in part, Jewish) circles. It has also been noted that the sparse informational reports from the republics are worked in as though they were supplementary to the quite extensive description of events in Russia, mostly

Moscow — this in and of itself creating a false impression of the situation in the USSR.

It is very hard to obtain information on the attitude toward the national question held by the various underground groups, organizations, and "parties" that have arisen in recent years in Russia (Leningrad, the Baltic fleet, the Volga region, etc.). The existence of these organizations has become known only after their being broken up by the KGB; likewise, their programmatic demands are known only in the broadest outline. From what is known, the conclusion can be drawn that none of these organizations had worked out a program for solving the national question in the USSR and none had stated its position on national demands and on the national movements in the USSR. The impression obtained is that the participants in these groups, while aiming at very radical changes in many spheres of social life, wished — to one degree or another — to preserve the status quo on the national question.

Along with organizations and groups that raise the question of democratic transformations in the USSR, others have appeared that criticize the government and the "liberals" from reactionary, openly chauvinist positions, seeking even a formal liquidation of the USSR and the creation of a military-democratic unitary state "of all the Russias." Let us quote the brief description of one such document of Russian samizdat given by the *Chronicle* in its issue No. 17, "Message to the Nation." [98]

Further on, the *Chronicle* No. 17 gave a similar brief summary of a samizdat reply to these patriots by V. Gusarov. . . . Judging by this summary, Gusarov's own position on the national question does not seem to be a constructive one outside of his assertion that "the national type"

---

98. [The following is the text of the description of "Message to the Nation" that appeared in *Chronicle* no. 17. The translation is by Amnesty International. "Signed: 'Russian patriots.' This document, a sort of declaration, is a manifesto of Russian nationalists. The authors vehemently take issue with Russian (and all) liberals, accusing them of having aims and views which are unsubstantiated, impotent, and objectively harmful. The 'Russian patriots' campaign for the purity of the white race, which is being tainted by 'random hybridization,' and for the rebirth of Russia ('great, united, and indivisible') and of the national religion."]

has not been preserved anywhere (consequently, there is no reason to try to preserve national types; let them all be leveled away). It is unclear what the author thinks the future of the non-Russian Soviet nationalities will be or what he would like it to be. The only thing that concerns him is that there be full public airing of issues and that there not be "the whip and the birch."

The *Chronicle*, giving an assessment of the typewritten journal of Russian nationalists, *Veche*, states that *Veche* differs from the above-mentioned manifesto "Message to the Nation" in its attitude of greater restraint and patience regarding the other nationalities. However, the *Chronicle* notes: "Judophobia [anti-Semitism] and Stalinist sympathies are characteristic of some of the contributors to *Veche*. . . ." As far as can be gathered from this assessment, *Veche* is published as a supposedly legal journal, and its editor Osipov is a real person.

AGAINST RUSSIFICATION

[The following open letter by seventeen Latvian Communists has been reprinted by several Western publications since it was first summarized in the January 30, 1972, issue of the Swedish newspaper *Dagens Nyheter* (Daily News). The attention it attracted occasioned a "rebuttal" by the official Soviet press, claiming that the letter is a forgery and that its contentions are all lies.

[The text was accompanied by a note reading "Please forward copies to Communist Party leaders in Rumania, Yugoslavia, France, Austria, and Spain, as well as to parties in any other countries you choose. Please forward copies to Comrades Aragon and Garaudy in France."

[This translation is from the July 3, 1972, *Intercontinental Press,* and is reprinted by permission.]

Dear comrades,

We are seventeen Latvian Communists, seeking your help. We are writing to you because we do not see any other way of affecting certain actions and events which cause great harm to the Communist movement, to Marxism-Leninism, and to our own and other small nations.

Many Communists have voiced in their party organizations the concerns we are expressing here, and some have appealed to the Central Committee of the Communist Party of the Soviet Union. Repressions have been the only results.

In order for you to understand us better, we would like to say a few words about ourselves. We are not opportunists, nor are we "leftists" or "rightists." We are Communists and most of us became Communists twenty-five to thirty-five or more years ago. We wish only success for socialism, for Marxism-Leninism, and for the whole of mankind. All of us were born and have lived in Latvia, and most of us have personally experienced the deficiencies of a bourgeois regime. We joined the party at a time when it was still underground. We endured repressions, were confined to prisons, and suffered under the yoke of bourgeois Latvia. The struggle to establish Soviet power and a socialistic order was our main goal in life. We all studied Marxism-Leninism. During the last world war, we were members of the Soviet armed forces or partisan groups and fought the Nazi aggressors. During the postwar years, we all actively participated in building socialism in our land. With a clear conscience, we did everything in our power to carry out the teachings of Marx, Engels, and Lenin. However, it became painfully clear to us that with each passing year their ideas became more distorted, that the teachings of Lenin are used here as a cover for Great Russian chauvinism, that deeds no longer agree with words, that we are complicating the work of Communists in other countries, that we are impeding this work instead of facilitating it.

Originally we believed that this was due simply to the errors of a few individual local officials who did not realize the harmful effects of their attitudes. With time, however, it became apparent to us that the leadership of the Soviet Communist Party had deliberately adopted a policy of Great Russian chauvinism and that the forcible assimilation of the small USSR nations had been set as one of the most immediate and important domestic policy goals.

Latvia is such a small country that its history, geography, and economic situation probably are not known to many outsiders. Already 2,000 years ago the Indo-European tribes of Kursi, Seli, Zemgali, and Letgali inhabited the eastern shores of the Baltic Sea. Because they inhabited the shores of sea gulfs and the estuaries of navigable rivers, such as Daugava, Visla, Venta, and others, their territories attracted the attention of nations both to the east and west, principally Germany and Russia. Consequently, these tribes were conquered in the thirteenth century with the cross and the sword of the German Crusaders. The ancestors of the Latvian people lived for 700 years under the oppression of the German Crusaders and barons.

But the Russian czars always dreamed of capturing the ice-free ports of Ventspils, Liepaja, Riga, and Tallinn. Czar Peter I fulfilled this dream and our ancestors came under Russian domination. From time to time various areas of Latvia were also occupied by the Poles and the Swedes. All these conquerors tried to assimilate the local tribes, but without success.

Later these tribes evolved as the nations of Lithuania, Latvia, and Estonia, gaining their independence in 1918, after World War I.

The territory of Latvia covered 66,000 square kilometers, with 2,000,000 inhabitants, 76 percent of them Latvians. Latvia established a democratic bourgeois government with a multiparty system. A political class struggle took place and, according to the division of power, the system was more or less democratic. The trade unions and the Social Democratic Party from 1918 to 1934 functioned legally, but the Communist Party was underground from 1919 to 1940.

Before World War II the Soviet Union forced Ulmanis, the head of the Latvian bourgeois government, to sign an agreement permitting the stationing of large garrisons of the Red Army in Latvia, but in 1940, with the help of the Red Army, the bourgeois government was overthrown and Latvia was annexed by the Soviet Union.

During the democratic bourgeois rule, Latvian economy and cultural life achieved significant progress. Latvia, along with Denmark and the Netherlands, supplied the world's markets with the highest quality butter, cheese, eggs, bacon, lumber, and flax. It also exported electrotechnical equipment, optical goods, and other industrial products. It had a national university with nine faculties, four other institutions for higher education, opera, a theater of music, several theaters of drama, and many groups of performing artists.

During World War II, approximately 40,000 people were evacuated to the interior of the Soviet Union. Two Latvian divisions fought in the ranks of the Red Army. The rest of the indigenous population remained in Latvia. Some of the people who had remained in Latvia were annihilated by the German fascists. Some died on the front in battle against the Red Army, and at the end of the war, some emigrated to Western countries (West Germany, Sweden, Australia, United States, etc.).

After World War II, the CPSU CC [Communist Party of the Soviet Union Central Committee] established as its goal to develop a permanent power base in the territories of Latvia, Lithuania, and Estonia, and began the forceful colonization of these territories with Russians, Byelorussians, and Ukrainians. It also began the forceful assimilation of Latvians, Lithuanians, and Estonians, as well as other minority nationalities, disregarding the fact that such actions clearly speak against the principles of Marxism-Leninism.

Since we cannot sign this letter, you may think that the things we have said are not true, that we have exaggerated certain shortcomings that are unavoidable in any endeavor. No, it is not so. Let the facts speak for themselves. Let us start with those truthful words that are written in the resolutions of the CPSU CC meeting on June 12, 1953 (the only such truthful resolution).

In his report about this resolution by the Presidium of the CPSU CC, the member of the CC and candidate of the Presidium of the CPSU CC Janis Kalnberzins said at the plenary session of the Latvian CP CC on June 22, 1953:

"The Presidium of the CPSU CC resolved:

"1) To charge all party and state organs with the task of correcting thoroughly the situation in the national republics — to put an end to the mutilation of Soviet national policy.

"2) To organize the preparation, education, and wide selection for leadership positions of the members of local nationalities, to abandon the present practice of selecting leaders who are not of the local nationality, and to relieve individuals who do not have the command of the native language, and have them recalled by the CPSU CC.

"3) All official business in the national republics should be conducted in native languages."

Latvian CP CC First Secretary Kalnberzins stated in this Latvian CP CC plenary session that the CPSU CC Presidium's resolution was harsh, but in regard to the Latvian SSR it was correct. Stated in this ruling was that the Latvian CP CC and Council of Deputies (obviously under pressure from Moscow) up until then had grossly overstepped Lenin's principles of national policy. He further stated that numerous party, Soviet, and economic executives, basing their actions on false vigilance, expressed their distrust of the local cadres, and for leading positions picked mostly non-Latvians. These people did not understand the Latvian language and were ignorant of local conditions. Such a position taken against the local cadres had resulted in a situation such that in the Latvian CP CC only 42 percent of its members were Latvians, while among the party secretaries from cities and districts only 47 percent were Latvians. Besides, many of them were Latvians in name only and did not know the Latvian language, having lived many years, or their entire lives, in Russia.

Who knows to what extent this action had been directed from above, but Kalnberzins (very loyal to Moscow) then correctly said that there was an especially unsatisfactory situation from a national group viewpoint in the city of Riga party organization. In the City Council cadre division there were no Latvians, and among thirty-one instructors only two were Latvians.

The cadre policy and party organization membership was set by the regional organization division and the party's charter organization secretary. It was in these circles that there were the fewest Latvians — the regional committee divisions each had but one Latvian, and among the charter organization secretaries, only 17 percent were Latvians.

Such unfounded mistrust of Latvian workers, farmers, and working intelligentsia, combined with the described party cadre membership, had led to the situation that among Riga Communists there were only 18 percent Latvians. This gross distortion of national policies and discrimination against Latvians mentioned in the Latvian CP CC plenum was acknowledged by such a sycophant of power politics as Arvids Pelse, the then Latvian CP CC propaganda secretary, present CPSU CC policy bureau member, and CPSU CC Control Commission chairman. Speaking about the CPSU CC plenary resolution, he said: "The resolution gives clear and unequivocal instructions — first of all, to improve the basic situation in the republic, to end distortion of Soviet national policy . . . to prepare, to train, and to appoint Latvian cadres to leading positions in the near future, on a large-scale basis."

From this statement, it is obvious that it was officially acknowledged in 1953 (the only time since Lenin's death) that the Marxist-Leninist national policy in our country had been grossly distorted (and is still being grossly distorted today). But did this distortion end after this plenary session? No. The above-mentioned course continued but a short time. After that, even though the plenary resolution was never repealed, all intended changes were halted and everything remained as it had been before. Even more, in the national republics the determined program for the coercive assimilation of small nationality groups was enacted even more forcibly and consistently. What is the main course of this program and how is it enacted? The first main task is to transfer from Russia, White Russia, and the Ukraine as many Russians, White Russians, and Ukrainians as possible to Latvia (and to other Baltic states) for permanent settlement.

How is this first main task enacted? The CPSU CC did not trust the national republic CP CC. Thus:

1) For the Latvian CP CC, and likewise for all other republic CP CCs, a CPSU CC Organizational Bureau (Orgbureau)

was established for Latvian affairs. The bureau's function was to control and direct the Latvian CP CC and the republic's overall politics. Shatalin was chosen the Orgbureau's chairman, but was later replaced by Ryazanov.

2) For the Latvian CP CC second secretary position Moscow appointed Ivan Lebedev and for the Latvian CP CC first secretary in cadre affairs, Fyodor Titov. These positions are still held by appointed Russians. At the present time the Latvian CP CC second secretary position is held by Belucha, a Russian sent from Leningrad.

3) The Orgbureau and these "high commissars" from Moscow have continually directed the republic's cadre politics so that all leading positions — and primarily all party, state, and economic department head positions — are given to Russian newcomers. These people in turn grant other newcomers preference for registration in cities, provide apartments, and appoint them to better jobs.

4) To guarantee a massive influx of Russians, White Russians, and Ukrainians into the Latvian Republic, federal, interrepublican, and zonal government departments have been set up in Latvia, and the construction of new large industries, as well as expansion of existing plants, has been undertaken, disregarding any economic necessity. The construction personnel for these projects were collected and brought in from cities outside of the republic; raw materials were brought in from the Urals or the Don Basin (i.e., from places 3,000-4,000 kilometers away); similarly, the labor force and the specialists were imported, but the production was exported from the republic. For this reason a diesel equipment factory, a factory making electrical accessories for automobiles (Autoelektropribor), a hydrometric equipment factory (Gidrometpribor), and a turbine factory were built in Riga. Extensive synthetic-fiber plants were built in Daugavpils. The imported labor force for these plants has formed a fair-sized town with almost no Latvian inhabitants. A large tricot garment factory and many other plants have been established in Ogre.

Literally, in every regional city new plants are being built. The construction labor, specialists, and production labor are imported, but the products are sent to the entire USSR.

Although Latvia had a sufficient number of generating stations, which have provided electric power for the republic, and Russia has many large rivers, imported workers have built a hydroelectric station in the River Daugava at Plavinas, and a city — Stucka — has been built for the construction forces, and consequently a new region has been formed in the republic.

5) Although the depletion of forests has exceeded reforestation for every year since the war, forests are being barbarically destroyed, turning large areas into swamps and leading to the importing of raw materials for the local furniture industry. For the last few years lumberjacks have been and are still being brought into Latvia from Russia, White Russia, and the Ukraine. The destruction of the forests continues and the imported lumberjacks settle permanently in the republic. This policy has led to the present situation where between 25,000 and 35,000 additional people each year become permanent residents of Riga. Total population has increased by a factor of 2.5. As a result, whereas Latvinians in Latvia were 62 percent of the population in 1959, in 1970 they accounted for 57 percent of the population. Similarly, the population of Riga was 45 percent Latvian in 1959 and only 40 percent Latvian in 1970. The future of such a policy can be clearly discerned from the fate of the former Karelian Soviet Socialist Republic. It exists no more, as it has been liquidated because the local nationals make up less than half of the total population of the republic. Now Karelia is a part of the Russian Soviet Federated Socialist Republic. A similar fate awaits the Kazakh SSR and Latvia.

6) Absorption of the local population into the mass of arriving Russians, White Russians, and Ukrainians is also furthered by the establishment of large bases for the armed forces and border guards on Latvian soil, as well as the building of dozens of medical clinics, rest homes, and tourist facilities for the use of the entire Soviet Union. Rigas Yurmala (the beach area on the Baltic Sea) is now an official Soviet Union resort and there remain few local residents. This has been the policy ever since the end of World War II and in the last two years it has been further reinforced. In our republic there are already many large firms where almost no Latvians remain among the workers, technician-engineers, or management (e. g., "REZ," Diselestroitelniy zavod, Gidrometpribor, and many others), and there are other companies where the majority of workers are Latvian, but management does not understand the Latvian language (Popov radio factory, Wagon Car Mfg., Autoelektropribor, Rigas Audums, etc.). There are bureaus and departments where few Latvians are employed. For example, in the Interior Department system of Riga there are about

1,500 workers, but only about 300 of these are Latvians.

Among the employees in the Commerce Department, a majority (51 percent) do not speak Latvian and only 29 percent of the management positions are filled by Latvians. There are very few Latvians in construction. Approximately 65 percent of the physicians who work in Riga's medical institutions do not understand Latvian, and because of this there are often gross mistakes made in diagnosis as well as in prescribing treatment. All of this naturally leads to rightful indignation among the local population.

In achieving the first basic aim, the increase in the number of non-Latvians in the republic, steps are also being taken to achieve the second basic aim, which is to assimilate the Latvians and lead to the Russian way of life throughout Latvia. To achieve this the following things already have been done and are still being done:

1. The arrivals' demands for increased Russian-language radio and television programming have been met. Currently, one radio station and one television station broadcast programs only in Russian, while the others broadcast programs bilingually. Thus, approximately two-thirds of radio and television broadcasts are in Russian. Jelinskis, the former director of Riga's broadcast center, resisted the arrivals' demands and was fired.

2. Regardless of the accessibility in Latvia of all newspapers, magazines, and books published in the Soviet Union, approximately half of all periodicals issued in Latvia are in Russian. In Latvia there is a shortage of paper for publishing works of Latvians and for school books; however, works of Russian writers are published, as well as school books in Russian.

3. In the republic's city, regional, and most of the local municipal organizations, as well as in all enterprises, all business is conducted in Russian.

4. With the exception of such collectives as the Latvian newspapers and magazines, Latvian theaters and schools, and partially the farm collectives, all gatherings and meetings are conducted in Russian. There are many collectives where the absolute majority is Latvian; however, if there is only one Russian in the collective, his demand that meetings be conducted in Russian is met. If this is not done, the collective is accused of nationalism.

5. In cities and villages the formation of the so-called united schools, kindergartens, and children's homes continues. In practice this means that Russian-language kindergartens and

schools remain unchanged, but in all the formerly Latvian-language institutions classes in Russian are instituted. Thereafter, in these cases, all pedagogical meetings, teacher and student meetings, as well as the meetings of the Young Pioneers, are conducted in Russian. Excepting the rural districts of Kurzeme, Zemgale, and Vidzeme, few Latvian kindergartens, children's homes, and schools remain.

6. In all high schools and institutions of higher learning there are extensive study programs in Russian.

7. In newspapers, radio and television broadcasts, meetings, and books — everywhere, every day, friendship with Russians is encouraged; widely propagandized are cases where Latvian girls marry Russians or Latvian youths marry Russian girls.

8. In the production of consumer goods, everything national has been eliminated. Formerly in Latvia, as in any other country, there were unique foods, special brands of confectionery, chocolates, cigarettes, but now there are only the brands of the Soviet Union: Belock, Lastocka, Kara-Kum, Kazbek, Belomorkahal, and others. In cafeterias and restaurants food is prepared according to the Russian recipes. National foods are rarities.

9. The Latvian people have a very important festival called "Ligo," which has been celebrated for hundreds of years, even during the German fascist occupation. Until last year, it was expressly forbidden to hold this festival. This year the festival again was not recognized, although it was not officially banned.

10. There are two approaches to our literary heritage. There are repeated editions of the works of such Russian authors as Tolstoy, Turgenev, Dostoevsky, Gogol, Pushkin, Lermontov, and others. However, of the Latvian authors who wrote in the pre-Soviet era, only Rainis, Paegle, and Veidenbaums are fully recognized, and partial recognition is given to Aspazija, Blaumanis, and a handful of others.

11. Riga is divided into six administrative regions, none of which has a locally derived name. They are named Lenin, Kirov, Moscow, Leningrad, October, and Proletarian.

12. Riga has streets that have been renamed after Lenin, Kirov, Sverdlov, Pushkin, Lermontov, Gogol, and Gorky. One street is named after Suvarov, who was a czarist governor. The street names that were dropped include Aspazija Boulevard (named after the best-known Latvian poet) and Krisjana Voldemara Street (named after an unrelenting exponent of Latvian nationhood).

13. In Riga today there is a memorial museum not only for

Lenin, but also for Peter I—the Russian czar who conquered the Baltic states.

14. Latvian soldiers, called "strelnieki," played an important role in the October Revolution. Lenin himself gave them the important role of guarding the Kremlin during the most critical days of the revolution. During World War II, two Latvian divisions and a special aviation battalion heroically fought as part of the Red Army. Today, however, there are no separate Latvian military units; Latvian youths in the military are purposely not assigned to the Russian units stationed in Latvia, but are scattered throughout the Soviet Union as far from Latvia as possible.

15. Latvian professional and amateur theaters, ensembles, orchestras, and choirs cannot have a repertory offically approved unless it contains Russian plays or songs. However, the Russian collective repertories almost never include Latvian plays or songs.

We could continue enumerating more such facts and conditions that all support the same point, namely, that all expressions of Latvian nationalism are suppressed, that there is a forcible assimilation and no equality among nations, cultures, and traditions.

One could ask: Why are the Latvian people and Latvian Communists silent? They are not silent. There have been attempts to oppose this political policy. For example, the former first secretary of the Riga Committee of the Communist Party, who later became vice chairman of the Latvian Soviet Socialist Republic, E. Berklavs, always spoke out against this injustice. For a time he was also supported by other members of the Central Committee of the Latvian Communist Party. But when his support grew to include a majority of the Central Committee members, the then first secretary of the Communist Party of the USSR, Comrade Khrushchev, made a personal trip to Latvia and later sent the secretary of the CPSU, Muchitinov. As a result, E. Berklavs was dismissed from his post as vice chairman of the Council of Ministers and expelled from the Central Committee bureau and the Central Committee, and was sent out of the Latvian Republic.

For supporting E. Berklavs and opposing Great Russian chauvinism and opposing the mutilation of Marxism and Leninism, the following persons were also removed from their posts:

K. Ozolins, chairman of the Supreme Soviet of the Latvian Soviet Socialist Republic and Latvian Communist Party Central Committee bureau member;

Straujums, first secretary (after E. Berklavs) of the City of Riga Communist Party Committee and Latvian Communist Party Central Committee bureau member;

Pizans, editor of the Latvian Communist Party official newspaper, *Cina,* and Latvian Communist Party Central Committee candidate;

E. Mukins, deputy planning chairman for the republic;

V. Kreitus, first deputy chairman of the city of Riga party executive committee;

Bisenieks, Latvian Communist Party Central Committee bureau member and secretary;

V. Krumins, Latvian Communist Party Central Committee secretary;

P. Dzerve, director of the Economic Research Institute of the Latvian Soviet Socialist Republic's Academy of Science;

V. Kalpins, minister of culture and Latvian Communist Party Central Committee bureau member;

P. Cerkovskis, deputy minister of culture;

Prombergs, deputy health minister;

A. Nikonovs, minister of agriculture;

Vallis, deputy minister of agriculture;

Darbins, editor of the city of Riga official newspaper;

Ruskulis, first secretary of the Communist Youth League Central Committee;

Valters, Latvian Communist Youth League secretary;

Brencis, editor of the Latvian Communist Youth League official publication, *Padomju Jaunatne*;

Zandmanis, director of the cadre division of the Latvian Soviet Socialist Republic's Council of Ministers;

J. Kacens, supervisor of the Administrative Section of the Latvian Communist Party Central Committee;

E. Liberts, minister of highways;

Plesums, chairman of the Control Commission of the Latvian Communist Party Central Committee;

E. Erenstreite, senior adviser to the Council of Ministers;

J. Gibietis, member of the city of Riga Communist Party Central Committee and supervisor of the education section of the city of Riga Communist Party executive committee;

M. Vernere and Duskina and many other principals of intermediate schools.

All the significant party and government posts have now been filled with non-Latvians and Latvians who have spent their entire lives in Russia and who arrived in Latvia only after World War II. The majority of them either do not speak any

Latvian or speak very little. The facts speak for themselves.

The secretaries of the Central Committee of the Latvian Communist Party are the following:

First Secretary Voss, Russian-born Latvian; as a rule, he doesn't speak Latvian in public.

Second Secretary Belucha, born Russian; knows no Latvian at all.

Secretary of Propaganda Drizulis, Russian-born Latvian.

Secretary of Agriculture Verro, Estonian from Russia; knows no Latvian at all.

Secretary of Industry Petersons, Russian-born Latvian; speaks Latvian poorly.

Leaders of the Council of Ministers: Chairman Y. Ruben, Russian-born Latvian; speaks Latvian very poorly; Vice Chairman Bondaletov, born Russian; speaks no Latvian at all.

Chairman of the Supreme Soviet of the Latvian Soviet Republic V. P. Ruben, Russian-born Latvian; knows Latvian only superficially; does not speak Latvian in public.

It is almost a law that leading positions are filled by men without principles, men without personal views or opinions, sycophants, opportunists, and flatterers. Men of principles who have opinions and express them openly are barred from important positions.

Such are the conditions in Latvia; under such conditions live the people native to their republics in their own land.

Those Lithuanians, Estonians, Jews, Germans, Poles, and other minorities (except Russians) residing in Latvian territory do not have their ethnic heritages at all respected. Until 1940 (until the establishment of Soviet rule) in Latvia these minorities had their own elementary and secondary schools where they studied in their own language. They issued their own language newspapers, magazines, books; they had their own clubs, theaters, and other cultural and educational institutions. Now, in disregard of pertinent Marxist-Leninist principles dealing with ethnic questions, and contrary to the statements of USSR leaders that ethnic problems in the Soviet Union have been solved and that each nationality has been guaranteed complete freedom and equality, nothing of that kind is evident. In every republic the Russians have everything, people native to their republics have something, but others nothing at all. The 3,500,000 Jews residing in the Soviet Union have only one magazine in their native language, and that only in their autonomous region. They are denied the right to have their own theaters, clubs, cultural and educational institutions, even in those cities where they number tens of thousands.

Esteemed comrades! In this letter we briefly illuminated actual conditions in the Soviet Union only from one viewpoint—that of the rights of ethnic minorities. Just as cruelly mutilated in our midst are Marxist-Leninist teachings about inalienable human rights and freedoms, freedom of speech, Lenin's work ethic, and other fundamental principles of Marxism-Leninism.

Why are we writing to you about all this? Why have we waited so long to write? What are we asking you to do; what are we proposing?

As explained earlier in this letter, we became Communists a long time ago. We were acquainted with the teachings of Marxism-Leninism and the basics of the socialist state in theory only while being active in the Communist underground, or while suffering in the prisons and forced-labor camps of bourgeois Latvia, but we believed in these ideas unreservedly. When we first saw the socialist state (the only one in existence at that time) we immediately noticed the difference between theory and practice. But we firmly believed that the faults were of a transient character and that they could be overcome.

At first we did not recognize the seriousness of these faults. Through daily application of socialist ideas we gradually realized that much of the official written and spoken output of the government was for display purposes only—deliberate distortions and outright lies. All party conferences, meetings, and assemblies are carefully prearranged and executed shows. They are convened only to create an illusion of democracy within the party. In reality, these conferences, meetings, and assemblies merely have to approve everything that has been dictated from "above"; subsequently they expound the individual opinion of a single person—the head man in the government. Every attempt to object to these opinions is regarded as opposition to the ideals of the party and Leninism. Those who dare to object not only lose their positions but also their freedom, and often end up suffering subhuman conditions in prisons and concentration camps, are deported, or sometimes vanish without a trace.

Naturally, these conditions eliminate all arguments and discussions at party conferences and assemblies as well as at the meetings of workers' councils. In this way, an apparent unity is achieved.

We suppose you have heard of the situation here or know

part of it. However, knowledge of the conditions here based on information of official documents, or short visits to the USSR, is certain to be far from complete. That is why we are writing to you: we want to acquaint you with the facts.

We realize that no Communist Party has the right to interfere in the internal affairs of another Communist Party. Nevertheless, for this very purpose, in order to safeguard this principle we must unite against any violator. You now have the facts. Besides, world opinion judges the effectiveness of socialism and communism in general by our successes and failures here. Therefore, the actions of the USSR have a direct influence on your work. For this reason we feel that you should know the truth about the conditions here, so that you can take appropriate steps to sway the leaders of the Communist Party of the Soviet Union. We know that this will not be easy. These men are not used to opening their minds to outside ideas. They act from a position of power and recognize only force. But your parties play an important role in the world Communist movement and your proposals cannot be taken lightly. We have no intentions of suggesting any methods you might use to influence the leaders of the Communist Party of the Soviet Union. Nevertheless, we are convinced that the high prestige of Marxism-Leninism cannot be preserved if the distortions of its principles are accepted silently, without protest. If the leaders of the Communist Party of the Soviet Union decline to stop the actions described above, they have to be unmasked and boycotted.

The present policies of the Communist Party leaders in the Soviet Union are destroying the world Communist movement.

With a Communist greeting.

UKRAINIANS DENOUNCE
STALINIST PRACTICES

[The *Chronicle of Current Events,* no. 25, dated May 20, 1972, carried the following excerpts from a letter signed "A Group of Soviet Citizens, May 1972, Ukraine." It was written in response to the wave of arrests aimed at putting an end to the uncensored publication *Ukrainsky Visnyk* (see preface above to the "*Ukrainsky Visnyk* Statement of Principles").

[This translation, by the Committee for the Defense of Soviet Political Prisoners, is reprinted by permission from the September 25, 1972, *Intercontinental Press.*]

To the Supreme Soviet of the USSR; the Supreme Soviet of the Ukrainian SSR; *Izvestia;* and *Literaturnaya Ukraina.*

The decades of Stalinist arbitrary rule, later modestly called the "personality cult," are a phenomenon that has as yet been little studied. This was much more complex than the cult of personality of any other individual, and in its consequences comparable to the devastation brought to the USSR by the world war. This was a terrible social plague, giving birth to terror, suspicion, denunciations, a whole country of concentration camps for millions of innocent people. It led to profound corruption, psychological shock, which tormented the people like a serious spiritual illness. In the 1930s this illness began with the extraordinary growth of the role of state security organs, which exceeded their authority and were no longer under the control of the government. The NKVD became "a state within a state"; it created an entire industry of killing and in principle could discredit and destroy any person in the country. . . .

The change in climate in public life in the USSR in this direction is an extremely dangerous symptom. A number of events — the invasion of Czechoslovakia by Soviet forces, a secret veto passed against the exposure of Stalinist arbitrary rule and even against revealing the materials of the twentieth congress of the CPSU, the hounding of Aleksandr Solzhenitsyn, endless reminders to intensify the ideological struggle — all these evoke profound anxiety, for they indicate a tendency which is capable of leading to a new 1937. . . . The suppression of national consciousness, multiple arrests of leading representatives of the Ukrainian intelligentsia, threats, blackmail, persecution, and countless mass searches serve as a dangerous reminder of the fact that the year 1937 began in 1933; it began with represssions against national cultural activists. Herein the reason for our warning. . . .

In particular we wish to explain the circumstance that forced us to sign ourselves simply as the Committee for Human Rights in the USSR. . . . We guarantee the authenticity of the information reported in this appeal. Anonymity sickens us. But the situation is such that the organs of the KGB respond to every display of social activity with immediate repressions. At the present time we, therefore, do not consider it advisable to have anything to do with the faceless and irresponsible Committee for State Security [the KGB], which is steadily becoming a real threat to society. We would be prepared to openly sign our names and take part in a public discussion of the essence of our letter, if there were the slightest hope that it would be published in full.

A Group of Soviet Citizens, May 1972, the Ukraine.

OPPOSITION ACTIVISTS ASSESS
YAKIR'S ARREST

[On June 21, 1972, Pyotr Yakir was arrested under Article 70 of the Russian Criminal Code, which deals with "anti-Soviet agitation and propaganda." Until his arrest, he had been one of the few members of the Initiative Group who had not been imprisoned or confined to a psychiatric hospital-prison. The KGB had obviously been afraid that a legal case involving him would revive too many memories of the 1936-38 purges. Yakir's father, the civil war hero General Iona Yakir, was shot in 1937, along with most of the Red Army high command in Stalin's purge of the military.

[In December, after Yakir had undergone interrogation for five months in the notorious Lefortovo prison, he was reported to have "recanted" and called for the dissolution of the democratic movement. Nine months later, in August 1973, after a show trial complete with "confessions," in the style of 1937, the Kremlin police displayed him and his codefendant Viktor Krasin at a press conference. The two dissidents were given relatively mild sentences and paroled shortly thereafter — partly because they had cooperated but also because their trial evoked a new burst of protest both at home and abroad. At the time of his arrest Yakir had stated: "If I 'confess,' that means they have tortured me; if I 'commit suicide,' that means they have murdered me."

[The following excerpts from an open letter assessing the significance of Yakir's arrest appeared in the *Chronicle of Current Events,* no. 26, dated July 1972. The translation is from the September 25, 1972, *Intercontinental Press,* and is reprinted by permission.]

July 1972

Pyotr Yakir has been jailed.

The authorities have decided to add a new, somber page to the tragic fate of one of the most remarkable of our contemporaries, a man with a rare quality of civic concern, great force of character, inexhaustible energy, and courage that shies at nothing.

This opens up one more stage — possibly the culminating one — in the tactics of a creeping, but systematic, repression which the regime has been pursuing for several years now in an attempt to stifle the democratic movement.

We can and we must protest against this action. It is more important, however, to understand the essence of the new situation and to seriously, deliberately, but without hysteria (whether it be the hysteria of flinging oneself at the oppressor's bayonets or the hysteria of totally capitulating) adjust the life and struggle of every democrat — and that means the entire movement as well — to the present reality.

The arrest of Yakir, a man who consciously placed himself at the point of sharpest conflict, does not mean that "all is lost," that the policy of the authorities has resulted in victory for them. . . . The arrest of Yakir is neither the beginning nor the end, but an important landmark. . . .

To keep our people safe and to keep samizdat going, to preserve and strengthen the democratic movement — that is the main goal of today. That is the best response to the arrest of Yakir. . . .

A Group of Soviet Citizens

DEBATE ON TACTICS

[In the summer of 1970, the *Chronicle of Current Events* began carrying contributions by various participants in the democratic movement on the subject of the tactics and strategy for the opposition movement in the face of the intensified repression. We are reprinting some of the more interesting of these contributions: from *Chronicle* no. 14 (June 30, 1970), in a translation by the editor; and from *Chronicles* 17 (December 1970), 18 (March 1971), and 25 (May 20, 1972), in translations from the Russian by Amnesty International.]

Tactical Principles of the Democratic Movement of the Soviet Union [DMSU]—such is the title of a document which elaborates a particular set of tactics for the struggle to democratize our society, or which, perhaps, only has pretensions toward such an elaboration. The *Tactical Principles* appeared in samizdat subsequently to the *Program* [of the DMSU] and constitutes a continuation and concretization of the ideas in the *Program*. In the *Tactical Principles* as well as in the *Program*, an irreconcilable attitude toward totalitarianism is expressed and an aspiration toward freedom and democracy.

As far as the concrete programmatic and tactical theses of the DMSU are concerned, the *Chronicle* advises its readers to directly consult the two documents mentioned. However, we consider it necessary to call readers' attention to what we consider debatable—to put it delicately—about the *Principles*.

1) The authors of the *Principles* and of the *Program* speak in the name of all freedom-loving and democratically-minded citizens in our country, as though they had been authorized to do so.

2) The authors present matters in such a way as to suggest that mass democratic forces already exist in the Soviet Union, even centralized ones (they refer to a "coordinating council") and that all layers of the society are involved with these forces: the intelligentsia, the workers, the peasants, the military, even a section of "the party elite." (Nevertheless, the "absence of

445

democratic traditions among some sections of the people" is noted.)

3) The authors assert that "the democrats, accumulating their forces, did not develop a broad movement in the 1960s" solely out of tactical considerations, but now, in the 1970s, such a movement will unfailingly develop to the fullest extent (an immutable and indisputable prognosis: "the coming decade will be a decade of steady and constant growth for the democratic movement . . .").

4) The authors feel that "the legal forms of the movement, having fulfilled their historical role, have essentially exhausted themselves," and therefore, although they call for combining legal and illegal methods of struggle, in their discussion of tactics they place the center of gravity on underground work. For example, they say the following about conspiratorial methods: "Every participant in the movement . . . should be known personally to the most restricted possible circle of activists . . . most often to no more than three persons." Or, "Group organizers, committees, directing centers, should not be known to the participants in the movement. . . ." and further, "Even those closest to a person — wife, husband, children, parents, friends — should not know the secrets of the democratic movement."

Readers may find historical analogies to all this for themselves.

The one general comment which we will permit ourselves concerning the *Principles* is as follows: mature people who involve themselves in politics ought to understand that to present one's desires as reality is to orient the youth incorrectly, that is, in a way that can be ruinous.

A. Mikhailov (pseudonym): Thoughts on the Liberal Campaign of 1968

In view of the importance of the questions raised by the author of this article, the *Chronicle* gives a detailed resume of it. Let the reader compare Mikhailov's standpoints with his own ideas.

Since the beginning of the fifties the country has been in a state of crisis. This crisis consists of a conflict between the forces of production and the relations of production. The administrative-bureaucratic system by which the economy is governed excludes scientific methods of management. The crisis gave rise to a liberal trend, which matured beneath the surface among the intelligentsia during the Khrushchev period. In 1968 the liberal opposition came out into the open for the first time and was swiftly crushed. Reaction set in on the part of the government and continues to this day.

The opposition bore no fruit. It caused no positive shifts in public consciousness, leaving after its destruction disillusion and apathy. Sensible people were put off by it. But the majority of people were actually turned against it. The opposition not only failed to attract new supporters of liberalism, but to a certain extent compromised the very idea of opposition. The failure of the opposition lay in its incorrect orientation, in its lack of understanding of the real situation. A social conflict, objective in content, underwent a transformation in the consciousness of the oppositionists, turning for them into a subjective moral conflict between individuals and the state. This confusion of consciousness gave the movement a romantic character and made it ineffectual. These liberal-romantics acted according to their emotions and moral instincts, they wanted to save only their souls and to purge their consciences — and therefore they sacrificed themselves. They did not wish, nor were they able, to think of the whole of society, they were not concerned with the practical results of their actions, which had become an end in themselves. This was protest for the sake of protest — without a positive program, without constructive ideas, without a social foundation.

Inasmuch as the liberals spoke out openly (letters and petitions over their own signatures, demonstrations) they were attempting to look to the law for support, which is patently pointless in our state. They appealed to the authorities, who put them in prison — ignoring all laws, as is their wont. The movement's formal, constitutional-legalistic tenor gave rise to contradictions within it: people who speak out in the name of truth, striving towards absolute honesty, cannot criticize the essence of the regime (as a system), but are forced to limit themselves to criticism of its individual manifestations, its frequent injustices. The opposition's only general demand is a purely legalistic one: freedom of speech. "Don't imprison people for their beliefs, print everything — or at any rate more" — this, in effect, is the protesters' motto.

It is no coincidence that open protests began after the trials of a few free-thinking intellectuals. Meanwhile the broad sections of the population, oppressed by need and social imperfections, do not see the liberals as the defenders of their interests; the liberals are ready to suffer for Sinyavsky and Daniel (and others like them), but they ignore the man in the street with his needs and sufferings. The demand for freedom of speech

directly expresses only the class interests of the creative intelligentsia. The liberals' alienation from the people is only
partially unintended — to a considerable extent it conforms with
the purpose of the liberals themselves. The opposition is a
closed circle. Moralizing, legalistic name-calling and bombastic
phrases are the preserve of a narrow circle of people. Such
are the active liberals. The passive section of the liberal intelligentsia, however, is rushing about in all directions. Nihilism.
Individualism. Aristocratic aestheticism. "Pure moral philosophy." Religion. There is discord and degradation.

The spiritual games of the passive intellectuals are useless.
The activities of the active ones are harmful. They are worthy
of personal respect, but their actions are by their nature objectively (unintentionally) provocative. Activities aimed at
getting oneself arrested (e.g., the demonstration of August 25,
1968) are hysterical lunacy, which, by spreading, only causes
more and more casualties. Collective letters of protest and
petitions (often addressed to broad public opinion, of which
our government takes no notice) also play a provocative part.
Without any effort on its part the KGB acquires prepared lists
of liberals. At present the government allows some of the active
oppositionists to remain at liberty only because their activities
are useful to it — they enable it to monitor discontent.

The reality is that we are approaching a national and worldwide disaster. All humanity is threatened with extinction. The
situation must be radically altered. The regime in its present
form will not survive for long. Our task is not to administer
the coup de grace (revolutionary and violent methods are
unacceptable) but to prepare a worthy replacement for it. This
is the task of the thinking section of society, the intelligentsia.
This requires a scientific approach to social problems (which
is rejected almost on principle by the liberal-romantics, who
cultivate incompetence in questions of theory). We must work
out an effective political position which will offer a way out
of the blind alley; we must work out a concept explaining
modern society and its workings. The concept must be based
on democratic socialism (the transplantation here of the at-
tributes of bourgeois democracy is unrealistic and would not
solve our problems). At the moment no entirely satisfactory
concept of this sort exists anywhere. We must take our cue
from "macrosociology" (of the Marx variety). Such works as,
for instance, Burnham's *The Managerial Revolution* and Djilas's *New Class* are valuable. Academician Sakharov's approach to social phenomena is promising (but the form of

his essay — the romantic form of appealing to the leadership — makes impartial scientific analysis impossible).

The opposition of 1968 made no attempt to create a realistic and at the same time attractive social ideal. Our program must be both scientific and popular. The intelligentsia must find a common language with the masses and express their interests and demands.

The progressive movement must declare itself to be a united whole. This requires a common ideological platform; not an organization (any attempt to create it would at present be madness), but rather ten or twelve programmatic points, a symbol of faith. All the efforts of thinking people must be directed toward the drawing-up of this program. Samizdat, both anonymous and pseudonymous, must become the instrument for working out new ideas (we must put a stop to demonstrations and other acts liable to result in arrests). In this way the progressive social movement can become a serious force.

A. Strikh: A Reply to A. Mikhailov

The substance of this Open Letter is as follows:

The idea that the "lunatics" are the opponents of a scientific approach to the life of society is pure fantasy. The "liberal-romantics" (they could be given a more neutral name, e.g., public protesters) are not in the least isolated from social problems; if they do not attempt to solve them, it is solely because they do not regard themselves as sociologists (though some of them may possibly deal with sociology in their creative work). They are acquainted with Marxism. But *modern* "macro-sociology" is not regarded by everybody as sociology "of the Marx variety." Sociological thought did not stand still after Marx. Moreover the conclusions of Burnham and Djilas, although they contain a certain truth, do not provide the key to the solution of many of our problems. It has been established that economics does not determine the entire social process. Among the contradictions in our society the economic contradiction is of course one of the most important, but that does not mean that it is primary, or that its doctrine of "basis" and "superstructure" provides the correct approach to this contradiction. Our "superstructure" appeared before the "basis" and was its absolute determinant. In our country economics is derived from and subordinated to politics, rather than vice-versa.

The motives and actions of individuals, social groups, and

the masses are by no means always due to economic causes (the field of social psychology is not covered by Marxist theory). A. Mikhailov suggests "finding a common language with the broad masses"—but are the "broad masses" disposed to respond to the voice of the "progressive movement"? This is by no means clear.

This is just as debatable as the assertion that "the regime in its present form cannot survive for long"; that a ten- or twelve-point program could unite the entire "thinking section of society," and that it would thus be possible "to make radical changes in the situation." It is also doubtful whether a universal conceptual panacea could be worked out on the basis of samizdat, anonymous or pseudonymous. Even where there is unlimited scope for sociological research, where the funds necessary for it are provided, where there is easy access to information and the free exchange of opinions—even there the way out of many modern blind alleys has not yet been found. But even assuming that we succeed in working out a sociological model ideal for our circumstances, how are we to realize it? Put it to the government? But that, in A. Mikhailov's view, is "romanticism." Await the automatic collapse of the regime? But how long must this inactive waiting last? Put it to the masses? How? That would require (as A. Mikhailov remarks) not only propaganda but also agitation—direct influence on the consciousness of the masses; in any case, agitation cannot even begin without an underground organization. Meanwhile A. Mikhailov regards even the attempt to create such an organization as madness. And rightly so. That really would be an objectively provocative act, since besides themselves the agitators would bring disaster to many other people.

A. Mikhailov is right when he says that we need intensive thinking and searching, and that this is the task of the intelligentsia. But ideological searching is a many-sided and complex cultural process, which could not be confined within the channel of economic materialism or within any limits, whatever they might be. It would be natural for A. Mikhailov to try to define ("prompt") the principal direction of this search, but his attacks on "pure spirituality," "spiritual games," are beneath all criticism.

A. Mikhailov's reproaches to those who have spoken out in open protest—and who are still doing so—will also not bear examination. In a society where the majority is intrinsically convinced that the state is not merely able, but *has the right* to do whatever it likes with people, and that people have no rights at all—it is in this society that we have been given our first lesson in the consciousness of civil rights. The question of rights is not an academic question in a society where they do not exist. What we cannot do without, what is needed before anything else, is at least a minimal level of democratic freedoms. The first of these is freedom of speech. That means freedom of thought. What social activity or "constructive solutions" are possible without it? Those who first demonstrated that freedom, who started introducing it "without asking permission," knew what they were doing. They had no recipes for the salvation of mankind—they were trying to protect people. They protested against individual acts of tyranny and violence where tyranny was most apparent (trials), where violence was most blatant (Czechoslovakia). They said, and are still saying, what they thought they had to, and this is an honest attitude. Sacrificing oneself does not mean inducing others to commit rash acts. At the moment the only ones who are actually being put in prison are those who were conscious of what they were facing. The government has been given a list of liberals, moans A. Mikhailov, but it is only where liberalism does not manifest itself in any way that it will *not* have such a list.

A. Mikhailov is also mistaken in supposing that open protest is of absolutely no practical benefit. It is not true that the government never in any way takes the slightest notice of public opinion—in particular of foreign public opinion. It is sufficient to recall the case of Zh. Medvedev [see *Chronicle* No. 14] or the last trial of the "hijackers" in Leningrad. But what's true is true: as regards practical results, the situation is bad. But A. Mikhailov's ideas contain absolutely nothing practical. His position objectively leads to total inactivity. Everyone who is unable to work out a "popular and scientific" program will sit doing nothing and await the magic "concept" like some sort of revelation, meanwhile averting their eyes from specific evil.

It is worth lending an ear to Albert Einstein's practical recommendations:

"Reactionary politicians have sown suspicion of intellectual activity by intimidating the public by means of external danger. . . . What must the intelligentsia do when confronted with this evil? To tell the truth I see only one way—the revolutionary way of disobedience in the spirit of Gandhi . . . if a sufficient number take that perilous way, it will lead to success. If not, then the intelligentsia of that country deserves nothing better than slavery."

Einstein further said: "One man alone is able only to serve as an example for others and to uphold with courage the moral principle. . . ."

K. Demov: I Am the Guardian

The points on which K. Demov takes issue with A. Mikhailov (see *Chronicle* No. 17) are essentially as follows:

The science of society, like any other science, is a matter for professionals, not for dilettantes. Samizdat cannot construct a scientific sociology — at best it is capable of generalizing data which sociology has already obtained (and then only if academic sociologists enter the field of samizdat). In Demov's opinion A. Mikhailov's aim of "overcoming the ideological chaos" and working out a unified program of ten or twelve points is not a scientific aspiration but a purely political one, which will later lead inevitably to a party-based power struggle (like the one which took place [early in the century]). The subjugation of samizdat to such guidelines (a unified program) would, the author thinks, put an end to freedom of speech in samizdat. Mikhailov's notion that the intelligentsia must give the people a "model of democratic socialism" is sharply criticized. What is needed is not yet another socialist scheme, but freedom; the people themselves, Demov maintains, are capable of expressing their own interests and formulating their own demands, without external assistance (e. g., in Poland at present). The author vigorously argues against Mikhailov's thesis about the ruinousness of getting oneself arrested (in particular he sets a high value on the demonstration of 25 August 1968, which Mikhailov condemns). He adheres to the view that the opposition must be legal, and that in order to achieve freedom it is essential to observe legality. "Better political inactivity than political extremism" — this is K. Demov's central idea. The conclusion of the article states that democrats must protect society from extremes, from the left as well as the right (it is in this sense that the author declares: "I am the guardian").

From "Democrat," No. 5, 1971: On the Question of Illegal Forms of Struggle

"October 1969 saw the publication of the 'Program of the Democratic Movement of the Soviet Union,' which had been drawn up and adopted by the democrats of Russia, Ukraine, and the Baltic lands. In June 1970 the democrats published their 'Tactical Principles of the Democratic Movement of the Soviet Union,' a document which explains and in many respects expands the program's tenets" (see *Chronicle* Nos. 11, 14). The article goes on: "The democrats replied to all the critical observations made about the 'program' in the 'Memorandum of the Democrats to the USSR Supreme Soviet.' . . ." (The authors state that the "memorandum" came out on 5 December 1970.)

The article addresses several reproaches to the *Chronicle:* "The *Chronicle*'s editors, when condemning illegal methods of struggle, somehow forget that the *Chronicle* itself operates in illegal conditions, observing the strictest rules of conspiracy. . . . So why does it censure us democrats, who are operating under identical conditions? Is the author of the critical note really so naive as to believe that the *Chronicle* on its own is sufficient for the whole of the Soviet Union, and that therefore it alone has the right to operate illegally, while everyone else who reads it must act legally? If one were to adhere to this notion, the KGB, in the space of a few days, or even hours, would isolate not only its readers but also the persons who gather information and those who circulate the *Chronicle.* . . .

"We cannot agree with the interpretation of the 'Tactical Principles of the DMSU' published in No. 14 of the *Chronicle of Current Events.* We value the *Chronicle* highly, copy it, and circulate it widely. It is difficult to overestimate the importance of the *Chronicle* for the DMSU. At the same time we should like to point out in a friendly spirit that, since the publication of the 'Tactical Principles,' circles closely connected with the *Chronicle*'s editors have not been sufficiently active in circulating official documents of the DMSU, in particular the 'Memorandum of the Democrats to the Supreme Soviet.' . . ."

The *Chronicle* repeats its belief that by using such expressions as "Organ of Democratic Forces," "Publisher — the Democratic Movement," or "The journal . . . has been authorized to state," the publishers of *Democrat* are indulging in wishful thinking and thereby confusing the reader.

In reply to *Democrat's* rebuke of inconsistency, the *Chronicle* states: the necessary precautions involved in the publication of an information bulletin such as the *Chronicle* in the conditions of our country are one thing; an underground organization (see *Chronicle* No. 14 on "The Tactical Principles of the Democratic Movement of the Soviet Union") is another.

Leaders of the Left Opposition before being sent to Siberian exile in early 1928. Seated (l. to r.): Serebriakov, Radek, Trotsky, Boguslavsky, Preobrazhensky. Standing (l. to r.): Rakovsky, Drobnis, Beloborodov, Sosnovsky.

APPENDIX:
Transitional Demands — The USSR and Problems of the Transitional Epoch
by Leon Trotsky

[The major problem the new Soviet opposition has to solve is how to link up with the masses, in particular the workers. There is a key concept that could be of enormous help in solving this problem — that of transitional demands, a concept developed in the Comintern in 1919-22 and further elaborated by the Fourth International. Transitional demands are ones that can serve as bridges for mobilizing the masses at their existing stage of consciousness, draw them into struggles whose logic tends to raise fundamental questions about the structure of society, thus leading large numbers to draw revolutionary conclusions on the basis of experience in action.

[Trotsky's discussion of transitional demands for Soviet society are included in this volume for their value if introduced into the discussion going on today over programmatic, tactical, and related organizational questions. For example, what attitude should Soviet rebels take toward the party? or the soviets? Trotsky's discussion can make a major contribution toward answering such questions.

[The Fourth International was founded on the basis of revolutionary internationalism in September 1938. Trotsky, then exiled in Mexico, was unable to attend the founding conference, but in the spring of 1938 he wrote the *Transitional Program*, which was adopted by the conference as its basic programmatic document.

[Reprinted here by permission is the section, dealing with the Soviet Union, of *The Transitional Program for Socialist Revolution* (Pathfinder Press, 1973).]

The Soviet Union emerged from the October Revolution as a workers' state. State ownership of the means of production, a necessary prerequisite to socialist development, opened up the possibility of rapid growth of the productive forces. But the apparatus of the workers' state underwent a complete degeneration at the same time: it was transformed from a weapon of the working class into a weapon of bureaucratic violence against the working class and more and more a weapon for the sabotage of the country's economy. The bureaucratization of a backward and isolated workers' state and the transformation of the bureaucracy into an all-powerful privileged caste constitute the most convincing refutation — not only theoretically but this time practically — of the theory of socialism in one country.

The USSR thus embodies terrific contradictions. But it still remains a *degenerated workers' state.* Such is the social diagnosis. The political prognosis has an alternative character: either the bureaucracy, becoming ever more the organ of the world bourgeoisie in the workers' state, will overthrow the new forms of property and plunge the country back to capitalism; or the working class will crush the bureaucracy and open the way to socialism.

To the sections of the Fourth International, the Moscow trials came not as a surprise and not as a result of the personal madness of the Kremlin dictator, but as the legitimate offspring of the Thermidor. They grew out of the unbearable conflicts within the Soviet bureaucracy itself, which in turn mirror the contradictions between the bureaucracy and the people, as well as the deepening antagonisms among the "people" themselves. The bloody "fantastic" nature of the trials gives the measure of the intensity of the contradictions and by the same token predicts the approach of the denouement.

The public utterances of former foreign representatives of the Kremlin, who refused to return to Moscow, irrefutably confirm in their own way that all shades of political thought are to be found among the bureaucracy: from genuine Bolshevism (Ignace Reiss) to complete fascism (F. Butenko). The revolutionary elements within the bureaucracy, only a small minority, reflect, passively it is true, the socialist interests of the proletariat. The fascist, counterrevolutionary elements, growing uninterruptedly, express with ever greater consistency the interests of world imperialism. These candidates for the role of compradors consider, not without reason, that the new ruling layer can insure their positions of privilege only through rejection of nationalization, collectivization, and monopoly of foreign trade in the name of the assimilation of "Western civilization," i. e., capitalism. Between these two poles, there are intermediate, diffused Menshevik-SR-liberal tendencies which gravitate toward bourgeois democracy.

Within the very ranks of that so-called "classless" society

there unquestionably exist groupings exactly similar to those in the bureaucracy, only less sharply expressed and in inverse proportions: conscious capitalist tendencies distinguish mainly the prosperous part of the collective farms (*kolkhozi*) and are characteristic of only a small minority of the population. But this layer provides itself with a wide base for petty-bourgeois tendencies of accumulating personal wealth at the expense of general poverty, and are consciously encouraged by the bureaucracy.

Atop this system of mounting antagonisms, trespassing ever more on the social equilibrium, the Thermidorian oligarchy, today reduced mainly to Stalin's Bonapartist clique, hangs on by terroristic methods. The latest judicial frameups were aimed as a blow *against the left.* This is true also of the mopping up of the leaders of the Right Opposition, because the Right group of the old Bolshevik Party, seen from the viewpoint of the bureaucracy's interests and tendencies, represented a *left* danger. The fact that the Bonapartist clique, likewise in fear of its own right allies of the type of Butenko, is forced in the interests of self-preservation to execute the generation of Old Bolsheviks almost to a man, offers indisputable testimony of the vitality of revolutionary traditions among the masses as well as of their growing discontent.

Petty-bourgeois democrats of the West, having but yesterday assayed the Moscow trials as unalloyed gold, today repeat insistently that there is "neither Trotskyism nor Trotskyists within the USSR." They fail to explain, however, why all the purges are conducted under the banner of a struggle with precisely this danger. If we are to examine "Trotskyism" as a finished program, and, even more to the point, as an organization, then unquestionably "Trotskyism" is extremely weak in the USSR. However, its indestructible force stems from the fact that it expresses not only revolutionary tradition but also today's actual opposition of the Russian working class. The social hatred stored up by the workers against the bureaucracy — that is precisely what from the viewpoint of the Kremlin clique constitutes "Trotskyism." It fears with a deathly and thoroughly well-grounded fear the bond between the deep but inarticulate indignation of the workers and the organization of the Fourth International.

From this perspective, impelling concreteness is imparted to the question of the "defense of the USSR." If tomorrow the bourgeois-fascist grouping, the "faction of Butenko," so to speak, should attempt the conquest of power, the "faction of Reiss" inevitably would align itself on the opposite side of the barricades. Although it would find itself temporarily the ally of Stalin, it would nevertheless defend not the Bonapartist clique but the social base of the USSR, i. e., the property wrenched away from the capitalists and transformed into state property. Should the "faction of Butenko" prove to be in alliance with Hitler, then the "faction of Reiss" would defend the USSR from military intervention, inside the country as well as on the world arena. Any other course would be a betrayal.

The extermination of the generation of Old Bolsheviks and of the revolutionary representatives of the middle and young generations has acted to disrupt the political equilibrium still more in favor of the right, bourgeois wing of the bureaucracy, and of its allies throughout the land. From them, i. e., from the right, we can expect ever more determined attempts in the next period to revise the socialist character of the USSR and bring it closer in pattern to "Western civilization" in its fascist form.

Although it is thus impermissible to deny in advance the possibility, in strictly defined instances, of a "united front" with the Thermidorian section of the bureaucracy against open attack by capitalist counterrevolution, the chief political task in the USSR still remains the *overthrow of this same Thermidorian bureaucracy*. Each day added to its domination helps rot the foundations of the socialist elements of economy and increases the chances for capitalist restoration. It is in precisely this direction that the Comintern moves as the agent and accomplice of the Stalinist clique in strangling the Spanish revolution and demoralizing the international proletariat.

As in fascist countries, the chief strength of the bureaucracy lies not in itself but in the disillusionment of the masses, in their lack of a new perspective. As in fascist countries, from which Stalin's *political* apparatus does not differ save in its more unbridled savagery, only preparatory propagandistic work is possible today in the USSR. As in fascist countries, the impetus to the Soviet workers' revolutionary upsurge will probably be given by events outside the country. The struggle against the Comintern on the world arena is the most important part today of the struggle against the Stalinist dictatorship. There are many signs that the Comintern's downfall, because it does not have a *direct* base in the GPU, will precede the downfall of the Bonapartist clique and the Thermidorian bureaucracy as a whole.

A fresh upsurge of the revolution in the USSR will undoubtedly begin under the banner of the struggle against *social inequality* and *political oppression.* Down with the privileges of the bureaucracy! Down with Stakhanovism! Down with the Soviet aristocracy and its ranks and orders! Greater equality of wages for all forms of labor!

The struggle for the freedom of the trade unions and the factory committees, for the right of assembly and freedom of the press, will unfold in the struggle for the regeneration and development of *Soviet democracy.*

The bureaucracy replaced the soviets as class organs with the fiction of universal electoral rights — in the style of Hitler-Goebbels. It is necessary to return to the soviets not only their free democratic form but also their class content. As once the bourgeoisie and kulaks were not permitted to enter the soviets, so now *it is necessary to drive the bureaucracy and the new aristocracy out of the soviets.* In the soviets there is room only for representatives of the workers, rank-and-file collective farmers, peasants, and Red Army men.

Democratization of the soviets is impossible without *legalization of soviet parties.* The workers and peasants themselves by their own free vote will indicate what parties they recognize as soviet parties.

A revision of *planned economy* from top to bottom in the interests of producers and consumers! Factory committees should be returned the right to control production. A democratically organized consumers' cooperative should control the quality and price of products.

Reorganization of the collective farms in accordance with the will and in the interests of the workers there engaged!

The reactionary *international policy* of the bureaucracy should be replaced by the policy of proletarian internationalism. The complete diplomatic correspondence of the Kremlin to be published. *Down with secret diplomacy!*

All political trials staged by the Thermidorian bureaucracy to be reviewed in the light of complete publicity and controversial openness and integrity. Only the victorious revolutionary uprising of the oppressed masses can revive the Soviet regime and guarantee its further development toward socialism. There is but one party capable of leading the Soviet masses to insurrection — the party of the Fourth International!

Down with the bureaucratic gang of Cain-Stalin!

Long live Soviet democracy!

Long live the international socialist revolution!

INDEX